THE PEARSON CUSTOM LIBRARY OF

American Literature

Cover Art: courtesy of Purestock/Getty Images

Please visit our website at *www.pearsonlearningsolutions.com.*

Attention bookstores: For permission to return any unsold stock, contact us at *pe-uscustomreturns@pearson.com.*

Pearson Learning Solutions, 501 Boylston Street, Suite 900, Boston, MA 02116
A Pearson Education Company
www.pearsoned.com

PEARSON

ISBN 10: 1-269-70298-X
ISBN 13: 978-1-269-70298-0

Acknowledgments

The idea of a customizable set of Anchor Volumes drawn from a comprehensive library of American literary texts that is both representative and flexible in its offerings of the canonical and new, and which would be assembled by a group of innovative and experienced scholars, was first conceived by Virginia Blanford and John Bryant in 1993. The project was brought to Pearson Custom Publishing by acquisitions editor Ellen Kuhl and freelance development editor Janice Wiggins, who advanced its growth with the help of in-house development editor Katherine Gehan and editorial assistant Amy Hurd. Sponsoring editor Natalie Danner joined the project in 2002 and, along with production manager Kathleen Masse, copyeditor Lydia Stuart Horton, Jim O'Malley at Stratford, permissions editors Karl Christian Krumpholtz and Deborah Schwartz, and designer Renée Sartell, squired the project through its final phases of production. Marketing manager Annabel Cellini conceived and implemented the plan for bringing the project intelligently and effectively into the hands of sales representatives, bookstores, faculty, and students. From the beginning, the project received enthusiastic support from executives at Pearson including President of Pearson Custom Publishing, Don Kilburn, Vice President: Editorial, Marketing and Media, Patrick Boles, and in particular Assistant Vice President and Director of Database Publishing, Michael Payne, who along with the previously mentioned individuals has, with patience and insight, contributed to the intellectual scope as well as practical dimensions of the Pearson Custom Library of American Literature.

The five editors of PCLAL worked closely in developing the table of contents, in selecting and editing texts, and in writing period introductions, author head notes, and textual annotations as well as special pedagogical features for over three hundred authors and more than 1700 texts. They could not have completed these tasks without the help and feedback of numerous scholars. They wish to thank Jane Aldrich, Kevin Armitage, Ralph Bauer, Dennis Berthold, Bruce Bickley, Virginia Blanford, Joanna Brooks, Eliza Bryant, Christy Burns, Kathy Cain, Gregg Camfield, Beth Widmaier Capo, Barbara Clonts, Stanley Corkin, Robert Dawidoff, Richard Dillman, John Ernest, Antonia Garcia-Orozco, Ann Gilmartin, Walter Graffin, Nancy L. Gray, Jane C. Harred, Sharon Harris, Henry W. Hart, Robert Hass, Beverly Haviland, John Hildebidle, Sue E. Houchins, Ken Johnson, David Kadlec, David Kann, Jim Kinney, Lucinda Kriete, Jasmin L. Lambert, Elaine Limbaugh, Bennett Lovett-Graff, Richard Lowry, Lucy Maddox, Joseph Malof, William Marling, Darlene McElfresh, Susan McKay, Janice Neuleib, Margaret Darlene O'Dell, John Parks, Catherine E. Paul, Michael Pearson, Kimberley Phillips, Hermine D. Pinson, Victoria Ramirez,

Bethany Reid, Paige Reynolds, David Robinson, James Rocks, Lois Rudnick, Stephen Ruffus, Maria Sanchez, Jonathan Smith, Steve Spence, Suzette A. Spencer, Andrew Stambuk, Judith Stanford, Elizabeth Sumner, Sheila Teahan, Donald Weber, Shira Wolosky, Hilary Wyss, John Young, and Lee Zimmerman.

Table of Contents

Literature of the 20th Century (1900-1945)

Literature of the 20th Century (1945-Present)

Fateful Lightning
Writing in America, 1820–1865

John Bryant

The first half of the nineteenth century brought forth on this continent a new nation-state, and its near demise. Politically, economically, and culturally, the United States "were" struggling through a kind of adolescence. The verb here is "were" because, at this time, the "nation" considered itself a collection of semi-self-determined states, and "the United States" did not become singular, grammatically, until after the Civil War violently insisted on the notion of a single Union of states. In these decades, the nation-state called the United States was decidedly adolescent, experiencing a period of exuberance and growth coupled with depression, violence, and self-destructive behavior.

This characterization is not meant to reduce the nation's formative age to "merely a passing phase." For just as the problems of anyone's adolescent years establish the issues that invariably govern the rest of their lives, so too have the conflicts of the nation's early years perpetuated themselves into the twenty-first century. The social, political, and ethical problems confronted today have their roots in the years leading to the cataclysmic Civil War: centralized government versus states' rights; women's rights and property rights; religious fundamentalism but also transcendental spiritual expansion; free markets but no free lunch; capitalism and imperialism but also genocide, poverty, and slavery; "America-First" patriotism but also multiculturalism. This antebellum age is often dismissed as if it were a primitive era, and yet this time "before the war"—The Civil War—is, in fact, a recognizable version of the United States today.

The writing during this period was also extraordinary, not only for the sudden, voluminous output of novels, tales, essays, poetry, and plays, but also for the daring and excellence of the writers and works themselves. In 1776 colonists had declared themselves politically independent, but it was not until the 1820s that citizens of the newly formed nation could begin to make their cultural declaration of independence from Britain and the rest of

Europe. Seeking to discover their own genius and voice, the nation's writers engaged in much sentiment but also much fire to ignite a uniquely American and modern national literature.

For all its impact, the American Revolution could not and did not slam the door on European ways, nor could "Young America" (as one group of writers called themselves) ignore its largely European past. Thus, early fictions transplanted Europe's ideals of civility and domesticity into the frontier in order to preach a new code of democratic manners; and darker narratives transformed Europe's gothic knights, monks, and castles into wilderness settings inhabited by adventurers, settlers, Native Americans, and nature's renegades to explore the limits of freedom and the self. At the same time, the nation's newest product—the freedom to pursue happiness—affected the people's freedom of self expression. Liberty had freed the white middle-class, property-owning male. But thousands of others had something more to say about liberty, freedom, and the dimensions of selfhood. Thus, new classes of dispossessed and underprivileged men and women—runaway slaves, Native Americans, frontier daughters and mothers—wrote out their lives in both protest and self-exploration, in a variety of styles and forms that Europe and most privileged males gave little attention to.

Eventually, writers as diverse as Emerson, Longfellow, and Poe; Cooper, Hawthorne, Lydia Maria Child, and Harriet Jacobs; Melville, Stowe, and Douglass; Bryant, Dickinson and Whitman exceeded the goal of a national literature by rejuvenating such exhausted literary forms as the gothic, romance, and epic, and giving new meaning to current forms such as the nature poem, travel writing, life writing, slave narrative, and the novel. Writing for America and themselves, they ended up writing for the world.

It is never entirely clear why volatile times generate great writing. Perhaps passionate conflicts over elemental issues such as freedom, spirituality, self-awareness, and sexuality naturally urge even the least of the populace to speak up and write it all down. But this does not necessarily explain the inventive, experimental nature of the literature produced during this age. The poetic lines—Dickinson's concision, Whitman's expansion, Melville's contortion, Poe's incessant rhyme—seem to exult in their nonconformity. The fictions (Poe's gothic hoaxes, Melville's dramatic prose-poem epic) deconstruct: the plots don't hold; the wording, like the emotions expressed, is excessive or perverse; the psychology plunges deep to the inexplicable. Narrators (benighted, neurotic, sometimes mad) try to con the reader, but why? The symbols (Poe's raven, Hawthorne's scarlet letter, Melville's whale, Whitman's leaf of grass, Dickinson's buzzing fly) lure readers into deep self-inspection and then implode. Even the humor is strained and dark, as if laughter is something the reader must do or go nuts.

These literary excesses and irregularities are not the work of impetuous over-achievers; they derive from a cultural paradox. During this nation-forming time, the nation was, in fact, falling apart. Nullifiers in the South were pushing the Declaration of Independence to their own misguided but seemingly logical conclusion that states had the right to secede from the Union and declare themselves independent, sovereign nations. At the same time, abolitionists were preaching freedom for all, even at the expense of war. Both were taking the nation's gravest self-contradictions—states' rights and slavery—to an inevitable self-destruction. To keep the nation intact and prevent war, each successive generation of Americans forged a political compromise between North and South, but despite these political efforts, fathers were digging in their heels and brothers making fists. The Mexican War of 1846–48—an expansionist land grab that pushed out Mexicans to make room for slaves—became a training ground for the likes of Grant and Lee whose encounter in the American Civil War of 1861–65 would shock the world and leave wounds still festering today. Given these seemingly irresolvable conflicts inherent in the democracy, it is only natural that the culture would generate, not a literature of resolution and independence, but a literature of breakdown.

This is not to say that all antebellum writing is about the looming Civil War. It is safe to say, however, that the instability inherent in the culture's experiment with liberal democracy and unbridled capitalism created an inherently unstable American sense of self. In his novel *The House of the Seven Gables* (1851), Nathaniel Hawthorne hit the nail on the head: "In this republican country, amid the fluctuating waves of our social life, somebody is always at the drowning-point. The tragedy is enacted with as continual a repetition as that of a popular drama on a holiday, and, nevertheless, is felt as deeply, perhaps, as when an hereditary noble sinks below his order." What Americans began to learn as the nation endured its adolescence was that the freedom to speak their mind beyond sexual, social, and religious conventions often meant confronting the possibility of gender confusion, alienation, even atheism; that the freedom to move West, or just move out, often meant rootlessness and homelessness; that the freedom to succeed invariably meant the freedom to fail. The fact that American freedom was in many ways at the expense of Africa was only part of the problem. Democracy and capitalism are inherently unstable systems—they require revolution, progress, and bankruptcy—and with them there is always the threat of going under; the systems are always at Hawthorne's "drowning-point." The democracy makes this so, and the literature of this age addresses this tragic and ennobling instability by being unstable itself in its form and destabilizing in its effect on readers. The great writing of the antebellum period is great, in one way or another, because it acts out the threatening instability of the culture itself. Whether in its oceanic embrace or tight concision, its obsessive coherencies or formal breakdowns, it is the fateful lightning of a nation forming itself, and falling apart.

Forming the Nation-State

It is one thing to gain power, and quite another to maintain it. So said Nicolo Machiavelli in 1526 to his Florentine Prince hoping to guide him toward a unified and republican Italy. In the early days of America's republic (from the ratification of the constitution in 1789 to the War of 1812) the problem in maintaining power was not when to use the iron fist of a Prince but how to invent anti-authoritarian traditions of governance from scratch. It was no longer enough for founding fathers including Washington, Adams, Jefferson, Madison, and Hamilton to articulate (as they had in 1776) certain principles of self-government and the rights of life, liberty, and the pursuit of happiness. Their job was to transform those principles into everyday laws and procedures, and the sticking point was this right to pursue happiness. Of course, no one can legislate happiness, but a government can be built to ensure its citizens equal opportunity in pursuing it. Thus, to maintain power, the architects of the new nation-state erected a system of balanced powers and sought ways to extend that system into the community as well as the wilderness, into business and on the plantation. They had a lot of work to do, never mind they did not agree on such fundamentals as how much power to give to Congress, the president, and the people—or even how to define "the people" (would that term include women, renters as opposed to property owners, and slaves?); whether to support industry as well as agriculture; who should control the banks; when to stop the African slave trade; and what foreign nations to recognize.

Federalists (chiefly among them John Adams and Alexander Hamilton) had a healthy fear of popular governance (i.e., the mob) and argued for a strong, centralized executive authority, tightly held money, and an economy based on business and industry as well as farms. Thomas Jefferson was more fearful of the capitalist system and the poverty it generated (as witnessed by industrialized Europe) than he was of the threat of "mobocracy," and he and his fellow Republican Democrats favored a small-scale agrarian system run by independent farmers. (Although himself an independent farmer, Jefferson never gave up his dependency on slaves). These were the political parties that gave voice to the fledgling nation's earliest internal conflicts.

Compounding the problem was that on the international scene, Britain, France, and Spain (and later Germany and Italy) were complicating their own nation status through aggressive acts of imperialism and revolutions of their own. Britain held claim to Canada and the Pacific Northwest; France to the center of the continent west of the Mississippi; and Spain to Mexico, which included Texas, California, and the territory in between. All three had eyes on the Caribbean. The French Revolution of 1789 and the advent of Napoleon as, first, dictator of France, and then emperor of Europe, had the happy effect of turning Europe's attention away from the New World, but

America's attempts to maintain neutrality only made its merchant ships prey to all parties concerned. And Jefferson's Embargo Act (1807–09), which was designed to punish England and France for their seizing of American ships by curtailing European imports, only managed to throw the nation into its first major economic crisis.

At the same time, Napoleon found himself in need of cash. Having acquired Louisiana when he seized Spain, and irritated by Toussaint L'Ouverture's costly revolt against him in Haiti, he was happy to get out of the New World and sold Louisiana and its adjoining territories to the United States for $15 million. The Louisiana Purchase (1803) virtually doubled the size of the nation. But this only exacerbated Northern border tensions with Britain, angered by America's neutrality in the Napoleonic Wars, and led to the War of 1812. In this two-year affair, the nation-state suffered attacks by the British and Indians from the North and on the Eastern seaboard. Despite the sacking of the nation's new capital, Washington D.C., the United States claimed a "decisive" victory in New Orleans, even though Britain had already decided weeks earlier to accept peace. The United States had survived its first great challenge to its sovereignty among nations. At home the split between Federalists and Democrats cooled down into an "era of good feelings," and the Monroe Doctrine made it clear that further European incursions into the New World would not be tolerated. With its borders relatively secure, the nation-state was ready to define itself culturally, and grow.

Expansions and Exploitation

By 1820 the United States had almost doubled its number of states and more than doubled its territory. Today, Americans recognize themselves as a nation of great size, wealth, and population, and this has been the case for more than fifty years. But while the nation's growth in these dimensions has been significant since World War II, it cannot compare to the incredible rate of growth of the antebellum age. From 1810 to 1860, each new census reported a thirty percent increase in population, due in part to the greatest influx of immigrants the nation had at that time ever seen. And to accommodate everyone, first- and then second-growth forests were mowed down for lumber to build cities. Most of the trees now seen east of Appalachia are the re-growth the country has allowed to return to mountains and fields long ago denuded by the nation's relentless movement West. Roads from Baltimore to Terre Haute cut through passes. Shipping lines up and down New York's navigable rivers were not enough to meet business and travel needs, so canals were dug where rivers would not go. But water is slow, so railroads were laid beside rivers to get to places faster. Soon enough the electric telegraph lined the roads, canals, and rails with wire. The nation was expanding, and everyone had to get somewhere now, even if the pace was only thirty miles an hour. The impact on the land and its original inhabitants was devastating. At the same time, the culture's connection to Nature as a source of value, self-identity, and even spiritual attachment grew.

By the 1840s, the Native American population was sufficiently "pacified" and marginalized to ensure their eventual demise. In 1790, the government had enacted peace treaties with various tribes, conferring on them certain lands and a quasi-nation status. But Westward moving settlers were continually encroaching on Indian lands. Just before the War of 1812, two Shawnee chieftains, Tecumseh and his brother called The Prophet, attempted to confederate their tribe with the Cherokee and Creek to present an organized front against white America, but their premature defeat in 1811 to future President William Henry Harrison on Indiana's Tippecanoe River spelled the end for the resistance. In 1818, another future president, Andrew Jackson (hero of the Battle of New Orleans), led a raid against Seminole Indians and runaway slaves holed up in an old Spanish fort in Florida. Killing Indians became a reliable route to the White House. In 1832 during his first administration, Jackson defied the Supreme Court's decision supporting Native-American sovereignty and saw to it that Indians inhabiting reservations in Georgia were removed to Arkansas. From this time on, the government continued its shameful pattern of displacing Native Americans, forcing them to march a "Trail of Tears" from their woodlands in the South and East out to the dusty districts of Oklahoma and the Dakotas.

In compensation for the eradication of a race, the Anglo-American establishment was happy to sentimentalize the Indian, by adorning their coins and folding money with images of idealized and ennobled Indian figures and by setting up charitable institutions and schools—for the further eradication Native-American culture. Images of the Indian have also appeared in American writing from the beginning. The "captivity narrative" of the seventeenth and eighteenth centuries, which related personal accounts of white settlers held captive by Indians, registered a general disgust and confusion over Indian customs, but nevertheless depicted the individuals realistically, with respect, and without sentiment. However, by the 1820s and 1830s the Native American was less of a threat and more a source of cultural guilt; hence, they began to play roles as either formidable villains or noble savages in several of the nation's more popular domestic fictions and heroic plays. In their own right these "romances," such as James Fenimore Cooper's Leather-Stocking novels (1823–41), Lydia Maria Child's *Hobomok* (1824), Catharine Sedgwick's *Hope Leslie* (1827), William Gilmore Simms's *The Yemassee* (1835), and Robert Montgomery Bird's stage production of *Metamora* (1836) used the conventions of the novel or drama of social manners to bend the rigidities of class into a democratic frame in which class lines and racial lines are called into question even as they are melodramatically reinforced.

Set in the colonial past and in the wilderness, these works convey a social world intimately tied to nature as though true republican values, rooted in the land, can emerge from the struggle to combine community and forest. In this context, the Indian became a symbol of both Nature's threatening chaos and yet its sublime, unspoken power, nobility, and truth. Cooper, in *The Pioneers* (1823), *The Last of the Mohicans* (1826), and *The Prairie* (1827), gives a remarkable range of fantasy Indians—villain, lover, sage, and loyal companion; virile and toothless; noble, evil, or comic; fighting, chanting and dying—each more virtuous than the common lot of reckless, spendthrift, "wasty" white settlers (whom the patrician Cooper generally disdained in real life). And needless to say, Cooper's white readers applauded these virtuous noble savages as they read along in their parlors, situated on stolen lands.

Slightly more realistic Indians appear in such travel literature as Washington Irving's A *Tour on the Prairies* (1835) and histories such as Francis Parkman's *Oregon Trail* (1849) and *The Conspiracy of Pontiac* (1851), or William H. Prescott's *Conquest of Mexico* (1843). But even here, the depictions tend toward the comic or sentimental or epic. Serious anthropological studies (apart from much earlier linguistic studies), in particular the work of Henry Rowe Schoolcraft (1793–1864), were only beginning to be written. Meanwhile, Native Americans such as Chief Seattle (1786–1866), William Apess (1798–1839), and George Copway (1818–1869), as well as white activist Lydia Maria Child (1802–1860) wrote eloquent messages of protest on behalf of Indian life and culture.

Two of the more moving poetic treatments of the Indian and of nature are William Cullen Bryant's "Prairies" (1834) and Henry Wadsworth Longfellow's epic *The Song of Hiawatha* (1855), which evoke an ancient, mythic past to connect readers to an Indian culture preceding colonization and more closely united to the rhythms of primeval nature. Bryant adapted to the American experience Wordsworth's poeticizing of common speech into blank verse and used such language to reflect on time and nature. In some cases, he out-Wordsworthed Wordsworth. "Prairies" is Bryant's "Tintern Abbey," for just as Wordsworth's poem uses present memory amid cathedral ruins to link past and future thoughts, Bryant's poem discovers through a kind of memory in the land itself a symbolic link between the ancient Indian mounds of a race no longer present and a frontier republican society to come. Longfellow drew on the incessant rhythms of the Finnish epic tradition to give his Indian heroes and lovers a link not only to nature but to a universalized folk culture. Beyond their use of the Indian, both Bryant and Longfellow found in nature a comfort and repose capable of containing the anxieties of men and women confronting America's relentless demand for movement. They were the nation's first poets to achieve success at home and abroad.

Toward a National Literature

If a nation is to establish a cultural identity and voice of its own, let alone something as presumptuous as a national literature, it must have the means to produce, or rather reproduce and distribute, that identity and voice. It must have a publishing industry. While settlers were moving into the wilderness, printers and book dealers were slowly setting up shop in town, the better to serve readers. But the readers of the day had simple reading needs: their Bible, a newspaper (in a growing variety of languages), a farmer's almanac, surveying and navigational texts, the occasional sermon or religious tract, school books, and commercial ads. They had little need for novels, tales, and poems. Besides, what demand there was for such literary fare could be met by imports from abroad. Getting home-grown writers to produce a body of uniquely American literature required consumers in need of such a thing and publishers willing to take the risk to meet that need. This would take time.

And there was a further complication. From 1800 on, while big publishing firms were being established—the Harper Brothers (New York, 1817), Matthew Carey's (Philadelphia, 1829), Little, Brown (Boston, 1847)—they, nevertheless, had little interest in American writers and no qualms about stealing the writing of established authors already published abroad. During these decades, American publishers reprinted foreign works for American distribution without bothering to send royalties (i.e., a percentage of the profit) to authors; and such "pirated" editions of, say, Sir Walter Scott and Charles Dickens were cheaper than books by America's own writers— Bryant, Cooper, Longfellow, and Irving—whose need for royalties to survive meant their works were necessarily more costly and thus less likely to gain wide circulation. Writers on both sides of the Atlantic complained bitterly of this situation and pleaded for an International Copyright Law to remedy the market inequity, but Congress would not come through until 1891. Until then, American writers hoping to make a name resorted to the scheme of getting their books published with royalties first in England, and then perhaps in America with similar terms. Therefore, until the great explosion of magazines in the 1850s, American writers had little recourse but to try to gain acceptance in England first before they could be read by friends at home. But the British were not entirely inclined to publish Americans unless they sounded enough like themselves. Thus, to make a national literature happen, Americans needed more than genius and vision; they needed readers and a marketplace at home, both of which were heavily restricted.

The vicious cycle began to break in 1819 when Washington Irving's *Sketch Book*, purportedly the work of an American "Gentleman" named Geoffrey Crayon, appeared with descriptions of English life and scenery but also a handful of American tales, including "Rip Van Winkle." This modern fairy tale of a henpecked idler who sleeps through the American Revolution and emerges free of his wife and the democracy's new anxieties managed to critique the bustle and rancor of partisan republican life without stooping to rancorous and divisive political satire, which had been the common lot of early comic writing. Instead, the tale's genial humor and nostalgia for older, calmer days underscore pre-Revolutionary values while still giving moral support to a rising generation eager to get ahead but also anxious just to relax. The British adored Irving because he reminded them of their own genial essayists Oliver Goldsmith and Charles Lamb; the Americans loved him because he articulated in comic tones the serious psychological condition of the democrat caught between conflicting desires for freedom and stability and, of course, because the British adored him first. Irving's reputation as America's great humorist and an international writer brought him a consulate abroad and continued reverence into the twentieth century.

But despite the international acclaim, Irving remained "America's Goldsmith," which is as much to say that American writing could only be comprehended in terms of British antecedents. Not until 1850, with Herman Melville's exuberant literary manifesto in praise of "Hawthorne and His Mosses," would someone complain of this situation so forthrightly: "We want no American Goldsmiths. . . . Call him an American, and have done; for you can not say a nobler thing of him.—But it is not meant that all American writers should studiously cleave to nationality in their writings, only this, no American writer should write like an Englishman, or a Frenchman; let him write like a man, for then he will be sure to write like an American." Putting aside the manly chest-thumping, there is a deeper point: It was time for America's national literature to emerge on its own terms, and to do that it needed to transcend mere nationality. American literature had to become a world literature.

Transcendental Urges: Emerson and Poe

Two writers, quite different from each other—Emerson and Poe—were able to write to the nation but beyond nationality, each in quite different ways, and thus, paradoxically, each established a legitimate claim to a uniquely American national literature.

Ralph Waldo Emerson (1803–1882) was a Harvard-educated, Unitarian minister who in 1832 renounced the pulpit and became a lecturer, essayist, and poet. His ideas, expressed in the philosophical tract *Nature* (1836) and in several volumes of essays including "Self-Reliance," "Compensation," "Experience," "Fate," and "The Poet" became the core of one of the nation's earliest and most compelling ethical and philosophical contributions: Transcendentalism. At the height of his career in the 1840s and 1850s, he drew around him a circle of like-minded New Englanders: Thoreau (author of

Walden), feminist Margaret Fuller, social critic Theodore Parker, utopian planner Bronson Alcott, educator Elizabeth Peabody, and mystic poet Jones Very. Their impact continues to be felt on thinkers and writers of today.

Transcendentalism has its most immediate philosophical source in the work of the German idealist Immanuel Kant (1724–1804), but Emerson also drew on Plato and the neo-Platonists, Puritan theology, the rational mystic Swedenborg, Hinduism, Confucianism, and Zen, as well as such modern British contemporaries as Coleridge and Carlyle, with whom he corresponded. Essentially, Transcendentalism begins with the understanding that the mind is limited by social constraints and anxieties that keep a person tied to a material world when, in fact, reality is governed by deeper universal forces or ideals (ultimately the concept of Beauty). To expand inner consciousness is to receive these forces and will allow an individual to be at One with all mankind and all nature.

Although also a poet, Emerson distinguished himself primarily as an essayist in the seemingly circular and digressive manner of the great French progenitor of the personal essay, Michel de Montaigne. His prose style is both fluid and terse, at times inscrutable, at times commonsensical, even suitable for calendar quotation. Following Emerson through a paragraph, and from one paragraph to the next, is an adventure in deep thinking and self-exploration involving leaps that, very much in keeping with his philosophy, induces the reader to seek out in seemingly unexpected places a unifying oneness of disparate things, including god, nature, and self. This challenging reading experience not only articulates transcendental principles; it is an enactment of them.

Given America's persistent focus on the practical, material, and down to earth, it is remarkable that Emerson's writing and brand of Transcendentalism even took root, much less that its spirituality continues in today's sensual age of consumerism to serve as a social equivalent of religion. The reason for this may lie in the consequences of liberal democracy's anti-authoritarianism and doctrine of self-reliance, which discourage organized or state-sponsored religion. While this tradition encourages a preference for a personal, unmediated engagement with God, it nevertheless leaves a person problematically structure-free in seeking out spirituality. The freedom to *find* one's own religious experience led in the days of the early republic to the opportunity to *found* one's own religion—Mormonism being one structure that took root, went West, became a nation of sorts, then a state, and now has its own missionary empire throughout the world. Less ambitious structures developed in the "camp meeting" in which traveling circuit preachers, such as Lorenzo Dow, gave week-long programs devoted to revival, conversion, and rebirth (as well as the occasional birth nine months later). This uniquely American religious experience has served generations of seekers perpetually in need of "spiritual uplift" through religious experimentation, born-again fundamentalism, even twelve-step programs. Although far more cerebral than revivalism, Transcendentalism may be placed in the context of America's penchant for independent spiritual engagement in that it seeks if not rebirth then "re-attachment" (see Emerson's "The Poet") to a universal sense of life, and finds structure not in a tent or temple but in nature.

For Americans living in or near a wilderness, nature was vast, unknown, and frightening, but as a resource for material sustenance and wealth, it was worth confronting. And for those seeking to find meaning in life, or to fill a void not met by material gain, nature also became a resource for spiritual growth. Getting back to nature is a logical step for the American democrat. But Emerson's "nature" is not simply the mountains, rivers, and trees; these "beautiful things" are merely material representations of higher ideal concepts—sublimity, fluidity, growth—all of which are components of an even higher unifying ideal: Beauty itself. For Emerson, "Beauty is the creator of the universe." Not God but Beauty is a Oneness, a force of Creativity that suffuses the outwardly confusing diversity of material things. It is a force anyone may experience, if one is willing to ignore social conventions and materiality, and wait for a moment of transcendence to occur. Such passivity, like the more traditional "waiting upon the Lord for deliverance," strained the patience of many, including Emerson's social-activist friends such as Alcott, Parker, Thoreau, and Fuller. Politically, Emerson was cognizant of, if not deeply engaged in, the issues of power and economy that had brought the nation to conflict, but his philosophy of waiting to achieve a moment of transcendence distanced him from the philanthropists and abolitionists seeking to end injustice here and now, regardless of beauty and oneness. Although philosophically abstract, Emerson's politics did have an activism of its own, for to transcend, if even for a moment, is to find the One in many and God in the street, an advanced consciousness that obviates the root causes of poverty and injustice. In this way, transcendental spirituality is deeply political; it is immediate, unstructured, democratic, universal, and hence American.

All this made Edgar Allan Poe (1809–1849) sick. A Southerner transplanted in Philadelphia and New York, or wherever his life as a magazine editor took him, he disdained New England's Transcendental Club, or "Frog Pond" as he called it, and derided its self-assured "German Idealism." This is not to say he was not drawn to his own version of Transcendentalism and a spiritual ideality beyond the material world. He, like Hawthorne and Melville, could not deny the human capacity for the "all feeling" of spiritual transcendence. But equally compelling for Poe was the Nothingness implied by death, the utter cessation of consciousness, and the fact that some impish, perverse death wish in everyone urges each individual toward self-annihilation. Beauty, Poe concluded, is not an ideal a person transcends to; it is merely an effect, something to make up in compensation for the fact humans cannot transcend. For Beauty to be beautiful, it must evoke a sense of loss and vacancy rather than sublimity and creativity. For it to have an effect, it must be strange, uncanny, and suggestive. Where Emerson required poets to make a "meter-making argument," Poe parodied argumentation (and all things didactic or preachy); his later poems, like "Ulalume" (1847) were increasingly musical and evocative. His best, "The Raven" (1845), which pulled together his ideas of symbol, musicality and the inability to transcend, became a national sensation only a few brief years before his untimely death.

Poe famously excelled in short stories. At first he wrote lampoons and hoaxes; later, he created a series of gothic tales, such as "Ligeia" (1838) and "The Fall of the House of Usher" (1839), which toyed with narrative voice and the supernatural in ways that make readers vaguely suspicious that they have been hoaxed yet again. His super-rational detective tales (a genre he invented), such as "The Murders in the Rue Morgue" (1841), also delight in stringing readers along. For all his spoofing of the reader, Poe limited his political satire of America to only a few fairly conventional attacks on politicians and the mob. Like Emerson, his interest in ideality and deep psychology distanced him from the hurly-burly of politics. His last prose work, *Eureka* (1848), is a philosophical treatise attempting to prove a transcendent reality through material evidence alone. Poe carried his love-hate relationship with Transcendentalism, and with his readers, to the end.

No two writers could be as far apart in temperament and style than Emerson and Poe, yet they merge, oddly enough, in their refusal "to cleave to nationality." Each insisted on taking readers beyond America, either into Nature or the Supernatural. And in becoming writers for the world, they revealed a simple truth for writers to come: that writing for the self and not one's party, and writing the truth, no matter how dark or ludicrous, opens an author to a readership worldwide, if the writing is palatable and the symbols suggestive.

Two other writers, this time quite similar to each other—Hawthorne and Melville—took this route. They did not, however, ignore America's politics, past, or social problems. But to get at these two, it is useful to consider more fully the impending crisis brought on by imperialism and slavery in American life, and the new growth in the literary world they inhabited as well. As the nation-state moved west to the Pacific, its vision of empire grew, and that growth brought to a head the question of whether empire would extend slavery or freedom for all. At this time, a new brand of frontier humor gave expression to the culture's exuberance, doubts, and diversified populace while an energetic new medium, the magazine, provided writers a new forum for their ideas. Stage spectacles and popular drama began to proliferate across the nation. At the same time, the horrifying paradox of slavery in a democracy gave birth to new kinds of writing altogether, including the deeply wrenching slave narrative.

Empire and Slavery

The Logic of Compromise

The problem with America's Manifest Destiny to expand to the Pacific was not how to populate the vast tracts of land—the people were coming and quickly—or where to draw international borders—if Britain would not accept 54° 40′ as the line between Canada and the United States, they would settle on the 49th parallel. The problem was whether the new territories would allow slavery. The founding fathers, many of whom abhorred the institution of slavery and yet kept their slaves, had put off the matter of manumission to ensure the union of Northern and Southern states, assuming that slavery would die out or that more efficient labor practices would evolve. But growing markets for cotton at home and abroad and the invention of the Cotton Gin for processing the product enhanced the Southern plantation system, causing many to realize that there is no labor practice more efficient than forcing workers to work for free. Even though the African Slave Trade was prohibited in 1808, and slavery abolished in the North—with New York finally complying in 1827—the Southern slave population grew over 1,000% from 1810 to 1860 to almost four million people, much of that growth occurring in the newly settled Western states of Alabama, Mississippi, and Texas. The business of slavery was not about to evolve out of existence on its own, nor were Northern and Southern politicians inclined to work out a gradual elimination of what was euphemistically called the South's "peculiar institution" and what Herman Melville called "man's foulest crime."

In addition, Southern politicians made it clear that their states would exercise their "right" to secede from the union before giving up slavery. Whether this was a sanctioned right was a matter hotly denied in the North and articulately defended by Senator John C. Calhoun, a brilliant if misguided debater from South Carolina. The logic was that if in ratifying the constitution, each constituent state was simply signing a contract, then each state had a right to nullify the contract whenever the contracted terms were not being met. And if the federal government were to force a sovereign state to end slavery against its will, then the original contract was broken, and the state had no further obligation to that contract. It could secede from the Union. The logic is valid, although its basic premise of a contract is not. And Calhoun's great adversaries, Henry Clay, Daniel Webster, and even the revered Southerner Andrew Jackson, told him so: The amendable document called the U.S. Constitution is not a temporary contract meeting short-term needs; it is a set of rules for working out problems and striking mutually beneficial compromises when states disagree. For decades, political compromise had become the chief mode of survival for the Union. But in the long run, the wisdom of compromise had only disastrous effects.

In order to prevent Congress from enacting a federal emancipation nationwide, the House, controlled by the more populous North, had to be balanced by the Senate, which was evenly divided by free and slave states. This equal-balance approach was codified by the Missouri Compromise of 1820, which admitted Missouri and Maine into the Union as slave and free states, respectively, and proclaimed the rest of the Louisiana Purchase free. Over the next thirty years, six states would be added, three slave, three free. Even so, tensions over slavery mounted. With the abolitionist movement gaining momentum in the 1830s, and with the slave revolts led by Denmark Vesey (1822), Nat Turner (1831), and Joseph Cinque of the Amistad (1841), the Southern states began to harden its repressive practices, forbidding the teaching of reading to African Americans; preaching white superiority; restricting slave travel; and censoring abolitionist writings. Meanwhile, the average price of a slave rose from $300 in 1820 to $1,200 and more in 1860.

Inevitably, the Westward movement threatened the fragile compromise and balance in the Senate. Northerners and Southerners alike began to look beyond the Louisiana Purchase at Mexico's land between Texas and California, a new empire up for grabs by free soilers and slave owners alike. People crowding up in the East eager for work, land, and wealth had great incentives to claim this empire. To begin with, money in the form of credit was suddenly more available to more people. For decades, U.S. currency had been controlled by a single federal Bank of the United States and only a limited number of state branches; thus getting a loan had not been easy. In 1832, Jackson campaigned to refuse to re-charter the Bank and thus allow state banks to proliferate into the Western states. Banks quickly issued credit more freely, and they printed up a colorful array of bank notes (folding paper money) for wide distribution. Tremendous growth, building, and spending ensued, and with it, of course, inflation, bankruptcy, and larceny, culminating in the Panic of 1837, America's biggest depression to date. Unemployment sent people West; the discovery of California gold in 1848 sent them running. Hundreds of women's diaries record the excitement, boredom, hardship, childbirth and death, and occasional Indian encounter as families essentially walked twenty miles a day along the Oregon or Santa Fe Trails, and over the notorious Donner Pass, where a group of pioneers stranded in winter were forced to eat their deceased in order to survive.

America's Humor: Getting to the Other Side

The economic instabilities, the boom or bust mentality, and uncertainties of the frontier (which despite its Emersonian Beauty included bears, Indians, and con men) made this a time ripe for humor. For a nation of diverse inhabitants—Yankees, Southerners, frontiersmen, Africans, preachers, farmers, low class and high, dudes and rubes, Frenchmen, Brits, urbanites and cosmopolites—it was not entirely clear what exactly an American was. Today it is called multiculturalism—the simple fact is that no American is really "native." All Americans originated somewhere else, if not recently then generations ago. Even America's Native Americans crossed over from Siberia. To be American is to have a dual identity—Anglo American, African American, German American, Irish American, Italian American, Hispanic American, Jewish American, Asian American. Today's dilemma is how to come to terms with this duality: to wonder when and with what sense of loss or guilt or relief a citizen becomes just American; to learn how to subsume a heritage with "American-ness" and keep the integrity of both. What exactly "American-ness" might be is a matter of perpetual debate as the definition of the term changes with every new wave of immigration.

This inherent identity crisis in the culture was addressed indirectly in the days of the early republic with comic self-portraits of regional character types: the sharp Yankee peddler, the extraverted frontiersman or "gamecock of the woods," the tuneful Negro minstrel. Each defined through laughter a slice of American life and social identity, and their multiplicity gave a color-ful presence to the nation's wide-flung regions and an implied tolerance for diversity. But the varied character types had one thing in common; each played a role in a vast confidence game called America. They were tricksters, liars, and confidence artists; they were dupes, ninnies, and fools. And in this brand of humor, no one character type played only one role: Con men were conned, and everybody played the fool. On the frontier, laughter was an equal opportunity offender.

Writers such as Davy Crockett (1786–1836), Augustus B. Longstreet (1790–1870), and George Washington Harris (1814–1869) offered up a humor of exaggeration and a rhetoric of deceit that let readers observe hoaxes, or be hoaxed and laugh at themselves in the process. It was good practice to laugh this way; it allowed readers to loosen social conventions and the rigidities of class while exercising a healthy doubt about venturing too confidently into the wilderness or business, or into the frontier where the two were likely to merge. The best of these identity-forming comic tales is T. B. Thorpe's "The Big Bear of Arkansas" (1841) in which a bear hunter dupes a crowd of native Mississippi riverboat "gentlemen" into believing his mythic tale of capturing a "creation bear." For jokesters or snake oil ped-dlers, America's new empire was ripe for the taking.

The Failure of Compromise

Southern plantation owners—who though relatively few in number held power over the Southern state legislatures—were hunting even bigger bear. Fully conscious that the prairies were simply not conducive to the plantation system, they turned their imperial eyes on Cuba and the Yucatan as potential colonies of a possible confederation of Southern states. At the same time, the major political parties (Jackson's Democrats and the Whig coalition of Clay in the West, Webster up North, and Calhoun down South) were beginning to fragment along ideological lines. Radical democrats against slavery (such as the Loco Focos and New York's Barnburners) joined with Free Soilers who supported Senator David Wilmot's "Proviso" that Western territories should not be open to slavery. By 1854 these splinter groups formed into the Republican Party, which in due course led Lincoln into office and the nation into Civil War.

But Texas was the beginning of the end. In 1821 Mexico had gained independence from Spain but had kept loose reins on its Northern territories. By 1836 enough American settlers had populated the wedge of fertile land between the Rio Grande and the gulf shores to make a bid for their own independence. After bloody fighting at the Alamo and San Jacinto, they proclaimed a new republic called Texas, which lasted as a sovereign nation (with a succession of presidents and ministers to European nations) until it entered the Union in 1845. A subsequent border dispute triggered war with Mexico in 1846. The United States invaded Mexico City from the seaport of Vera Cruz, and took control of several other Spanish towns—Santa Fe, San Diego, Los Angeles, and San Francisco—by inland routes. By war's end in 1848, the United States had stretched its empire beyond Texas to the Pacific. Like Vietnam, the Mexican War was a controversial affair, not because it was an obvious land grab, but because the land grabbed threatened to extend the Southern slavocracy. Would gold-rich California (now itself a republic) enter the Union, and as a slave state or free? Immediately, Henry Clay set about erecting a new set of compromise laws that declared California a free state, gave Texas and New Mexico self-determination, abolished slavery in Washington D.C., and renewed the Fugitive Slave law, which forced the return of escaped slaves to their owners.

In stalling the Civil War, this Compromise of 1850, as it came to be called, made the conflict all the more inevitable. Ironically, Clay's measures only weakened his own Whig party, thus putting Democrats with Southern sympathies in the White House and angering Abolitionists. The Kansas-Nebraska Act (1854), which gave the citizens of these territories the right to determine for themselves whether to be slave or free, led to a land rush of Northern and Southern ideologues bent on influencing the territorial legislatures. With them came the so-called "border ruffians," fanatics from both sides who terrorized innocent settlers. The violence of "Bleeding Kansas"—righteous John Brown murdered five of his neighbors—was the harbinger of bloodier battles to come. But the Dred Scott decision (1857) was the ultimate polarization of slave and free factions. Scott, a Missouri slave, had resided for a while in the free state of Illinois and sued for freedom on the basis of this residency. The Supreme Court ruled not only that, as property, Scott remained a piece of property wherever he traveled and that, as a piece of property, he had no right to sue. It further ruled that the Missouri Compromise, which had declared the Louisiana Purchase exempt from slavery, was, in fact, an unconstitutional restriction on property rights. Abolitionists were right in seeing that the nation was regressing in its efforts to rid itself of slavery. In light of their outrage, Southern nullifiers and secessionists saw little recourse but to declare themselves independent. On April 12, 1861, soon after Lincoln's inauguration, they fired on Fort Sumter.

The Language of Protest and the Slave Narrative

Well before the Compromise of 1850 insisted on the enforcement of the Fugitive Slave Law, anti-slavery activists had been particularly outraged by the return of fugitive slaves to their owners; and in response they lectured, demonstrated, sometimes rioted, and wrote voluminously. The fiery New Englander William Lloyd Garrison (1805–1879) edited the abolitionist newspaper *The Liberator;* former slave Frederick Douglass (1818?–1895) edited the more moderate *North Star.* Others such as David Garnet, Theodore Weld, Angelina and Sarah Grimké, Sojourner Truth, James Redpath, and Harriet Tubman circulated orations, essays, and political tracts. A unique literary genre, the slave narrative, grimly reflective in content and form of the "peculiar" conditions of American life, also emerged. Recounting dramatic escapes to freedom, often along the famous Underground Railroad (a system of safe houses for hiding fugitives headed for Canada), these accounts were mostly dictated by illiterate runaways to earnest white editors, who heavily edited and revised the narrative. But some were written by the slaves themselves, including Douglass's 1845 autobiography of how he "became a man;" Henry "Box" Brown's tale of his audacious escape by mailing himself to freedom in a shipping crate; and Harriet Jacobs's female perspective on the sexual abuses inherent in the slave system.

The increasingly violent conflict over slavery—and the concurrent issues of race, gender, and sexuality—inevitably seeped more deeply into the nation's popular consciousness and literary works. By the 1830s, one of the most popular entertainments available to citizens in both the North and South was the minstrel show, a highly stylized spectacle with white men and women in black face mimicking African Americans in dance, pantomime, jokes, and song. This odd phenomenon of white audiences watching white actors debase black folk through sentimentalized and rudely comic stereotyping while the nation was so deeply conflicted over the issue of slavery is a classic instance of victimizers working hard to dehumanize their victims and thus minimize guilt through seemingly humanistic performance art. In 1852

17

Harriet Beecher Stowe (1811–1896) proposed an alternative fiction that did not entirely escape stereotyping itself, but which used rich strands of sentiment and irony to humanize America's slaves and get American readers to confront their guilt. Her *Uncle Tom's Cabin* became the nation's first, enduring bestseller. Stowe's use of the sentimental convention of domesticity (resilient women, Christ-like men, demented villains, and lovable dying children) as well as cagey direct addresses to male and female readers skewered Northern and Southern hypocrites alike, while providing some of the most memorable dramatic figures and scenes in popular American fiction. Making this novel even more popular was the appearance of a stage version by George Aikens that not only gave theater-goers a further alternative to black minstrels, as well as Broadway's standard fare of tawdry spectacles and melodramatized Shakespeare, but also spawned decades of "Tom Shows" in theaters across the country and paved the way for Dion Boucicault's immensely popular stage production, *The Octoroon* (1857).

African Americans fought against black minstrelsy on their own, mostly by composing work songs and spirituals that subversively yearn for freedom under the guise of religious symbols, but also by supplying re-writes of popular songs, as with Henry "Box" Brown's black lyrics to the white tune "Old Ned" by minstrelsy's chief composer, Stephen Foster. On a grander scale, African Americans were also writing their own fictional narratives. William Wells Brown, who wrote his own slave narrative, is also credited with publishing the first African-American novel, *Clotel,* or *the President's Daughter* (1853). In addition, Frances Harper's poems and her novel *Iola Leroy* (1892), Frank Webb's *The Garies and Their Friends* (1857), Harriet Wilson's *Our Nig* (1859), and Martin Delany's *Blake* (1861) establish themes of revolt, escape, class, and "passing" for white that would continue into the twentieth century.

Breakdown and Voice

Even as the nation was heading toward breakdown, its literary community was growing. The demand for an American literature was being met by a more receptive reading public at home and a broader acceptance abroad for things American. The means of production was expanding, and not only in the book trade. Magazines addressing all kinds of interest groups beyond the political parties—merchants, "ladies," and sportsmen—and beginning in the 1830s with subscriptions in only the hundreds suddenly took hold in the 1840s and 50s with circulations in the tens of thousands. All that was needed to launch the nation's literature into the world arena was a voice to tell its tales and talents to express that voice. In the decade before the Civil War, the nation suddenly found many voices.

Writing for the Magazines: Women in the Marketplace

Initially, magazines and newspapers took as their organizing principle a particular political stance or party allegiance—whether it be Jeffersonian, Jacksonian, Whig, or Republican; abolitionist, secessionist, feminist, liberal, or conservative—and to some degree this pattern continued well past the Civil War and into the present (although with less overt party affiliation). Periodicals, then as now, provided the kind of eclectic mix of news, commentary, useful information, and entertainment that the word "magazine," or storehouse, implies. They also catered to special interests. Specialty journals independent of particular parties, such as *The Dial,* a transcendental monthly, or Boston's *Ladies' Journal,* or *Spirit of the Times* for New York's sportsmen, emerged throughout the country giving writers steady jobs. Poe not only wrote for journals; he made his living editing them—*The Southern Literary Messenger, Burton's Gentleman's Magazine,* and *Graham's*—and his lifelong dream of running his own magazine was realized in *The Broadway Journal,* if only for a year.

Women were a significant and growing audience for the magazine industry. Although they contributed their equal share in populating America and more than their share in nurturing its children, they were not themselves accorded full citizenship in terms of voting until the ratification of the Nineteenth Amendment in 1920, and a married woman's property fell under the husband's ownership. In 1848, with the Seneca Falls Convention led by Lucretia Mott (1793–1880) and Elizabeth Cady Stanton (1815–1902), these inequities were formally addressed, and the slow progress toward suffrage and equal rights in ownership, divorce, employment, and education began to get on track.

In the meantime, as suffragists worked to ease the plight of women in the home and in public, women also found a niche in publishing. Not only did they write for the journals, they became printers, editors, and publishers in their own right, putting out magazines for children, parents, Native Americans, farmers, and teachers, and addressing such issues as temperance, abolition, as well as suffrage. They also contributed solidly to the fields of arts, sciences, and home economics. Hundreds of writers throughout the century, such as Amelia Bloomer, Alice and Phoebe Cary, Margaret Fuller, Julia Ward Howe, Lydia Sigourney, and Ann Stephens proved early on the strength of women's professionalism in magazine publishing. They challenged the notion that women and men must occupy "separate spheres" (home and public forum). As editors, they made the very public world of publication their home, thus spreading notions of domesticity into business and politics and giving women a platform from which they might finally gain equal rights with men. Lydia Maria Child (*The National Anti-Slavery Standard*) was a patient, unflinching speaker against slavery. The more moderate Sarah

Josepha Hale (*Godey's Lady's Book*) advocated rational approaches to "Home Management" and what Stowe's sister Catharine Beecher called "Domestic Economy," freeing women from the relentless drudgery of housework and child rearing.

Writing for the Magazines: Hawthorne and Melville

While the magazines served as an early form of social liberation for countless talented women, it helped to advance the careers of two of the nation's most talented literary men: Nathaniel Hawthorne and Herman Melville. In the one case, magazine publication launched a career; in the other, it helped rejuvenate a flagging readership.

Nathaniel Hawthorne (1804–1864), who made his reputation writing for the magazines, was, generally speaking, favorably disposed toward the female sex, but as writers they were serious competition, and in one ungracious moment he referred to them as a "mob of scribbling women." Hawthorne was a descendent of Judge John Hathorne who presided over the Salem Witch Trials of 1692, and his sense of ancestral guilt drew him into fictional investigations of the Puritan mind. He set his tales in a colonial world, which even for his readers in the 1830s and 1840s would have seemed like ancient times, but which he made to resonate with the problems of sin, faith, and community richly applicable to the nation's present world of disintegrative imperialism. In such magazine pieces as "The Minister's Black Veil," "Young Goodman Brown," and "The Maypole of Merry Mount," he pushed allegory into complex human conflicts to explore self-loathing, sensuality and the loss of faith, and humanity's paradoxical "doom of care." Despite their narrowmindedness, the Puritans, in Hawthorne's view, had a deep understanding of the heart, betrayal, and the most "unforgivable sin," letting the mind's obsession for perfection eclipse love and fellow feeling. These themes he developed as well in tales with more contemporaneous settings such as "Rappaccini's Daughter," "The Artist of the Beautiful," and "Ethan Brand."

Poe, who had much to say in his criticism about magazine writing, thought highly of Hawthorne's mastery of the short story genre, but disdained his allegorizing, by which he meant Hawthorne's tendency to moralize rather than let his symbols be suggestive. But in turning next from tale to novel, Hawthorne made in *The Scarlet Letter* (1850) his allegorical "A" (standing for "adultery" but emblematic of deeper psychological workings) evolve in meaning beyond any simple or easy moral. Elsewhere, he defended his method by saying that he did not wish to use fiction as a pin with which to impale the butterfly of thought and desire. He preferred to call his books not allegories, or even novels, but "romances" in which plot, character, and symbol ignore mundane social realities for more deeper probings of the mind.

Although he was friendly enough with President Franklin Pierce (an old college chum and Southern sympathizer) to win a consulate abroad, Hawthorne had no real taste for politics. It was to him a bore. Nevertheless, works such as his pre-Revolutionary tale "My Kinsman Major Molineux"; his great comic novel of an old family overtaken by progress, *The House of the Seven Gables* (1851); and his satire of a transcendental utopian community, *The Blithedale Romance* (1852) reveal a sharp social consciousness. But it was Hawthorne's persistent plummeting into the darker reaches of the mind that appealed the most to Melville.

Herman Melville (1819–1891) inverted and extended Hawthorne's career path. He began as a novelist before moving on to magazine writing, and once finished with short fiction, he became a poet. His first work, *Typee* (1846), relating his mostly factual but romanticized adventures among the South Sea islanders of Nuku Hiva, was an instant success, but was attacked by the religious press for its criticism of missionaries and Western imperialism. Unlike Hawthorne, Melville was not shy of overt political commentary, but as a consequence, *Typee* was censored in subsequent editions. The lesson was that during the volatile Mexican War era, it was best to avoid politics or rather to develop plot, character, and symbol in ways that present the truth covertly and in snatches as if it were "a scared white doe in the woodlands." Melville's greatest achievement, *Moby-Dick* (1851), does this with its symbol of the white whale, but more, it was the nation's most experimental "Romance" to date, combining its sea narrative with stage play, essay-like chapters on whales and whaling, and a poetic prose line that continues to whelm and overwhelm readers. At the same time, the novel's ostensible story-line—an obsessive and dictatorial sea captain seeks vengeance on the whale that chewed off his leg but destroys himself and all but one of his cosmopolitan crew in the process—was a remarkable symbolic commentary on the capitalist and imperialistic nation's ship of state heading toward its doom. The pivotal role of the black cabin-boy Pip made the connection between the ship's fate and slavery all the more obvious. Not surprisingly, the novel failed to sell.

Exhausted by publishing seven books in as many years, Melville turned to the magazines. He wrote for two new journals, *Harper's Magazine* and *Putnam's Monthly Magazine,* both intent on paying top dollar for American writing, and he created some the culture's most innovative and enduring works. The tragicomic "Bartleby" recounts the suicide of an office worker who simply "prefers not" to participate in business; "The Paradise of Bachelors and the Tartarus of Maids" is an unusual "diptych" of paired tales concerning male and female sexualities; and "Benito Cereno" is the ambitious narrative of a disastrous slave revolt seen from varying points of view. In all three a genial voice chips away at the pretenses of capitalism, gender, imperialism, and race.

Unlike Hawthorne, Melville was never able to secure a diplomatic post that would allow him to travel and write. By 1857, with his last novel *The Confidence-Man,* a dark comedy of faith and the republic, he gave up fiction writing. Ten years later, the Civil War gave him a subject for a poetic revival of his career, and he responded with *Battle-Pieces* (1866), a brilliant book of poems that proposed reconciliation but which disgusted readers who were weary of war and bent on a merciless "reconstruction" of the South. Not surprisingly, the book failed. Beset by a faltering marriage, the suicide of his teenage son, and a dreary job in New York City's custom house, Melville braved through his mid-life crisis and lapsed into obscurity; but he continued to write poetry in his remaining twenty-five years as well as several "prose and poem" works, including *Billy Budd,* the story of a martyred sailor falsely accused of mutiny. This short novel remained in manuscript at Melville's death in 1891, and was not published until its discovery in a bread box in 1919. The nation's most complex voice—novelist, magazinist, and poet—would not be fully heard until today's modern age.

Getting a New Line: Poetry in the Republic

Poetry and nation-building go hand in hand. The great epics from earliest recorded civilizations—*Exodus,* the *Iliad* and *Odyssey,* the *Aeneid,* and *Mahabharata*—derive from a period (c. 500 B.C.E.) when songs of heroic tribal conflict were first preserved in written language: These were classic instances in which a people unite in verse and project a cultural identity. More modern instances of epic literature in the emerging nations of Europe include Spenser's *The Faerie Queene,* and such dramas in verse as Shakespeare's history plays and Corneille's *Le Cid* might be seen as epic in their promotion of national heroes. Of course, most English poetry being written while Americans were forging a nation was writing that favored the shorter, balladic, more deeply introspective writing of lyric poetry that epics typically lacked. There were the innovative works of Wordsworth and Coleridge who in blank verse or rhyme applied a seemingly everyday language to common people in common settings. Or the more fiery Byron and Shelley who wrote passionately of human confrontations with nature and the self. Or Keats whose odes on beauty, time, and death were the epitome of romantic introspection. To be sure, these poets, who became models for writers of English on both sides of the Atlantic, experimented with new versions of epic writing, but these were largely inverted forms such as Byron's rakish *Don Juan* or nostalgic pastorals such as Tennyson's *Idylls of the King* and Arnold's *Sohrab and Rustum.* As England solidified its empire throughout the nineteenth century, its modern epics (comic and tragic) had more to do with formations of the inner self than with the building of a nation-state. In catching up to England's poetic tradition, America had to compress the dynamics of nation-building, empire, and self-formation into a voice and form suitable to its own reality and its own evolving identity.

Sentiment and Fire: Ameria's Early Poets

Excellence in poetry was a long time coming in North America. Utilitarian and practical-minded colonists, both puritan and deist alike, found prose (or at best mere sing-song poetry) to be the more serviceable mode of communication than lyric or epic poems. Moreover, colonists and early republican writers had little time and fewer resources for the kind of close study of metrical forms and literary precedents that the writing of effective poetry requires. Great poetry emerges when individual men and women have the talent to put their time and resources together; great poets emerge, too, when they discover an overwhelming personal need to write, either because of internal imperatives or because of some cultural, national, or spiritual calling.

In their brief moment, the seventeenth century puritans produced the likes of Edward Taylor, Anne Bradstreet, and Michael Wigglesworth. But with the exception of Philip Freneau's nature poems, colonial America contributed nothing to the rise of modern poetry. The urge to create an American epic was met in the early days of the republic with Joel Barlow's *Columbiad* (1805) and Richard Emmons's *Fredoniad.* But these tedious metrical affairs were caught up too much in the partisan and often petty politics of the day. Epics are about universalized conflicts that come to a resolution. America had conflicts but no resolutions; it had yet to achieve its promised land, or a splendor to rival Athens, or a glory that was Rome. Nor did it have a Moses, Homer, or Virgil to write it all down. This would begin to change in the first half of the nineteenth century when time, resources, talent, and personal need coalesced in several remarkable men and women.

In 1817, readers of the *North American Review* in Boston were astonished by "Thantopsis," a sophisticated poem by William Cullen Bryant (1794–1878), composed seven years earlier when he was only sixteen. This deeply engaged but readable "meditation on death" (as its Greek title indicates) developed its argument of consolation in democratic terms and in a Wordsworthian line that Bryant would perfect later on. Bryant quickly gained national fame and then international recognition, but his versatility and reputation as a poet did not match that of Henry Wadsworth Longfellow (1807–1882). This moody often depressive fellow (Harvard's first professor of modern languages) converted his depressions into lyrics both jaunty and haunting, and produced a body of work that ranged from the patriotic "Paul Revere's Ride" and the epics *Evangeline* and *Hiawatha,* to the inspirational "Psalm of Life" and sentimental "Village Blacksmith." He published poems for "the Fireside" that made Queen Victoria weep, and which school children were still reciting in the 1950s. Today, Longfellow (along with other so-called "Fireside Poets" such as the nostalgic Oliver Wendell Holmes, abolitionist John Whittier, and humorist James Russell Lowell) is ignored largely because of his sentimentalism, but such skillful and probing lyrics as "Mezzo Cammin," "Hymn to the Night," *Poems on Slavery*, and numerous sonnets including his famous remembrance of his deceased wife, "The Cross of Snow," argue for his restoration.

For the transcendentalists such as Emerson and the mystic Jones Very, poets were the "children of fire," and yet their own poems—mostly brief, short-lined ballads—were designed to contain the ecstatic emotions of transcendence rather than to let them run amok; the result was a spare poetry that is all the more spiritual for its restraint. Perhaps the most memorable test of such restraint is Emerson's "Threnody," a meditation on the death of his young son, which maintains a remarkable balance between sentiment and transcendental theory. Edgar Allan Poe, the nemesis of Transcendentalism, was himself (as noted earlier) a closet transcendentalist, at least in his intense longing for, if not faith in, ideality. Unlike his transcendental rivals, or any other poet for that matter, his poems are distinctively awash in music. Like Longfellow, whom he also vilified; and later Whitman, whom he predeceased and therefore could not attack, Poe experimented with rhythms and rhymes in such works as "The Raven," "Annabel Lee," and "The Bells." But unlike Longfellow and Whitman, he let this music become the poem's meaning, as if the feelings evoked (vague, suggestive, but real) might transport the reader toward ideal realms of beauty beyond death. This semblance of transcendence was Poe's poetic answer to Longfellow's sentiment and Emerson's fire.

As good, or even great as these new American poets were, they would not have the power or impact of the three yet to come.

Whitman, Melville, Dickinson

In his formative years as a writer, Whitman (1819–1892) was a printer, journalist, editor of Democratic party papers, and a free-soil advocate, who composed occasional verse, tales, and the temperance novel, *Franklin Evans* (1842), but none of this had much impact on the literary scene. In the early 1850s, he changed all that: He came to terms with himself, his talent, vision, and sexuality, and went bohemian. Freeing himself from emotional, social, political, and poetic constraints, he began to write a new lyrical kind of modern epic. What he eventually produced was essentially his accumulated life's work placed in an ever-growing and re-issued volume of poems called *Leaves of Grass*. It was not about heroes or quests or warriors in battle, but was a "Song of Myself," as the first and greatest poem of this collection was called. It was an epic-size voicing of one individual's search for self-awareness, and the potential to become all things.

Published first in 1855 and then revised, augmented, and republished repeatedly throughout his life, the single, ever-expanding volume not only offered a vision of democratic unity in the form of Walt's own sensual, exuberant, meditative, and expansive consciousness, but it also put forth its ideas in a new poetic form—free verse—with unrhymed lines of varying length and meter. With a freer sense of symbolism similar to Hawthorne's and Melville's, and with an innovative, operatic sense of musicality similar but more complex than Poe's or Longfellow's, he was able to bring Emerson and Thoreau's isolationist sensibilities out of New England and into the streets of New York, Ohio, Texas, and California. This, in turn, led to a cosmic consciousness embracing white and black, male and female, North and South. This was a hot, sensual, experiential, and accessible Transcendentalism. For all his extroverted personality, Whitman was never willing to admit publicly to his homosexuality, but he used it brilliantly, for readers of all sexual orientations, especially in his *Calamus* poems, which he added to the 1860 edition of *Leaves of Grass.* Here he transforms his sexual love of men into a democratic love of mankind, promoting personal longing into a civic comradeship that is more sensual than sexual, more communitarian than personal. Whitman's vision and new poetic line liberated American poetry and gave the world a new standard, still fresh today.

Unlike Whitman who achieved international fame (if not wealth) in his lifetime, Melville and the reclusive Emily Dickinson, for separate reasons, kept their poetry to themselves. For Melville, this was not for want of trying to become a famous poet. He studied poetic form as diligently as Longfellow and Poe, and his first published collection, *Battle-Pieces,* consists of over seventy hard, brittle, innovative poems in response to the Civil War. Whitman, who served as a nurse during the conflict and contributed his elegiac and finally patriotic "cluster" of poems called *Drum-Taps,* received far more acclaim than Melville. But Melville's more thoughtful, battle by battle, collection made the deadly mistake of playing too much and too well with rhyme schemes and point of view, and the deadlier mistake of promoting respect for, forgiveness of, and reconciliation with the defeated South. The book's failure triggered in Melville a personal breakdown to match the nation's crisis and pushed the poet into decades of obscurity, but he continued to write producing his own epic of faith and doubt in the Holy Land, *Clarel* (1876). Today's readers are only beginning to recognize Melville's enormous poetic talent.

Recognition for Emily Dickinson (1830–1886) came more quickly, but only after her death and only through the editorial labors of various male and female enthusiasts. Her poems are not epic narratives but short lyrical pieces following a deceptively conventional ballad form. And yet the wording is so concise as to reduce language to bare bones imagery alone. The antithesis of Whitman, her poems have the look of light verse but the feel of a blow to the chest. They number over a thousand, and Dickinson bound most of them in "fascicles" or booklets for private use. The bulk of her work, with its naturalism and psychological realism had little to do with the war or the nation's struggle with its wounds. Even so, Dickinson's quiet feminism and unsentimental treatment of death coupled with her defiantly fragmentary lines make her poetry, like Melville's and Whitman's, decidedly modern.

Coda: The War

When the war came, it was to preserve the Union, not to free the slaves. But to win the war and to preserve the nation's principles, the Union did free the slaves, and thus removed the cancer that was killing the culture. The bitterness of that war, however, caused new cancers whose growth the nation has yet to remedy. At the outset of the war in the spring of 1861 when cannons bombarded Fort Sumter in Charleston harbor, the South had banked on the false belief that the North had little taste for warfare, and that Britain and France would help them achieve political and economic independence. The more populous North at first saw the whole affair as a picnic to be concluded in a few months, even though their enemy was fighting *on* its own land *for* its land and traditions (no matter how misguided). The routing of Union troops at Bull Run, twice during the war's first two years, quickly gave credence to the Confederacy's surmise concerning Northern military incompetence and the shallowness of the Union's predictions of a holiday. The war went badly for the North until Antietam and Gettysburg in 1863. With Grant in control, and England declining the opportunity to intervene, it was the Confederacy's turn to be "undeceived" in its theory of victory. The loss of life on both sides; the invention of a new style of mechanized warfare aimed at civilian attack; the destruction of the Southern economy; and Lincoln's assassination stunned the world and scarred the nation. Those scars remain—but the legacy of America's nation-forming adolescence, the lessons of its political and economic conflicts, and its brilliant antebellum literature also remain as texts for the country's future growth.

The writing of America's coming of age confronted the joys, fears, and anxieties of a nation struggling to achieve its founding principles. It found uniquely talented voices amid its diverse and commonplace populace; it created new literary forms to meet the many needs for expression in a modern liberal democracy. It confronted cultural breakdown by allowing itself strategic literary breakdowns. It was the kind of writing that only a nation trying to make sense of its odd self-contradictions could make, a kind of writing, too, that was, to borrow from the words of Julia Ward Howe's "Battle Hymn of the Republic," the "fateful lightning" of a literature soon to match the world's.

Literature of the Late 19th Century

NATHANIEL HAWTHORNE
[1804–1864]

Deeply rooted in New England culture, Nathaniel Hawthorne was among the first American writers to draw on the history, scenery, characters, and values of a particular region to create distinctive and lasting works of fiction. A dedicated, professional writer with high literary ambitions, Hawthorne spent twenty–five years developing his craft before he reached fame with his first novel, The Scarlet Letter *(1850). Since this his reputation has never flagged, and he is regarded as one of the most influential and accomplished American writers of the nineteenth century.*

Hawthorne was born in Salem, Massachusetts, on July 4, 1804, the descendant of six generations of New England Hathornes (he changed the spelling to ensure correct pronunciation). His ancestors included William Hathorne, famous for his persecutions of Quakers in seventeenth century Boston; John Hathorne, one of the judges at the Salem witchcraft trials in 1692; and a grandfather and father who were ship captains, a common vocation in Salem. When his father died on a voyage in 1808, Hawthorne moved with his mother and two sisters into the Salem home of the Mannings, his maternal grandparents. He made several childhood visits to the family house in Raymond, Maine, near Lake Sebago, and long remembered his days fishing, hunting, and running wild in the woods. He obtained a good education from private tutors and in a few years of local schooling, and from 1821 to 1825 attended Bowdoin College in Brunswick, Maine. Among his fellow students were Franklin Pierce, later fourteenth president of the United States, and Henry Wadsworth Longfellow, eventually one of America's most popular poets.

After graduating, Hawthorne returned to the Manning household in Salem and began writing fiction. His first publication, Fanshawe *(1828), a short romantic novel based on his college days, failed to sell, and he later destroyed all the copies he could find. He had more success with short tales and sketches, and during the 1830s contributed over sixty short pieces to such publications as his local newspaper, the* Salem Gazette, *the* New-England Magazine, *and* The Token, *an annual giftbook. Only some of his early works were stories in the modern sense. Many were historical narratives, descriptions of local manners and customs, moralistic fables, gothic fantasy pieces, and travel sketches based on his extensive journeys through New England. "Mrs. Hutchinson" (1830), for example, reveals Hawthorne's command of early New England history and its inherent drama and psychological complexity. Yet the piece also presents a compelling portrait of a strong-willed, independent women who might foreshadow the aspiring women of his present day. New England, in Hawthorne's hands, provided materials not only for understanding the American past, but also for representing the American present. By reading widely in the Salem Athenaeum Library and keenly observing his neighbors and countrymen, Hawthorne found ample resources for plots, situations, and characters he could turn into fiction of unusual power and scope.*

Yet Hawthorne was not just interested in the Puritan past, nor was he a Puritan himself. He read history to dramatize and criticize it, to bring it alive and give it wider relevance, and to help Americans understand how, from humble beginnings, they had arrived at nationhood. In "My Kinsman Major Molineux" (1832), national history and individual psychology converge in a tale resonant with the symbolism one finds in dreams, hallucinations, fantasies, and fears. Young Robin Molineux's visit to the provincial capital, presumably Boston, simultaneously records an adolescent's initiation into political rebellion and the terrors of maturity. Robin's perplexing night-journey exposes him to mobs like those that preceded the American Revolution even as it separates him from home and family. He must find his own way through this political and moral labyrinth and confront life on his own, a liberated but anxious youth embarking on the difficult road toward individual freedom.

Hawthorne's best-known tale, "Young Goodman Brown" (1835), directly asks whether Brown has "only dreamed a wild dream of a witch meeting?" "Be it so, if you will," the narrator replies, offering readers multiple choices that deliberately create ambiguity. The point is not to play parlor games with serious historical events, in this case the Salem witchcraft trials, but to force readers to consider more than one view of historical events and their effect on individuals. Brown's experience probes into the relationship between personal and institutional religious beliefs; gender roles; illusion and reality; family traits; sexuality; the effects of the wilderness; and ultimately the nature and source of good and evil themselves. No one, with the possible exception of Philadelphia novelist Charles Brockden Brown, had used American materials for such powerful symbolic dramas of the self, or marshaled them into such elegantly constructed, tightly wound narratives. With such tales, Hawthorne was laying the foundation for the modern short story.

Similarly, "The Minister's Black Veil" (1836) studies the effect of religious dogmatism on both community and individual psychology. On the one hand, Father Hooper becomes a powerful preacher because of his sense of sin; on the other, he dies alone, separated from his parishioners, his fellow minister, and his fiancee's love. The mysterious veil focuses meaning around a central symbol and multiplies it depending on the perspective of the beholder. It is a source of both strength and weakness, an avenue into understanding sin and evidence of sinfulness, a way to communicate spiritual insight and a barrier to communication, an ironic symbol that invites the reader to consider why people view such a simple object in so many opposing ways. Such considerations contribute to readers' understanding of the story as well as themselves.

Although Hawthorne initially published anonymously, making him, as he said in 1851, "the obscurest man in American letters," his first collection of stories brought him fame if not profit. Twice-Told Tales *(1837) included eighteen works previously published in newspapers, magazines, and annuals, and received favorable reviews from some of the leading journals in New England. He published a second, expanded edition in 1842, adding seventeen tales, and a third edition in 1851. While he still could not support himself solely through his writing, he had established himself as one of America's leading writers of tales. In 1837 he began courting Sophia Peabody, daughter of a prominent Salem family and sister of Elizabeth Peabody, an intellectual who ran a famous bookstore in Boston. With marriage in view, he accepted the job of coal measurer in the Boston Custom House in 1839, the first of several government appointments in his career. While there he wrote four collections of children's stories, three of them published by Elizabeth Peabody, and began a long and emotional correspondence with Sophia. In another attempt at gaining financial independence, he joined Brook Farm in early 1841, a gathering of New England intellectuals who hoped to create a utopian socialist farming community on the outskirts of Boston. Hawthorne, ever skeptical of idealist projects, left after six months.*

In 1842 Hawthorne married Sophia and couple moved to the small village of Concord, Massachusetts, into a house known as the "Old Manse," the former residence of several Concord clergymen. Neighbors included Ralph Waldo Emerson, Henry David Thoreau, Margaret Fuller, William Ellery Channing, and Bronson Alcott, all writers associated with transcendentalism, the new secular gospel of spiritual self-reliance and Nature's essential goodness. Hawthorne valued their company, but remained skeptical of their idealism and optimism. He "admired Emerson as a poet of deep beauty and austere tenderness," he wrote in an 1846 preface, "but sought nothing from him as a philosopher," and found many of Concord's residents to be "simply bores of a very intense water." Nevertheless, these were the happiest years of his life, years that witnessed the birth of his first daughter, Una, in 1844, and saw an important turn in his writing away from the New England past and toward more contemporary issues such as women's rights, transcendentalism, scientific progress, industrialization, and the place of art in an increasingly commercial and capitalist economy. He published almost exclusively in The United States Magazine and Democratic Review, *a periodical of social and political commentary, and widened his reach by placing scattered pieces in* The Pioneer, *a short-lived but distinguished journal edited by James Russell Lowell,* Graham's Magazine, *a widely distributed periodical published in Philadelphia, and* Godey's Magazine, *perhaps the most popular magazine of the day. In 1846 he published another collection of tales,* Moses from an Old Manse, *emphasizing his most recent productions.*

"The Birth-Mark" (1843) demonstrates Hawthorne's move away from regional themes and characters. Devoid of the historical particulars that mark his earlier stories, this tale seems more like science fiction than historical fable, taking place as it does in a nonspecific, symbolic realm of scientific inquiry and marital anxiety. Aylmer's quest to "perfect" his wife might represent any human wish to reshape nature into forms of personal desire, a Faustian goal that takes Aylmer out of history into the realm of obsessive psychology. Similarly, "The Artist of the Beautiful" (1844) allegorizes one man's quest for artistic perfection, a quest that separates him from humanity yet results in the creation of a marvelous object that seems to transcend the material world. In these tales Hawthorne interrogates the role of the artist in society, and opposes artistic to material creativity in a contest with ambiguous results. "Rappaccini's Daughter" (1844), Hawthorne's only tale set outside America, focuses on a love relationship entangled with patriarchal lust for scientific achievement. Intermixing the passions of the two loves (Giovanni Guasconti and Beatrice) with the rationalism of the head (Rappacini) leads to the terrifying psychological insight that love and hate can be two sides of the same emotion, and that passion, however essential to the human condition, can destroy as well as create. In all three of these stories, Hawthorne uses a central symbol— birthmark, butterfly, garden—to create unity without sacrificing complexity in tales with multiple interpretive possibilities.

In April 1846, with a second child, his son Julian, now in the family, Hawthorne accepted a political appointment as Surveyor of Customs at Salem, a position obtained through his associations with the Democratic Party. For the next three years he wrote almost nothing, his imagination having become, as he said, "a tarnished mirror." It probably didn't help that he and his family had taken up housekeeping with his mother and sisters. In 1849, after the Whigs won the election of 1848, Hawthorne was dismissed, and once more found himself without a stable income. His mother died in July 1849, an event that reinvigorated his imagination and led him to write The Scarlet Letter *(1850), his first novel and the work that would finally win him the combination of popular and literary success he had always desired.*

The Scarlet Letter, *set in seventeenth century Boston, draws once more on Hawthorne's historical knowledge, yet infuses it with Concord transcendentalism and the political and social upheaval of the American 1840s. Hester Prynne, unwed mother of Pearl, is one of the strongest female characters in American fiction, a combination of Ann Hutchinson and contemporary feminists. Her refusal* to name Pearl's father or leave the community challenges male religious and social authority. She and Pearl stand as living reproaches to Arthur Dimmesdale, the guilt-ridden Puritan minister who fathers Pearl and then disowns her. Dimmesdale combines the hypocrisy of Young Goodman Brown with the idealism of Father Hooper and the sexual yearnings of Giovanni Gausconti. In Roger Chillingworth, Hester's elderly husband, Hawthorne paints a villain of unsurpassed evil, another man of science whose materialism denies him full humanity. Secrecy, concealment, and deception fuel the plot of this compact novel whose central symbol, the scarlet "A," radiates the dilemma of personal freedom confronting social authority. The Christian press roundly condemned the book for its frank themes of ministerial adultery, illegitimacy, religious hypocrisy, and sexual passion, yet its popularity gave Hawthorne his widest audience so far and encouraged him to continue his career as a novelist instead of a teller of tales.

After the gloomy theme of The Scarlet Letter, Hawthorne consciously set out to write a cheerier novel in The House of the Seven Gables (1851). Although the narrative begins in the Puritan past, it quickly moves into the busy, present-day life of Salem. Hepzibah and Clifford Pyncheon, an elderly sister and brother, are living isolated lives in the family mansion. With the help of Phoebe Pyncheon, a fresh young cousin who comes to live with them, and Holgrave, a young lodger, they gradually come into the sunshine of the present. Judge Jaffray Pyncheon, the family patriarch, symbolizes the evil of the Puritan past, and with his death Hepzibah and Clifford can finally leave the oppressive house, and Phoebe and Holgrave can marry. The House of the Seven Gables, along with The Wonder-Book (1851), a retelling of classical myths for children, and The Snow-Image (1851), a final collection of tales, demonstrated Hawthorne's ability to reach ever wider audiences and finally succeed in the literary marketplace.

The Blithedale Romance (1852) concluded an extraordinary three-year outburst of creativity, and continued Hawthorne's move toward contemporary topics by drawing on his experiences at Brook Farm. Best read as topical satire, incorporating his skepticism toward reformers and idealists of all stripes, the novel describes life in a socialist community through the eyes of Miles Coverdale, one of Hawthorne's rare first-person narrators. A vain, self-deceptive poet of little talent and less human sympathy, Coverdale discovers in others the shortcomings he fails to see in himself, allowing Hawthorne to expose both his narrator and the utopian community he describes to ironic authorial ridicule. Zenobia, the transcendental heroine; Hollingsworth, the prison reformer; and even Priscilla, the sentimental waif, all come in for Coverdale's criticism. Wary readers understand Coverdale's self-delusions, his unreliability, and lack of warmth, and realize that Hawthorne once more writes about the forces that blunt genuine human feeling and make love difficult.

With the birth of his third child, Rose, in 1851, and the financial success of his novels and story collections, Hawthorne purchased a large home in Concord in

1852, the first place he could truly call his own. He published a campaign biography of Franklin Pierce, and in 1853 produced a second volume of myths for children, Tanglewood Tales. *The Pierce biography led to Hawthorne's appointment as U.S. consul in Liverpool, England, a position he held from 1853 to 1857. A remunerative but tedious job, the consulship gave him little time for imaginative writing but allowed him to save $30,000, enough to spend two years in Italy and a year in England before returning to the United States in 1860.*

While abroad he began his final published novel, The Marble Faun *(1860). This story of two couples caught in a web of intrigue among the expatriate artists of Rome and Florence drew heavily on Hawthorne's voluminous Italian travel notebooks, and painstakingly described the landscapes, architecture, statues, and paintings the author had observed in Italy. The title character Donatello, a young Italian nobleman who reminds his friends of Praxiteles' statue of a faun, falls in love with Miriam, a mysterious sculptress with a secret past. The Americans Kenyon and Hilda, a sculptor and a copyist, observe the budding relationship with fascination and eventually fall in love themselves. The backdrop of Italian history and art dominates these personal relationships and gives the novel a sprawling, digressive structure unlike Hawthorne's earlier, tightly organized works. His longest novel,* The Marble Faun *creates varied symbols from Old World materials and characters and addresses a wide range of moral and aesthetic issues.*

Hawthorne produced comparatively little in his last four years. "Chiefly About War Matters" (1862), an essay on the Civil War, reveals Hawthorne's growing distaste for the rise of the commonplace in American life, even while recognizing that a certain rudeness may be the price of egalitarianism. Our Old Home *(1863) draws heavily on his English notebooks for a series of essays on contemporary English life that combine travelogue with social and political commentary to reveal the author's mixed nostalgia, admiration, and disdain for England. Hawthorne tried to complete four additional novels between 1860 and 1864, but his imaginative powers seem to have evaporated, perhaps due to undiagnosed illness. He died in 1864 on a journey to New Hampshire with his old friend Franklin Pierce, and was buried in Sleepy Hollow Cemetery in Concord.*

For most of his life, Hawthorne remained an outsider, perhaps the vantage point from which, like Miles Coverdale, he could best view American history and values. By the time of his death, Americans recognized his central place in the new nation's literature, and honored his memory with posthumous publications of his notebooks, letters, travel journals, unfinished romances, and numerous handsomely bound editions of his complete works. As a fabricator of searching, carefully wrought allegories of the American mind and the human heart, Hawthorne has few peers, and exercised influence on writers from Herman Melville and Henry James, through William Faulkner, Eudora Welty, Flannery O'Connor, John Updike, and even foreign writers such as Jorge Luis Borges. Truly, Hawthorne is an American writer for the world whose works repay close reading and lifelong scrutiny as they mirror the dilemmas not only of his own time, but of today.

For Further Reading

Primary Works

Fanshawe (1828); *Twice-Told Tales* (1837, 1842, 1851); *Grandfather's Chair: A History for Youth* (1841); *Famous Old People: Being the Second Epoch of Grandfather's Chair* (1841); *Liberty Tree: With the Last Words of Grandfather's Chair* (1841); *Biographical Stories for Children* (1842); *Mosses from an Old Manse* (1846a); *The Scarlet Letter, a Romance* (1850); *The House of the Seven Gables, a Romance* (1851); *The Snow-Image, and Other Twice-told Tales* (1851); *The Blithedale Romance* (1852); *Life of Franklin Pierce* (1852); *Tanglewood Tales for Girls and Boys: Being a Second Wonder-book* (1853); *The Marble Faun; or The Romance of Monte Beni* (1860); *Our Old Home: A Series of English Sketches* (1863); *Passages from the American Note-Books of Nathaniel Hawthorne* (1868); *Passages from the English Note-Books of Nathaniel Hawthorne* (1870); *Passages from the French and Italian Note-Books of Nathaniel Hawthorne* (1872); *Septimius Felton; or The Elixir of Life* (1872); *The Dolliver Romance and other Pieces* (1876); *Doctor Grimshawe's Secret: A Romance* (1883); *Twenty Days with Julian and Little Bunny: A Diary* (1904); *Hawthorne as Editor: Selections from His Writings in The American Magazine of Useful and Entertaining Knowledge*, edited by Arlin Turner (Baton Rouge: Louisiana State University Press, 1941); *The Centenary Edition of the Works of Nathaniel Hawthorne*, 23 volumes, ed. William Charvat et al. (Columbus: Ohio State University Press, 1962–94).

Biographies

Julian Hawthorne, *Nathaniel Hawthorne and His Wife: A Biography* (Boston: James R. Osgood, 1885); Henry James, *Hawthorne* (London, 1879); Edward C. Wagenknecht, *Nathaniel Hawthorne: Man and Writer* (New York: Oxford University Press, 1961); Beatrice Ricks, Joseph D. Adams, and Jack O. Hazling, *Nathaniel Hawthorne: A Reference Bibliography, 1900–1971* (Boston: G. K. Hall, 1972): Lea Newman, Bertani Vozar, *A Reader's Guide to the Short Stories of Nathaniel Hawthorne* (Boston: G. K. Hall, 1979); James R. Mellow, *Nathaniel Hawthorne in His Times* (Boston: Houghton Mifflin, 1980); Arlin Turner, *Nathaniel Hawthorne: A Biography* (New York: Oxford University Press, 1980); Robert L. Gale, *A Hawthorne Encyclopedia* (Westport, Conn.: Greenwood Press, 1988); Gary Scharnhorst, *Nathaniel Hawthorne: An Annotated Bibliography of Comment and Criticism Before 1900* (Metuchen, N.J.: Scarecrow Press, 1988); Edwin Haviland Miller, *Salem Is My Dwelling Place: A Life of Nathaniel Hawthorne* (Iowa City: University of Iowa Press, 1991); John L. Idol, Jr. and Buford Jones, eds., *Nathaniel Hawthorne: The Contemporary Reviews* (New York: Cambridge University Press, 1994).

Secondary Works

Hyatt Waggoner, HawthorneA: A Critical Study (Cambridge, Mass.: Harvard University Press, 1955); Roy R. Male, *Hawthorne's Tragic Vision* (Austin: University of Texas Press, 1957); Millicent Bell, Hawthorne's View *of the Artist* (Albany: State University of New York Press, 1962); Richard Harter Fogle, *Hawthorne's Fiction: The Light and the Dark,* revised edition (Norman: University of Oklahoma Press, 1964); Neal F. Doubleday, *Hawthorne's Early Tales: A Critical Study* (Durham, N.C.: Duke University Press, 1972); Nina Baym, *The Shape of Hawthorne's Career* (Ithaca, N.Y.: Cornell University Press, 1976); Edgar A. Dryden, *Nathaniel Hawthorne: The Poetics of Enchantment (Ithaca:* Cornell University Press, 1977); Rita K. Gollin, *Nathaniel Hawthorne and the Truth of Dreams* (Baton Rouge: Louisiana State University Press, 1979); Claudia D. Johnson, *The Productive Tension in Hawthorne's Art* (Tuscaloosa: University of Alabama Press, 1981); Terence Martin, *Nathaniel Hawthorne,* rev. edition (Boston: Twayne, 1983); Michael J. Colacurcio, *The Province of Piety: Moral History in Hawthorne's Early Fiction* (Cambridge, Mass.: Harvard University Press, 1984); Gloria C. Erlich, *Family Themes and Hawthorne's Fiction: The Tenacious Web* (New Brunswick, N.J.: Rutgers University Press, 1984); Richard Brodhead, *The School of Hawthorne* (New York: Oxford University Press, (1986); Frederick Newberry, *Hawthorne's Divided Loyalties: England and America in His Works* (Teaneck, N.J.: Fairleigh Dickinson University Press, 1987); Kenneth Marc Harris, *Hypocrisy and Self-Deception in Hawthorne's Fiction* (Charlottesville: University Press of Virginia, 1988); Gordon Hutner, *Secrets and Sympathy: Forms of Disclosure in Hawthorne's Novels* (Athens: University of Georgia Press, 1988); Edwin H. Cady and Louis J. Budd, eds., *On Hawthorne: The Best from American Literature* (Durham, N.C.: Duke University Press, 1990); Frederick Crews, *The Sins of the Fathers: Hawthorne's Psychological Themes,* with a new afterword (Berkeley: University of California Press, 1989); Sacvan Bercovitch, *The Office of The Scarlet Letter* (Baltimore: Johns Hopkins University Press, 1991); Joel Pfister, *The Production of Personal Life: Class, Gender, and the Psychological in Hawthorne's Fiction* (Stanford, Calif.: Stanford University Press, 1991); Charles Swann, *Nathaniel Hawthorne, Tradition and Revolution* (Cambridge: Cambridge University Press, 1991); Laura Laffrado, *Hawthorne's Literature for Children* (Athens: University of Georgia Press, 1992); Richard H. Millingston, *Practicing Romance: Narrative Form and Cultural Engagement in Hawthorne's Fiction* (Princetion, N.J.: Princetion University Press, 1992); T. Walter Herbert, *Dearest Beloved: The Hawthornes and the Making of the Middle-Class Family* (Berkely: University of California Press, 1993); Alison Easton, *The Making of the Hawthorne Subject* (Columbia: University of Missouri Press, 1996). Margaret B. Moore, *The Salem World of Nathaniel Hawthorne* (Columbia: University of Missouri Press, 1998); John L. Idol, Jr. and Melinda M. Ponder, eds., *Hawthorne and Women: Engendering and Expanding the Hawthorne Tradition* (Amherst: University of Massachusetts Press, 1999).

Young Goodman Brown[*]

NATHANIEL HAWTHORNE

Young Goodman Brown came forth, at sunset, into the street of Salem village, but put his head back, after crossing the threshold, to exchange a parting kiss with his young wife.[1] And Faith, as the wife was aptly named, thrust her own pretty head into the street, letting the wind play with the pink ribbons of her cap, while she called to Goodman Brown.

"Dearest heart," whispered she, softly and rather sadly, when her lips were close to his ear, "pr'y thee, put off your journey until sunrise, and sleep in your own bed to-night. A lone woman is troubled with such dreams and such thoughts, that she's afeard of herself, sometimes. Pray, tarry with me this night, dear husband, of all nights in the year!"

"My love and my Faith," replied young Goodman Brown, "of all nights in the year, this one night must I tarry away from thee. My journey, as thou callest it, forth and back again, must needs be done 'twixt now and sunrise. What, my sweet, pretty wife, dost thou doubt me already, and we but three months married!"

"Then, God bless you!" said Faith, with the pink ribbons, "and may you find all well when you come back."

"Amen!" cried Goodman Brown. "Say thy prayers, dear Faith, and go to bed at dusk, and no harm will come to thee."

So they parted; and the young man pursued his way, until, being about to turn the corner by the meeting-house, he looked back, and saw the head of Faith still peeping after him, with a melancholy air, in spite of her pink ribbons.

"Poor little Faith!" thought he, for his heart smote him. "What a wretch am I, to leave her on such an errand! She talks of dreams, too. Methought, as she spoke, there was trouble in her face, as if a dream had warned her what work is to be done to-night. But, no, no! 'twould kill her to think it. Well;

---

[*]First published in the *New England Magazine* (April 1835); collected in *Mosses from an Old Manse* (1846). This text is from volume 10 of *The Centenary Edition of the Works of Nathaniel Hawthorne* (1974).

[1]"Goodman" and "Goodwife" (or "Goody") were terms of polite address for ordinary men and women. Salem village, the present Danvers, was a few miles north of Salem, Massachusetts, site of the witchcraft trials of 1692.

she's a blessed angel on earth; and after this one night, I'll cling to her skirts and follow her to Heaven."

With this excellent resolve for the future, Goodman Brown felt himself justified in making more haste on his present evil purpose. He had taken a dreary road, darkened by all the gloomiest trees of the forest, which barely stood aside to let the narrow path creep through, and closed immediately behind. It was all as lonely as could be; and there is this peculiarity in such a solitude, that the traveller knows not who may be concealed by the innumerable trunks and the thick boughs overhead; so that, with lonely footsteps, he may yet be passing through an unseen multitude.

"There may be a devilish Indian behind every tree," said Goodman Brown, to himself; and he glanced fearfully behind him, as he added, "What if the devil himself should be at my very elbow!"

His head being turned back, he passed a crook of the road, and looking forward again, beheld the figure of a man, in grave and decent attire, seated at the foot of an old tree. He arose, at Goodman Brown's approach, and walked onward, side by side with him.

"You are late, Goodman Brown," said he. "The clock of the Old South[2] was striking as I came through Boston; and that is full fifteen minutes agone."

"Faith kept me back awhile," replied the young man, with a tremor in his voice, caused by the sudden appearance of his companion, though not wholly unexpected.

It was now deep dusk in the forest, and deepest in that part of it where these two were journeying. As nearly as could be discerned, the second traveller was about fifty years old, apparently in the same rank of life as Goodman Brown, and bearing a considerable resemblance to him, though perhaps more in expression than features. Still, they might have been taken for father and son. And yet, though the elder person was as simply clad as the younger, and as simple in manner too, he had an indescribable air of one who knew the world, and would not have felt abashed at the governor's dinner-table, or in King William's court,[3] were it possible that his affairs should call him thither. But the only thing about him, that could be fixed upon as remarkable, was his staff, which bore the likeness of a great black snake, so curiously wrought, that it might almost be seen to twist and wriggle itself, like a living serpent. This, of course, must have been an ocular deception, assisted by the uncertain light.

"Come, Goodman Brown!" cried his fellow-traveller, "this is a dull pace for the beginning of a journey. Take my staff, if you are so soon weary."

---

[2]church about sixteen miles from Salem village.
[3]William III (1650–1702) ruled England jointly with his wife, Queen Mary II (1662–1694), from 1689–1702.

"Friend," said the other, exchanging his slow pace for a full stop, "having kept covenant by meeting thee here, it is my purpose now to return whence I came. I have scruples, touching the matter thou wot'st of."[4]

"Sayest thou so?" replied he of the serpent, smiling apart. "Let us walk on, nevertheless, reasoning as we go, and if I convince thee not, thou shalt turn back. We are but a little way in the forest, yet."

"Too far, too far!" exclaimed the goodman, unconsciously resuming his walk. "My father never went into the woods on such an errand, nor his father before him. We have been a race of honest men and good Christians, since the days of the martyrs.[5] And shall I be the first of the name of Brown, that ever took this path, and kept—"

"Such company, thou wouldst say," observed the elder person, interpreting his pause. "Well said, Goodman Brown! I have been as well acquainted with your family as with ever a one among the Puritans; and that's no trifle to say. I helped your grandfather, the constable, when he lashed the Quaker woman so smartly through the streets of Salem. And it was I that brought your father a pitch-pine knot, kindled at my own hearth, to set fire to an Indian village, in King Philip's war.[6] They were my good friends, both; and many a pleasant walk have we had along this path, and returned merrily after midnight. I would fain be friends with you, for their sake."

"If it be as thou sayest," replied Goodman Brown, I marvel they never spoke of these matters. Or, verily, I marvel not, seeing that the least rumor of the sort would have driven them from New-England. We are a people of prayer, and good works, to boot, and abide no such wickedness."

"Wickedness or not," said the traveller with the twisted staff, "I have a very general acquaintance here in New-England. The deacons of many a church have drunk the communion wine with me; the selectmen, of divers towns, make me their chairman; and a majority of the Great and General Court[7] are firm supporters of my interest. The governor and I, too—but these are state-secrets."

"Can this be so!" cried Goodman Brown, with a stare of amazement at his undisturbed companion. "Howbeit, I have nothing to do with the governor and council; they have their own ways, and are no rule for a simple husbandman,[8] like me. But, were I to go on with thee, how should I meet the eye

---

[4]knowest of

[5]Almost three hundred Protestants were executed under the reign of Mary I (1516–1558), also known as Mary Tudor and "Bloody Mary," the Roman Catholic queen of England from 1553–58.

[6]A 1661 Massachusetts law required that disobedient Quakers be stripped to the waist, led through the streets, and whipped. King Philip's War was named for Metacom, also known as King Philip, a Wampanoag chief who led several New England Indian tribes in a war against the English from 1675–76.

[7]colonial legislature

[8]usually a farmer, but here any man of ordinary means.

of that good old man, our minister, at Salem village? Oh, his voice would make me tremble, both Sabbath-day and lecture-day!"[9]

Thus far, the elder traveller had listened with due gravity, but now burst into a fit of irrepressible mirth, shaking himself so violently, that his snake-like staff actually seemed to wriggle in sympathy.

"Ha! ha! ha!" shouted he, again and again; then composing himself, "Well, go on, Goodman Brown, go on; but pr'y thee, don't kill me with laughing!"

"Well, then, to end the matter at once," said Goodman Brown, considerably nettled, "there is my wife, Faith. It would break her dear little heart; and I'd rather break my own!"

"Nay, if that be the case," answered the other, "e'en go thy ways, Goodman Brown. I would not, for twenty old women like the one hobbling before us, that Faith should come to any harm."

As he spoke, he pointed his staff at a female figure on the path, in whom Goodman Brown recognized a very pious and exemplary dame, who had taught him his catechism, in youth, and was still his moral and spiritual adviser, jointly with the minister and Deacon Gookin.[10]

"A marvel, truly, that Goody Cloyse[11] should be so far in the wilderness, at night-fall!" said he. "But, with your leave, friend, I shall take a cut through the woods, until we have left this Christian woman behind. Bring a stranger to you, she might ask whom I was consorting with, and whither I was going."

"Be it so," said his fellow-traveller. "Betake you to the woods, and let me keep the path."

Accordingly, the young man turned aside, but took care to watch his companion, who advanced softly along the road, until he had come within a staff's length of the old dame. She, meanwhile, was making the best of her way, with singular speed for so aged a woman, and mumbling some indistinct words, a prayer, doubtless, as she went. The traveller put forth his staff, and touched her withered neck with what seemed the serpent's tail.

"The devil!" screamed the pious old lady.

"Then Goody Cloyse knows her old friend?" observed the traveller, confronting her, and leaning on his writhing stick.

"Ah, forsooth, and is it your worship, indeed?" cried the good dame. "Yea, truly is it, and in the very image of my old gossip, Goodman Brown, the grandfather of the silly fellow that now is. But—would your worship believe it?—my broomstick hath strangely disappeared, stolen, as I suspect,

---

[9]a midweek day for sermons.

[10]perhaps Daniel Gookin (1612–1687), Massachusetts official, but never a church deacon.

[11]Sarah Cloyse, sentenced to death for witchcraft in 1692, but never executed.

by that unhanged witch, Goody Cory, and that, too, when I was all anointed with the juice of smallage and cinque-foil and wolf's-bane—"[12]

"Mingled with fine wheat and the fat of a new-born babe," said the shape of old Goodman Brown.

"Ah, your worship knows the receipt," cried the old lady, cackling aloud. "So, as I was saying, being all ready for the meeting, and no horse to ride on, I made up my mind to foot it; for they tell me, there is a nice young man to be taken into communion to-night. But now your good worship will lend me your arm, and we shall be there in a twinkling."

"That can hardly be," answered her friend. I may not spare you my arm, Goody Cloyse, but here is my staff, if you will."

So saying, he threw it down at her feet, where, perhaps, it assumed life, being one of the rods which its owner had formerly lent to the Egyptian Magi.[13] Of this fact, however, Goodman Brown could not take cognizance. He had cast up his eyes in astonishment, and looking down again, beheld neither Goody Cloyse nor the serpentine staff, but his fellow-traveller alone, who waited for him as calmly as if nothing had happened.

"That old woman taught me my catechism!" said the young man; and there was a world of meaning in this simple comment.

They continued to walk onward, while the elder traveller exhorted his companion to make good speed and persevere in the path, discoursing so aptly, that his arguments seemed rather to spring up in the bosom of his auditor, than to be suggested by himself. As they went, he plucked a branch of maple, to serve for a walking-stick, and began to strip it of the twigs and little boughs, which were wet with evening dew. The moment his fingers touched them, they became strangely withered and dried up, as with a week's sunshine. Thus the pair proceeded, at a good free pace, until suddenly, in a gloomy hollow of the road, Goodman Brown sat himself down on the stump of a tree, and refused to go any farther.

"Friend," said he, stubbornly, "my mind is made up. Not another step will I budge on this errand. What if a wretched old woman do choose to go to the devil, when I thought she was going to Heaven! Is that any reason why I should quit my dear Faith, and go after her?"

"You will think better of this, by-and-by," said his acquaintance, composedly. "Sit here and rest yourself awhile; and when you feel like moving again, there is my staff to help you along."

Without more words, he threw his companion the maple stick, and was as speedily out of sight, as if he had vanished into the deepening gloom. The young man sat a few moments, by the road-side, applauding himself greatly,

---

[12]Martha Cory was hanged for witchcraft in 1692; smallage, cinquefoil, and wolf's-bane are wild plants with supposed magical powers.

[13]Exodus 7:9–12 describes Egyptian priests turning their rods into serpents.

and thinking with how clear a conscience he should meet the minister, in his morning-walk, nor shrink from the eye of good old Deacon Gookin. And what calm sleep would be his, that very night, which was to have been spent so wickedly, but purely and sweetly now, in the arms of Faith! Amidst these pleasant and praiseworthy meditations, Goodman Brown heard the tramp of horses along the road, and deemed it advisable to conceal himself within the verge of the forest, conscious of the guilty purpose that had brought him thither, though now so happily turned from it.

On came the hoof-tramps and the voices of the riders, two grave old voices, conversing soberly as they drew near. These mingled sounds appeared to pass along the road, within a few yards of the young man's hiding-place; but owing, doubtless, to the depth of the gloom, at that particular spot, neither the travellers nor their steeds were visible. Though their figures brushed the small boughs by the way-side, it could not be seen that they intercepted, even for a moment, the faint gleam from the strip of bright sky, athwart which they must have passed. Goodman Brown alternately crouched and stood on tip-toe, pulling aside the branches, and thrusting forth his head as far as he durst, without discerning so much as a shadow. It vexed him the more, because he could have sworn, were such a thing possible, that he recognized the voices of the minister and Deacon Gookin, jogging along quietly, as they were wont to do, when bound to some ordination or ecclesiastical council. While yet within hearing, one of the riders stopped to pluck a switch.

"Of the two, reverend Sir," said the voice like the deacon's, "I had rather miss an ordination-dinner than to-night's meeting. They tell me that some of our community are to be here from Falmouth and beyond, and others from Connecticut and Rhode-Island; besides several of the Indian powows,[14] who, after their fashion, know almost as much deviltry as the best of us. Moreover, there is a goodly young woman to be taken into communion."

"Mighty well, Deacon Gookin!" replied the solemn old tones of the minister. "Spur up, or we shall be late. Nothing can be done, you know, until I get on the ground."

The hoofs clattered again, and the voices, talking so strangely in the empty air, passed on through the forest, where no church had ever been gathered, nor solitary Christian prayed. Whither, then, could these holy men be journeying, so deep into the heathen wilderness? Young Goodman Brown caught hold of a tree, for support, being ready to sink down on the ground, faint and overburthened with the heavy sickness of his heart. He looked up to the sky, doubting whether there really was a Heaven above him. Yet, there was the blue arch, and the stars brightening in it.

---

[14]Falmouth is a village on southern Cape Cod, about seventy miles from Salem; powows, usually spelled powwow, are medicine men.

"With Heaven above, and Faith below, I will yet stand firm against the devil!" cried Goodman Brown.

While he still gazed upward, into the deep arch of the firmament, and had lifted his hands to pray, a cloud, though no wind was stirring, hurried across the zenith, and hid the brightening stars. The blue sky was still visible, except directly overhead, where this black mass of cloud was sweeping swiftly northward. Aloft in the air, as if from the depths of the cloud, came a confused and doubtful sound of voices. Once, the listener fancied that he could distinguish the accents of town's-people of his own, men and women, both pious and ungodly, many of whom he had met at the communion-table, and had seen others rioting at the tavern. The next moment, so indistinct were the sounds, he doubted whether he had heard aught but the murmur of the old forest, whispering without a wind. Then came a stronger swell of those familiar tones, heard daily in the sunshine, at Salem village, but never, until now, from a cloud of night. There was one voice, of a young woman, uttering lamentations, yet with an uncertain sorrow, and entreating for some favor, which, perhaps, it would grieve her to obtain. And all the unseen multitude, both saints and sinners, seemed to encourage her onward.

"Faith!" shouted Goodman Brown, in a voice of agony and desperation; and the echoes of the forest mocked him, crying—"Faith! Faith!" as if bewildered wretches were seeking her, all through the wilderness.

The cry of grief, rage, and terror, was yet piercing the night, when the unhappy husband held his breath for a response. There was a scream, drowned immediately in a louder murmur of voices, fading into far-off laughter, as the dark cloud swept away, leaving the clear and silent sky above Goodman Brown. But something fluttered lightly down through the air, and caught on the branch of a tree. The young man seized it, and beheld a pink ribbon.

"My Faith is gone!" cried he, after one stupefied moment. "There is no good on earth; and sin is but a name. Come, devil! for to thee is this world given."

And maddened with despair, so that he laughed loud and long, did Goodman Brown grasp his staff and set forth again, at such a rate, that he seemed to fly along the forest-path, rather than to walk or run. The road grew wilder and drearier, and more faintly traced, and vanished at length, leaving him in the heart of the dark wilderness, still rushing onward, with the instinct that guides mortal man to evil. The whole forest was peopled with frightful sounds; the creaking of the trees, the howling of wild beasts, and the yell of Indians; while, sometimes, the wind tolled like a distant church-bell, and sometimes gave a broad roar around the traveller, as if all Nature were laughing him to scorn. But he was himself the chief horror of the scene, and shrank not from its other horrors.

"Ha! ha! ha!" roared Goodman Brown, when the wind laughed at him. "Let us hear which will laugh loudest! Think not to frighten me with your deviltry! Come witch, come wizard, come Indian powow, come devil himself! and here comes Goodman Brown. You may as well fear him as he fear you!"

In truth, all through the haunted forest, there could be nothing more frightful than the figure of Goodman Brown. On he flew, among the black pines, brandishing his staff with frenzied gestures, now giving vent to an inspiration of horrid blasphemy, and now shouting forth such laughter, as set all the echoes of the forest laughing like demons around him. The fiend in his own shape is less hideous, than when he rages in the breast of man. Thus sped the demoniac on his course, until, quivering among the trees, he saw a red light before him, as when the felled trunks and branches of a clearing have been set on fire, and throw up their lurid blaze against the sky, at the hour of midnight. He paused, in a lull of the tempest that had driven him onward, and heard the swell of what seemed a hymn, rolling solemnly from a distance, with the weight of many voices. He knew the tune; it was a familiar one in the choir of the village meeting-house. The verse died heavily away, and was lengthened by a chorus, not of human voices, but of all the sounds of the benighted wilderness, pealing in awful harmony together. Goodman Brown cried out; and his cry was lost to his own ear, by its unison with the cry of the desert.

In the interval of silence, he stole forward, until the light glared full upon his eyes. At one extremity of an open space, hemmed in by the dark wall of the forest, arose a rock, bearing some rude, natural resemblance either to an altar or a pulpit, and surrounded by four blazing pines, their tops aflame, their stems untouched, like candles at an evening meeting. The mass of foliage, that had overgrown the summit of the rock, was all on fire, blazing high into the night, and fitfully illuminating the whole field. Each pendent twig and leafy festoon was in a blaze. As the red light arose and fell, a numerous congregation alternately shone forth, then disappeared in shadow, and again grew, as it were, out of the darkness, peopling the heart of the solitary woods at once.

"A grave and dark-clad company!" quoth Goodman Brown.

In truth, they were such. Among them, quivering to-and-fro, between gloom and splendor, appeared faces that would be seen, next day, at the council-board of the province, and others which, Sabbath after Sabbath, looked devoutly heavenward, and benignantly over the crowded pews, from the holiest pulpits in the land. Some affirm, that the lady of the governor was there. At least, there were high dames well known to her, and wives of honored husbands, and widows, a great multitude, and ancient maidens, all of excellent repute, and fair young girls, who trembled, lest their mothers should espy them. Either the sudden gleams of light, flashing over the obscure field, bedazzled Goodman Brown, or he recognized a score of the churchmembers of Salem village, famous for their especial sanctity. Good old Deacon Gookin had arrived, and waited at the skirts of that venerable saint, his revered pastor. But, irreverently consorting with these grave, reputable, and pious people, these elders of the church, these chaste dames and dewy virgins, there were men of dissolute lives and women of spotted fame, wretches given over to all mean and filthy vice, and suspected even of horrid crimes. It was strange to see, that the good shrank not from the wicked, nor were the sinners abashed by the saints. Scattered, also, among their pale-faced enemies, were the Indian priests, or powows, who had often scared their native forest with more hideous incantations than any known to English witchcraft.

"But, where is Faith?" thought Goodman Brown; and, as hope came into his heart, he trembled.

Another verse of the hymn arose, a slow and mournful strain, such as the pious love, but joined to words which expressed all that our nature can conceive of sin, and darkly hinted at far more. Unfathomable to mere mortals is the lore of fiends. Verse after verse was sung, and still the chorus of the desert swelled between, like the deepest tone of a mighty organ. And, with the final peal of that dreadful anthem, there came a sound, as if the roaring wind, the rushing streams, the howling beasts, and every other voice of the unconverted wilderness, were mingling and according with the voice of guilty man, in homage to the prince of all. The four blazing pines threw up a loftier flame, and obscurely discovered shapes and visages of horror on the smoke-wreaths, above the impious assembly. At the same moment, the fire on the rock shot redly forth, and formed a glowing arch above its base, where now appeared a figure. With reverence be it spoken, the figure bore no slight similitude, both in garb and manner, to some grave divine of the New-England churches.

"Bring forth the converts!" cried a voice, that echoed through the field and rolled into the forest.

At the word, Goodman Brown stept forth from the shadow of the trees, and approached the congregation, with whom he felt a loathful brotherhood, by the sympathy of all that was wicked in his heart. He could have well nigh sworn, that the shape of his own dead father beckoned him to advance, looking downward from a smoke-wreath, while a woman, with dim features of despair, threw out her hand to warn him back. Was it his mother? But he had no power to retreat one step, nor to resist, even in thought, when the minister and good old Deacon Gookin seized his arms, and led him to the blazing rock. Thither came also the slender form of a veiled female, led between Goody Cloyse, that pious teacher of the catechism, and Martha Carrier,[15] who had received the devil's promise to be queen of hell. A rampant hag was she! And there stood the proselytes, beneath the canopy of fire.

"Welcome, my children," said the dark figure, "to the communion of your race! Ye have found, thus young, your nature and your destiny. My children, look behind you!"

---

[15]Martha Carrier was hanged as a witch in 1692.

They turned; and flashing forth, as it were, in a sheet of flame, the fiend-worshippers were seen; the smile of welcome gleamed darkly on every visage.

"There," resumed the sable form, "are all whom ye have reverenced from youth. Ye deemed them holier than yourselves, and shrank from your own sin, contrasting it with their lives of righteousness, and prayerful aspirations heavenward. Yet, here are they all, in my worshipping assembly! This night it shall be granted you to know their secret deeds; how hoary-bearded elders of the church have whispered wanton words to the young maids of their households; how many a woman, eager for widow's weeds, has given her husband a drink at bedtime, and let him sleep his last sleep in her bosom; how beardless youths have made haste to inherit their fathers' wealth; and how fair damsels—blush not, sweet ones!—have dug little graves in the garden, and bidden me, the sole guest, to an infant's funeral. By the sympathy of your human hearts for sin, ye shall scent out all the places—whether in church, bed-chamber, street, field, or forest—where crime has been committed, and shall exult to behold the whole earth one stain of guilt, one mighty blood-spot. Far more than this! It shall be yours to penetrate, in every bosom, the deep mystery of sin, the fountain of all wicked arts, and which inexhaustibly supplies more evil impulses than human power—than my power, at its utmost!—can make manifest in deeds. And now, my children, look upon each other."

They did so; and, by the blaze of the hell-kindled torches, the wretched man beheld his Faith, and the wife her husband, trembling before that unhallowed altar.

"Lo! there ye stand, my children," said the figure, in a deep and solemn tone, almost sad, with its despairing awfulness, as if his once angelic nature could yet mourn for our miserable race. "Depending upon one another's hearts, ye had still hoped, that virtue were not all a dream. Now are ye undeceived! Evil is the nature of mankind. Evil must be your only happiness. Welcome, again, my children, to the communion of your race!"

"Welcome!" repeated the fiend-worshippers, in one cry of despair and triumph.

And there they stood, the only pair, as it seemed, who were yet hesitating on the verge of wickedness, in this dark world. A basin was hollowed, naturally, in the rock. Did it contain water, reddened by the lurid light? or was it blood? or, perchance, a liquid flame? Herein did the Shape of Evil dip his hand, and prepare to lay the mark of baptism upon their foreheads, that they might be partakers of the mystery of sin, more conscious of the secret guilt of others, both in deed and thought, than they could now be of their own. The husband cast one look at his pale wife, and Faith at him. What polluted wretches would the next glance shew them to each other, shuddering alike at what they disclosed and what they saw!

"Faith! Faith!" cried the husband. "Look up to Heaven, and resist the Wicked One!"

Whether Faith obeyed, he knew not. Hardly had he spoken, when he found himself amid calm night and solitude, listening to a roar of the wind, which died heavily away through the forest. He staggered against the rock and felt it chill and damp, while a hanging twig, that had been all on fire, besprinkled his cheek with the coldest dew.

The next morning, young Goodman Brown came slowly into the street of Salem village, staring around him like a bewildered man. The good old minister was taking a walk along the grave-yard, to get an appetite for breakfast and meditate his sermon, and bestowed a blessing, as he passed, on Goodman Brown. He shrank from the venerable saint, as if to avoid an anathema. Old Deacon Gookin was at domestic worship, and the holy words of his prayer were heard through the open window. "What God doth the wizard pray to?" quoth Goodman Brown. Goody Cloyse, that excellent old Christian, stood in the early sunshine, at her own lattice, catechising a little girl, who had brought her a pint of morning's milk. Goodman Brown snatched away the child, as from the grasp of the fiend himself. Turning the corner by the meeting-house, he spied the head of Faith, with the pink ribbons, gazing anxiously forth, and bursting into such joy at sight of him, that she skipt along the street, and almost kissed her husband before the whole village. But, Goodman Brown looked sternly and sadly into her face, and passed on without a greeting.

Had Goodman Brown fallen asleep in the forest, and only dreamed a wild dream of a witch-meeting?

Be it so, if you will. But, alas! it was a dream of evil omen for young Goodman Brown. A stern, a sad, a darkly meditative, a distrustful, if not a desperate man, did he become, from the night of that fearful dream. On the Sabbath-day, when the congregation were singing a holy psalm, he could not listen, because an anthem of sin rushed loudly upon his ear, and drowned all the blessed strain. When the minister spoke from the pulpit, with power and fervid eloquence, and, with his hand on the open Bible, of the sacred truths of our religion, and of saint-like lives and triumphant deaths, and of future bliss or misery unutterable, then did Goodman Brown turn pale, dreading, lest the roof should thunder down upon the gray blasphemer and his hearers. Often, awakening suddenly at midnight, he shrank from the bosom of Faith, and at morning or eventide, when the family knelt down at prayer, he scowled, and muttered to himself, and gazed sternly at his wife, and turned away. And when he had lived long, and was borne to his grave, a hoary corpse, followed by Faith, an aged woman, and children and grand-children, a goodly procession, besides neighbors, not a few, they carved no hopeful verse upon his tomb-stone; for his dying hour was gloom.

[1835]

EDGAR ALLAN POE
[1809–1849]

Edgar Allan Poe has the reputation of being the "bad boy" of early American literature: an alcoholic, drug-addicted cradle-robber who lived wild and died young. Most of this is legend based on slanders created by Poe's enemies and perpetuated by the reader's tendency to confuse a writer with his characters and by the general desire to have "bad boys" among literary heroes. Of course, there is some truth amid the falsity: Poe drank too much and married his thirteen-year-old cousin. But his worst sin was his ability to irritate his peers with his insistence upon intellectual integrity and literary brilliance in them, and in himself.

Poe resists easy classification; he was a literary movement of his own, always rubbing against the establishment despite his own establishment views. He inclined toward idealism yet disdained the New England transcendentalists. He was a poet, (not a moralizer) striving for beauty and "suggestiveness," and yet he was a hoaxer who indulged in gross fantasies. He had no desire to promote a national literature; for him, literature existed beyond nationality. Thus, he rarely indulged in the culture's standard themes of individualism, race, revolution, domesticity, and nature, but pursued deeper problems of the mind, science, creation, and the supernatural.

Born in Boston into a family of minor actors, Poe was orphaned at the age of two but immediately taken under the wing of John and Frances Allan of Richmond, Virginia. Frances doted over Edgar as if he were her own, and John, a merchant of substantial wealth, treated this only child as the heir to his fortune. In 1815, business took the Allans and Edgar to England, where for five formative years, the boy excelled in Latin and French. Back home Edgar continued to read and translate. However, his adolescence was shaped by a troubling relationship to his foster father. John Allan, who never legally adopted Poe, was a parent in every sense of the word: by turns loving and exasperating to his trying ward. As a family man, he was decidedly flawed; he cheated on his wife (producing several illegitimate children) and thereby scarred the teenage boy. Up to the day of Allan's death, Edgar's dealings with his foster father would be a tumultuous history of self-destructive screw-ups and reconciliations, ending sadly with an estrangement between the two that left Edgar without an inheritance.

In 1826, Poe attended the University of Virginia where, apparently, matriculation was his license to gamble and outspend his father's allowance. Gone by the following spring, he joined the U.S. Army under the name Edgar A. Perry and was stationed in Boston where he published his long poem "Tamerlane," about an ambitious world conqueror who deserts the girl he loves and dies regretting his pursuit of fame and power. Transferred to Charleston and then back to Virginia, Sergeant Major Poe produced a second, more widely received volume of poetry, Al Aaraaf, Tamerlane, and Minor Poems, which includes some of Poe's best works, not only the tough and lengthy title poems but also "Sonnet—To Science," which pairs off the seemingly contradictory worlds of thought and creativity. The more ambitious "Al Aaraaf" is the first (and perhaps best) of several cosmological works (including his last treatise Eureka) that create a celestial world symbolic of human passions and the inherent nothingness of existence.

Three years in the Army disciplined Poe. With renewed support from his father he enrolled at West Point in 1830. Just prior to this, his mother died, freeing John Allan to re-marry one woman despite having just fathered twins with another. Perhaps with this exemplary father figure in mind, Poe began to sabotage his West Point career before it even started. He charmed officers and students, but drinking got him dismissed before the end of the year. In the spring of 1831, he published Poems by Edgar A. Poe. Second Edition, which he dedicated to "the U.S. corps of cadets." Featured in this new volume are poems about creativity and ruin prefaced by the essay "Letter to B—" and including the memorable poem "Israfel"; Poe's paeon to female beauty in "To Helen"; his facetious "Fairy-Land"; and the haunting "The City in the Sea."

Now thoroughly estranged from his father, Poe moved to Baltimore. Living with his aunt, he supported himself, barely, with short comic and gothic fictions published in Philadelphia and Baltimore magazines. By 1833 Poe proposed to include these dozen or so mostly forgettable pieces into "The Tales of the Folio Club." The organizing principle of the collection is that each month a member of the Folio Club—they have ridiculous names such as Convolvulus Gondola and Solomon Seadrift—composes a tale that parodies contemporary writing and writers. Poe never managed to convince a publisher to accept the Folio Club project, and its exact contents is still a matter of conjecture. The best of these tales—"Metzengerstein" and "MS Found in a Bottle"—are gothic tales that play effortlessly and concisely upon the thin line separating the supernatural and bunkum. Others, such as "The Duke de L'Omlette" and "Loss of Breath," take on familiar situations (betting against the devil or losing one's breath) and run them into the ground. Poe's aim was to make his mark in the growing American literary scene through satires on the worst of European sensationalism, as found in Blackwood's Magazine and the worst of America's scribblers, such as Nathaniel Parker Willis. But his joking in these tales is too obvious to be an effective hoax, the wit too strained to be effective parody. The more lasting and resilient comic mode of Washington Irving's nostalgic humor, as opposed to his own brand of satiric attack, was what American culture rewarded, and Poe seemed constitutionally unable to engage in such sentiment; he preferred excess and "the ludicrous heightened to the grotesque."

While publishers were not convinced the public needed a volume of Poe's obscure satire, they recognized his talent, and in 1835 the Southern Literary Messenger, Richmond's newest journal, hired him as editor. This was the beginning of Poe's career as a man of letters, and as a man given to drink. In that year, his grandmother died, leaving his Aunt Marie and thirteen-year-old cousin Virginia Clemm without income. Rather than have this small remnant of his original family dissolve any further, he quickly married Virginia and brought both aunt and wife under his roof. The marriage to the girl thirteen years his junior lasted until Virginia's death twelve years later but, according to Poe, it was never consummated. Poe drank heavily at this time; however, the need to support a family forced him to moderate, and he produced a prodigious amount of writing for the Messenger—reviews (treating his most important critical ideas concerning the emotional intensity and unity of literary works), filler (such as "Autography" and "Pinakidia"), an unfinished play (Politian), and more tales, including "Berenice" (concerning one man's experiments in dental extraction), and "Hans Phaal" (a science fiction hoax concerning space travel).

Under Poe's two-year editorship, the Southern Literary Messenger grew from a local rag to a national journal, but Poe's drinking got him fired. In 1837 he moved to New York City where he completed his only novel, The Narrative of Arthur Gordon Pym (1838). This sea-gothic relates young Pym's survival in a wild storm, entombment in a dark hold, defeat of a mutinous crew, and encounter with a plague-ridden ghost ship. Rescued, his new ship is pulled to the Antarctic, which oddly enough is rather hot and populated by black natives. The novel ends in riot with the apocalyptic emergence of a great white god. The novel's racialized ending contains a political allegory of various meanings. Given Poe's ardent anti-Jacksonian views against "the mob," the conclusion may warn against the extension of freedom to the masses and in particular African-Americans, or more liberally articulate America's precarious racial condition.

After less than a year in New York, Poe moved to Philadelphia where in 1839 he signed on as editor for Burton's Gentleman's Magazine, and published (in various journals) some of his best short fiction: "The Fall of the House of Usher," "Ligeia," and "William Wilson." The first two deal with the will to conquer death. In "Usher" the narrator witnesses the actual disintegration of Usher castle as its occupants (the family's last brother and sister about whom there are vague hints of incest) sicken and die, but not before the premature burial of the sister. In "Ligeia" a less reliable narrator tells of the death of his first, transcendently beautiful wife and her apparent return from the dead through the possession of his second, also deceased, wife's body. But here the narrator's intentions may be to hoax the reader into believing his rather convenient transcendental wishes. "William Wilson" is a doppelgänger tale in which a young con man is plagued by his double who represents his conscience. In these three works, Poe moved his gothic art from the entertainingly grotesque to the deeply psychological, or what in symbolic terms Poe called "the arabesque," and in 1840 his Tales of the Grotesque and Arabesque finally found a willing publisher.

In 1840 Burton's changed hands and combined with another journal to become Graham's Magazine, and Poe, whose reputation as an audacious but effective editor had continued to grow, stayed on. In the following years, he invented a new form of fiction, the tale of ratiocination or detective story. In "The Murders in the Rue Morgue" (1841), "The Mystery of Marie Roget" (1843), and "The Purloined Letter" (1845), Poe's sleuth, C. Auguste Dupin, makes a creative art out of his masterful analytical skills. He not only deduces but imagines in creative ways the solution to his mystery, playing upon a sharp sense of human nature. Of course, in writing these "mysteries," Poe had the advantage of knowing the mystery in advance and was always amused by dull readers who praised his skill in uncovering the very mysteries he had invented and purposefully concealed in order to achieve an effect of sublime ratiocination. In short, his detective tales were another form of hoax.

By 1842 Poe had lifted Graham's circulation to 20,000. But the self-destructive behavior that would come to characterize his life was about to begin. In this year, Virginia burst a blood vessel while singing, exhibiting the ghastly symptoms of tuberculosis. Moving her and the family into the countryside, Poe began drinking more heavily. He was dismissed from Graham's but made ends meet by publishing new tales, including "The Masque of the Red Death" about the insinuation of disease (the plague) into a castle despite the king's attempt to block its entry, no doubt a response to Virginia's condition. Despite this kind of allegorical writing, he made cogent arguments against this overly determined symbolic form, but did so by castigating (in separate reviews) Longfellow's and Hawthorne's use of allegory, thus bringing to a higher pitch his antagonisms against the literary establishment.

For years, Poe had wanted to head a journal of his own; his first proposal had been for a periodical he wanted to call Penn Magazine and then Stylus, but few wanted to invest in the brainchild of such an erratic personality. However, in 1845 with the instant and remarkable success of his best-known poem "The Raven" (about a student tormented by the memory of his dead lover), Poe's notoriety was tempered with admiration; he was asked to recite the poem and lecture on it. Later that year Wiley and Putnam published The Raven and Other Poems as well as a volume of Tales. With his career at its highest point, Poe's dream of magazine ownership was finally realized when *he joined novelist Charles F. Briggs, in New York City, as co-owner of Broadway Journal; within a year, he was its sole proprietor. In it, he revised and reprinted many of his tales and poems, but he also published in other journals such new works as "The Imp of the Perverse" (about the death wish) and the overlooked classic "The System of Dr. Tarr and Prof. Fether" (about the inability to distinguish madness and sanity). Poe also engaged at this time in a wreckless attack upon Longfellow (charging the popular poet professor with plagiarism) that created a minor sensation in both Boston and New York. The so-called "Longfellow War" increased circulation for the Broadway Journal but only underscored Poe's edgy personality. In one episode, his anger became physical when he got in a brawl with the minor poet Thomas Dunn English. The more substantial James Russell Lowell had admired Poe during these years and had earlier published "The Tell-Tale Heart" (about a murderer's inability to keep his perfect crime a secret), but when Lowell finally met Poe in 1845, he found him drunk, and Poe's relationship with one of the nation's more influential writers ended. Nor did it help his reputation when he began overly praising the poetry of Frances Sargent Osgood, and then dating the woman, even as his wife Virginia was slowly dying at home.*

Poe fell quickly. Although he was creating some of his best tales — "The Black Cat" and "The Cask of Amontillado"—he could not pay his bills, and in 1846 the Broadway Journal folded. A year later, Virginia died at their Fordham (The Bronx) cottage. Devastated, Poe considered suicide but instead wrote "Ulalume," a moving musical poem about a lost love and the separation of body and soul. He also composed a grim fairy tale, "Hop-Frog," about a jester (himself) and a dancer (Virginia) who dress the king and courtiers (critics) as monkeys and burn them to death. Despite his desperate condition or perhaps because of it, Poe's lectures drew large crowds, and out of one of them he composed his last semi-scientific, semi-hoax treatise on being and nothingness, Eureka. Poe's final months were wrenching. He frantically sought female companions while desperately trying to curb his drinking. Death came in the streets. One theory holds that his drinking coupled with undiagnosed diabetes (Type II) led to a series of strokes that left him disoriented and seemingly deranged. He was found dying in a Baltimore gutter, on Election Day, 1849.

Poe grabs young readers (with his lurid tales and rhythmic poems) and holds them into adulthood (with his fierce penetrations into darkness). Poe's enemies, in particular his own literary executor Rufus Griswold, reviled his memory and lied about his life. But the lies only fed his popularity, first among French symbolists and now universally. In his poems, gothic tales, hoaxes, mysteries, and essays, Poe used language to trick his readers into fear and wonder; he used language like music to suggest what can never be spoken directly. In this regard, "bad boy" Poe has survived into the modern age.

For Further Reading

Primary Works

Tamerlane and Other Poems. By a Bostonian (1827); *Al Aaraaf, Tamerlane, and Minor Poems* (1829); *Poems by Edgar A. Poe. Second Edition* (1831); *The Narrative of Arthur Gordon Pym of Nantucket* (1838); *Tales of the Grotesque and Arabesque* (1840); *The Prose Romances of Edgar A. Poe* (1843); *Tales by Edgar A. Poe* (1845); *The Raven and Other Poems* (1845); *Eureka: A Prose Poem by Edgar A. Poe* (1848); *Works of Edgar Allan Poe, with a Memoir by Rufus Wilmot Griswold and Notices of his Life and Genius by N. P. Willis and J. R. Lowell* (ed. Griswold, 1850–1856); *The Complete Works of Edgar Allan Poe* (ed. James A. Harrison, 1902); *The Letters of Edgar Allan Poe* (ed. John Ward Ostrom,1948); *Collected Works of Edgar Allan Poe* (ed. Thomas Ollive Mabbott, 1969–78); *Collected Writings of Edgar Allan Poe* (ed. Burton R. Pollin, 1981 and 1985); *Edgar Allan Poe: Poetry and Tales* (ed. Patrick F. Quinn, 1984); *Edgar Allan Poe: Essays and Reviews* (ed. G. R. Thompson, 1984).

Secondary Works

Arthur Hobson Quinn, *Edgar Allan Poe: A Critical Biography* (1941); Daniel Hoffman, *Poe Poe Poe Poe Poe Poe Poe* (1973); G. R. Thompson, *Poe's Fiction: Romantic Irony in the Gothic Tales* (1973); Esther F. Hyneman, *Edgar Allan Poe: An Annotated Bibliography* (1974); David Ketterer, *The Rationale of Deception in Poe* (1979); *The Poe Log: A Documentary Life* (ed. Dwight Thomas and David K. Jackson, 1987); John Bryant, "Poe's Ape of Unreason: Humor, Ritual, and Culture," in *Nineteenth-Century Literature* 51 (June 1996); *A Companion to Poe Studies* (ed. Eric W. Carlson, 1996); Kenneth Silverman, *Edgar A. Poe: A Biography* (1991).

The Cask of Amontillado[*]

EDGAR ALLAN POE

The thousand injuries of Fortunato I had borne as I best could, but when he ventured upon insult I vowed revenge. You, who so well know the nature of my soul, will not suppose, however, that I gave utterance to a threat. *At length* I would be avenged; this was a point definitively settled—but the very definitiveness with which it was resolved precluded the idea of risk. I must not only punish but punish with impunity. A wrong is unredressed when retribution overtakes its redresser. It is equally unredressed when the avenger fails to make himself felt as such to him who has done the wrong.

It must be understood that neither by word nor deed had I given Fortunato cause to doubt my good will. I continued, as was my wont, to smile in his face, and he did not perceive that my smile *now* was at the thought of his immolation.[1]

He had a weak point—this Fortunato—although in other regards he was a man to be respected and even feared. He prided himself upon his connoisseurship in wine. Few Italians have the true virtuoso spirit. For the most part their enthusiasm is adopted to suit the time and opportunity, to practice imposture upon the British and Austrian *millionaires.* In painting and gemmary, Fortunato, like his countrymen, was a quack, but in the matter of old wines he was sincere. In this respect I did not differ from him materially;—I was skilful in the Italian vintages myself, and bought largely whenever I could.

It was about dusk, one evening during the supreme madness of the carnival[2] season, that I encountered my friend. He accosted me with excessive warmth, for he had been drinking much. The man wore motley.[3] He had on a

---

[*]First published in November 1846 in *Godey's Magazine and Lady's Book,* this tale was not reprinted in Poe's life; however, it is now considered a model of suspense, horror, and irony, appearing in countless anthologies. Amontillado is a dry, light-colored sherry. The text here is the 1846 magazine version.

[1]Sacrifice

[2]Carnival (from the Latin meaning farewell to meat) is a period of celebration and feasting culminating on Shrove Tuesday (Mardi Gras), the day before the beginning of Lent and its forty days of fasting before Easter.

[3]A clown's or harlequin's outfit of mixed colors and shapes.

tight-fitting parti-striped dress, and his head was surmounted by the conical cap and bells. I was so pleased to see him that I thought I should never have done wringing his hand.

I said to him—"My dear Fortunato, you are luckily met. How remarkably well you are looking to-day. But I have received a pipe[4] of what passes for Amontillado, and I have my doubts."

"How?" said he. "Amontillado? A pipe? Impossible! And in the middle of the carnival!"

"I have my doubts," I replied; "and I was silly enough to pay the full Amontillado price without consulting you in the matter. You were not to be found, and I was fearful of losing a bargain."

"Amontillado!"

"I have my doubts."

"Amontillado!"

"And I must satisfy them."

"Amontillado!"

"As you are engaged, I am on my way to Luchresi. If any one has a critical turn it is he. He will tell me— —"

"Luchresi cannot tell Amontillado from Sherry."

"And yet some fools will have it that his taste is a match for your own."

"Come, let us go."

"Whither?"

"To your vaults."

"My friend, no; I will not impose upon your good nature. I perceive you have an engagement. Luchresi— —"

"I have no engagement;—come."

"My friend, no. It is not the engagement, but the severe cold with which I perceive you are afflicted. The vaults are insufferably damp. They are encrusted with nitre."[5]

"Let us go, nevertheless. The cold is merely nothing. Amontillado! You have been imposed upon. And as for Luchresi, he cannot distinguish Sherry from Amontillado."

Thus speaking, Fortunato possessed himself of my arm; and putting on a mask of black silk and drawing a *roquelaire*[6] closely about my person, I suffered him to hurry me to my palazzo.

There were no attendants at home; they had absconded to make merry in honour of the time. I had told them that I should not return until the morning, and had given them explicit orders not to stir from the house. These

---

[4]A cask containing four barrels of wine.

[5]Saltpeter, or potassium nitrate, found naturally encrusted on stones and used to make gunpowder.

[6]A roquelaire is a knee-length cloak of the seventeenth century.

orders were sufficient, I well knew, to insure their immediate disappearance, one and all, as soon as my back was turned.

I took from their sconces two flambeaux, and giving one to Fortunato, bowed him through several suites of rooms to the archway that led into the vaults. I passed down a long and winding staircase, requesting him to be cautious as he followed. We came at length to the foot of the descent, and stood together upon the damp ground of the catacombs of the Montresors.

The gait of my friend was unsteady, and the bells upon his cap jingled as he strode.

"The pipe," said he.

"It is farther on," said I; "but observe the white web-work which gleams from these cavern walls."

He turned towards me, and looked into my eyes with two filmy orbs that distilled the rheum of intoxication.[7]

"Nitre?" he asked, at length.

"Nitre," I replied. "How long have you had that cough?"

"Ugh! ugh! ugh!—ugh! ugh! ugh!—ugh! ugh! ugh!—ugh! ugh! ugh!— ugh! ugh! ugh!"

My poor friend found it impossible to reply for many minutes.

"It is nothing," he said, at last.

"Come," I said, with decision, "we will go back; your health is precious. You are rich, respected, admired, beloved; you are happy, as once I was. You are a man to be missed. For me it is no matter. We will go back; you will be ill, and I cannot he responsible. Besides, there is Luchresi——"

"Enough," he said; "the cough is a mere nothing; it will not kill me. I shall not die of a cough."

"True—true," I replied; "and, indeed, I had no intention of alarming you unneccessarily—but you should use all proper caution. A draught of this Medoc[8] will defend us from the damps."

Here I knocked off the neck of a bottle which I drew from a long row of its fellows that lay upon the mould.

"Drink," I said, presenting him the wine.

He raised it to his lips with a leer. He paused and nodded to me familiarly, while his bells jingled.

"I drink," he said, "to the buried that repose around us."

"And I to your long life."

He again took my arm, and we proceeded.

"These vaults," he said, "are extensive."

"The Montresors," I replied, "were a great and numerous family."

---

[7]Rheum is any watery discharge, in this case tears; perhaps a pun on rum.

[8]A Bordeaux wine.

"I forget your arms."[9]

"A huge human foot d'or, in a field azure; the foot crushes a serpent rampant whose fangs are imbedded in the heel."

"And the motto?"

"Nemo me impune lacessit."

"Good!" he said.

The wine sparkled in his eyes and the bells jingled. My own fancy grew warm with the Medoc. We had passed through long walls of piled skeletons, with casks and puncheons[10] intermingling, into the inmost recesses of the catacombs. I paused again, and this time I made bold to seize Fortunato by an arm above the elbow.

"The nitre!" I said; "see, it increases. It hangs like moss upon the vaults. We are below the river's bed. The drops of moisture trickle among the bones. Come, we will go back ere it is too late. Your cough——"

"It is nothing," he said; "let us go on. But first, another draught of the Medoc."

I broke and reached him a flaçon of De Grâve.[11] He emptied it at a breath. His eyes flashed with a fierce light. He laughed and threw the bottle upwards with a gesticulation I did not understand.

I looked at him in surprise. He repeated the movement—a grotesque one.

"You do not comprehend?" he said.

"Not I," I replied.

"Then you are not of the brotherhood."

"How?"

"You are not of the masons."[12]

"Yes, yes," I said; "yes, yes."

"You? Impossible! A mason?"

"A mason," I replied.

"A sign," he said, "a sign."

"It is this," I answered, producing from beneath the folds of my *roquelaire* a trowel.

"You jest," he exclaimed, recoiling a few paces. "But let us proceed to the Amontillado."

---

[9]Coat of arms, or a family's heraldic emblem. In the following line, Montresor uses heraldic terminology to describe his arms: it is a gold ("d'or ") foot crushing an upright ("rampant") snake depicted on a blue ("azure") background ("field"). The family motto is the motto of Scotland: "No one provokes me with impunity."

[10]Large casks

[11]Small bottle with a stopper. De Grâve is a Bordeaux wine.

[12]Masons or Freemasons are members of a fraternal order, with secret rituals and symbols, established in the eighteenth century and dedicated to free thinking, tolerance, and charitable acts. In the 1820s, American nativists and isolationists reacted against masonry's liberalism and secrecy, which created a widespread disdain for masons and led to the anti-masonic movement.

"Be it so," I said, replacing the tool beneath the cloak and again offering him my arm. He leaned upon it heavily. We continued our route in search of the Amontillado. We passed through a range of low arches, descended, passed on, and descending again, arrived at a deep crypt, in which the foulness of the air caused our flambeaux rather to glow than flame.

At the most remote end of the crypt there appeared another less spacious. Its walls had been lined with human remains, piled to the vault overhead, in the fashion of the great catacombs of Paris.[13] Three sides of this interior crypt were still ornamented in this manner. From the fourth side the bones had been thrown down, and lay promiscuously upon the earth, forming at one point a mound of some size. Within the wall thus exposed by the displacing of the bones, we perceived a still interior crypt or recess, in depth about four feet, in width three, in height six or seven. It seemed to have been constructed for no especial use within itself, but formed merely the interval between two of the colossal supports of the roof of the catacombs, and was backed by one of their circumscribing walls of solid granite.

It was in vain that Fortunato, uplifting his dull torch, endeavoured to pry into the depth of the recess. Its termination the feeble light did not enable us to see.

"Proceed," I said; "herein is the Amontillado. As for Luchresi——"

"He is an ignoramus," interrupted my friend, as he stepped unsteadily forward, while I followed immediately at his heels. In an instant he had reached the extremity of the niche, and finding his progress arrested by the rock, stood stupidly bewildered. A moment more and I had fettered him to the granite. In its surface were two iron staples, distant from each other about two feet, horizontally. From one of these depended a short chain, from the other a padlock. Throwing the links about his waist, it was but the work of a few seconds to secure it. He was too much astounded to resist. Withdrawing the key I stepped back from the recess.

"Pass your hand," I said, "over the wall; you cannot help feeling the nitre. Indeed, it is very damp. Once more let me *implore* you to return. No? Then I must positively leave you. But I will first render you all the little attentions in my power."

"The Amontillado!" ejaculated my friend, not yet recovered from his astonishment.

"True," I replied; "the Amontillado."

As I said these words I busied myself among the pile of bones of which I have before spoken. Throwing them aside, I soon uncovered a quantity of building stone and mortar. With these materials and with the aid of my trowel, I began vigorously to wall up the entrance of the niche.

---

[13]Catacombs are underground passages used for burial. The Roman catacombs are ancient; however, the catacombs of Paris are abandoned stone quarries not used for burial until 1787.

I had scarcely laid the first tier of the masonry when I discovered that the intoxication of Fortunato had in great measure worn off. The earliest indication I had of this was a low moaning cry from the depth of the recess. It was not the cry of a drunken man. There was then a long and obstinate silence, I laid the second tier, and the third, and the fourth; and then I heard the furious vibration of the chain. The noise lasted for several minutes, during which, that I might hearken to it with the more satisfaction, I ceased my labours and sat down upon the bones. When at last the clanking subsided, I resumed the trowel, and finished without interruption the fifth, the sixth, and the seventh tier. The wall was now nearly upon a level with my breast. I again paused, and holding the flambeaux over the mason-work, threw a few feeble rays upon the figure within.

A succession of loud and shrill screams, bursting suddenly from the throat of the chained form, seemed to thrust me violently back. For a brief moment I hesitated, I trembled. Unsheathing my rapier, I began to grope with it about the recess; but the thought of an instant reassured me. I placed my hand upon the solid fabric of the catacombs and felt satisfied. I re-approached the wall. I replied to the yells of him who clamoured. I re-echoed, I aided, I surpassed them in volume and in strength. I did this, and the clamourer grew still.

It was now midnight, and my task was drawing to a close. I had completed the eighth, the ninth and the tenth tier. I had finished a portion of the last and the eleventh; there remained but a single stone to be fitted and plastered in. I struggled with its weight; I placed it partially in its destined position. But now there came from out the niche a low laugh that erected the hairs upon my head. It was succeeded by a sad voice, which I had difficulty in recognizing as that of the noble Fortunato. The voice said—

"Ha! ha! ha!—he! he! he!—a very good joke, indeed—an excellent jest. We will have many a rich laugh about it at the palazzo—he! he! he!—over our wine—he! he! he!"

"The Amontillado!" I said.

"He! he! he!—he! he! he!—yes, the Amontillado. But is it not getting late? Will not they be awaiting us at the palazzo—the Lady Fortunato and the rest? Let us be gone."

"Yes," I said, "let us be gone."

"For the love of God, Montresor!"

"Yes," I said, "for the love of God!"

But to these words I hearkened in vain for a reply. I grew impatient. I called aloud—

"Fortunato!"

No answer. I called again—

"Fortunato!"

No answer still. I thrust a torch through the remaining aperture and let it fall within. There came forth in return only a jingling of the bells. My heart grew sick; it was the dampness of the catacombs that made it so. I hastened to make an end of my labour. I forced the last stone into its position; I plastered it up. Against the new masonry I re-erected the old rampart of bones. For the half of a century no mortal has disturbed them. *In pace requiescat!*

[1846]

FREDERICK DOUGLASS
[1818–1895]

One of the most prolific and influential writers of the nineteenth century is known to most readers today for a single, slim book: Narrative of the Life of Frederick Douglass, An American Slave, Written by Himself *(1845). There's good reason to remember this book in particular, for it is considered by many to be the classic example of the genre of writing commonly called "slave narratives," and it remains an eloquent, wise, and compelling commentary on slavery and the struggle for freedom—a book from which readers still have much to learn these many years later. But today's recognition of Douglass's power as a writer should not be limited to his first book, however compelling, for throughout his life Douglass remained devoted to the conviction that the written word was a powerful weapon in the cause of social justice, and that literature could change the world. In three autobiographies, a novella ("The Heroic Slave"), newspaper writings (for his papers* The North Star *and Frederick Douglass' Paper), and published orations (among many others, "What to the Slave Is the Fourth of July?"), Douglass demonstrated this faith throughout his long public career as the most celebrated African-American leader of the nineteenth century, and as one of the most influential men in American history.*

Much of Douglass's writing career can be understood as an attempt to promote his own life as a representative story of African-American life in the nineteenth century, and then to meet the responsibilities that follow from that role. In part, this challenge led Douglass back to autobiographical writing throughout his career—including his 1845 Narrative, My Bondage and My Freedom, *published in 1855, and* Life and Times of Frederick Douglass, *published in 1881 and expanded in 1892. Douglass recognized the importance of this genre of writing to African Americans, for their experience, and the perspectives and understanding shaped by that experience, were largely either unrepresented or misrepresented in the publications of the day. "My part," Douglass wrote in the last of the autobiographies, "has been to tell the story of the slave. The story of the master never wanted for narrators. The masters, to tell their story, had at call all the talent and genius that wealth could command. They have had their day in court. Literature, theology, philosophy, law, and learning have come willingly to their service, and, if condemned, they have not been condemned unheard." Marshaling the forces of literature, Douglass was determined that others would have their day in court as well, and in his newspaper writing, fiction, and orations he brought theology, philosophy, law, and learning to the antislavery movement, to the women's rights movement, and broadly to the cause of educational, social, and occupational opportunity for African Americans.*

Douglass was enslaved at birth in Talbot County, Maryland, in February 1818, and years later would speak of himself, with considerable justice, as a "self-made man," the topic of one of his most popular lectures. His mother, Harriet Bailey, was enslaved; his father was a white man whose identity Douglass could never determine with certainty. A turning point in Douglass's life came when he was sent to Baltimore in 1826 to be a house servant for Sophia and Hugh Auld. Initially kind, Sophia Auld began to teach the young Douglass to read, but both her kindness and the lessons soon came to a halt. Convinced of the importance of that which was denied to him, Douglass continued the lessons on his own, sometimes recruiting the help of young white boys in the city. He was sent back to his rural plantation in 1833, but was sent back to Baltimore in 1836 following his unsuccessful attempt to escape. Finally, in 1838, and with the help of a free black woman in Baltimore, Anna Murray, Douglass escaped by posing as a sailor and taking a train to New York City. Anna followed shortly after that, and she and Douglass married and settled in New Bedford, Massachusetts. Douglass, who had heard of abolitionists while enslaved, began reading William Lloyd Garrison's antislavery newspaper the Liberator *in 1839. Within a few years Douglass joined his own voice to the movement, and his power as a speaker was so great that he was quickly invited, after his initial speech in 1841, to become a lecturing agent for the Massachusetts Anti-Slavery Society. From 1841 to 1845 he traveled the antislavery lecture circuit, gaining recognition and prominence within the movement, speaking so powerfully and eloquently that some audiences doubted that he could have been born a slave.*

In part to put such doubts to rest, Douglass wrote his Narrative of the Life of Frederick Douglass, an American Slave, Written by Himself, *a book instantly recognized in its own time as a singular achievement and celebrated ever since as a classic of American literary history. Published by the American Anti-Slavery Society of Boston, the* Narrative *sold close to five thousand copies in its first four months, and nearly thirty thousand copies in the United States and Great Britain by 1850. The 1845 American edition was followed by a Dutch translation in 1846 and a French translation in 1848. In the* Narrative, *Douglass tells the story of coming of age under the system of slavery, learning to read, and struggling to realize his developing dreams of freedom. Many episodes in the* Narrative *presented readers with horrors and struggles they would expect to hear, with eloquent testament to the ideal of liberty. As Douglass writes in one* of the Narrative's best-known statements, "You have seen how a man was made a slave; you shall see how a slave was made a man." But the Narrative is notable as well for what Douglass chooses not to relate—the details of the story of his escape, for example, and the personal story of his relationship with Anna. The Narrative is a strategic story, denying readers certain intimacies of his life, and specific information about his means of escape from slavery. The Narrative is a critique of slavery, one designed to enlist support; and it was a sufficiently sharp critique that Douglass added an Appendix to defend his representation of white slaveholding religion, drawing a sharp distinction "between the Christianity of this land, and the Christianity of Christ."

The Narrative succeeded in establishing Douglass's credentials as one who had experienced slavery firsthand—to the point that, for personal safety, Douglass was forced to leave the country. The narrative of enslavement could too easily become the tool of Douglass's reenslavement, for he was a fugitive under American law. From 1845 to 1847 Douglass worked in Great Britain for the antislavery movement by giving lectures in England, Ireland, and Scotland. His efforts inspired significant support for his cause and for his leadership, and when he returned to the United States (following the indignity of having to purchase, with the assistance of white supporters, his own liberty), he returned with funds to start his own weekly newspaper, the North Star. Douglass established the new antislavery paper (which heightened developing tensions with William Lloyd Garrison, editor of the Liberator) at his new home, Rochester, New York, in December 1847, proclaiming its guiding philosophy in its masthead: "Right is of no Sex—Truth is of no Color—God is the Father of us all, and we are all Brethren." In 1851, the North Star would become Frederick Douglass' Paper, and in 1858 Douglass initiated a monthly publication as well, Douglass' Monthly. In all of these periodicals Douglass reprinted articles from other papers, and enlisted black and white abolitionists as contributors—but necessarily, filled the paper with his own writing.

Some of Douglass' most influential work of this period followed his conviction that "the people want to do what is best," but that "they must be shown that to do right is best." In 1853, Douglass wrote "The Heroic Slave," a fictionalized novella of the true story of Madison Washington, leader of the successful mutiny on the slave ship Creole in 1841. Douglass begins the narrative by associating Washington with the white founding fathers and heroes of the American Revolution—but Douglass notes that while the story of white revolutionary heroism is amply documented, Washington's story can only be pieced together, and he focuses much of the story on the experiences, the partial understanding and the occasional resolve, of a white character, Mr. Listwell, whose ability to listen well to Washington's experiences converts him to the antislavery movement and inspires him to act on his convictions.

Douglass's hesitations about the sincerity of white antislavery efforts became increasingly a subject of his writing, and was suggested dramatically *in his 1855 autobiography,* My Bondage and My Freedom. *Whereas the 1845* Narrative *included a preface by white abolitionist William Lloyd Garrison,* My Bondage and My Freedom *begins with a preface from black abolitionist James McCune Smith, one of the preeminent African-American scholars of his time and an established critic of Garrison's methods. Douglass draws from the earlier autobiography, but his portrayal of slavery is more harsh, and his consideration of it as a political and cultural system is more detailed than in the 1845* Narrative. *Moreover, Douglass extends his story to a glimpse into racial prejudice in the North and into the antislavery movement itself. In many of his newspaper editorials, Douglass was even more frank about life in the "free" North—asserting, for example, in an 1850 article that "properly speaking,* prejudice against color *does not exist in this country. The feeling (or whatever it is) which we call* prejudice *is no less than a* murderous, hell-born hatred *of every virtue which may adorn the character of a* black man." *Much of Douglass's writing during this period was devoted to the full range of African-American experience, and to the various aspects of a cultural system that supported and encouraged the restriction of African-American opportunity and the misrepresentation of black identity.*

Douglass's frustrations are clear in one of his most famous speeches from this period, "What to the Slave Is the Fourth of July?" On July 5, 1852, Douglass responded to an invitation to speak in Rochester, New York, by asking his audience, "Do you mean, citizens, to mock me, by asking me to speak to-day?" Douglass begins his speech by reviewing, with admiration, the great events of the American Revolution so ceremoniously celebrated on the Fourth of July, but he argues that the ideals of the American Revolution have been violated and the national founders dishonored by subsequent events, for rather than follow through on their devotion to liberty they had instead abandoned it to the system of slavery. Douglass accordingly asks and answers what is, for him, the question of the day: "What, to the American slave, is your Fourth of July? I answer: a day that reveals to him, more than all other days in the year, the gross injustice and cruelty to which he is the constant victim." The force of Douglass's comments, though, is only increased by his expressed admiration for the ideals that drove the American Revolution. Indeed, through his most trying times as a prominent critic of slavery and racism, Douglass remained a staunch friend to those white Americans who had similarly devoted themselves to the cause. Throughout his career, in fact, Douglass held onto his remarkable faith that things could and would change, and that Americans could come to view themselves differently and embrace a community based on the belief that "a diverse origin does not disprove a common nature, nor does it disprove a united destiny. The essential characteristics of humanity are everywhere the same."

As the Civil War approached, Douglass's convictions were both challenged and seemingly vindicated. He was sufficiently militant in his resistance to things as they were that he consulted with the white abolitionist John Brown before Brown's raid at Harpers Ferry, though Douglass did not have the faith in Brown's plan to join the raid himself. His association with Brown was sufficiently incriminating, however, to force Douglass to leave the country briefly after Brown was captured. But with the arrival of the Civil War in 1861, Douglass believed that the nation was finally in a position to confront the sins of the past, and he was influential in finally convincing Abraham Lincoln to recruit African Americans for the Union army and in guiding the recruitment efforts. After the war, Douglass tried to convince President Andrew Johnson to guide the nation toward African-American rights.

In the years that followed, Douglass's leadership was broadly acknowledged, if often frustrated and limited. He held various public offices, including United States Marshal of the District of Columbia (1877–81), Recorder of Deeds for the District of Columbia (1881–86), president of the Freedman's Bureau Bank, consul to Haiti and chargé d'affaires for the Dominican Republic (1889–91). When he returned to autobiography in his 1881 publication, Life and Times of Frederick Douglass, *and when he expanded that final story of his life in 1892, he could write of his belief, after the Civil War, that his life's work had been completed—but he had to write as well of the great work that remained in education, civil rights, and economic opportunity. Telling the story of his life remained the great work of his life, as he looked in his own experience for evidence that African Americans would be recognized as free and equal citizens in a nation that had learned to finally embrace its own professed ideals. As he states toward the end of* Life and Times, *"it will be seen in these pages that I have lived several lives in one: first, the life of slavery; secondly, the life of a fugitive from slavery; thirdly, the life of comparative freedom; fourthly, the life of conflict and battle; and fifthly, the life of victory, if not complete, at least assured." That his story remains important, but still unfinished, is evident in the many biographies and poems devoted to him by various American writers, black and white, who recognize the importance of understanding the first four stories if Americans are to complete the fifth.*

John Ernest
University of New Hampshire

For Further Reading

Primary Works

Narrative of the Life of Frederick Douglass, an American Slave, Written by Himself *(1845);* What to the Slave Is the Fourth of July? An Address Delivered in Rochester, New York, on 5 July 1852 *(1852);* The Heroic Slave *(1853);* My Bondage and My Freedom *(1855);* Life and Times of Frederick Douglass *(1881,*

1892); *Introduction, The Reason Why the Colored American Is Not in the World Columbian Exposition* (1893); *The Lessons of the Hour* (1894); *Life and Writings of Frederick Douglass,* ed. Philip S. Foner. 5 vols. New York: International, 1950–75; *The Frederick Douglass Papers*, ed. John W. Blassingame. 5 vols. New Haven: Yale University Press, 1979–.

Biography

Blight, David W., *Frederick Douglass' Civil War* (Baton Rouge: Louisiana State University Press, 1989). Chesnutt, Charles Waddell, *Frederick Douglass* (London: K. Paul, Trench, Trübner & Co., 1899). Huggins, Nathan Irvin, *Slave and Citizen: The Life of Frederick Douglass* (Boston: Little, Brown, 1980). Martin, Waldo E., *The Mind of Frederick Douglass,* (Chapel Hill: University of North Carolina Press, 1982). McFeely, William S., *Frederick Douglass* (New York: W.W. Norton, 1991). Preston, Dickson, J., *Young Frederick Douglass: The Maryland Years* (Baltimore: Johns Hopkins University Press, 1980). Quarles, Benjamin, *Frederick Douglass* (Washington, D.C.: Associated Publishers, 1948). Washington, Booker T., *Frederick Douglass* (New York: Haskell House, 1968).

Secondary Works

Andrews, William L., ed., *Critical Essays on Frederick Douglass* (Boston: G.K. Hall, 1991). Andrews, William L., *To Tell a Free Story: The First Century of Afro-American Autobiography, 1760–1865* (Urbana: University of Illinois Press, 1986). Baker, Houston A., Jr., *Blues, Ideology, and Afro-American Literature* (Chicago: University of Chicago Press, 1984). Butterfield, Stephen, *Black Autobiography in America,* (Amherst: University of Massachusetts Press, 1974). Davis, Charles T., and Henry Louis Gates, Jr., eds., *The Slave's Narrative* (New York: Oxford University Press, 1985). Ernest, John, *Resistance and Reformation in Nineteenth-Century African-American Literature: Brown, Wilson, Jacobs, Delany, Douglass, and Harper* (Jackson: University Press of Mississippi, 1995). Fisch, Audrey, *American Slaves in Victorian England: Abolitionist Politics in Popular Literature and Culture* (Cambridge: Cambridge University Press, 2000). Foster, Frances Smith, *Witnessing Slavery: The Development of Ante-bellum Slave Narratives,* 1979. 2nd ed. (Madison: University of Wisconsin Press, 1994). Gates, Henry Louis, Jr., ed., *Black Literature & Literary Theory* (New York: Routledge, 1984). Gates, Henry Louis, Jr., *Figures in Black: Words, Signs, and the "Racial" Self* (New York: Oxford University Press, 1987). Hall, Jim, ed., *Approaches to Teaching The Narrative of the Life of Frederick Douglass* (New York: The Modern Language Association of America, 1999). Howard-Pittney, David, *The Afro-American Jeremiad: Appeals for Justice in America* (Philadelphia: Temple University Press, 1990). Levine, Robert S., *Martin Delany, Frederick Douglass, and the Politics of Representative Identity* (Chapel Hill: The University of North Carolina Press, 1997). Lott, Tommy L., ed., *Subjugation & Bondage: Critical Essays on Slavery and Social Philosophy* (Lanham: Rowman & Littlefield, 1998). Rice, Alan J., and Martin Crawford, eds., *Liberating Sojourn:*

Frederick Douglass & Transatlantic Reform (Athens: The University of Georgia Press, 1999). Rogers, William B., *"We Are All Together Now": Frederick Douglass, William Lloyd Garrison, and the Prophetic Tradition* (New York: Garland, 1995). Sale, Maggie Montesinos, *The Slumbering Volcano: American Slave Ship Revolts and the Production of Rebellious Masculinity* (Durham: Duke University Press, 1997). Sartwell, Crispin, *Act Like You Know: African-American Autobiography and White Identity* (Chicago: The University of Chicago Press, 1998). Smith, Valerie, *Self-Discovery and Authority in Afro-American Narrative* (Cambridge: Harvard University Press, 1991). Starling, Marion Wilson, *The Slave Narrative: Its Place in American History* (Washington, D.C.: Howard University Press, 1988). Stuckey, Sterling, *Going Through the Storm: The Influence of African American Art in History* (New York: Oxford University Press, 1994). Sundquist, Eric J., ed., *Frederick Douglass: New Literary and Historical Essays* (Cambridge: Cambridge University Press, 1990). Sundquist, Eric J., *To Wake the Nations: Race in the Making of American Literature* (Cambridge, Mass: Belknap Press of Harvard University Press, 1993). Wald, Priscilla, *Constituting Americans: Cultural Anxiety and Narrative Form* (Durham: Duke University Press, 1995). Wood, Marcus, *Blind Memory: Visual Representations of Slavery in England and America, 1780–1865* (New York: Routledge, 2000).

What to the Slave Is the Fourth of July?*

*AN ADDRESS DELIVERED IN ROCHESTER, NEW YORK,
ON 5 JULY 1852*

FREDERICK DOUGLASS

Mr. President, Friends and Fellow Citizens: He who could address this audience without a quailing sensation, has stronger nerves than I have. I do not remember ever to have appeared as a speaker before any assembly more shrinkingly, nor with greater distrust of my ability, than I do this day. A feeling has crept over me, quite unfavorable to the exercise of my limited powers of speech. The task before me is one which requires much previous thought and study for its proper performance. I know that apologies of this sort are generally considered flat and unmeaning. I trust, however, that mine will not be so considered. Should I seem at ease, my appearance would much misrepresent me. The little experience I have had in addressing public meetings, in country school houses, avails me nothing on the present occasion.

The papers and placards say, that I am to deliver a 4th of July oration. This certainly sounds large, and out of the common way, for me. It is true that I have often had the privilege to speak in this beautiful Hall, and to address many who now honor me with their presence. But neither their familiar faces, nor the perfect gage I think I have of Corinthian Hall, seems to free me from embarrassment.

The fact is, ladies and gentlemen, the distance between this platform and the slave plantation, from which I escaped, is considerable—and the difficulties to be overcome in getting from the latter to the former, are by no means slight. That I am here to-day is, to me, a matter of astonishment as well as of gratitude. You will not, therefore, be surprised, if in what I have to say, I evince no elaborate preparation, nor grace my speech with any high sounding exordium. With little experience and with less learning, I have been able to throw my thoughts hastily and imperfectly together; and trusting to your patient and generous indulgence, I will proceed to lay them before you.

---

*The text of this speech is based on the pamphlet published by Lee, Mann and Company shortly after Douglass delivered the speech at Corinthian Hall, *What to the Slave Is the Fourth of July?*

This, for the purpose of this celebration, is the 4th of July. It is the birthday of your National Independence, and of your political freedom. This, to you, is what the Passover was to the emancipated people of God. It carries your minds back to the day, and to the act of your great deliverance; and to the signs, and to the wonders, associated with that act, and that day. This celebration also marks the beginning of another year of your national life; and reminds you that the Republic of America is now 76 years old. I am glad, fellow-citizens, that your nation is so young. Seventy-six years, though a good old age for a man, is but a mere speck in the life of a nation. Three score years and ten is the allotted time for individual men; but nations number their years by thousands. According to this fact, you are, even now, only in the beginning of your national career, still lingering in the period of childhood. I repeat, I am glad this is so. There is hope in the thought, and hope is much needed, under the dark clouds which lower above the horizon. The eye of the reformer is met with angry flashes, portending disastrous times; but his heart may well beat lighter at the thought that America is young, and that she is still in the impressible stage of her existence. May he not hope that high lessons of wisdom, of justice and of truth, will yet give direction to her destiny? Were the nation older, the patriot's heart might be sadder, and the reformer's brow heavier. Its future might be shrouded in gloom, and the hope of its prophets go out in sorrow. There is consolation in the thought that America is young. Great streams are not easily turned from channels, worn deep in the course of ages. They may sometimes rise in quiet and stately majesty, and inundate the land, refreshing and fertilizing the earth with their mysterious properties. They may also rise in wrath and fury, and bear away, on their angry waves, the accumulated wealth of years of toil and hardship. They, however, gradually flow back to the same old channel, and flow on as serenely as ever. But, while the river may not be turned aside, it may dry up, and leave nothing behind but the withered branch, and the unsightly rock, to howl in the abyss-sweeping wind, the sad tale of departed glory. As with rivers so with nations.

Fellow-citizens, I shall not presume to dwell at length on the associations that cluster about this day. The simple story of it is that, 76 years ago, the people of this country were British subjects. The style and title of your "sovereign people" in which you now glory was not then born. You were under the British Crown. Your fathers esteemed the English Government as the home government; and England as the fatherland. This home government, you know, although a considerable distance from your home, did, in the exercise of its parental prerogatives, impose upon its colonial children, such restraints, burdens and limitations, as, in its mature judgement, it deemed wise, right and proper.

But, your fathers, who had not adopted the fashionable idea of this day, of the infallibility of government, and the absolute character of its acts, presumed to differ from the home government in respect to the wisdom and the justice of some of those burdens and restraints. They went so far in their excitement as to pronounce the measures of government unjust, unreasonable, and oppressive, and altogether such as ought not to be quietly submitted to. I scarcely need say, fellow-citizens, that my opinion of those measures fully accords with that of your fathers. Such a declaration of agreement on my part would not be worth much to anybody. It would, certainly, prove nothing, as to what part I might have taken, had I lived during the great controversy of 1776. To say *now* that America was right, and England wrong, is exceedingly easy. Everybody can say it; the dastard, not less than the noble brave, can flippantly discant on the tyranny of England towards the American Colonies. It is fashionable to do so; but there was a time when to pronounce against England, and in favor of the cause of the colonies, tried men's souls.[1] They who did so were accounted in their day, plotters of mischief, agitators and rebels, dangerous men. To side with the right, against the wrong, with the weak against the strong, and with the oppressed against the oppressor! *here* lies the merit, and the one which, of all others, seems unfashionable in our day. The cause of liberty may be stabbed by the men who glory in the deeds of your fathers. But, to proceed.

Feeling themselves harshly and unjustly treated by the home government, your fathers, like men of honesty, and men of spirit, earnestly sought redress. They petitioned and remonstrated; they did so in a decorous, respectful, and loyal manner. Their conduct was wholly unexceptionable. This, however, did not answer the purpose. They saw themselves treated with sovereign indifference, coldness and scorn. Yet they persevered. They were not the men to look back.

As the sheet anchor takes a firmer hold, when the ship is tossed by the storm, so did the cause of your fathers grow stronger, as it breasted the chilling blasts of kingly displeasure. The greatest and best of British statesmen admitted its justice, and the loftiest eloquence of the British Senate came to its support. But, with that blindness which seems to be the unvarying characteristic of tyrants, since Pharoah and his hosts were drowned in the Red Sea, the British Government persisted in the exactions complained of.

The madness of this course, we believe, is admitted now, even by England; but we fear the lesson is wholly lost on our present rulers.

Oppression makes a wise man mad. Your fathers were wise men, and if they did not go mad, they became restive under this treatment. They felt themselves the victims of grievous wrongs, wholly incurable in their colonial capacity. With brave men there is always a remedy for oppression. Just here, the idea of a total separation of the colonies from the crown was born! It was

---

[1]Douglass here refers to Thomas Paine's pamphlet titled *The American Crisis* (1776), which opens with the words, "These are the times that try men's souls." Thomas Paine (1737–1809) was an important voice in the American Revolution, but a controversial figure later for his challenge to established religion in *The Age of Reason.*

a startling idea, much more so, than we, at this distance of time, regard it. The timid and the prudent (as has been intimated) of that day, were, of course, shocked and alarmed by it.

Such people lived then, had lived before, and will, probably, ever have a place on this planet; and their course, in respect to any great change, (no matter how great the good to be attained, or the wrong to be redressed by it), may be calculated with as much precision as can be the course of the stars. They hate all changes, but silver, gold and copper change! Of this sort of change they are always strongly in favor.

These people were called tories in the days of your fathers; and the appellation, probably, conveyed the same idea that is meant by a more modern, though a somewhat less euphonious term, which we often find in our papers, applied to some of our old politicians.

Their opposition to the then dangerous thought was earnest and powerful; but, amid all their terror and affrighted vociferations against it, the alarming and revolutionary idea moved on, and the country with it.

On the 2d of July, 1776, the old Continental Congress, to the dismay of the lovers of ease, and the worshippers of property, clothed that dreadful idea with all the authority of national sanction. They did so in the form of a resolution; and as we seldom hit upon resolutions, drawn up in our day, whose transparency is at all equal to this, it may refresh your minds and help my story if I read it.

> "Resolved, That these united colonies are, and of right, ought to be free and Independent States; that they are absolved from all allegiance to the British Crown; and that all political connection between them and the State of Great Britain is, and ought to be, dissolved."[2]

Citizens, your fathers made good that resolution. They succeeded; and to-day you reap the fruits of their success. The freedom gained is yours; and you, therefore, may properly celebrate this anniversary. The 4th of July is the first great fact in your nation's history—the very ring-bolt in the chain of your yet undeveloped destiny.

Pride and patriotism, not less than gratitude, prompt you to celebrate and to hold it in perpetual remembrance. I have said that the Declaration of Independence is the RING-BOLT to the chain of your nation's destiny; so, indeed, I regard it. The principles contained in that instrument are saving principles. Stand by those principles, be true to them on all occasions, in all places, against all foes, and at whatever cost.

From the round top of your ship of state, dark and threatening clouds may be seen. Heavy billows, like mountains in the distance, disclose to the

---

[2]Here and throughout this oration, Douglass quotes from or paraphrases the Declaration of Independence.

leeward huge forms of flinty rocks! That *bolt* drawn, that *chain* broken, and all is lost. *Cling to this day—cling to it,* and to its principles, with the grasp of a storm-tossed mariner to a spar at midnight.

The coming into being of a nation, in any circumstances, is an interesting event. But, besides general considerations, there were peculiar circumstances which make the advent of this republic an event of special attractiveness.

The whole scene, as I look back to it, was simple, dignified and sublime.

The population of the country, at the time, stood at the insignificant number of three millions. The country was poor in the munitions of war. The population was weak and scattered, and the country a wilderness unsubdued. There were then no means of concert and combination, such as exist now. Neither steam nor lightning had then been reduced to order and discipline. From the Potomac to the Delaware was a journey of many days. Under these, and innumerable other disadvantages, your fathers declared for liberty and independence and triumphed.

Fellow Citizens, I am not wanting in respect for the fathers of this republic. The signers of the Declaration of Independence were brave men. They were great men too—great enough to give fame to a great age. It does not often happen to a nation to raise, at one time, such a number of truly great men. The point from which I am compelled to view them is not, certainly, the most favorable; and yet I cannot contemplate their great deeds with less than admiration. They were statesmen, patriots and heroes, and for the good they did, and the principles they contended for, I will unite with you to honor their memory.

They loved their country better than their own private interests; and, though this is not the highest form of human excellence, all will concede that it is a rare virtue, and that when it is exhibited, it ought to command respect. He who will, intelligently, lay down his life for his country, is a man whom it is not in human nature to despise. Your fathers staked their lives, their fortunes, and their sacred honor, on the cause of their country. In their admiration of liberty, they lost sight of all other interests.

They were peace men; but they preferred revolution to peaceful submission to bondage. They were quiet men; but they did not shrink from agitating against oppression. They showed forbearance; but that they knew its limits. They believed in order; but not in the order of tyranny. With them, nothing was *"settled"* that was not right. With them, justice, liberty and humanity were *"final";* not slavery and oppression. You may well cherish the memory of such men. They were great in their day and generation. Their solid manhood stands out the more as we contrast it with these degenerate times.

How circumspect, exact and proportionate were all their movements! How unlike the politicians of an hour! Their statesmanship looked beyond the passing moment, and stretched away in strength into the distant future. They seized upon eternal principles, and set a glorious example in their defence. Mark them!

Fully appreciating the hardship to be encountered, firmly believing in the right of their cause, honorably inviting the scrutiny of an on-looking world, reverently appealing to heaven to attest their sincerity, soundly comprehending the solemn responsibility they were about to assume, wisely measuring the terrible odds against them, your fathers, the fathers of this republic, did, most deliberately, under the inspiration of a glorious patriotism, and with a sublime faith in the great principles of justice and freedom, lay deep the corner-stone of the national superstructure, which has risen and still rises in grandeur around you.

Of this fundamental work, this day is the anniversary. Our eyes are met with demonstrations of joyous enthusiasm. Banners and pennants wave exultingly on the breeze. The din of business, too, is hushed. Even Mammon seems to have quitted his grasp on this day. The ear-piercing fife and the stirring drum unite their accents with the ascending peal of a thousand church bells. Prayers are made, hymns are sung, and sermons are preached in honor of this day; while the quick martial tramp of a great and multitudinous nation, echoed back by all the hills, valleys and mountains of a vast continent, bespeak the occasion one of thrilling and universal interest—a nation's jubilee.

Friends and citizens, I need not enter further into the causes which led to this anniversary. Many of you understand them better than I do. You could instruct me in regard to them. That is a branch of knowledge in which you feel, perhaps, a much deeper interest than your speaker. The causes which led to the separation of the colonies from the British crown have never lacked for a tongue. They have all been taught in your common schools, narrated at your firesides, unfolded from your pulpits, and thundered from your legislative halls, and are as familiar to you as household words. They form the staple of your national poetry and eloquence.

I remember, also, that, as a people, Americans are remarkably familiar with all facts which make in their own favor. This is esteemed by some as a national trait—perhaps a national weakness. It is a fact, that whatever makes for the wealth or for the reputation of Americans, and can be had *cheap*! will be found by Americans. I shall not be charged with slandering Americans, if I say I think the American side of any queston may be safely left in American hands.

I leave, therefore, the great deeds of your fathers to other gentlemen whose claim to have been regularly descended will be less likely to be disputed than mine!

The Present

My business, if I have any here to-day, is with the present. The accepted time with God and his cause is the ever-living now.

"Trust no future, however pleasant,
  Let the dead past bury its dead;
Act, act in the living present,
  Heart within, and God overhead."[3]

We have to do with the past only as we can make it useful to the present and to the future. To all inspiring motives, to noble deeds which can be gained from the past, we are welcome. But now is the time, the important time. Your fathers have lived, died, and have done their work, and have done much of it well. You live and must die, and you must do your work. You have no right to enjoy a child's share in the labor of your fathers, unless your children are to be blest by your labors. You have no right to wear out and waste the hard-earned fame of your fathers to cover your indolence. Sydney Smith[4] tells us that men seldom eulogize the wisdom and virtues of their fathers, but to excuse some folly or wickedness of their own. This truth is not a doubtful one. There are illustrations of it near and remote, ancient and modern. It was fashionable, hundreds of years ago, for the children of Jacob to boast, we have "Abraham to our father," when they had long lost Abraham's faith and spirit.[5] That people contented themselves under the shadow of Abraham's great name, while they repudiated the deeds which made his name great. Need I remind you that a similar thing is being done all over this country to-day? Need I tell you that the Jews are not the only people who built the tombs of the prophets, and garnished the sepulchers of the righteous? Washington could not die till he had broken the chains of his slaves.[6] Yet his monument is built up by the price of human blood, and the traders in the bodies and souls of men, shout—"We have Washington to *our father.*" Alas! that it should be so; yet so it is.

"The evil that men do, lives after them,
The good is oft' interred with their bones."[7]

Fellow-citizens, pardon me, allow me to ask, why am I called upon to speak here to-day? What have I, or those I represent, to do with your national independence? Are the great principles of political freedom and of natural justice, embodied in that Declaration of Independence, extended to us? and am I, therefore, called upon to bring our humble offering to the

---

[3]From "A Psalm of Life" (1838) by Henry Wadsworth Longfellow (1807–1882).

[4]Sydney Smith (1771–1845) was an Anglican minister best known for asking in an essay who "reads an American book."

[5]Luke 3:8

[6]Douglass is not quite accurate here, though Washington did state in his will that the slaves he owned should be freed after his wife's death.

[7]From William Shakespeare's *Julius Caesar,* Act III, Scene 2, line 76.

national altar, and to confess the benefits and express devout gratitude for the blessings resulting from your independence to us?

Would to God, both for your sakes and ours, that an affirmative answer could be truthfully returned to these questions! Then would my task be light, and my burden easy and delightful. For *who* is there so cold, that a nation's sympathy could not warm him? Who so obdurate and dead to the claims of gratitude, that would not thankfully acknowledge such priceless benefits? Who so stolid and selfish, that would not give his voice to swell the hallelujahs of a nation's jubilee, when the chains of servitude had been torn from his limbs? I am not that man. In a case like that, the dumb might eloquently speak, and the "lame man leap as an hart."[8]

But, such is not the state of the case. I say it with a sad sense of the disparity between us. I am not included within the pale of this glorious anniversary! Your high independence only reveals the immeasurable distance between us. The blessings in which you, this day, rejoice, are not enjoyed in common. The rich inheritance of justice, liberty, prosperity and independence, bequeathed by your fathers, is shared by you, not by me. The sunlight that brought life and healing to you, has brought stripes and death to me. This Fourth [of] July is *yours,* not *mine. You* may rejoice, *I* must mourn. To drag a man in fetters into the grand illuminated temple of liberty, and call upon him to join you in joyous anthems, were inhuman mockery and sacrilegious irony. Do you mean, citizens, to mock me, by asking me to speak to-day? If so, there is a parallel to your conduct. And let me warn you that it is dangerous to copy the example of a nation whose crimes, towering up to heaven, were thrown down by the breath of the Almighty, burying that nation in irrecoverable ruin! I can to-day take up the plaintive lament of a peeled and woe-smitten people!

"By the rivers of Babylon, there we sat down. Yea! we wept when we remembered Zion. We hanged our harps upon the willows in the midst thereof. For there, they that carried us away captive, required of us a song; and they who wasted us required of us mirth, saying, Sing us one of the songs of Zion. How can we sing the Lord's song in a strange land? If I forget thee, O Jerusalem, let my right hand forget her cunning. If I do not remember thee, let my tongue cleave to the roof of my mouth."[9]

Fellow-citizens; above your national, tumultuous joy, I hear the mournful wail of millions! whose chains, heavy and grievous yesterday, are, to-day, rendered more intolerable by the jubilee shouts that reach them. If I do forget, if I do not faithfully remember those bleeding children of sorrow this day, "may my right hand forget her cunning, and may my tongue cleave to the roof of my mouth!" To forget them, to pass lightly over their wrongs, and to chime in with the popular theme, would be treason most scandalous and shocking,

[8]Isaiah 35:6
[9]Psalm 137:1–6

and would make me a reproach before God and the world. My subject, then fellow-citizens, is AMERICAN SLAVERY. I shall see, this day, and its popular characteristics, from the slave's point of view. Standing, there, identified with the American bondman, making his wrongs mine, I do not hesitate to declare, with all my soul, that the character and conduct of this nation never looked blacker to me than on this 4th of July! Whether we turn to the declarations of the past, or to the professions of the present, the conduct of the nation seems equally hideous and revolting. America is false to the past, false to the present, and solemnly binds herself to be false to the future. Standing with God and the crushed and bleeding slave on this occasion, I will, in the name of humanity which is outraged, in the name of liberty which is fettered, in the name of the constitution and the Bible, which are disregarded and trampled upon, dare to call in question and to denouce, with all the emphasis I can command, everything that serves to perpetuate slavery—the great sin and shame of America! "I will not equivocate; I will not excuse";[10] I will use the severest language I can command; and yet not one word shall escape me that any man, whose judgment is not blinded by prejudice, or who is not at heart a slaveholder, shall not confess to be right and just

But I fancy I hear some one of my audience say, it is just in this circumstance that you and your brother abolitionists fail to make a favorable impression on the public mind. Would you argue more, and denounce less, would you persuade more, and rebuke less, your cause would be much more likely to succeed. But, I submit, where all is plain there is nothing to be argued. What point in the anti-slavery creed would you have me argue? On what branch of the subject do the people of this country need light? Must I undertake to prove that the slave is a man? That point is conceded already. Nobody doubts it. The slaveholders themselves acknowledge it when they punish disobedience on the part of the slave. There are seventy-two crimes in the State of Virginia, which, if committed by a black man, (no matter how ignorant he be), subject him to the punishment of death; while only two of the same crimes will subject a white man to the like punishment. What is this but the acknowledgement that the slave is a moral, intellectual and responsible being? The manhood of the slave is conceded. It is admitted in the fact that Southern statute books are covered with enactments forbidding, under severe fines and penalties, the teaching of the slave to read or to write. When you can point to any such laws, in reference to the beasts of the field, then I may consent to argue the manhood of the slave. When the dogs in your streets, when the fowls of the air, when the cattle on your hills, when the fish of the sea, and the reptiles that crawl, shall be unable to distinguish the slave from a brute, *then* will I argue with you that the slave is a man!

For the present, it is enough to affirm the equal manhood of the negro race. Is it not astonishing that, while we are ploughing, planting and reaping,

---

[10]From William Lloyd Garrison's opening editorial for the *Liberator,* January 1, 1831.

using all kinds of mechanical tools, erecting houses, constructing bridges, building ships, working in metals of brass, iron, copper, silver and gold; that, while we are reading, writing and cyphering, acting as clerks, merchants and secretaries, having among us lawyers, doctors, ministers, poets, authors, editors, orators and teachers; that, while we are engaged in all manner of enterprises common to other men, digging gold in California, capturing the whale in the Pacific, feeding sheep and cattle on the hill-side, living, moving, acting, thinking, planning, living in families as husbands, wives and children, and, above all, confessing and worshipping the Christian's God, and looking hopefully for life and immortality beyond the grave, we are called upon to prove that we are men!

Would you have me argue that man is entitled to liberty? that he is the rightful owner of his own body? You have already declared it. Must I argue the wrongfulness of slavery? Is that a question for Republicans? Is it to be settled by the rules of logic and argumentation, as a matter beset with great difficulty, involving a doubtful application of the principle of justice, hard to be understood? How should I look to-day, in the presence of Americans, dividing, and subdividing a discourse, to show that men have a natural right to freedom? speaking of it relatively, and positively, negatively, and affirmatively. To do so, would be to make myself ridiculous, and to offer an insult to your understanding. There is not a man beneath the canopy of heaven, that does not know that slavery is wrong *for him.*

What, am I to argue that it is wrong to make men brutes, to rob them of their liberty, to work them without wages, to keep them ignorant of their relations to their fellow men, to beat them with sticks, to flay their flesh with the lash, to load their limbs with irons, to hunt them with dogs, to sell them at auction, to sunder their families, to knock out their teeth, to burn their flesh, to starve them into obedience and submission to their masters? Must I argue that a system thus marked with blood, and stained with pollution, is *wrong*? No! I will not. I have better employments for my time and strength, than such arguments would imply.

What, then, remains to be argued? Is it that slavery is not divine; that God did not establish it; that our doctors of divinity are mistaken? There is blasphemy in the thought. That which is inhuman, cannot be divine! *Who* can reason on such a proposition? They that can, may; I cannot. The time for such argument is past.

At a time like this, scorching irony, not convincing argument, is needed. O! had I the ability, and could I reach the nation's ear, I would, to-day, pour out a fiery stream of biting ridicule, blasting reproach, withering scarcasm, and stern rebuke. For it is not light that is needed, but fire; it is not the gentle shower, but thunder. We need the storm, the whirlwind, and the earthquake. The feeling of the nation must be quickened; the conscience of the nation must be roused; the propriety of the nation must be startled; the hypocrisy of the nation must be exposed; and its crimes against God and man must be proclaimed and denounced.

What, to the American slave, is your 4th of July? I answer: a day that reveals to him, more than all other days in the year, the gross injustice and cruelty to which he is the constant victim. To him, your celebration is a sham; your boasted liberty, an unholy license; your national greatness, swelling vanity; your sounds of rejoicing are empty and heartless; your denunciations of tyrants, brass fronted impudence; your shouts of liberty and equality, hollow mockery; your prayers and hymns, your sermons and thanksgivings, with all your religious parade, and solemnity, are, to him, mere bombast, fraud, deception, impiety, and hypocrisy—a thin veil to cover up crimes which would disgrace a nation of savages. There is not a nation on the earth guilty of practices, more shocking and bloody, than are the people of these United States, at this very hour.

Go where you may, search where you will, roam through all the monarchies and despotisms of the old world, travel through South America, search out every abuse, and when you have found the last, lay your facts by the side of the everyday practices of this nation, and you will say with me, that, for revolting barbarity and shameless hypocrisy, America reigns without a rival.

The Internal Slave Trade

Take the American slave-trade, which, we are told by the papers, is especially prosperous just now. Ex-Senator Benton[11] tells us that the price of men was never higher than now. He mentions the fact to show that slavery is in no danger. This trade is one of the peculiarities of American institutions. It is carried on in all the large towns and cities in one-half of this confederacy; and millions are pocketed every year, by dealers in this horrid traffic. In several states, this trade is a chief source of wealth. It is called (in contradistinction to the foreign slave-trade) *"the internal slave-trade."* It is, probably, called so, too, in order to divert from it the horror with which the foreign slave-trade is contemplated. That trade has long since been denounced by this government, as piracy. It has been denounced with burning words, from the high places of the nation, as an execrable traffic. To arrest it, to put an end to it, this nation keeps a squadron, at immense cost, on the coast of Africa. Everywhere, in this country, it is safe to speak of this foreign slave-trade, as a most inhuman traffic, opposed alike to the laws of God and of man. The duty to extirpate and destroy it, is admitted even by our DOCTORS OF DIVINITY. In order to put an end to it, some of these last have consented that

---

[11]Thomas Hart Benton (1782–1858) was Missouri's United States Senator from 1821–1851.

their colored brethren (nominally free) should leave this country, and establish themselves on the western coast of Africa! It is, however, a notable fact that, while so much execration is poured out by Americans upon those engaged in the foreign slave-trade, the men engaged in the slave-trade between the states pass without condemnation, and their business is deemed honorable.

Behold the practical operation of this internal slave-trade, the American slave-trade, sustained by American politics and American religion. Here you will see men and women reared like swine for the market. You know what is a swine-drover? I will show you a man-drover. They inhabit all our Southern States. They perambulate the country, and crowd the highway of the nation, with droves of human stock. You will see one of these human flesh-jobbers, armed with pistol, whip and bowie-knife, driving a company of a hundred men, women, and children, from the Potomac to the slave market at New Orleans. These wretched people are to be sold singly, or in lots, to suit purchasers. They are food for the cotton-field, and the deadly sugar-mill. Mark the sad procession, as it moves wearily along, and the inhuman wretch who drives them. Hear his savage yells and his blood-chilling oaths, as he hurries on his affrighted captives! There, see the old man, with locks thinned and gray. Cast one glance, if you please, upon that young mother, whose shoulders are bare to the scorching sun, her briny tears falling on the brow of the babe in her arms. See, too, that girl of thirteen, weeping, *yes*! weeping, as she thinks of the mother from whom she has been torn! The drove moves tardily. Heat and sorrow have nearly consumed their strength; suddenly you hear a quick snap, like the discharge of a rifle; the fetters clank, and the chain rattles simultaneously; your ears are saluted with a scream, that seems to have torn its way to the centre of your soul! The crack you heard, was the sound of the slave-whip; the scream you heard, was from the woman you saw with the babe. Her speed had faltered under the weight of her child and her chains! that gash on her shoulder tells her to move on. Follow this drove to New Orleans. Attend the auction; see men examined like horses; see the forms of women rudely and brutally exposed to the shocking gaze of American slave-buyers. See this drove sold and separated forever; and never foget the deep, sad sobs that arose from that scattered multitude. Tell me citizens, WHERE, under the sun, you can witness a spectacle more fiendish and shocking. Yet this is but a glance at the American slave-trade, as it exists, at this moment, in the ruling part of the United States.

I was born amid such sights and scenes. To me the American slave-trade is a terrible reality. When a child, my soul was often pierced with a sense of its horrors. I lived on Philpot Street, Fell's Point, Baltimore, and have watched from the wharves, the slave ships in the Basin, anchored from the shore, with their cargoes of human flesh, waiting for favorable winds to waft them down the Chesapeake. There was, at that time, a grand slave mart kept at the head of Pratt Street, by Austin Woldfolk.[12] His agents were sent into every town and county in Maryland, announcing their arrival, through the papers, and on flaming *"hand-bills,"* headed CASH FOR NEGROES. These men were generally well dressed men, and very captivating in their manners. Ever ready to drink, to treat, and to gamble. The fate of many a slave has depended upon the turn of a single card; and many a child has been snatched from the arms of its mother by bargains arranged in a state of brutal drunkenness.

The flesh-mongers gather up their victims by dozens, and drive them, chained, to the general depot at Baltimore. When a sufficient number have been collected here, a ship is chartered, for the purpose of conveying the forlorn crew to Mobile, or to New Orleans. From the slave prison to the ship, they are usually driven in the darkness of night; for since the anti-slavery agitation, a certain caution is observed.

In the deep still darkness of midnight, I have been often aroused by the dead heavy footsteps, and the piteous cries of the chained gangs that passed our door. The anguish of my boyish heart was intense; and I was often consoled, when speaking to my mistress in the morning, to hear her say that the custom was very wicked; that she hated to hear the rattle of the chains, and the heart-rending cries. I was glad to find one who sympathised with me in my horror.

Fellow-citizens, this murderous traffic is, to-day, in active operation in this boasted republic. In the solitude of my spirit, I see clouds of dust raised on the highways of the South; I see the bleeding footsteps; I hear the doleful wail of fettered humanity, on the way to the slave-markets, where the victims are to be sold like *horses, sheep,* and *swine,* knocked off to the highest bidder. There I see the tenderest ties ruthlessly broken, to gratify the lust, caprice and rapacity of the buyers and sellers of men. My soul sickens at the sight.

> "Is this the land your Fathers loved,
>   The freedom which they toiled to win?
> Is this the earth whereon they moved?
>   Are these the graves they slumber in?"[13]

But a still more inhuman, disgraceful, and scandalous state of things remains to be presented.

By an act of the American Congress, not yet two years old, slavery has been nationalized in its most horrible and revolting form. By that act, Mason & Dixon's line has been obliterated; New York has become as Virginia; and

---

[12]Austin Woolfolk was a slave trader in Baltimore whom Douglass mentions in the second chapter of his *Narrative of the Life of Frederick Douglass.*

[13]Douglass reprints, with slight alterations, the first four lines of John Greenleaf Whittier's "Stanzas for the Times." Whittier (1807–1872) was a Quaker abolitionist.

the power to hold, hunt, and sell men, women, and children as slaves remains no longer a mere state institution, but is now an institution of the whole United States. The power is co-extensive with the star-spangled banner and American Christianity. Where these go, may also go the merciless slave-hunter. Where these are, man is not sacred. He is a bird for the sportsman's gun. By that most foul and fiendish of all human decrees, the liberty and person of every man are put in peril. Your broad republican domain is hunting ground for *men. Not* for thieves and robbers, enemies of society, merely, but for men guilty of no crime. Your lawmakers have commanded all good citizens to engage in this hellish sport. Your President, your Secretary of State, your *lords, nobles,* and ecclesiastics, enforce, as a duty you owe to your free and glorious country, and to your God, that you do this accursed thing. Not fewer than forty Americans have, within the past two years, been hunted down and, without a moment's warning, hurried away in chains, and consigned to slavery and excruciating torture. Some of these have had wives and children, dependent on them for bread; but of this, no account was made. The right of the hunter to his prey stands superior to the right of marriage, and to *all* rights in this republic, the rights of God included! For black men there are neither law, justice, humanity, nor religion. The Fugitive Slave *Law* makes MERCY TO THEM, A CRIME; and bribes the judge who tries them. An American JUDGE GETS TEN DOLLARS FOR EVERY VICTIM HE CONSIGNS to slavery, and five, when he fails to do so. The oath of any two villains is sufficient, under this hell-black enactment, to send the most pious and exemplary black man into the remorseless jaws of slavery! His own testimony is nothing. He can bring no witnesses for himself. The minister of American justice is bound by the law to hear but *one* side; and *that* side, is the side of the oppressor. Let this damning fact be perpetually told. Let it be thundered around the world, that, in tyrant-killing, king-hating, people-loving, democratic, Christian America, the seats of justice are filled with judges, who hold their offices under an open and palpable *bribe,* and are bound, in deciding in the case of a man's liberty, *to hear only his accusers!*[14]

In glaring violation of justice, in shameless disregard of the forms of administering law, in cunning arrangement to entrap the defenceless, and in diabolical intent, this Fugitive Slave Law stands alone in the annals of tyrannical legislation. I doubt if there be another nation on the globe, having the brass and the baseness to put such a law on the statute-book. If any man in

---

[14]The Fugitive Slave Law was part of the Compromise of 1850, and was a restatement and radical extension of the previously existing fugitive slave law. States had attempted before to resist, by state law, the capturing of fugitive slaves within their boundaries; the new law was designed to control these attempts at the federal level. The Fugitive Slave Law was a measure that emphasized the extent to which the rights of African Americans were not recognized in the U.S. constitutional and legal processes, a point about which the Supreme Court was explicit in its decision on the Dred Scott case in 1857.

this assembly thinks differently from me in this matter, and feels able to disprove my statements, I will gladly confront him at any suitable time and place he may select.

Religious Liberty

I take this law to be one of the grossest infringements of Christian Liberty, and, if the churches and ministers of our country were not stupidly blind, or most wickedly indifferent, they, too, would so regard it.

At the very moment that they are thanking God for the enjoyment of civil and religious liberty, and for the right to worship God according to the dictates of their own consciences, they are utterly silent in respect to a law which robs religion of its chief significance, and makes it utterly worthless to a world lying in wickedness. Did this law concern the *"mint, anise* and *cummin"*[15]—abridge the right to sing psalms, to partake of the sacrament, or to engage in any of the ceremonies of religion, it would be smitten by the thunder of a thousand pulpits. A general shout would go up from the church, demanding *repeal, repeal, instant repeal*! And it would go hard with that politician who presumed to solicit the votes of the people without inscribing this motto on his banner. Further, if this demand were not complied with, another Scotland would be added to the history of religious liberty, and the stern old Covenanters would be thrown into the shade. A John Knox[16] would be seen at every church door, and heard from every pulpit, and Fillmore[17] would have no more quarter than was shown by Knox, to the beautiful, but treacherous Queen Mary of Scotland. The fact that the church of our country, (with fractional exceptions), does not esteem "the Fugitive Slave Law" as a declaration of war against religious liberty, implies that that church regards religion simply as a form of worship, an empty ceremony, and *not* a vital principle, requiring active benevolence, justice, love and good will towards man. It esteems sacrifice above mercy; psalm-singing above right doing; solemn meetings above practical righteousness. A worship that can be conducted by persons who refuse to give shelter to the houseless, to give bread to the hungry, clothing to the naked, and who enjoin obedience to a law forbidding these acts of mercy, is a curse, not a blessing to mankind. The Bible addresses all such persons as "scribes, pharisees, hypocrites, who pay tithe of *mint, anise,* and *cummin,* and have omitted the weightier matters of the law, judgment, mercy and faith."

---

[15]Here and at the end of this paragraph Douglass quotes from Matthew 23:23.
[16]John Knox (1514?–1572) was the founder of Scottish Presbyterianism.
[17]Millard Fillmore (1800–1874) was the thirteenth President of the United States (1850–1853).

The Church Responsible

But the church of this country is not only indifferent to the wrongs of the slave, it actually takes sides with the oppressors. It has made itself the bulwark of American slavery, and the shield of American slave-hunters. Many of its most eloquent Divines, who stand as the very lights of the church, have shamelessly given the sanction of religion and the Bible to the whole slave system. They have taught that man may, properly, be a slave; that the relation of master and slave is ordained of God; that to send back an escaped bondman to his master is clearly the duty of all the followers of the Lord Jesus Christ; and this horrible blasphemy is palmed off upon the world for Christianity.

For my part, I would say, welcome infidelity! welcome atheism! welcome anything! in preference to the gospel, *as preached by those Divines*! They convert the very name of religion into an engine of tyranny, and barbarous cruelty, and serve to confirm more infidels, in this age, than all the infidel writings of Thomas Paine, Voltaire, and Bolingbroke,[18] put together, have done! These ministers make religion a cold and flinty-hearted thing, having neither principles of right action, nor bowels of compassion. They strip the love of God of its beauty, and leave the throne of religion a huge, horrible, repulsive form. It is a religion for oppressors, tyrants, man-stealers, and *thugs.* It is not that *"pure and undefiled religion"* which is from above, and which is *"first pure, then peaceable, easy to be entreated,* full of mercy and good fruits, *without partiality, and without hypocrisy."*[19] But a religion which favors the rich against the poor; which exalts the proud above the humble; which divides mankind into two classes, tyrants and slaves; which says to the man in chains, *stay there;* and to the oppressor, *oppress on;* it is a religion which may be professed and enjoyed by all the robbers and enslavers of mankind; it makes God a respecter of persons, denies his fatherhood of the race, and tramples in the dust the great truth of the brotherhood of man. All this we affirm to be true of the popular church, and the popular worship of our land and nation—a religion, a church, and a worship which, on the authority of inspired wisdom, we pronounce to be an abomination in the sight of God. In the language of Isaiah, the American church might be well addressed, "Bring no more vain oblations; incense is an abomination unto me: the new moons and Sabbaths, the calling of assemblies, I cannot away with; it is iniquity, even the solemn meeting. Your new moons and your appointed feasts my soul hateth. They are a trouble to me; I am weary to bear them; and when ye spread forth

---

[18] Thomas Paine (1737–1809), Voltaire (1694–1778), and Henry St. John, Viscount Bolingbroke (1678–1751) were often placed together as representatives of infidelity because of their writings on religion.

[19] James 1:27

your hands I will hide mine eyes from you. Yea! when ye make many prayers, I will not hear. YOUR HANDS ARE FULL OF BLOOD; cease to do evil, learn to do well; seek judgment; relieve the oppressed; judge for the fatherless; plead for the widow."[20]

The American church is guilty, when viewed in connection with what it is doing to uphold slavery; but it is superlatively guilty when viewed in connection with its ability to abolish slavery.

The sin of which it is guilty is one of omission as well as of commission. Albert Barnes but uttered what the common sense of every man at all observant of the actual state of the case will receive as truth, when he declared that "There is no power out of the church that could sustain slavery an hour, if it were not sustained in it."[21]

Let the religious press, the pulpit, the Sunday school, the conference meeting, the great ecclesiastical, missionary, Bible and tract associations of the land array their immense powers against slavery and slave-holding; and the whole system of crime and blood would be scattered to the winds; and that they do not do this involves them in the most awful responsibility of which the mind can conceive.

In prosecuting the anti-slavery enterprise, we have been asked to spare the church, to spare the ministry; but *how,* we ask, could such a thing be done? We are met on the threshold of our efforts for the redemption of the slave, by the church and ministry of the country, in battle arrayed against us; and we are compelled to fight or flee. From what *quarter,* I beg to know, has proceeded a fire so deadly upon our ranks, during the last two years, as from the Northern pulpit? As the champions of oppressors, the chosen men of American theology have appeared—men, honored for their so-called piety, and their real learning. The LORDS of Buffalo, the SPRINGS of New York, the LATHROPS of Auburn, the COXES and SPENCERS of Brooklyn, the GANNETS and SHARPS of Boston, the DEWEYS of Washington,[22] and other great religious lights of the land, have, in utter denial of the authority of *Him,* by whom they professed to be called to the ministry, deliberately taught us, against the example of the Hebrews and against the remonstrance of the Apostles, they teach *"that we ought to obey man's law before the law of God."*

My spirit wearies of such blasphemy; and how such men can be supported, as the "standing types and representatives of Jesus Christ," is a mystery which

---

[20]Isaiah 1:13–17

[21]Albert Barnes (1798–1870) was a Presbyterian minister in Philadelphia and author of *An Inquiry into the Scriptural Views of Slavery* (1846), from which Douglass here quotes. Barnes writes to respond to those who argued that slavery was sanctioned by the Bible.

[22]Douglass here refers to men who publicly supported the Fugitive Slave Act and noted their opposition to what they perceived to be the radical aims of many abolitionists: John Chase Lord, Gardiner Spring, Leonard Elijah Lathrop, Samuel Hanson Cox, Ichabod Smith Spencer, Ezra Stiles Gannett, Daniel Sharp, and Orville Dewey.

I leave others to penetrate. In speaking of the American church, however, let it be distinctly understood that I mean the *great mass* of the religious organizations of our land. There are exceptions, and I thank God that there are. Noble men may be found, scattered all over these Northern States, of whom Henry Ward Beecher[23] of Brooklyn, Samuel J. May of Syracuse,[24] and my esteemed friend[25] on the platform, are shining examples; and let me say further, that upon these men lies the duty to inspire our ranks with high religious faith and zeal, and to cheer us on in the great mission of the slave's redemption from his chains.

Religion in England and Religion in America

One is struck with the difference between the attitude of the American church towards the anti-slavery movement, and that occupied by the churches in England towards a similar movement in that country. There, the church, true to its mission of ameliorating, elevating, and improving the condition of mankind, came forward promptly, bound up the wounds of the West Indian slave, and restored him to his liberty. There, the question of emancipation was a high[ly] religious question. It was demanded, in the name of humanity, and according to the law of the living God. The Sharps, the Clarksons, the Wilberforces, the Buxtons, and the Burchells and the Knibbs,[26] were alike famous for their piety, and for their philanthropy. The anti-slavery movement *there* was not an anti-church movement, for the reason that the church took its full share in prosecuting that movement: and the anti-slavery movement in this country will cease to be an anti-church movement, when the church of this country shall assume a favorable, instead of a hostile position towards that movement.

Americans! your republican politics, not less than your republican religion, are flagrantly inconsistent. You boast of your love of liberty, your superior civilization, and your pure Christianity, while the whole political power of the nation (as embodied in the two great political parties), is solemnly pledged to support and perpetuate the enslavement of three millions of your countrymen. You hurl your anathemas at the crowned headed

---

[23]Henry Ward Beecher, one of the most popular preachers of his time, was the brother of Harriet Beecher Stowe, author of *Uncle Tom's Cabin.*

[24]Samuel J. May (1810–1899) was a Unitarian clergyman who served as the general agent of the Massachusetts Anti-Slavery Society from 1847 to 1865.

[25]The Rev. Robert R. Raymond, to whom Douglass here refers, read the Declaration of Independence for this gathering.

[26]Douglass here refers to men who led the antislavery efforts in Great Britain that helped lead to the ending of the slave trade in Britain and its colonies: Granville Sharp, Thomas Clarkson, William Wilberforce, Thomas Fowell Buxton, Thomas Burchell, and William Knibb.

tyrants of Russia and Austria, and pride yourselves on your Democractic institutions, while you yourselves consent to be the mere *tools* and *body-guards* of the tyrants of Virginia and Carolina. You invite to your shores fugitives of oppression from abroad, honor them with banquets, greet them with ovations, cheer them, toast them, salute them, protect them, and pour out your money to them like water; but the fugitives from your own land you advertise, hunt, arrest, shoot and kill. You glory in your refinement and your universal education; yet you maintain a system as barbarous and dreadful as ever stained the character of a nation—a system begun in avarice, supported in pride, and perpetuated in cruelty. You shed tears over fallen Hungary, and make the sad story of her wrongs the theme of your poets, statesmen and orators, till your gallant sons are ready to fly to arms to vindicate her cause against her oppressors;[27] but, in regard to the ten thousand wrongs of the American slave, you would enforce the strictest silence, and would hail him as an enemy of the nation who dares to make those wrongs the subject of public discourse! You are all on fire at the mention of liberty for France or for Ireland; but are as cold as an iceberg at the thought of liberty for the enslaved of America. You discourse eloquently on the dignity of labor; yet, you sustain a system which, in its very essence, casts a stigma upon labor. You can bare your bosom to the storm of British artillery to throw off a threepenny tax on tea; and yet wring the last hard-earned farthing from the grasp of the black laborers of your country. You profess to believe "that, of one blood, God made all nations of men to dwell on the face of all the earth,"[28] and hath commanded all men, everywhere to love one another; yet you notoriously hate, (and glory in your hatred), all men whose skins are not colored like your own. You declare, before the world, and are understood by the world to declare, that you *"hold these truths to be self evident, that all men are created equal; and are endowed by their Creator with certain inalienable rights; and that, among these are, life, liberty, and the pursuit of happiness;"* and yet, you hold securely, in a bondage which, according to your own Thomas Jefferson, *"is worse than ages of that which your fathers rose in rebellion to oppose,"* a seventh part of the inhabitants of your country.

Fellow-citizens! I will not enlarge further on your national inconsistencies. The existence of slavery in this country brands your republicanism as a sham, your humanity as a base pretence, and your Christianity as a lie. It destroys your moral power abroad; it corrupts your politicians at home. It saps the foundation of religion; it makes your name a hissing, and a byword

---

[27]Hungary's republican government was overthrown in 1849 by Russia and Austria. The cause of Hungarian freedom fighters was widely celebrated in the United States, and the irony of that support for freedom in a nation supporting slavery was often noted in antislavery texts—perhaps most noably, Stowe's *Uncle Tom's Cabin.*

[28]Acts 17:26

to a mocking earth. It is the antagonistic force in your government, the only thing that seriously disturbs and endangers your *Union*. It fetters your progress; it is the enemy of improvement, the deadly foe of education; it fosters pride; it breeds insolence; it promotes vice; it shelters crime; it is a curse to the earth that supports it; and yet, you cling to it, as if it were the sheet anchor of all your hopes. Oh! be warned! be warned! a horrible reptile is coiled up in your nation's bosom; the venemous creature is nursing at the tender breast of your youthful republic; *for the love of God, tear away,* and fling from you the hideous monster, and *let the weight of twenty millions crush and destroy it forever!*

The Constitution

But it is answered in reply to all this, that precisely what I have now denounced is, in fact, guaranteed and sanctioned by the Constitution of the United States; that the right to hold and to hunt slaves is a part of that Constitution framed by the illustrious Fathers of this Republic.

Then, I dare to affirm, notwithstanding all I have said before, your fathers stooped, basely stooped

"To palter with us in a double sense:
And keep the word of promise to the ear,
But break it to the heart."[29]

And instead of being the honest men I have before declared them to be, they were the veriest imposters that ever practised on makind. *This* is the inevitable conclusion, and from it there is no escape. But I differ from those who charge this baseness on the framers of the Constitution of the United States. *It is a slander upon their memory,* at least, so I believe. There is not time now to argue the constitutional question at length; nor have I the ability to discuss it as it ought to be discussed. The subject has been handled with masterly power by Lysander Spooner, Esq., by William Goodell, by Samuel E. Sewall, Esq., and last, though not least, by Gerrit Smith, Esq.[30] These gentlemen have,

---

[29]From William Shakespeare's *Macbeth,* Act 5, scene 8, lines 20–22.

[30]Douglass refers to prominent white antislavery writers and activists. Particularly relevant here are Samuel E. Sewell's *Remarks on Slavery in the United States* (1827), William Goodell's *Views of American Constitutional Law: Its Bearing Upon American Slavery* (1844), Lysander Spooner's *The Unconstitutionality of Slavery* (1845), and *Letter of Gerrit Smith to S. P. Chase on the Unconstitutionality of Every Part of American Slavery* (1847). Douglass's affiliation with Gerrit Smith, and his acceptance of the Constitution as an antislavery document, marked his increasing departure from William Lloyd Garrison's approach to the abolitionist cause, which argued against the Constitution as a document capable of securing liberty for all and therefore against political measures to end slavery.

as I think, fully and clearly vindicated the Constitution from any design to support slavery for an hour.

Fellow-citizens! there is no matter in respect to which, the people of the North have allowed themselves to be so ruinously imposed upon, as that of the pro-slavery character of the Constitution. In *that* instrument I hold there is neither warrant, license, nor sanction of the hateful thing; but, interpreted as it *ought* to be interpreted, the Constitution is a GLORIOUS LIBERTY DOCUMENT. Read its preamble, consider its purposes. Is slavery among them? Is it at the gateway? or is it in the temple? It is neither. While I do not intend to argue this question on the present occasion, let me ask, if it be not somewhat singular that, if the Constitution were intended to be, by its framers and adopters, a slave-holding instrument, why neither *slavery, slaveholding,* nor *slave* can anywhere be found in it. What would be thought of an instrument, drawn up, *legally* drawn up, for the purpose of entitling the city of Rochester to a track of land, in which no mention of land was made? Now, there are certain rules of interpretation, for the proper understanding of all legal instruments. These rules are well established. They are plain, common-sense rules, such as you and I, and all of us, can understand and apply, without having passed years in the study of law. I scout the idea that the question of the constitutionality or unconstitutionality of slavery is not a question for the people. I hold that every American citizen has a right to form an opinion of the constitution, and to propagate that opinion, and to use all honorable means to make his opinion the prevailing one. Without this right, the liberty of an American citizen would be as insecure as that of a Frenchman. Ex-Vice-President Dallas[31] tells us that the constitution is an object to which no American mind can be too attentive, and no American heart too devoted. He further says, the constitution, in its words, is plain and intelligible, and is meant for the home-bred, unsophisticated understandings of our fellow-citizens. Senator Berrien[32] tells us that the Constitution is the fundamental law, that which controls all others. The charter of our liberties, which every citizen has a personal interest in understanding thoroughly. The testimony of Senator Breese, Lewis Cass,[33] and many others that might be named, who are everywhere esteemed as sound lawyers, so regard the constitution. I take it, therefore, that it is not presumption in a private citizen to form an opinion of that instrument.

Now, take the constitution according to its plain reading, and I defy the presentation of a single pro-slavery clause in it. On the other hand it will be

---

[31]George Mifflin Dallas (1792–1864) was Vice President of the United States from 1845–49. Dallas, who was at this time seeking the Democratic nomination for President, supported the Fugitive Slave Law.

[32]John MacPherson Berrien (1781–1856) was U.S. Senator from Georgia, and author of the 1849 *Address to the People of the United States,* which called for compromise on the issue of slavery.

[33]Sidney Breese was a U.S. Senator from Illinois; Lewis Cass was a senator from Michigan.

found to contain principles and purposes, entirely hostile to the existence of slavery.

I have detained my audience entirely too long already. At some future period I will gladly avail myself of an opportunity to give this subject a full and fair discussion.

Allow me to say, in conclusion, not withstanding the dark picture I have this day presented of the state of the nation, I do not despair of this country. There are forces in operation, which must inevitably work the downfall of slavery. *The arm of the Lord is not shortened,* "[34] and the doom of slavery is certain. I, therefore, leave off where I began, with *hope.* While drawing encouragement from the Declaration of Independence, the great principles it contains, and the genius of American Institutions, my spirit is also cheered by the obvious tendencies of the age. Nations do not now stand in the same relation to each other that they did ages ago. No nation can now shut itself up from the surrounding world, and trot round in the same old path of its fathers without interference. The time *was* when such could be done. Long established customs of hurtful character could formerly fence themselves in, and do their evil work with social impunity. Knowledge was then confined and enjoyed by the privileged few, and the multitude walked on in mental darkness. But a change has now come over the affairs of mankind. Walled cities and empires have become unfashionable. The arm of commerce has borne away the gates of the strong city. Intelligence is penetrating the darkest corners of the globe. It makes its pathway over and under the sea, as well as on the earth. Wind, steam, and lightning are its chartered agents. Oceans no longer divide, but link nations together. From Boston to London is now a holiday excursion. Space is comparatively annihilated. Thoughts expressed on one side of the Atlantic are distinctly heard on the other.

The far off and almost fabulous Pacific rolls in grandeur at our feet. The Celestial Empire, the mystery of ages, is being solved. The fiat of the Almighty, *"Let there be Light,"*[35] has not yet spent its force. No abuse, no outrage whether in taste, sport or avarice, can now hide itself from the all-pervading light. The iron shoe, and crippled foot of China must be seen, in contrast with nature. *Africa must rise and put on her yet unwoven garment.* *"Ethiopia shall stretch out her hand unto God."*[36] In the fervent aspirations of William Lloyd Garrison, I say, and let every heart join in saying it:

God speed the year of jubilee
    The wide world o'er!

---

[34] See Isaiah 50:2 and 59:1.

[35] Genesis 1:3

[36] Psalm 68:31, one of the most frequently quoted biblical verses in nineteenth century African-American literature.

When from their galling chains set free,
Th' oppress'd shall vilely bend the knee,
And wear the yoke of tyranny
    Like brutes no more.
That year will come, and freedom's reign,
To man his plundered rights again
    Restore.

God speed the day when human blood
    Shall cease to flow!
In every clime be understood,
The claims of human brotherhood,
And each return for evil, good,
    Not blow for blow;
That day will come all feuds to end,
And change into a faithful friend
    Each foe.

God speed the hour, the glorious hour,
    When none on earth
Shall exercise a lordly power,
Nor in a tyrant's presence cower;
But all to manhood's stature tower,
    By equal birth!
THAT HOUR WILL COME, to each, to all,
And from his prison-house, the thrall
    Go forth.

Until that year, day, hour, arrive,
With head, and heart, and hand I'll strive,
To break the rod, and rend the gyve,
The spoiler of his prey deprive—
    So witness Heaven!
And never from my chosen post,
Whate'er the peril or the cost,
    Be driven.[37]

[1852]

---

[37]William Lloyd Garrison's "The Triumph of Freedom," published in the January 10, 1845 issue of the *Liberator.*

CHIEF SEATTLE (DUWAMISH)
[1786–1866]

Memorialized by the major city of Washington State, the civil polity that now encompasses the territory of his rule, Chief Seattle presided over two Christianized Indian tribes, the Suqumish and the Duwamish. His homeland around the Puget Sound was being inhabited by Anglo settlers who had crossed the continent on the Oregon Trail. A believer in the harmonious accommodation of the newcomers, he became in time disillusioned with his neighbors, for their hunger for land, selfishness, and violence. When the region was made a U.S. territory in 1853, the newly appointed governor Isaac Stevens settled in Washington. During his negotiations with the local tribes, he engaged in the diplomatic exchange that produced Seattle's famous oration. The result of the negotiation was the signing of the Port Elliot Treaty, an agreement that confined Natives to the reservations while recognizing a limited Native sovereignty. Dr. Henry A. Smith, one of the treaty party, purportedly took notes of Seattle's speech and in 1887 composed them into a formal English composition published in the Seattle Sunday Star *newspaper. It became an instant sensation, being popularly embraced as an authentic expression of Indian indignation, resignation, and fortitude in the face of a history whose tendency was to marginalize the Native. It was also accepted as a lustrous example of an ancient tradition of Native oratorical eloquence. How authentic the speech is remains a question, for like much of the oratorical and memoir literature of the eighteenth and nineteenth centuries, there is a mediating "white hand" at work. So readers must accept the complex nature of the text's meaning. Part of its meaning can be measured in the influence it has exerted on subsequent thinkers and writers. It has become a canonical text of American pan-Indian identity. It has inspired environmentalist and countercultural expansions of its ideas.*

For Further Reading

Primary Works

Henry A. Smith. "Early Reminiscences," in *Sunday Star* (Seattle, October 29, 1887).

Secondary Works

Rudolph Kiser. "Chief Seattle's Speech(es): *American Origin and European Reception, Recovering the Words: Essays in Native American Literature,* eds. Brian Swann and Arnold Krupat 1987; Vi Hubert, "When Chief Seattle Spoke," in *A Time of Gathering: Native Heritage in Washington State*, ed. Robin K. Wright (Seattle: University of Washington Press, 1990).

Speech of Chief Seattle

CHIEF SEATTLE (DUWAMISH)

Yonder sky that has wept tears of compassion upon my people for centuries untold, and which to us appears changeless and eternal, may change. Today is fair. Tomorrow it may be overcast with clouds. My words are like the stars that never change. Whatever Seattle says the great chief at Washington can rely upon with as much certainty as he can upon the return of the sun or the seasons. The White Chief says that Big Chief at Washington sends us greetings of friendship and goodwill. This is kind of him for we know he has little need of our friendship in return. His people are many. They are like the grass that covers vast prairies. My people are few. They resemble the scattering trees of a storm-swept plain. The great—and I presume—good White Chief sends us word that he wishes to buy our lands but is willing to allow us enough to live comfortably. This indeed appears just, even generous, for the Red Man no longer has rights that he need respect, and the offer may be wise also, as we are no longer in need of an extensive country.

There was a time when our people covered the land as the waves of a wind-ruffled sea cover its shell paved floor, but that time long since passed away with the greatness of tribes that are now but a mournful memory. I will not dwell on, nor mourn over, our untimely decay, nor reproach my paleface brothers with hastening it as we too may have been somewhat to blame.

Youth is impulsive. When our young men grow angry at some real or imaginary wrong, and disfigure their faces with black paint, it denotes that their hearts are black, and that they are often cruel and relentless, and our old men and old women are unable to restrain them. Thus it has ever been. Thus it was when the white man first began to push our forefathers westward. But let us hope that the hostilities between us may never return. We would have everything to lose and nothing to gain. Revenge by young men is considered gain, even at the cost of their own lives, but old men who stay at home in times of war, and mothers who have sons to lose, know better.

Our good father at Washington—for I presume he is now our father as well as yours, since King George[1] has moved his boundaries further north— our great and good father, I say, sends us word that if we do as he desires he will protect us. His brave warriors will be to us a bristling wall of strength, and his wonderful ships of war will fill our harbors so that our ancient enemies far to the northward—the Hydas and Tsimpsians—will cease to frighten our women, children, and old men. Then in reality will he be our father and we his children. But can that ever be? Your God is not our God! Your God loves your people and hates mine. He folds his strong protecting arms lovingly about the pale face and leads him by the hand as a father leads his infant son—but He has forsaken His red children—if they really are His. Our God, the Great Spirit, seems also to have forsaken us. Your God makes your people wax strong every day. Soon they will fill all the land. Our people are ebbing away like a rapidly receding tide that will never return. The white man's God cannot love our people or He would protect them. They seem to be orphans who can look nowhere for help. How then can we be brothers? How can your God become our God and renew our prosperity and awaken in us dreams of returning greatness. If we have a common heavenly father He must be partial—for He came to His paleface children. We never saw Him. He gave you laws but had no word for his red children whose teeming multitudes once filled this vast continent as stars fill the firmament. No; we are two distinct races with separate origins and separate destinies. There is little in common between us.

To us the ashes of our ancestors are sacred and their resting place is hallowed ground. You wander far from the graves of your ancestors and seemingly without regret. Your religion was written upon tables of stone by the iron finger of your God so that you could not forget. The Red Man could never comprehend nor remember it. Our religion is the traditions of our ancestors—the dreams of our old men, given them in the solemn hours of night by the Great Spirit; and the visions of our sachems, and is written in the hearts of our people.

Your dead cease to love you and the land of their nativity as soon as they pass the portals of the tomb and wander way beyond the stars. They are soon forgotten and never return. Our dead never forget the beautiful world that gave them being. They still love its verdant valleys, its murmuring rivers, its magnificent mountains, sequestered vales and verdant lined lakes and bays, and ever yearn in tender, fond affection over the lonely hearted living, and often return from the Happy Hunting Ground to visit, guide, console and comfort others.

[1]Queen Victoria was the actual ruling monarch in 1855. Seattle refers to past action by the Hanoverian monarchs of England.

Day and night cannot dwell together. The Red Man has ever fled the approach of the White Man, as the morning mist flees before the morning sun.

However, your proposition seems fair and I think that my people will accept it and will retire to the reservation you offer them. Then we will dwell in peace, for the words of the Great White Chief seem to be the words of nature speaking to my people out of dense darkness.

It matters little where we pass the remnant of our days. They will not be many. The Indians' night promises to be dark. Not a single star of hope hovers above his horizon. Sad-voiced winds moan in the distance. Grim fate seems to be on the Red Man's trail, and wherever he goes he will hear the approaching footsteps of his fell destroyer and prepare stolidly to meet his doom, as does the wounded doe that hears the approaching footsteps of the hunter.

A few more moons. A few more winters — and not one of the descendants of the mighty hosts that once moved over his broad land or lived in happy homes, protected by the Great Spirit, will remain to mourn over the graves of a people — once more powerful and hopeful than yours. But why should I mourn at the untimely fate of my people? Tribe follows tribe, and nation follows nation, like the waves of the sea. It is the order of nature, and regret is useless. Your time of decay may be distant, but it will surely come, for even the White Man whose God walked and talked with him as friend with friend, cannot be exempt from the common destiny. We may be brothers after all. We will see.

We will ponder your proposition and when we decide will let you know. But should we accept it, I here and now make this condition that we will not be denied the privilege without molestation of visiting at any time the tombs of our ancestors, friends and children. Every part of this soil is sacred in the estimation of my people. Every hillside, every valley, every plain and grove, has been hallowed by some sad or happy event in days long vanished. Even the rocks, which seem to be dumb and dead as they swelter in the sun along the silent shore, thrill with memories of stirring events connected with the lives of my people, and the very dust upon which you now stand responds more lovingly to their footsteps than to yours, because it is rich with the blood of our ancestors and our bare feet are conscious of the sympathetic touch. Our departed braves, fond mothers, glad, happy-hearted maidens, and even our little children who lived here and rejoiced here for a brief season, will love these somber solitudes and at eventide they greet shadowy returning spirits. And when the last Red Man shall have perished, and the memory of my tribe shall have become a myth among the White Men, these shores will swarm with the invisible dead of my tribe, and when your children's children think themselves alone in the field, the store, the shop, upon the highway, or in the silence of the pathless woods, they will not be alone. In all the earth there is no place dedicated to solitude. At night when the streets of your cities and villages are silent and you think them deserted, they will throng with the returning hosts that once filled them and still love this beautiful land. The White Man will never be alone.

Let him be just and deal kindly with my people, for the dead are not powerless. Dead, did I say? There is no death, only a change of worlds.

[1855]

RALPH WALDO EMERSON
[1803–1882]

Ralph Waldo Emerson, an innovative essayist and poet, articulated a set of ethical and literary principles in the decades immediately before the Civil War that made him America's most influential writer. Son of the minister of a prominent Boston church, Emerson prepared for the ministry himself, with some ambivalence, assuming a Boston pastorate in 1828 that was part of the emerging New England Unitarian movement. Emerson was influenced intellectually by the leading Unitarian minister of the day, William Ellery Channing, and also by his brilliant and deeply learned aunt, Mary Moody Emerson, who had helped to raise him and his four brothers after the death of their father in 1811. Adept as a preacher but somewhat uncomfortable with other ministerial duties, Emerson established himself as a well-liked and successful minister, growing increasingly liberal in his interpretation of Christian doctrines as he continued a voluminous reading of both ancient and contemporary philosophy and theology. The death of his wife Ellen in 1830, a severe emotional blow, led him to reconsider his course in life, and he eventually resigned from the pulpit in 1832, telling his congregation that he could no longer administer the Lord's Supper in good conscience.

Emerson then traveled to Europe, seeing Italy, France, and England, and meeting literary and social critic Thomas Carlyle in Scotland, a key influence on his outlook and style who would also become a lifelong friend and correspondent. He returned to America in 1833 to launch a career as a lecturer and essayist, presenting an annual series of lectures on such philosophical topics as "The Philosophy of History" (1836–37) and "Human Culture" (1837–38). In 1836 he published Nature, *a profound and highly original inquiry into the origins and purposes of the natural world. His call therein to reject the traditions of the past and rebuild the world signaled his determination to call for a new era in theology, philosophy, and literature. He began to attract young intellectuals who shared his discontent with the prevailing conservatism in American religion, literature, and cultural life.*

Two major addresses at Harvard thrust Emerson into controversy, and made him the leader of an intellectual avant-garde in New England. In "The

American Scholar" (1837) Emerson criticized the lethargy of American intellectual life and reminded his listeners that "in yourself is the law of all nature." He applied the same analysis to religion in the Divinity School Address (1838), castigating "a decaying church and a wasting unbelief" and urging the divinity students in his audience to "cast behind you all conformity, and acquaint men at firsthand with Deity."

Emerson and his followers came to be known as the "Transcendentalists," though their movement was hardly unified behind any particular agenda or set of articulated principles. Emerson defined Transcendentalism as "Idealism as it appears in 1842," linking it with the philosophical traditions of Plato and Kant; his use of the term idealism also captured the more widely understood meaning of high-minded aspiration toward the good, a quality that accounted for the aesthetic sensibility of many of his followers, and their growing engagement in causes of social and political reform in the 1840s and 1850s.

In 1840 Emerson helped to found The Dial, a magazine devoted to the writings of those sympathetic with the transcendentalist movement. It was first edited by Emerson's friend Margaret Fuller, an originating voice of American feminism, and then by Emerson. The Dial provided a venue of publication for developing writers such as Fuller, Henry David Thoreau, Amos Bronson Alcott, and Jones Very. Emerson and Thoreau also published a series of translations of "Ethnical Scriptures" in The Dial, including sacred texts of Hinduism, Confucianism, and Buddhism, then very little known in America.

Emerson married Lydia Jackson in 1835 and settled into Concord, Massachusetts, devoting much of his time to lecturing on the lyceum circuit in the Northeast, and gradually expanding his travels to the newly settled Midwest. One of his principal beliefs, which became very influential in American culture, was the necessity of individualistic nonconformity. He articulated this message most memorably in "Self-Reliance," published in his first collection of Essays (1841). Arguing against the damaging effects of social conformity and a lack of confidence and spontaneity, Emerson urged his readers to "affront the smooth mediocrity and squalid contentment of our times," and to act from within. Such absolute inner-directedness, he believed, was in fact a means of access to "the aboriginal Self," a universally shared spiritual nature that was the ultimate source of right perception and right action. Terming this fundamental source of thought and character "The Over-Soul" in another essay from the same volume, he reminded readers that "our being is descending into us from we know not whence," making every individual "conscious of attaining to a higher self-possession."

This message of individual capability and responsibility, moral aspiration, and spiritual trust was of vital importance to many in an age when scientific advance was weakening belief in traditional Christianity, and the market economy, industrialization, and urbanization were undermining community and familial relationships. Emerson offered a message that combined spiritual *assurance with ethical challenge, helping to ease for many the jarring transition into the modern world.*

Emerson's optimistic sense of human potential added to his popular appeal, but became a point of criticism for some later critics, who argued that he lacked a sense of evil and that his optimism was therefore shallow. But Emerson had struggled with his own doubts from the very beginning of his intellectual career, admitting in his journals his own difficulties in sustaining his affirmative stance. These difficulties were exacerbated by his increasing emphasis on dynamism and growth in such essays as "Circles" (1841), a text that has gained increasing importance among Emerson's essays. By positing a philosophy based almost entirely on energy and forward movement, in which every advance or achievement was only a prelude to the next, Emerson created a paradox of achievement, in which any sense of settlement or satisfaction could be read as complacency and thus be seen as the enemy of further advance.

Emerson's struggle with skepticism is evident in "Circles," but his attempt to shore up and maintain his optimism was dealt a serious blow by the death of his five-year-old son Waldo in 1842. Emerson eulogized his son in his poetry, but the most disturbing treatment of his grief and his resulting disillusionment was in "Experience" (1844), his greatest work, and one that marks a significant shift in his intellectual orientation. "Experience" is not a surrender of hope or affirmation, but an honest and deeply probing attempt to reconcile hope with reality. Admitting a sense of loss and benumbed alienation as the essay begins, Emerson works his way toward a new and more pragmatic recognition that sometimes must be called upon to continue to act even when assurance is denied, making action itself the source of assurance. "I am very content with knowing, if only I could know," he writes. In the face of uncertainty, however, it is crucial to continue to act with knowledge such as it is. "To finish the moment, to find the journey's end in every step of the road, to live the greatest number of good hours, is wisdom."

"Experience" marks a revision of Emerson's earlier optimism, and opens a new emphasis on ethical action and social criticism. This shift was accelerated by Emerson's visit to England and France in 1847–48, where he observed both the effects of the industrial revolution and of the revolutions of 1848 that were sweeping through Europe. Soon after his return, the conflict over slavery in America reached a new point of crisis with the passage of the Fugitive Slave Law of 1850. The law mandated the return of slaves who had escaped to the North, and inflamed northern antislavery sentiments. Emerson had been decidedly antislavery all his life, but the passage of the bill, "a filthy enactment" as he called it in his journal, outraged him. "I will not obey it, by God," he declared.

Emerson's blistering antislavery addresses of 1851, 1854, and 1855, long forgotten after the Civil War, show the full range of his rhetorical powers, and suggest the extent to which his thinking had now become dominated by ethical and social questions. Later volumes of essays, The Conduct of Life *(1869) and* Society and Solitude *(1870), reflect this new orientation, and include his recognition in "Fate" (1860) that people must realistically understand their limitations to live most effectively and meaningfully. His contention in "Worship" (1860) was that worship is often best expressed through dedicated work, and in "Success" (1870) he warned his readers of the unsatisfying and superficial definitions of success.*

A critic of the establishment in the 1830s, the decade of his intellectual emergence, Emerson delivered a message that became more and more ingrained into America's sense of its identity and values over the next three decades. By the 1860s he was an influential public figure and a central voice in American culture. Remaining in Concord his entire life, he was intellectually active until the early 1870s, when a gradual loss of memory and cognitive ability began to limit his capacities. He left unfinished one major intellectual project, A Natural History of Intellect, *some portions of which he delivered at Harvard in 1872.*

Emerson had a deep influence on younger contemporaries such as Henry David Thoreau, a pioneering environmentalist, Margaret Fuller, an early leader of the women's rights movement, and the innovative poet Walt Whitman. He also had a more subtle but pervasive influence on a whole panoply of nineteenth- and twentieth century authors and philosophers, and has become a touchstone for American literary and cultural history. An "Emerson Revival" among literary scholars and critics in the 1980s continues, placing Emerson at the center of ongoing discussions of America's values and cultural identity; the different stands of American poetry and philosophy; and questions of literary form, the artistic process, and cultural authority. The Emerson canon, once centered principally on his addresses of the 1830s, has now expanded to include later essays such as "Experience" and "Fate," and to incorporate his voluminous and intellectually rich journals, published in a modern edition from 1960 to 1982. Whether as a fiery young reformer, a meditative philosopher of nature, an apostle of innovation and newness in literature, or an American sage and social critic, Emerson promises to remain a prominent figure in American history throughout the twenty-first century.

David M. Robinson
Oregon State University

For Further Reading

Primary Works

Nature (1836); *Essays* (later titled *Essays: First Series*) (1841); *Essays: Second Series* (1844); *Poems* (1847); *Nature; Addresses, and Lectures* (1849); *Representative Men* (1850); *English Traits* (1865); *The Conduct of Life* (1860); *May-Day and Other Pieces* (1867); *Society and Solitude* (1870); *Letters and Social Aims* (1876); and *Selected Poems* (1876); *Collected Works*, eds. Alfred R. Ferguson *et al.*, 5 vols. to date (1971–   ); *Collected Poems and Translations*, eds. Harold Bloom and Paul Kane (1994); *Complete Sermons*, eds. Albert J. von Frank, *et al.*, 4 vols. (1989–92); *Complete Works*, ed. Edward Waldo Emerson [Centenary Edition], 12 vols. (1903–34); *Early Lectures*, eds. Stephen E. Whicher, Robert E. Spiller, and Wallace E. Williams, 3 vols. (1959–72); *Emerson's Antislavery Writings*, eds. Len Gougeon and Joel Myerson (1995); *Journals and Miscellaneous Notebooks*, eds. William H. Gilman, *et al.*, 16 vols. (1960–82); *Later Lectures*, eds. Ronald A. Bosco and Joel Myerson (2001); *Letters*, eds. Ralph L. Rusk and Eleanor Tilton, 10 vols. (1939–95); *Poetry Notebooks*, eds. Ralph H. Orth, *et al.* (1986); *Topical Notebooks*, eds. Ronald A. Bosco, Susan Sutton Smith, and Glen M. Johnson, 3 vols. (1990).

Biographies

Joel Myerson, *Ralph Waldo Emerson: A Descriptive Bibliography* (1982); Ralph L. Rusk, *The Life of Ralph Waldo Emerson* (1949); Albert J. von Frank, *An Emerson Chronology* (1994); Robert D. Richardson, Jr., *Emerson: The Mind on Fire* (1995).

Secondary Works

F. O. Matthiessen, *American Renaissance* (1941); Stephen E. Whicher, *Freedom and Fate* (1953); Lawrence Buell, *Literary Transcendentalism* (1973); Joel Porte, *Representative Man* (1979); Barbara Packer, *Emerson's Fall* (1982); Joel Myerson, ed., *Emerson Centenary Essays* (1982); David Van Leer, *Emerson's Epistemology* (1986); Richard Poirier, *The Renewal of Literature* (1987); Evelyn Barish, *Emerson: The Roots of Prophecy* (1989); Wesley T. Mott, *The Strains of Eloquence* (1989); Stanley Cavell, *Conditions Handsome and Unhandsome* (1990); Len Gougeon, *Virtue's Hero* (1990); Merton M. Sealts, Jr., *Emerson on the Scholar* (1992); David M. Robinson, *Emerson and the Conduct of Life* (1993); Lee Rust Brown, *The Emerson Museum* (1997); Albert J. von Frank, *The Trials of Anthony Burns: Freedom and Slavery in Emerson's Boston* (1998); Joel Porte and Saundra Morris, eds., *Cambridge Companion to Ralph Waldo Emerson* (1998); Gustaaf Van Cromphout, *Emerson's Ethics* (1999); Joel Myerson, ed., *Historical Guide to Ralph Waldo Emerson* (2000); and Sarah Ann Wider, *The Critical Reception of Emerson* (2001).

Self-Reliance[♦]

RALPH WALDO EMERSON

"Ne te quaesiveris extra."[1]

"Man is his own star; and the soul that can
Render an honest and a perfect man,
Commands all light, all influence, all fate;
Nothing to him falls early or too late.
Our acts our angels are, or good or ill,
Our fatal shadows that walk by us still."
    —Epilogue to Beaumont and Fletcher's *Honest Man's Fortune*

Cast the bantling on the rocks,
Suckle him with the she-wolf's teat;
Wintered with the hawk and fox,
Power and speed be hands and feet.

I read the other day some verses written by an eminent painter[2] which were original and not conventional. The soul always hears an admonition in such lines, let the subject be what it may. The sentiment they instil is of more value than any thought they may contain. To believe your own thought, to believe that what is true for you in your private heart, is true for all men,— that is genius. Speak your latent conviction and it shall be the universal sense; for the inmost in due time becomes the outmost,—and our first thought is rendered back to us by the trumpets of the Last Judgment. Familiar as the voice of the mind is to each, the highest merit we ascribe to Moses, Plato, and Milton, is that they set at naught books and traditions, and spoke not what

---

♦"Self-Reliance," published in Emerson's first collection of *Essays* (1841) has become his best-known and most influential essay. The individualism that Emerson advocates in this essay captures a vital element of the American spirit, whether that be manifest in social nonconformity, artistic experimentalism, political dissent, or economic entrepreneurship. Yet as the essay progresses, the private "self" becomes more and more clearly a universal "Self," and the stance of combative self-sufficiency evolves into a stance of patient humility and receptivity to the spirit.

[1]"Ne te quaesiveris extra": Look to no one outside yourself.

[2]an eminent painter: Washington Allston (1799–1843).

men but what they thought. A man should learn to detect and watch that gleam of light which flashes across his mind from within, more than the lustre of the firmament of bards and sages. Yet he dismisses without notice his thought, because it is his. In every work of genius we recognize our own rejected thoughts: they come back to us with a certain alienated majesty. Great works of art have no more affecting lesson for us than this. They teach us to abide by our spontaneous impression with good-humored inflexibility then most when the whole cry of voices is on the other side. Else, tomorrow a stranger will say with masterly good sense precisely what we have thought and felt all the time, and we shall be forced to take with shame our own opinion from another.

There is a time in every man's education when he arrives at the conviction that envy is ignorance; that imitation is suicide; that he must take himself for better, for worse, as his portion; that though the wide universe is full of good, no kernel of nourishing corn can come to him but through his toil bestowed on that plot of ground which is given to him to till. The power which resides in him is new in nature, and none but he knows what that is which he can do, nor does he know until he has tried. Not for nothing one face, one character, one fact makes much impression on him, and another none. This sculpture in the memory is not without preëstablished harmony. The eye was placed where one ray should fall, that it might testify of that particular ray. We but half express ourselves, and are ashamed of that divine idea which each of us represents. It may be safely trusted as proportionate and of good issues, so it be faithfully imparted, but God will not have his work made manifest by cowards. A man is relieved and gay when he has put his heart into his work and done his best; but what he has said or done otherwise, shall give him no peace. It is a deliverance which does not deliver. In the attempt his genius deserts him; no muse befriends; no invention, no hope.

Trust thyself: every heart vibrates to that iron string. Accept the place the divine Providence has found for you; the society of your contemporaries, the connexion of events. Great men have always done so and confided themselves childlike to the genius of their age, betraying their perception that the absolutely trustworthy was seated at their heart, working through their hands, predominating in all their being. And we are now men, and must accept in the highest mind the same transcendent destiny; and not minors and invalids in a protected corner, not cowards fleeing before a revolution, but guides, redeemers, and benefactors, obeying the Almighty effort, and advancing on Chaos and the Dark.

What pretty oracles nature yields us on this text in the face and behavior of children, babes and even brutes. That divided and rebel mind, that distrust of a sentiment because our arithmetic has computed the strength and means opposed to our purpose, these have not. Their mind being whole, their eye is as yet unconquered, and when we look in their faces, we are disconcerted.

Infancy conforms to nobody: all conform to it, so that one babe commonly makes four or five out of the adults who prattle and play to it. So God has armed youth and puberty and manhood no less with its own piquancy and charm, and made it enviable and gracious and its claims not to be put by, if it will stand by itself. Do not think the youth has no force because he cannot speak to you and me. Hark! in the next room his voice is sufficiently clear and emphatic. It seems he knows how to speak to his contemporaries. Bashful or bold, then, he will know how to make us seniors very unnecessary.

The nonchalance of boys who are sure of a dinner, and would disdain as much as a lord to do or say aught to conciliate one, is the healthy attitude of human nature. A boy is in the parlour what the pit is in the playhouse; independent, irresponsible, looking out from his corner on such people and facts as pass by, he tries and sentences them on their merits, in the swift summary way of boys, as good, bad, interesting, silly, eloquent, troublesome. He cumbers himself never about consequences, about interests: he gives an independent, genuine verdict. You must court him: he does not court you. But the man is, as it were, clapped into jail by his consciousness. As soon as he has once acted or spoken with eclat, he is a committed person, watched by the sympathy or the hatred of hundreds whose affections must now enter into his account. There is no Lethe for this. Ah, that he could pass again into his neutrality! Who can thus avoid all pledges, and having observed, observe again from the same unaffected, unbiassed, unbribable, unaffrighted innocence, must always be formidable. He would utter opinions on all passing affairs, which being seen to be not private but necessary, would sink like darts into the ear of men, and put them in fear.

These are the voices which we hear in solitude, but they grow faint and inaudible as we enter into the world. Society everywhere is in conspiracy against the manhood of every one of its members. Society is a joint-stock company in which the members agree for the better securing of his bread to each shareholder, to surrender the liberty and culture of the eater. The virtue in most request is conformity. Self-reliance is its aversion. It loves not realities and creators, but names and customs.

Whoso would be a man must be a nonconformist. He who would gather immortal palms must not be hindered by the name of goodness, but must explore if it be goodness. Nothing is at last sacred but the integrity of your own mind. Absolve you to yourself, and you shall have the suffrage of the world. I remember an answer which when quite young I was prompted to make to a valued adviser[3] who was wont to importune me with the dear old doctrines of the church. On my saying, What have I to do with the sacredness of traditions, if I live wholly from within? my friend suggested — "But

---

[3]valued adviser: probably Emerson's Aunt Mary Moody Emerson (1774–1863).

these impulses may be from below, not from above." I replied, "They do not seem to me to be such; but if I am the Devil's child, I will live then from the Devil." No law can be sacred to me but that of my nature. Good and bad are but names very readily transferable to that or this; the only right is what is after my constitution, the only wrong what is against it. A man is to carry himself in the presence of all opposition as if every thing were titular and ephemeral but he. I am ashamed to think how easily we capitulate to badges and names, to large societies and dead institutions. Every decent and well-spoken individual affects and sways me more than is right. I ought to go upright and vital, and speak the rude truth in all ways. If malice and vanity wear the coat of philanthropy, shall that pass? If an angry bigot assumes this bountiful cause of Abolition, and comes to me with his last news from Barbadoes, why should I not say to him, 'Go love thy infant; love thy wood-chopper: be good-natured and modest: have that grace; and never varnish your hard, uncharitable ambition with this incredible tenderness for black folk a thousand miles off. Thy love afar is spite at home.' Rough and graceless would be such greeting, but truth is handsomer than the affectation of love. Your goodness must have some edge to it—else it is none. The doctrine of hatred must be preached as the counteraction of the doctrine of love when that pules and whines. I shun father and mother and wife and brother, when my genius calls me. I would write on the lintels of the doorpost, *Whim.* I hope it is somewhat better than whim at last, but we cannot spend the day in explanation. Expect me not to show cause why I seek or why I exclude company. Then, again, do not tell me, as a good man did to-day, of my obligation to put all poor men in good situations. Are they *my* poor? I tell thee, thou foolish philanthropist, that I grudge the dollar, the dime, the cent I give to such men as do not belong to me and to whom I do not belong. There is a class of persons to whom by all spiritual affinity I am bought and sold; for them I will go to prison, if need be; but your miscellaneous popular charities; the education at college of fools; the building of meeting-houses to the vain end to which many now stand; alms to sots; and the thousandfold Relief Societies;—though I confess with shame I sometimes succumb and give the dollar, it is a wicked dollar which by and by I shall have the manhood to withhold.

Virtues are in the popular estimate rather the exception than the rule. There is the man *and* his virtues. Men do what is called a good action, as some piece of courage or charity, much as they would pay a fine in expiation of daily non-appearance on parade. Their works are done as an apology or extenuation of their living in the world,—as invalids and the insane pay a high board. Their virtues are penances. I do not wish to expiate, but to live. My life is for itself and not for a spectacle. I much prefer that it should be of a lower strain, so it be genuine and equal, than that it should be glittering and unsteady. I wish it to be sound and sweet, and not to need diet and bleeding.

I ask primary evidence that you are a man, and refuse this appeal from the man to his actions. I know that for myself it makes no difference whether I do or forbear those actions which are reckoned excellent. I cannot consent to pay for a privilege where I have intrinsic right. Few and mean as my gifts may be, I actually am, and do not need for my own assurance or the assurance of my fellows any secondary testimony.

What I must do, is all that concerns me, not what the people think. This rule, equally arduous in actual and in intellectual life, may serve for the whole distinction between greatness and meanness. It is the harder, because you will always find those who think they know what is your duty better than you know it. It is easy in the world to live after the world's opinion; it is easy in solitude to live after our own; but the great man is he who in the midst of the crowd keeps with perfect sweetness the independence of solitude.

The objection to conforming to usages that have become dead to you, is, that it scatters your force. It loses your time and blurs the impression of your character. If you maintain a dead church, contribute to a dead Bible-Society, vote with a great party either for the Government or against it, spread your table like base housekeepers,—under all these screens, I have difficulty to detect the precise man you are. And, of course, so much force is withdrawn from your proper life. But do your work, and I shall know you. Do your work, and you shall reinforce yourself. A man must consider what a blindman's-buff is this game of conformity. If I know your sect, I anticipate your argument. I hear a preacher announce for his text and topic the expediency of one of the institutions of his church. Do I not know beforehand that not possibly can he say a new and spontaneous word? Do I not know that with all this ostentation of examining the grounds of the institution, he will do no such thing? Do I not know that he is pledged to himself not to look but at one side,—the permitted side, not as a man, but as a parish minister? He is a retained attorney, and these airs of the bench are the emptiest affectation. Well, most men have bound their eyes with one or another handkerchief, and attached themselves to some one of these communities of opinion. This conformity makes them not false in a few particulars, authors of a few lies, but false in all particulars. Their every truth is not quite true. Their two is not the real two, their four not the real four: so that every word they say chagrins us, and we know not where to begin to set them right. Meantime nature is not slow to equip us in the prison-uniform of the party to which we adhere. We come to wear one cut of face and figure, and acquire by degrees the gentlest asinine expression. There is a mortifying experience in particular which does not fail to wreak itself also in the general history; I mean "the foolish face of praise," the forced smile which we put on in company where we do not feel at ease in answer to conversation which does not interest us. The muscles, not spontaneously moved, but moved by a low usurping wilfulness, grow tight about the outline of the face with the most disagreeable sensation.

For nonconformity the world whips you with its displeasure. And therefore a man must know how to estimate a sour face. The bystanders look askance on him in the public street or in the friend's parlor. If this aversation had its origin in contempt and resistance like his own, he might well go home with a sad countenance; but the sour faces of the multitude, like their sweet faces, have no deep cause, but are put on and off as the wind blows, and a newspaper directs. Yet is the discontent of the multitude more formidable than that of the senate and the college. It is easy enough for a firm man who knows the world to brook the rage of the cultivated classes. Their rage is decorous and prudent, for they are timid as being very vulnerable themselves. But when to their feminine rage the indignation of the people is added, when the ignorant and the poor are aroused, when the unintelligent brute force that lies at the bottom of society is made to growl and mow, it needs the habit of magnanimity and religion to treat it godlike as a trifle of no concernment.

The other terror that scares us from self-trust is our consistency; a reverence for our past act or word, because the eyes of others have no other data for computing our orbit than our past acts, and we are loath to disappoint them.

But why should you keep your head over your shoulder? Why drag about this corpse of your memory, lest you contradict somewhat you have stated in this or that public place? Suppose you should contradict yourself; what then? It seems to be a rule of wisdom never to rely on your memory alone, scarcely even in acts of pure memory, but to bring the past for judgment into the thousand-eyed present, and live ever in a new day. In your metaphysics you have denied personality to the Deity; yet when the devout motions of the soul come, yield to them heart and life, though they should clothe God with shape and color. Leave your theory as Joseph his coat in the hand of the harlot, and flee.

A foolish consistency is the hobgoblin of little minds, adored by little statesmen and philosophers and divines. With consistency a great soul has simply nothing to do. He may as well concern himself with his shadow on the wall. Speak what you think now in hard words, and to-morrow speak what to-morrow thinks in hard words again, though it contradict every thing you said to-day.—'Ah, so you shall be sure to be misunderstood.'—Is it so bad then to be misunderstood? Pythagoras was misunderstood, and Socrates, and Jesus, and Luther, and Copernicus, and Galileo, and Newton, and every pure and wise spirit that ever took flesh. To be great is to be misunderstood.

I suppose no man can violate his nature. All the sallies of his will are rounded in by the law of his being as the inequalities of Andes and Himmaleh are insignificant in the curve of the sphere. Nor does it matter how you gauge and try him. A character is like an acrostic or Alexandrian stanza;—read it forward, backward, or across, it still spells the same thing. In this pleasing contrite wood-life which God allows me, let me record day by day my honest thought without prospect or retrospect, and, I cannot doubt, it will be found symmetrical, though I mean it not, and see it not. My book should smell of pines and resound with the hum of insects. The swallow over my window should interweave that thread or straw he carries in his bill into my web also. We pass for what we are. Character teaches above our wills. Men imagine that they communicate their virtue or vice only by overt actions and do not see that virtue or vice emit a breath every moment.

There will be an agreement in whatever variety of actions, so they be each honest and natural in their hour. For of one will, the actions will be harmonious, however unlike they seem. These varieties are lost sight of at a little distance, at a little height of thought. One tendency unites them all. The voyage of the best ship is a zigzag line of a hundred tacks. See the line from a sufficient distance, and it straightens itself to the average tendency. Your genuine action will explain itself and will explain your other genuine actions. Your conformity explains nothing. Act singly, and what you have already done singly, will justify you now. Greatness appeals to the future. If I can be firm enough to-day to do right and scorn eyes, I must have done so much right before, as to defend me now. Be it how it will, do right now. Always scorn appearances, and you always may. The force of character is cumulative. All the foregone days of virtue work their health into this. What makes the majesty of the heroes of the senate and the field, which so fills the imagination? The consciousness of a train of great days and victories behind. They shed an united light on the advancing actor. He is attended as by a visible escort of angels. That is it which throws thunder into Chatham's[4] voice, and dignity into Washington's port, and America into Adams's[5] eye. Honor is venerable to us because it is no ephemeris. It is always ancient virtue. We worship it to-day, because it is not of to-day. We love it and pay it homage, because it is not a trap for our love and homage, but is self-dependent, self-derived, and therefore of an old immaculate pedigree, even if shown in a young person.

I hope in these days we have heard the last of conformity and consistency. Let the words be gazetted and ridiculous henceforward. Instead of the gong for dinner, let us hear a whistle from the Spartan fife. Let us never bow and apologize more. A great man is coming to eat at my house. I do not wish to please him: I wish that he should wish to please me. I will stand here for humanity, and though I would make it kind, I would make it true. Let us affront and reprimand the smooth mediocrity and squalid contentment of

---

[4]Chatham: William Pitt, Earl of Chatham (1708–1778), English politician.
[5]Samuel Adams (1772–1803), American Revolutionary leader; or John Adams (1735–1826), second U.S. President.

the times, and hurl in the face of custom, and trade, and office, the fact which is the upshot of all history, that there is a great responsible Thinker and Actor working wherever a man works; that a true man belongs to no other time or place, but is the centre of things. Where he is, there is nature. He measures you, and all men, and all events. Ordinarily every body in society reminds us of somewhat else or of some other person. Character, reality, reminds you of nothing else; it takes place of the whole creation. The man must be so much that he must make all circumstances indifferent. Every true man is a cause, a country, and an age; requires infinite spaces and numbers and time fully to accomplish his design;—and posterity seem to follow his steps as a train of clients. A man Cæsar is born, and for ages after, we have a Roman Empire. Christ is born, and millions of minds so grow and cleave to his genius, that he is confounded with virtue and the possible of man. An institution is the lengthened shadow of one man; as, Monachism, of the Hermit Antony; the Reformation, of Luther; Quakerism, of Fox; Methodism, of Wesley; Abolition, of Clarkson.[6] Scipio,[7] Milton called "the height of Rome;" and all history resolves itself very easily into the biography of a few stout and earnest persons.

Let a man then know his worth, and keep things under his feet. Let him not peep or steal, or skulk up and down with the air of a charity-boy, a bastard, or an interloper, in the world which exists for him. But the man in the street finding no worth in himself which corresponds to the force which built a tower or sculptured a marble god, feels poor when he looks on these. To him a palace, a statue, or a costly book have an alien and forbidding air, much like a gay equipage, and seem to say like that, 'Who are you, sir?' Yet they all are his, suitors for his notice, petitioners to his faculties that they will come out and take possession. The picture waits for my verdict: it is not to command me, but I am to settle its claims to praise. That popular fable of the sot who was picked up dead drunk in the street, carried to the duke's house, washed and dressed and laid in the duke's bed, and, on his waking, treated with all obsequious ceremony like the duke, and assured that he had been insane, owes its popularity to the fact, that it symbolizes so well the state of man, who is in the world a sort of sot, but now and then wakes up, exercises his reason, and finds himself a true prince.

Our reading is mendicant and sycophantic. In history, our imagination plays us false. Kingdom and lordship, power and estate are a gaudier vocabulary than private John and Edward in a small house and common day's work: but the things of life are the same to both: the sum total of both is the same.

---

[6]Hermit Antony (251–356), religious ascetic and patron saint of monks; Martin Luther (1483–1546), Protestant leader; George Fox (1624–1691), founder of Quakerism; John Wesley (1703–1791), founder of Methodism; Thomas Clarkson (1760–1846), English antislavery advocate.
[7]Scipio Africanus Major (234?–183 B.C.E.), Roman leader who defeated Hannibal.

Why all this deference to Alfred, and Scanderbeg, and Gustavus?[8] Suppose they were virtuous: did they wear out virtue? As great a stake depends on your private act to-day, as followed their public and renowned steps. When private men shall act with original views, the lustre will be transferred from the actions of kings to those of gentlemen.

The world has been instructed by its kings, who have so magnetized the eyes of nations. It has been taught by this colossal symbol the mutual reverence that is due from man to man. The joyful loyalty with which men have everywhere suffered the king, the noble, or the great proprietor to walk among them by a law of his own, make his own scale of men and things, and reverse theirs, pay for benefits not with money but with honor, and represent the Law in his person, was the hieroglyphic by which they obscurely signified their consciousness of their own right and comeliness, the right of every man.

The magnetism which all original action exerts is explained when we inquire the reason of self-trust. Who is the Trustee? What is the aboriginal Self on which a universal reliance may be grounded? What is the nature and power of that science-baffling star, without parallax, without calculable elements, which shoots a ray of beauty even into trivial and impure actions, if the least mark of independence appear? The inquiry leads us to that source, at once the essence of genius, of virtue, and of life, which we call Spontaneity or Instinct. We denote this primary wisdom as Intuition, whilst all later teachings are tuitions. In that deep force, the last fact behind which analysis cannot go, all things find their common origin. For the sense of being which in calm hours rises, we know not how, in the soul, is not diverse from things, from space, from light, from time, from man, but one with them, and proceeds obviously from the same source whence their life and being also proceed. We first share the life by which things exist, and afterwards see them as appearances in nature, and forget that we have shared their cause. Here is the fountain of action and of thought. Here are the lungs of that inspiration which giveth man wisdom, and which cannot be denied without impiety and atheism. We lie in the lap of immense intelligence, which makes us receivers of its truth and organs of its activity. When we discern justice, when we discern truth, we do nothing of ourselves, but allow a passage to its beams. If we ask whence this comes, if we seek to pry into the soul that causes, all philosophy is at fault. Its presence or its absence is all we can affirm. Every man discriminates between the voluntary acts of his mind, and his involuntary perceptions, and knows that to his involuntary perceptions a perfect faith is due. He may err in the expression of them, but he knows that these things are so, like day and night, not to be disputed. My wilful actions and acquisitions are but roving;—the idlest reverie, the faintest native emotion, command my

---

[8]Alfred (849–899), Anglo-Saxon King; Scanderberg, originally George Castriota (1404?–1468), Albanian patriot; Gustavus Adolphus (1594–1632), King of Sweden.

curiosity and respect. Thoughtless people contradict as readily the statement of perceptions as of opinions, or rather much more readily; for, they do not distinguish between perception and notion. They fancy that I choose to see this or that thing. But perception is not whimsical, but fatal. If I see a trait, my children will see it after me, and in course of time, all mankind,—although it may chance that no one has seen it before me. For my perception of it is as much a fact as the sun.

The relations of the soul to the divine spirit are so pure that it is profane to seek to interpose helps. It must be that when God speaketh, he should communicate not one thing, but all things; should fill the world with his voice; should scatter forth light, nature, time, souls, from the centre of the present thought; and new date and new create the whole. Whenever a mind is simple, and receives a divine wisdom, old things pass away,—means, teachers, texts, temples fall; it lives now and absorbs past and future into the present hour. All things are made sacred by relation to it,—one as much as another. All things are dissolved to their centre by their cause, and in the universal miracle petty and particular miracles disappear. If, therefore, a man claims to know and speak of God, and carries you backward to the phraseology of some old mouldered nation in another country, in another world, believe him not. Is the acorn better than the oak which is its fulness and completion? Is the parent better than the child into whom he has cast his ripened being? Whence then this worship of the past? The centuries are conspirators against the sanity and authority of the soul. Time and space are but physiological colors which the eye makes, but the soul is light; where it is, is day; where it was, is night; and history is an impertinence and an injury, if it be anything more than a cheerful apologue or parable of my being and becoming.

Man is timid and apologetic; he is no longer upright; he dares not say 'I think,' 'I am,' but quotes some saint or sage. He is ashamed before the blade of grass or the blowing rose. These roses under my window make no reference to former roses or to better ones; they are for what they are; they exist with God to-day. There is no time to them. There is simply the rose; it is perfect in every moment of its existence. Before a leaf-bud has burst, its whole life acts; in the full-blown flower, there is no more; in the leafless root, there is no less. Its nature is satisfied, and it satisfies nature, in all moments alike. But man postpones or remembers; he does not live in the present, but with reverted eye laments the past, or, heedless of the riches that surround him, stands on tiptoe to foresee the future. He cannot be happy and strong until he too lives with nature in the present, above time.

This should be plain enough. Yet see what strong intellects dare not yet hear God himself, unless he speak the phraseology of I know not what David, or Jeremiah, or Paul. We shall not always set so great a price on a few texts, on a few lives. We are like children who repeat by rote the sentences of grandames and tutors, and, as they grow older, of the men of talents and character they chance to see,—painfully recollecting the exact words they spoke; afterwards, when they come into the point of view which those had who uttered these sayings, they understand them, and are willing to let the words go; for, at any time, they can use words as good, when occasion comes. If we live truly, we shall see truly. It is as easy for the strong man to be strong, as it is for the weak to be weak. When we have new perception, we shall gladly disburden the memory of its hoarded treasures as old rubbish. When a man lives with God, his voice shall be as sweet as the murmur of the brook and the rustle of the corn.

And now at last the highest truth on this subject remains unsaid; probably, cannot be said; for all that we say is the far off remembering of the intuition. That thought, by what I can now nearest approach to say it, is this. When good is near you, when you have life in yourself, it is not by any known or accustomed way; you shall not discern the foot-prints of any other; you shall not see the face of man; you shall not hear any name;—the way, the thought, the good shall be wholly strange and new. It shall exclude example and experience. You take the way from man, not to man. All persons that ever existed are its forgotten ministers. Fear and hope are alike beneath it. There is somewhat low even in hope. In the hour of vision, there is nothing that can be called gratitude, nor properly joy. The soul raised over passion beholds identity and eternal causation, perceives the self-existence of Truth and Right, and calms itself with knowing that all things go well. Vast spaces of nature, the Atlantic Ocean, the South Sea,—long intervals of time, years, centuries,—are of no account. This which I think and feel underlay every former state of life and circumstances, as it does underlie my present, and what is called life, and what is called death.

Life only avails, not the having lived. Power ceases in the instant of repose; it resides in the moment of transition from a past to a new state, in the shooting of the gulf, in the darting to an aim. This one fact the world hates, that the soul *becomes;* for, that forever degrades the past, turns all riches to poverty, all reputation to a shame, confounds the saint with the rogue, shoves Jesus and Judas equally aside. Why then do we prate of self-reliance? Inasmuch as the soul is present, there will be power not confident but agent. To talk of reliance, is a poor external way of speaking. Speak rather of that which relies, because it works and is. Who has more obedience than I, masters me, though he should not raise his finger. Round him I must revolve by the gravitation of spirits. We fancy it rhetoric when we speak of eminent virtue. We do not yet see that virtue is Height, and that a man or a company of men plastic and permeable to principles, by the law of nature must overpower and ride all cities, nations, kings, rich men, poets, who are not.

This is the ultimate fact which we so quickly reach on this as on every topic, the resolution of all into the ever blessed ONE. Self-existence is the attribute of the Supreme Cause, and it constitutes the measure of good by the degree in which it enters into all lower forms. All things real are so by so much virtue as they contain. Commerce, husbandry, hunting, whaling, war, eloquence, personal weight, are somewhat, and engage my respect as examples of its presence and impure action. I see the same law working in nature for conservation and growth. Power is in nature the essential measure of right. Nature suffers nothing to remain in her kingdoms which cannot help itself. The genesis and maturation of a planet, its poise and orbit, the bended tree recovering itself from the strong wind, the vital resources of every animal and vegetable, are demonstrations of the self-sufficing, and therefore self-relying soul.

Thus all concentrates; let us not rove; let us sit at home with the cause. Let us stun and astonish the intruding rabble of men and books and institutions by a simple declaration of the divine fact. Bid the invaders take the shoes from off their feet, for God is here within. Let our simplicity judge them, and our docility to our own law demonstrate the poverty of nature and fortune beside our native riches.

But now we are a mob. Man does not stand in awe of man, nor is his genius admonished to stay at home, to put itself in communication with the internal ocean, but it goes abroad to beg a cup of water of the urns of other men. We must go alone. I like the silent church before the service begins, better than any preaching. How far off, how cool, how chaste the persons look, begirt each one with a precinct or sanctuary. So let us always sit. Why should we assume the faults of our friend, or wife, or father, or child, because they sit around our hearth, or are said to have the same blood? All men have my blood, and I have all men's. Not for that will I adopt their petulance or folly, even to the extent of being ashamed of it. But your isolation must not be mechanical, but spiritual, that is, must be elevation. At times the whole world seems to be in conspiracy to importune you with emphatic trifles. Friend, client, child, sickness, fear, want, charity, all knock at once at thy closet door and say, — 'Come out unto us.' But keep thy state; come not into their confusion. The power men possess to annoy me, I give them by a weak curiosity. No man can come near me but through my act. "What we love that we have, but by desire we bereave ourselves of the love."

If we cannot at once rise to the sanctities of obedience and faith, let us at least resist our temptations; let us enter into the state of war, and wake Thor and Woden, courage and constancy, in our Saxon breasts. This is to be done in our smooth times by speaking the truth. Check this lying hospitality and lying affection. Live no longer to the expectation of these deceived and deceiving people with whom we converse. Say to them, O father, O mother, O wife, O brother, O friend, I have lived with you after appearances hitherto. Henceforward I am the truth's. Be it known unto you that henceforward I obey no law less than the eternal law. I will have no covenants but proximities. I shall endeavor to nourish my parents, to support my family, to be the chaste husband of one wife,—but these relations I must fill after a new and unprecedented way. I appeal from your customs. I must be myself. I cannot break myself any longer for you, or you. If you can love me for what I am, we shall be the happier. If you cannot, I will still seek to deserve that you should. I will not hide my tastes or aversions. I will so trust that what is deep is holy, that I will do strongly before the sun and moon whatever inly rejoices me, and the heart appoints. If you are noble, I will love you; if you are not, I will not hurt you and myself by hypocritical attentions. If you are true, but not in the same truth with me, cleave to your companions; I will seek my own. I do this not selfishly, but humbly and truly. It is alike your interest and mine and all men's, however long we have dwelt in lies, to live in truth. Does this sound harsh to-day? You will soon love what is dictated by your nature as well as mine, and if we follow the truth, it will bring us out safe at last.—But so you may give these friends pain. Yes, but I cannot sell my liberty and my power, to save their sensibility. Besides, all persons have their moments of reason when they look out into the region of absolute truth; then will they justify me and do the same thing.

The populace think that your rejection of popular standards is a rejection of all standard, and mere antinomianism; and the bold sensualist will use the name of philosophy to gild his crimes. But the law of consciousness abides. There are two confessionals, in one or the other of which we must be shriven. You may fulfil your round of duties by clearing yourself in the *direct,* or, in the *reflex* way. Consider whether you have satisfied your relations to father, mother, cousin, neighbor, town, cat, and dog; whether any of these can upbraid you. But I may also neglect this reflex standard, and absolve me to myself. I have my own stern claims and perfect circle. It denies the name of duty to many offices that are called duties. But if I can discharge its debts, it enables me to dispense with the popular code. If any one imagines that this law is lax, let him keep its commandment one day.

And truly it demands something godlike in him who has cast off the common motives of humanity, and has ventured to trust himself for a taskmaster. High be his heart, faithful his will, clear his sight, that he may in good earnest be doctrine, society, law to himself, that a simple purpose may be to him as strong as iron necessity is to others.

If any man consider the present aspects of what is called by distinction *society,* he will see the need of these ethics. The sinew and heart of man seem to be drawn out, and we are become timorous desponding whimperers. We are afraid of truth, afraid of fortune, afraid of death, and afraid of each other. Our age yields no great and perfect persons. We want men and women who shall renovate life and our social state, but we see that most natures are insolvent, cannot satisfy their own wants, have an ambition out of all proportion to their practical force, and do lean and beg day and night continually. Our housekeeping is mendicant,[9] our arts, our occupations, our marriages, our religion we have not chosen, but society has chosen for us. We are parlor soldiers. We shun the rugged battle of fate, where strength is born.

If our young men miscarry in their first enterprizes, they lose all heart. If the young merchant fails, men say he is *ruined.* If the finest genius studies at one of our colleges, and is not installed in an office within one year afterwards in the cities or suburbs of Boston or New York, it seems to his friends and to himself that he is right in being disheartened and in complaining the rest of his life. A sturdy lad from New Hampshire or Vermont, who in turn tries all the professions, who *teams it, farms it, peddles,* keeps a school, preaches, edits a newspaper, goes to Congress, buys a township, and so forth, in successive years, and always, like a cat, falls on his feet, is worth a hundred of these city dolls. He walks abreast with his days, and feels no shame in not 'studying a profession,' for he does not postpone his life, but lives already. He has not one chance, but a hundred chances. Let a Stoic open the resources of man, and tell men they are not leaning willows, but can and must detach themselves; that with the exercise of self-trust, new powers shall appear; that a man is the word made flesh, born to shed healing to the nations, that he should be ashamed of our compassion, and that the moment he acts from himself, tossing the laws, the books, idolatries, and customs out of the window, we pity him no more but thank and revere him,—and that teacher shall restore the life of man to splendor, and make his name dear to all History.

It is easy to see that a greater self-reliance must work a revolution in all the offices and relations of men; in their religion; in their education; in their pursuits; their modes of living; their association; in their property; in their speculative views.

1. In what prayers do men allow themselves! That which they call a holy office, is not so much as brave and manly. Prayer looks abroad and asks for some foreign addition to come through some foreign virtue, and loses itself in endless mazes of natural and supernatural, and mediatorial and miraculous. Prayer that craves a particular commodity,—any thing less than all good,—is vicious. Prayer is the contemplation of the facts of life from the highest point of view. It is the soliloquy of a beholding and jubilant soul. It is the spirit of God pronouncing his works good. But prayer as a means to effect a private end, is meanness and theft. It supposes dualism and not unity in nature and consciousness. As soon as the man is at one with God, he will not beg. He will then see prayer in all action. The prayer of the farmer kneeling in his field to weed it, the prayer of the rower kneeling with the stroke of his oar, are true prayers heard throughout nature, though for cheap ends.

---

[9]mendicant: beggarly. Emerson means that one's reading is dependent on the suggestions and approval of others.

Caratach, in Fletcher's Bonduca,[10] when admonished to inquire the mind of the god Audate, replies,—

"His hidden meaning lies in our endeavors,
Our valors are our best gods."

Another sort of false prayers are our regrets. Discontent is the want of self-reliance: it is infirmity of will. Regret calamities, if you can thereby help the sufferer; if not, attend your own work, and already the evil begins to be repaired. Our sympathy is just as base. We come to them who weep foolishly, and sit down and cry for company, instead of imparting to them truth and health in rough electric shocks; putting them once more in communication with their own reason. The secret of fortune is joy in our hands. Welcome evermore to gods and men is the self-helping man. For him all doors are flung wide: him all tongues greet, all honors crown, all eyes follow with desire. Our love goes out to him and embraces him, because he did not need it. We solicitously and apologetically caress and celebrate him, because he held on his way and scorned our disapprobation. The gods love him because men hated him. "To the persevering mortal," said Zoroaster, "the blessed Immortals are swift."[11]

As men's prayers are a disease of the will, so are their creeds a disease of the intellect. They say with those foolish Israelites, 'Let not God speak to us, lest we die. Speak thou, speak any man with us, and we will obey.' Everywhere I am hindered of meeting God in my brother, because he has shut his own temple doors, and recites fables merely of his brother's, or his brother's brother's God. Every new mind is a new classification. If it prove a mind of uncommon activity and power, a Locke, a Lavoisier, a Hutton, a Bentham, a Fourier,[12] it imposes its classification on other men, and lo! a new system. In proportion to the depth of the thought, and so to the number of the objects it touches and brings within reach of the pupil, is his complacency. But chiefly is this apparent in creeds and churches, which are also classifications of some powerful mind acting on the elemental thought of Duty, and man's relation to the Highest. Such is Calvinism, Quakerism, Swedenborgianism. The pupil takes the same delight in subordinating every thing to the new terminology, as a girl who has just learned botany in seeing a new earth and new seasons thereby. It will happen for a time, that the pupil will find his intellectual

---

[10]*Bonduca* (1614), a play by John Fletcher.

[11]"To the persevering mortal . . . ": from *The Chaldean Oracles of Zoroaster* (1832).

[12]John Locke (1632–1704), English philosopher associated with empiricism; Antoine Lavoisier (1743–1794), French scientist who made important contributions to the founding of modern chemistry; James Hutton (1726–1797), English geologist; Jeremy Bentham (1748–1832), English philosopher associated with utilitarianism; Charles Fourier (1772–1832), French utopian social theorist.

power has grown by the study of his master's mind. But in all unbalanced minds, the classification is idolized, passes for the end, and not for a speedily exhaustible means, so that the walls of the system blend to their eye in the remote horizon with the walls of the universe; the luminaries of heaven seem to them hung on the arch their master built. They cannot imagine how you aliens have any right to see,—how you can see; 'It must be somehow that you stole the light from us.' They do not yet perceive, that light, unsystematic, indomitable, will break into any cabin, even into theirs. Let them chirp awhile and call it their own. If they are honest and do well, presently their neat new pinfold will be too strait and low, will crack, will lean, will rot and vanish, and the immortal light, all young and joyful, million-orbed, million-colored, will beam over the universe as on the first morning.

2. It is for want of self-culture that the superstition of Travelling, whose idols are Italy, England, Egypt, retains its fascination for all educated Americans. They who made England, Italy, or Greece venerable in the imagination, did so by sticking fast where they were, like an axis of the earth. In manly hours, we feel that duty is our place. The soul is no traveller: the wise man stays at home, and when his necessities, his duties, on any occasion call him from his house, or into foreign lands, he is at home still, and shall make men sensible by the expression of his countenance, that he goes the missionary of wisdom and virtue, and visits cities and men like a sovereign, and not like an interloper or a valet.

I have no churlish objection to the circumnavigation of the globe, for the purposes of art, of study, and benevolence, so that the man is first domesticated, or does not go abroad with the hope of finding somewhat greater than he knows. He who travels to be amused, or to get somewhat which he does not carry, travels away from himself, and grows old even in youth among old things. In Thebes, in Palmyra, his will and mind have become old and dilapidated as they. He carries ruins to ruins.

Travelling is a fool's paradise. Our first journeys discover to us the indifference of places. At home I dream that at Naples, at Rome, I can be intoxicated with beauty, and lose my sadness. I pack my trunk, embrace my friends, embark on the sea, and at last wake up in Naples, and there beside me is the stern Fact, the sad self, unrelenting, identical, that I fled from. I seek the Vatican, and the palaces. I affect to be intoxicated with sights and suggestions, but I am not intoxicated. My giant goes with me wherever I go.

3. But the rage of travelling is a symptom of a deeper unsoundness affecting the whole intellectual action. The intellect is vagabond, and our system of education fosters restlessness. Our minds travel when our bodies are forced to stay at home. We imitate; and what is imitation but the travelling of the mind? Our houses are built with foreign taste; our shelves are garnished with foreign ornaments; our opinions, our tastes, our faculties, lean, and follow the Past and the Distant. The soul created the arts wherever they have flourished. It was in his own mind that the artist sought his model. It was an application of his own

thought to the thing to be done and the conditions to be observed. And why need we copy the Doric or the Gothic model? Beauty, convenience, grandeur of thought, and quaint expression are as near to us as to any, and if the American artist will study with hope and love the precise thing to be done by him, considering the climate, the soil, the length of the day, the wants of the people, the habit and form of the government, he will create a house in which all these will find themselves fitted, and taste and sentiment will be satisfied also.

Insist on yourself; never imitate. Your own gift you can present every moment with the cumulative force of a whole life's cultivation; but of the adopted talent of another, you have only an extemporaneous, half possession. That which each can do best, none but his Maker can teach him. No man yet knows what it is, nor can, till that person has exhibited it. Where is the master who could have taught Shakspeare? Where is the master who could have instructed Franklin, or Washington, or Bacon, or Newton? Every great man is a unique. The Scipionism of Scipio is precisely that part he could not borrow. Shakspeare will never be made by the study of Shakspeare. Do that which is assigned you, and you cannot hope too much or dare too much. There is at this moment for you an utterance brave and grand as that of the colossal chisel of Phidias,[13] or trowel of the Egyptians, or the pen of Moses, or Dante, but different from all these. Not possibly will the soul all rich, all eloquent, with thousand-cloven tongue, deign to repeat itself; but if you can hear what these patriarchs say, surely you can reply to them in the same pitch of voice: for the ear and the tongue are two organs of one nature. Abide in the simple and noble regions of thy life, obey thy heart, and thou shalt reproduce the Foreworld again.

4. As our Religion, our Education, our Art look abroad, so does our spirit of society. All men plume themselves on the improvement of society, and no man improves.

Society never advances. It recedes as fast on one side as it gains on the other. It undergoes continual changes: it is barbarous, it is civilized, it is christianized, it is rich, it is scientific; but this change is not amelioration. For every thing that is given, something is taken. Society acquires new arts and loses old instincts. What a contrast between the well-clad, reading, writing, thinking American, with a watch, a pencil, and a bill of exchange in his pocket, and the naked New Zealander, whose property is a club, a spear, a mat, and an undivided twentieth of a shed to sleep under. But compare the health of the two men, and you shall see that the white man has lost his aboriginal strength. If the traveller tell us truly, strike the savage with a broad axe, and in a day or two the flesh shall unite and heal as if you struck the blow into soft pitch, and the same blow shall send the white to his grave.

---

[13]Phidias (c. 500–c. 432 B.C.E.), greatest of the ancient Greek sculptors.

The civilized man has built a coach, but has lost the use of his feet. He is supported on crutches, but lacks so much support of muscle. He has a fine Geneva watch, but he fails of the skill to tell the hour by the sun. A Greenwich nautical almanac he has, and so being sure of the information when he wants it, the man in the street does not know a star in the sky. The solstice he does not observe; the equinox he knows as little; and the whole bright calendar of the year is without a dial in his mind. His note-books impair his memory; his libraries overload his wit; the insurance office increases the number of accidents; and it may be a question whether machinery does not encumber; whether we have not lost by refinement some energy, by a christianity entrenched in establishments and forms, some vigor of wild virtue. For every stoic was a stoic; but in Christendom where is the Christian?

There is no more deviation in the moral standard than in the standard of height or bulk. No greater men are now than ever were. A singular equality may be observed between the great men of the first and of the last ages; nor can all the science, art, religion and philosophy of the nineteenth century avail to educate greater men than Plutarch's[14] heroes, three or four and twenty centuries ago. Not in time is the race progressive. Phocion, Socrates, Anaxagoras, Diogenes,[15] are great men, but they leave no class. He who is really of their class will not be called by their name, but will be his own man, and, in his turn the founder of a sect. The arts and inventions of each period are only its costume, and do not invigorate men. The harm of the improved machinery may compensate its good. Hudson and Behring accomplished so much in their fishing-boats, as to astonish Parry and Franklin, whose equipment exhausted the resources of science and art.[16] Galileo, with an opera-glass, discovered a more splendid series of celestial phenomena than any one since. Columbus found the New World in an undecked boat. It is curious to see the periodical disuse and perishing of means and machinery which were introduced with loud laudation, a few years or centuries before. The great genius returns to essential man. We reckoned the improvements of the art of war among the triumphs of science, and yet Napoleon conquered Europe by the Bivouac, which consisted of falling back on naked valor, and disencumbering it of all aids. The Emperor held it impossible to make a perfect army, says Las Cases, "without abolish-ing our arms, magazines, commissaries, and carriages, until in imitation of

---

[14]Plutarch (46?–c. 120 C.E.), Greek biographer.

[15]Phocion (402–318 B.C.E.), prominent Greek military leader; Socrates (469–399 B.C.E.), Greek philosopher and teacher of Plato; Anaxagoras (c. 500–428 B.C.E.), Greek philosopher; Diogenes (c. 412–323 B.C.E.), Greek philosopher noted for his search for a man of truth.

[16]Emerson compares explorers who lived a century apart from each other: Henry Hudson (d. 1611); Vitus Bering (1680–1714); Sir William Percy (1790–1855); Sir John Franklin (1786–1847).

the Roman custom, the soldier should receive his supply of corn, grind it in his hand-mill, and bake his bread himself."[17]

Society is a wave. The wave moves onward, but the water of which it is composed, does not. The same particle does not rise from the valley to the ridge. Its unity is only phenomenal. The persons who make up a nation to-day, next year die, and their experience with them.

And so the reliance on Property, including the reliance on governments which protect it, is the want of self-reliance. Men have looked away from themselves and at things so long, that they have come to esteem the religious, learned, and civil institutions, as guards of property, and they deprecate assaults on these, because they feel them to be assaults on property. They measure their esteem of each other, by what each has, and not by what each is. But a cultivated man becomes ashamed of his property, out of new respect for his nature. Especially he hates what he has, if he see that it is accidental,–came to him by inheritance, or gift, or crime; then he feels that it is not having; it does not belong to him, has no root in him, and merely lies there, because no revolution or no robber takes it away. But that which a man is, does always by necessity acquire, and what the man acquires is living property, which does not wait the beck of rulers, or mobs, or revolutions, or fire, or storm, or bankruptcies, but perpetually renews itself wherever the man breathes. "Thy lot or portion of life," said the Caliph Ali,[18] "is seeking after thee; therefore be at rest from seeking after it." Our dependence on these foreign goods leads us to our slavish respect for numbers. The political parties meet in numerous conventions; the greater the concourse, and with each new uproar of announcement, The delegation from Essex! The Democrats from New Hampshire! The Whigs of Maine! the young patriot feels himself stronger than before by a new thousand of eyes and arms. In like manner the reformers summon conventions, and vote and resolve in multitude. Not so, O friends! will the God deign to enter and inhabit you, but by a method precisely the reverse. It is only as a man puts off all foreign support, and stands alone, that I see him to be strong and to prevail. He is weaker by every recruit to his banner. Is not a man better than a town? Ask nothing of men, and in the endless mutation, thou only firm column must presently appear the upholder of all that surrounds thee. He who knows that power is inborn, that he is weak because he has looked for good out of him and elsewhere, and so perceiving, throws himself unhesitatingly on his thought, instantly rights himself, stands in the erect position, commands his limbs, works miracles; just as a man who stands on his feet is stronger than a man who stands on his head.

---

[17]Napoleon's tactics described by Emmanuel Augustin de Las Cases (1766–1842), a French historian.
[18]Caliph Ali (c. 600–661), fourth Caliph of Islam.

So use all that is called Fortune. Most men gamble with her, and gain all, and lose all, as her wheel rolls. But do thou leave as unlawful these winnings, and deal with Cause and Effect, the chancellors of God. In the Will work and acquire, and thou hast chained the wheel of Chance, and shalt sit hereafter out of fear from her rotations. A political victory, a rise of rents, the recovery of your sick, or the return of your absent friend, or some other favorable event, raises your spirits, and you think good days are preparing for you. Do not believe it. Nothing can bring you peace but yourself. Nothing can bring you peace but the triumph of principles.

[1841, 1847]

EMILY DICKINSON

———————

Tell all the truth but tell it slant - ♦
Success in Circuit lies
Too bright for our infirm Delight
The Truth's superb surprise
As Lightening to the Children eased   5
With explanation kind
The Truth must dazzle gradually
Or every man be blind -

[c. 1872] (F1263)♦♦

EMILY DICKINSON

I dwell in Possibility - ♦
A fairer House than Prose -
More numerous of Windows -
Superior - for Doors -

Of Chambers as the Cedars -   5
Impregnable of eye -
And for an everlasting Roof
The Gambrels of the Sky -

Of Visitors - the fairest -
For Occupation - This -   10
The spreading wide my narrow Hands
To gather Paradise -

                    [c. late 1862] (F466)♦♦

From *The Poems of Emily Dickinson*, edited by Ralph W. Franklin, Cambridge, Mass.: the Belknap Press of Harvard University Press, Copyright © 1988 by the President and Fellows of Harvard College. Copyright © 1951, 1955, 1979 by the President and Fellows of Harvard College. Reprinted by permission of Harvard University Press and the Trustees of Amherst College.
♦Included in fascicle 22. One variant: line 8 Gambrels] Gables -.
♦♦The *F* indicates Ralph W. Franklin's numbering from his Reading Edition of *The Poems of Emily Dickinson* (1999); the poems are numbered chronologically according to the date of the first handwritten copy.

EMILY DICKINSON

Because I could not stop for Death - ♦
He kindly stopped for me -
The Carriage held but just Ourselves -
And Immortality.

We slowly drove - He knew no haste   5
And I had put away
My labor and my leisure too,
For His Civility -

We passed the School, where Children strove
At Recess - in the Ring -   10
We passed the Fields of Gazing Grain -
We passed the Setting Sun -

Or rather - He passed Us -
The Dews drew quivering and Chill -
For only Gossamer, my Gown -   15
My Tippet - only Tulle - ¹

We paused before a House that seemed
A Swelling of the Ground -
The Roof was scarcely visible -
The Cornice - in the Ground -   20

From *The Poems of Emily Dickinson*, edited by Ralph W. Franklin, Cambridge, Mass.: the Belknap Press of Harvard University Press, Copyright © 1988 by the President and Fellows of Harvard College. Copyright © 1951, 1955, 1979 by the President and Fellows of Harvard College. Reprinted by permission of Harvard University Press and the Trustees of Amherst College.
♦Included in fascicle 23.
¹Flimsy, fine material; a "tippet" is a shoulder cape.

Since then - 'tis Centuries - and yet
Feels shorter than the Day
I first surmised the Horses' Heads
Were toward Eternity -

[c. late 1862] (F479)♦♦

♦♦The *F* indicates Ralph W. Franklin's numbering from his Reading Edition of *The Poems of Emily Dickinson* (1999); the poems are numbered chronologically according to the date of the first handwritten copy.

EMILY DICKINSON

Some keep the Sabbath going to Church - ♦
I keep it, staying at Home -
With a Bobolink for a Chorister -
And an Orchard, for a Dome -

Some keep the Sabbath in Surplice - ¹   5
I, just wear my Wings -
And instead of tolling the Bell, for Church,
Our little Sexton² - sings.

God preaches, a noted Clergyman -
And the sermon is never long,   10
So instead of getting to Heaven, at last -
I'm going, all along.

[c. 1861] (F236)♦♦

From *The Poems of Emily Dickinson*, edited by Ralph W. Franklin, Cambridge, Mass.: the Belknap Press of Harvard University Press, Copyright © 1988 by the President and Fellows of Harvard College. Copyright © 1951, 1955, 1979 by the President and Fellows of Harvard College. Reprinted by permission of Harvard University Press and the Trustees of Amherst College.
♦Published during Dickinson's lifetime in *The Round Table* on March 12, 1864; one of the editors, Charles H. Sweetser, may have obtained the manuscript during 1861, while he was still a neighbor of the Dickinsons and attending Amherst College. Dickinson mailed another copy to T. W. Higginson.
¹A white robe with full, flowing sleeves worn by clergymen during services.
²One who maintains church property and rings the church bells.
♦♦The *F* indicates Ralph W. Franklin's numbering from his Reading Edition of *The Poems of Emily Dickinson* (1999); the poems are numbered chronologically according to the date of the first handwritten copy.

Regions and Realisms
Writing in America, 1865–1914

Cristanne Miller

The period from 1865 to 1914 was one of radical changes and contrasts, in almost every sphere of life. It began with the end of a war that irretrievably altered the United States and ended with the beginning of another war that would do the same. Between the Civil War and World War I, the United States changed from a relatively rural and parochial nation into a major economic power on the world stage. As often occurs in periods of extreme change, what was good for one segment of the population harmed or angered another. Hence, this period witnessed the making of extraordinary fortunes, and widespread impoverishment; a swing from legislative and civic power for African Americans and white Southern outrage, to a white-dominated Southern culture of Jim Crow laws and mob lynchings; a shift from masculine war heroism and sharp distinctions between the spheres of activity assumed appropriate for men and women, to widespread male anxiety about the erosion of masculinity and increasing legal, economic, and political powers for women. Perhaps because such contrasts and fluctuations stimulated uncertainty about what remained stable even in human values, the literature written from 1865 to 1914 turned with particular fervor to the ordinary, every day, and nitty-gritty, or what it called the "real" aspects of life.

Literary "realism" of the second half of the nineteenth and early twentieth centuries has been called local color writing, regionalism, social realism, scientific or psychological realism, and naturalism, and critics still debate the parameters of this international movement as it occurred in the United States. The most important American literary spokesman of the end of the century, William Dean Howells, defined "realism" broadly: it is "nothing more and nothing less than the truthful treatment of material." His good friend Henry James was similarly vague; realists, he claimed, have a "powerful impulse to mirror the unmitigated realities of life." The question of what constituted the "realities of life" or what was most "real," however, was answered variously by different writers, or even by the same writers at different points in their career. The realest reality, as it were, was found in domestic or rural life, physical suffering, urban slums, economic desires or disaster, sex, death, class hierarchies, social tensions and needs, and in the workings of the human mind. It was expressed through regionally marked speech, detailed physical description, muckraking journalistic fiction, and the exploration of subjectivity or psychological processes. In short, no single set of topics or style characterized this vast and diverse body of writing called "realism." Generally, however, literary emphasis shifted slowly and irregularly from the small heroisms of regional, daily life, to a still relatively optimistic focus on major social issues and complex psychological processes, to a "naturalistic" anti-capitalist and anti-imperialist outrage at the result of several decades of unfettered industrial and financial expansion. This turn-of-the-century literature of angry, sometimes even bitter, didactic commentary, in turn, gave way to the more conceptual and formal experimentalism of modernism that eschewed direct social or political critique for indirect approaches to the problems of the "new" century. The period from 1865 to 1914 therefore moved the nation not just from a local to a world perspective and economy, but from a primarily regional focus in the literature to the beginnings of international modernism.

The cataclysmic event of the nineteenth century was the Civil War. All late nineteenth century political, social, cultural, and literary events and transformations could in some way be said to develop out of or in reaction to it. Over six hundred thousand people died, and hundred of thousands more were wounded or disabled, or incapacitated by disease incurred during imprisonment, in hospitals, or in army camps. The South and Border States suffered great loss of property and destruction of livestock and agricultural produce, while in the North, several industries were stimulated, encouraging technological innovation and great increases in production. Small towns were ineradicably altered in the North and South by the departure of men to armies and the growth of factories with their resulting influx of immigrants to work in them. Moreover, whole families were dispersed by the war's battles and ravages. To African Americans in the South, however, the war also brought the first possibility for free movement throughout the country to relocate family members and friends, as well as protection and employment by the Union army as it slowly advanced into the South.

Following the war, African American lives were even more radically transformed by the thirteenth, fourteenth, and fifteenth amendments to the Constitution, prohibiting slavery, securing citizenship for all persons born or naturalized in the United States, granting suffrage to black men, and (at least on the books) prohibiting discrimination on the basis of "race, color, or previous condition of servitude." General William Sherman promised "forty acres and a mule" (the latter, on loan from the army) to every newly liberated family along a stretch of the South Carolina and Georgia coasts and on the

126

Georgia Sea Islands, enabling black ownership of land through the forced redistribution of property. Freedmen's Bureau schools set about educating African-American adults and youth, bringing large-scale literacy for the first time to a population legally denied the right to learn to read in the antebellum South, and attempting to oversee the monumental transition from slave to free labor. At the same time, 1866 saw the founding of the Ku Klux Klan by Confederate army veterans, and although the Klan was outlawed in 1870–71 by President Ulysses Grant, white southerners found alternate political, economic, and physically violent routes to reimpose white control of land, jobs, and government in the South. The South was, in effect, conquered territory, and its white inhabitants reacted in multiple and contradictory ways—with bitterness, relief, sorrow, anger, and with fear at what the future would bring. With the withdrawal of Federal troops in 1877, as Reconstruction was formally declared at an end, systematic terror and violence reigned privately in much of the South, and Jim Crow laws publicly established a separate and unequal system of rights and privileges for black and white populations that was not dismantled until the 1960s.

White women's lives were also dramatically affected by the war. White and black women's involvement in the antebellum abolitionist movement led to similar participation in other areas of social reform after the war, including temperance, child labor, and Indian rights. Even more significantly, during the war, white women of the North and South were forced into more public work by the absence or death of their fathers, husbands, and sons. Because of the war's death toll, the distinct shortage of manpower, and of men, continued after the war. In 1869, the *New York Times* estimated that a quarter of a million young women in the eastern-seaboard states were unlikely ever to marry since they outnumbered men to that extent—a figure that does not include the number of older women widowed by the war or women living in the Midwest or West. This so-called surplus population of women enormously increased pressure on legal and public structures to support more varied and highly paid employment (hence, also more adequate education and training) for women. By the 1870s, even conservative, bourgeois white women initially drawn into the public sphere by male patriotic rhetoric were instrumental in creating extra-domestic roles for women and in demanding equal education, employment, and wages. This, in turn, gave a tremendous boost to the (white-dominated) women's movement, which gathered great force by the end of the century.

It was not only the infrastructure of family life that changed after the war. The need to move massive army units over large tracts of territory and to produce and move materials to support army efforts had transformed transportation, communication, and industrial efficiency and techniques. While both the railroad and telegraph were features of antebellum life in the United States, it wasn't until 1861 that the first intercontinental telegraph line was

127

laid, and 1869 that the first transcontinental railroad was completed. People even told time differently: to facilitate railroad commerce, the fifty-six time zones of the continent were reduced to four. In 1866 the first Transatlantic telegraph cable was laid, revolutionizing communication between the United States and Europe. Edison's 1879 invention of the light bulb and the subsequent large-scale introduction of electricity into businesses and houses revolutionized both business dealings and daily life—as did the invention of the telephone. By 1900 there were 1,356,000 telephones in the country, twice as many as in all Europe, and the United States owned nearly half the railroad mileage in the world.

While the war was the single most significant event, industrialization was the most striking fact of the period. As factory employment nearly doubled, major industries consolidated into monopolies, driving small shopkeepers, farmers, and entrepreneurs out of business and placing vast wealth and power in the hands of a few men—euphemistically called "captains of industry" by those who held them up as a model of the American dream of wealth, but called "robber barons" by others. Andrew Carnegie dominated steel production through Carnegie Steel; John Jay Gould was a railroad financier and speculator, who sold fraudulent stock to the likes of New York Tamany Hall's "Boss" Tweed; J.P. Morgan consolidated U.S. Steel, International Harvester, and General Electric and established one of the most powerful banking houses in the world; and John D. Rockefeller founded Standard Oil, the first great U.S. business trust and eventual target of antitrust suits and laws. Many of these men became significant philanthropists; for example, Carnegie funded the construction of a great number of public and college libraries in the United States and his native Scotland. They were known primarily, however, as ambitious if not ruthless businessmen of fabulous personal wealth. By 1890, one percent of the population owned over twenty-five percent of the nation's wealth.

Because of this rapid and massive industrialization, people were on the move. Young men and women left rural areas to work in the manufacturing centers. African Americans also migrated to cities, especially in the North, to find jobs and escape the cycle of violence and oppression overwhelming their lives in the South; the black population of New York increased four hundred percent between 1900 and 1920—and similar increases occurred in Chicago, Detroit, St. Louis, and other industrial cities. A country whose populace lived primarily on farms or in small towns before the war had become one of extreme urban density: by 1900, only a third of the U.S. populace still lived on farms; Philadelphia's population had tripled, New York's had quadrupled (bringing the city to a population of 3.5 million), and Chicago had grown from about 20,000 at mid-century to over two million inhabitants.

At the same time, better transcontinental transportation encouraged many people to relocate in the West, putting increased pressure on the government to remove Midwestern and Plains Indian populations, often forcibly and without regard to traditional ways of life or territories. In 1871, Congress downgraded the status of all Indian peoples by ending the policy of making treaties—a policy based on the assumption that Native-American tribes were independent nations. The end of this policy, governmental neglect of Indian complaints about the destruction of their way of life, and continued stealing of their land by the government led eventually to violent military conflict, ending with the defeat of the Lakota people at Wounded Knee in 1890. After this massacre, Native Americans—who had once inhabited an area of three billion acres—were restricted to around 150 million acres of "reservation" land. The 1887 passage of the Dawes Severalty Act had already transferred ownership of Indian land from the tribe to individuals, thereby opening the way for white settlers to purchase that land. Consequently, by 1934, when the Act was rescinded, Native Americans owned a mere 48 million acres—less than one percent of their earlier territory.

In keeping with its ruthless disregard for its own previous treaties and agreements with Native Americans during this period, by the end of the century the United States had also begun to exercise more obvious imperialistic designs. In 1893, U.S. sugar growers cooperated with the Navy to overthrow the Hawaiian monarchy; victory in the Spanish-American War of 1898 then led to U.S. annexation of Hawaii and—through a combination of treaty, purchase, and military aggression—acquisition of the Philippines, Puerto Rico, and Guam, and domination of Cuba. During his first term, President Theodore Roosevelt used the U.S. Navy to support an engineered local revolt in Panama and then purchased the Panama Canal from the new government, along with complete control of a ten-mile wide canal zone. This was in keeping with changing U.S. policy toward its southern neighbors. Between 1898 and 1930, the United States intervened in Latin America thirty-two times, following Roosevelt's "big stick" policy of international policing, and his successor William Taft's "dollar diplomacy." In 1909, for example, the powerful U.S.-Nicaraguan Concession organized a revolution that placed one of its own employees as president of the new government. When that president was threatened by another revolt, Taft sent in the Marines, who then remained stationed in Nicaragua for twenty-one years.

Part of the surge in urban population came from unprecedented levels of immigration to the United States. While antebellum immigration had come primarily from England, Germany, Ireland, and Scandinavia, post-war immigration came primarily from Russia and Italy. On the West coast, immigration from China and (to a lesser extent) Japan also increased; Chinese were the primary laborers on the railroad lines that proceeded from the West. In total, fourteen million people formally moved into the United States between the end of the war and the turn of the century. Unlike most earlier arrivals, these immigrants were largely Catholic or non-Christian. For example, immigration from Russia consisted largely of Jews fleeing local and national repressive anti-Semitic policies; by 1910, thirty-one percent of the population of New York City was Jewish, and within a few more years Hebrews dominated a twenty-block square area of Manhattan. There were Yiddish newspapers and theaters—the latter drawing crowds of up to two million people a year in their heyday in the mid-teens. Many immigrant populations developed their own journalistic and literary productions. By one count, in 1896 approximately 1,200 periodicals were being published in the United States in a language other than English.

The increasing visibility of populations not speaking English caused a resurgence of xenophobia. For example, in 1882 Congress passed the Chinese Exclusion Act, following various outbreaks of violence against the Chinese. In 1885 and 1886, more anti-Chinese riots and massacres occurred in the West, and in 1888 Congress passed further legislation preventing even those Chinese previously living in the United States holding official reentry permits from returning. After the 1882 Exclusion Act, Chinese immigration dropped from 40,000 a year to 23,000. In 1915, the Ku Klux Klan was revived by Southern white Protestants reacting defensively against large-scale immigration, especially of Bolsheviks (the communist movement that was to seize power in Russia in 1917), Catholics, and Jews. Within a decade, the Klan had attained a national membership of up to six million.

By the turn of the century, the scope and scale of these changes transformed the United States into a modern nation, with all the characteristics now associated with twentieth century life. It became the world's most highly industrialized nation, with densely inhabited cities and nation-wide systems of communication and transportation. It was characterized by advanced technology; the concentration of capital and wealth in banks, businesses, and monopolistic corporations; and by imperialistic designs on neighboring or satellite countries. The pace of life seemed to have accelerated. Families could no longer assume their children would settle nearby or in their home towns, or that anyone could be raised to enter a single occupation. By the turn of the century, a majority of the people living in New York City was not born there and a third of the population in America's largest cities was foreign born.

Regional Writing

Immediately preceding the Civil War, the United States enjoyed the production of innovative and ambitious works of literature attempting to create a national literary identity. Following the war, writers largely abandoned the Romantic, heroic, and mythic narratives that had provided the basis for much of this literature, and turned to stories based on regional events or ways of life. Various explanations for this trend have been given. Among the most persuasive are, first, that the increasing industrialization and urbanization of the 1860s and 1870s generated an acute consciousness that many rural ways of life were about to disappear. This was certainly the case in the Northeast, Midwest, and—because of the war as well as industrialization—in the South. Second, the war left the country morally exhausted, leading writers to concentrate on the local rather than the national or ideological. Writers and readers were glad to see ordinary aspects of everyday life in each part of the country as revealing human worth and values. Third, the increased prosperity of part of the populace directly following the war led to the practice of taking vacations, purchasing summer houses, and traveling for leisure purposes. Hence, people wanted to know what other regions were like. The phenomenal growth of the magazine industry also created a demand for short fiction, met in large part by, as well as encouraging, regionalist realism. Whatever its stimulus, this writing tended to focus on the everyday lives of ordinary people, often used local dialect or idiom, included precise detail about natural and social geographies, and typically celebrated small heroisms of endurance or character. Using a high proportion of dialogue, such literature eschewed authorial intrusion or commentary—except in the plainest of language and relatively simple terms; it was documentary in style. Regional realist fiction (like the social and psychological realism of Howells and James) was also influenced by the domestic detail of bestselling novels written before the war by women such as Fanny Fern, E.D.E.N. Southworth, Susan Warner, and Harriet Beecher Stowe. Sometimes denigrated as "local color writing," in fact regional realism contributed importantly to the rebuilding of a more nationally conceived literature and is indistinguishable in its primary characteristics from social and urban realism.

Among the earliest unmistakably realist works published in the United States was Rebecca Harding Davis's *Life in the Iron Mills* (1861), revealing the back-breaking and emotionally deadening working conditions and lives of Welsh iron workers near Wheeling, Virginia. The thrust of Davis's story, like that of all important regional writing, goes far beyond the local. Any detailed account, however, must be localized to be credible. Davis's story both depicted individual lives among a particular immigrant community, and revealed the general plight of "life in the iron mills" for thousands of urban workers. While much regional writing leaned toward the charming or humorous rather than toward social reform, magazine editors eagerly bought a range of stories accurately describing the various regions of the now vast nation and its various classes. Bret Harte's 1860s stories of California mining towns and scoundrels were the first such accounts to become nationally popular. As editor of the *Overland Monthly* from 1868 to 1871, Harte also published stories by other Western writers—including Samuel Clemens (Mark Twain) and Ambrose Beirce. Several years later, Mary Austin became popular for a very different kind of Western tale, depicting the stark and subtle conditions of the desert and its inhabitants, especially indigenous and Hispanic people maintaining traditional ways of life and arts. Native-American writers such as Charles Eastman, Gertrude Bonnin (Zitkala-Sa), and John Oskison also wrote about the people of the West.

In the Northeast, Mary Wilkins Freeman, Harriet Beecher Stowe, and Sarah Orne Jewett wrote of individuals in small communities, those whose lives followed patterns relatively untouched by the currents of change. These stories have a nostalgic edge for the readers who knew such character types, but they are also sharp psychological and social studies of aging, impoverishment, sexism, and the abandonment of villages by the young. In her verse, Emily Dickinson proclaims, "I see—New Englandly," and that "The Queen, discerns like me—//Provincially." Louisa May Alcott became internationally famous for her portrayal of New England family life in *Little Women* (1868–69) and its several sequels.

Almost all regionalist writers, as indeed most writers of the period, depended on magazine publication both to gain an initial local and national audience, and as a continuing source of income. Because of technical improvements in printing, lower costs for paper and transportation (facilitated by the construction of canals and national railroad lines), and the rise of national corporations interested in publishing, the cost of literary production and distribution fell dramatically following the Civil War, causing a tremendous surge in magazine publication. Between 1865 and 1905, the number of periodicals in the United States increased from 700 to more than 6,000. East and West Coast monthly magazines gained national circulations—especially *Harper's Monthly*, the *Atlantic Monthly*, and *Scribners* in the East, and the *Overland Monthly* in California. Book production also became cheaper, giving rise to highly popular, widely distributed pulp fiction, epitomized by Erastus Beadle's dime novels. Stories about Deadeye Dick in the wild West and other larger-than-life characters from highly mythologized regions were produced by a stable of writers, repeating a simplified ideology of self-reliance and white American manhood. The popularity of such stock story lines can also be seen in Horatio Alger's production of more than one hundred urban novels between the 1860s and 1890s, each preaching that financial success would award virtue and hard work, enabling the fabled Andrew Carnegie-like rise from rags to riches.

In the Midwest, Hamlin Garland focused on the privations of small farm life, as corporations gobbled up land and profits, running the small farmer out of business or into increasingly harsh conditions of living. Frank Norris wrote about similar deprivation in the urban Midwest in short stories and in the second of his two "Epic of Wheat" novels, depicting speculation on the grain market in Chicago (*The Pit*, 1903; and the first novel of this epic, *The Octopus*, 1901, portrayed wheat farmers in California).

In the South, what was called plantation literature constructed a nostalgic antebellum land of genteel living and affection between the races; while most of this fiction has not survived, a later novel of this genre, Margaret Mitchell's *Gone With The Wind* (1936), was a national bestseller. Joel Chandler Harris made use of, and departed from, the plantation genre in his wildly popular Uncle Remus tales (first published, 1880). These tales recounted African-American folk traditions in a narrative style and dialect widely praised for their accuracy, as did Charles Chesnutt's later stories in collections such as *The Conjure Woman* (1899). Both Chesnutt's folktale based short stories and his novels were deliberately set against the myths and stereotypes of the plantation genre. Similarly, George Washington Cable and Kate Chopin wrote charming and subtle tales about the complex interactions of the mixed racial populations of Louisiana—Creoles, Cajuns, blacks, and Euro-Americans.

The publication of regional realism peaks in the 1880s, and is perhaps best represented by Mark Twain's *Huckleberry Finn* (1884), which exemplifies the broadest reach of the genre in its portrayal of the young white Huck and the older black Jim escaping briefly into a realm of fully human interaction on the Mississippi River in the midst of a racist, violent, and selfish dominant society. Twain's earlier humorous tales of the West and sketches of life on the Mississippi had by this point developed into his brilliant use of first-person narration, dialect, local geography, and humor to explore the complexities of racial relations, black manhood, rural class systems, and adolescence in a story popular across the United States and Europe. While, as with Harris's Uncle Remus tales, some critics at the time (and more in the late twentieth century) criticized nostalgic elements of Twain's novel, the vast majority acknowledge *Huckleberry Finn* as one of America's great novels and a classic of American realism.

Social and Psychological Realism

Twain's unvarnished depiction of human meanness in towns along the Mississippi River reveals the bleaker aspects of realist writing. Yet Huck's free moral agency in deciding to renounce social respectability and "go to hell" in order to save the enslaved Jim is also typical of American realism—as is Jim's equally difficult moral decision to sacrifice his freedom to save Tom Sawyer's life. By the 1880s, American realism was more closely associated with William Dean Howells than with any other writer or critic, and Howells's realism combined an acute recognition of the economic, social, and ethical problems facing ordinary people with an optimistic conviction that individuals could finally act as independent moral agents.

Howells exemplified his theories of realism preeminently in novels such as *A Modern Instance* (1882), *The Rise of Silas Lapham* (1885), and *A Hazard of New Fortune* (1890), which portray the social customs, achievements, and failures of America's middle class, with a focus on questions of character. In his six decades of writing, Howells published over a hundred books of various genres, mostly fiction, and much of this writing dealt with issues immediately pertinent to the times: the ethics of self-made business men, divorce, spousal abuse, and the "hazard" of unchecked capitalism. According to Howells, such attention to the real problems of common people's lives was not just realistic but necessary to the production of "good" fiction in both senses of the word: In his view, if a book treats the ordinary materials of American life truthfully, "the book *cannot* be wicked and cannot be weak"; without that truth, "all graces of style and feats of invention and cunning of construction are so many superfluities of naughtiness." Through his editorial positions first at the *Atlantic Monthly* and then *Harper's Monthly*, Howells had ample opportunity to express such convictions: He wrote numerous reviews and essays of literary criticism and social commentary. Tremendously influential and generous in his personal responses to others' writing, Howells helped further the careers of writers as diverse as George Washington Cable, Abraham Cahan, Charles Chesnutt, Samuel Clemens, Stephen Crane, Paul Lawrence Dunbar, Mary Wilkins Freeman, Hamlin Garland, Henry James, and Sarah Orne Jewett.

A great admirer of Howells, Henry James took realism in yet another direction, struggling in his novels to represent the complexity of the inner life and the unfixed quality of human perception. While his earlier novels shared with Howells's work deep attention to individual character in a particular scene—"Daisy Miller" in Rome (1879), Christopher Newman in Paris in *The American* (1877), Isabelle Archer in a variety of English and (American-owned) Italian houses in *The Portrait of a Lady* (1881)—his later fiction dealt increasingly with surfaces and depths of thought. These are works more of language than of action, or of ways that subtle, nuanced, complex syntax and wording can express the fluctuations of perception and consciousness registered in the mind. Although frequently parodied for the complex syntax and fine distinctions of his late fiction, both the theory and form of James's style influenced the development of modernist fiction. More clearly in the dominant realist vein of his own times, in works such as *The Princess Casamassima* (1886) or *The Bostonians* (1886), James depicted major characters involved in radical social movements to redistribute wealth and political power, and in women's rights. His last novel, *The Ivory Tower* (1917), records how vividly he felt that unequal distribution of wealth crippled even the wealthy.

Psychological processes had long been the province of literature, and earlier writers much admired by James—especially Nathaniel Hawthorne and Gustave Flaubert—had excelled in a literature of deep psychological complexity. Yet the new science of psychology heralded by writers including Sigmund Freud, Carl Jung, and Henry's brother William James gave new impetus and provided new language for literary examination of the mind. Many realist writers saw parallels between their work and that of the scientific discourses of their times—anthropology, sociology, and biological sciences as well as psychology; they borrowed terminology and ideas from science for their fictional explorations of similar areas of concern. Such association implicitly entitled literature to a cultural authority parallel to that of science, which was rapidly becoming the most authoritative discourse of the modern world—as though the writer, too, could claim the myth of objective mastery. The authority of science, however, demanded the possibility of experimental repetition and an objectivity based on numerical calculations as well as a detached perspective. In contrast, the authority of literature relied paradoxically on both a detached perspective and the artist's empathetic understanding of his or her subject. Moreover, the author's characters themselves must embody both the singularities of particular selfhood and the common characteristics of recognizable human types. The mechanics of repetition were the stock-in-trade of the dime novel. In contrast, James's great narrative skill lay in part in his transformation of the most tawdry and common of life's situations—adultery, greed, egocentric self-blindness, psychological cruelty within marriage, national and class prejudice—into complex examinations of human character, carried out in language simultaneously impressionistic and as precise as math.

Fiction dominates realist literature of the late nineteenth century, but James's closest contemporary in the realistic examination of psychological processes, and in the construction of a distinctive style that both anticipates modernist practice and bases itself on nineteenth century models is the poet Emily Dickinson. Especially in her numerous poems on pain, loss, and dying, Dickinson gives extraordinary glimpses into moments of intense personal feeling. That many of these poems were written during the Civil War helps to explain her focus on these topics, when the whole nation was consumed with the war's violence and death tolls. Writing with a compression and lack of narrative frame unique in her era, Dickinson produced hundreds of poems describing moments of perception without specifying who registered them and in what circumstances. Consequently, her "I" takes on the ring of commonplace experience characteristic of other realist writing, even while her speakers are highly idiosyncratic in their expressions: "I felt a Funeral, in my Brain," she writes, in describing intense depression or grief—or, similarly, "It was not Death, for I stood up, / And all the Dead, lie down." In other poems she writes more philosophically: "Success is counted sweetest / By those who ne'er succeed," or joyfully: "Exhilaration –is within - / There can no Outer Wine / So royally intoxicate / As that diviner Brand." Another poet, Edwin Arlington Robinson, turns to Arthurian narrative in his late poetry, but his poems from around the turn of the century contain memorable realistic portraits of bewildered, drunken, or despairing figures—from the wealthy

"Richard Corey" who "put a bullet through his head" to the bittersweet play-fulness of a lonely, drunken old man in "Mr. Flood's Party."

Paul Laurence Dunbar was another realist poet anticipating the emphases of modernism. Dunbar constructed moving portraits of ordinary and exemplary African Americans in poems such as "When Malindy Sings," "Frederick Douglass," and "The Colored Soldiers." At times using dialect but often writing in standard English and traditional verse forms, he both contributed to the realist representation of the multiple, rich idioms of the Unites States, and paved the way for the use of dialect and the inflection of speech rhythms in the work of Harlem Renaissance poets, including Langston Hughes. In "The Poet," however, Dunbar also lamented that the "world" is more eager to hear "a jingle in a broken tongue" from its black poets than the "high" or "deeper" tones of poems written in elegant standard English.

Several writers brought the insights of their own experience to bear on their versions of social realism. Like James, and influenced by his fiction, Edith Wharton wrote complex short stories and novels involving the lives of the well-to-do in American and European cities—a class whose prejudices and foibles she knew firsthand. Like the many domestic realists who preceded her, Wharton makes restrictive gender conventions, bourgeois morality, and narrowly conceived social proprieties a primary focus of much of her fiction. Louisa May Alcott published stories stemming from her hospital work during the War (*Hospital Sketches*, 1863) and, following years of attempts to support her mother and siblings, a trenchant account of the narrowness and hazards of work options for women (*Work: A Story of Experience*, 1873). The poet Emma Lazarus became interested in the Jewish experience and her own Jewish ancestry after she read about Russian persecution of the Jews, and as Jewish immigration to the United States increased. Her poem "The New Colossus" became nearly synonymous with U.S. refuge for immigrants after its closing lines were inscribed on the Statue of Liberty: "Give me your tired, your poor, / Your huddled masses yearning to breathe free . . . Send these, the homeless, tempest-tost to me." Russian-Jewish writers Abraham Cahan and Mary Antin and the Cuban José Martí were among the many immigrants who contributed to the growing diversity of American literature, and to the growing diversity of published perspectives on being in and part of the United States.

Naturalisms

All realists responded directly or indirectly to the currents of the times—the new sciences, the pressures of capitalist industrialism, the increasing chasm between rich and poor, and people's overwhelming consciousness of money in its human and social significance. Some, however, wrote with greater directness than others about the disasters of turn-of-the-century capitalism and America's urban and rural poor, and were less optimistic than Howells and other social realists about the resilience of human nature. Ambrose Beirce, Stephen Crane, Frank Norris, Theodore Dreiser, Jack London, Henry Adams, Upton Sinclair, and Abraham Cahan are among those writers—often called Naturalists—who saw the most pressing realities of the late nineteenth and early twentieth centuries in the inhumane, physically exhaustive, emotionally draining conditions of Americans' lives.

Samuel Clemens referred to this period as the "Gilded Age" in reference to the fraudulence and superficiality of its glitter. Behind the conspicuous consumption of the country's millionaires were millions of ordinary laborers, caught increasingly in a system that exploited the labor of men, women, and children without regard for the effects on these workers of long working hours, dangerous conditions, and inadequate wages. Even Walt Whitman, who vibrantly proclaimed the hopes of his age before the Civil War, wrote in *Democratic Vistas* (1871), "the problem of the future of America is in certain respects as dark as it is vast." This was an age known for corruption and scandal—typified by the infamous Tweed Ring in New York, which systematically plundered the city's resources of what may have been as much as 200 million dollars. Every level of government seemed guilty of spoils and bribery, from Congress, to the neighborhood or small town bureau. A series of panics and Depressions beginning in 1873 made the economic situation of the middle and lower classes unstable. By the end of an especially devastating and prolonged Depression in 1893–94, twenty percent of the labor force was unemployed.

As more people entered the ranks of the poor and the conditions of their lives grew less tolerable, strife between capital and labor erupted—in 1892, for example, with the Homestead Strike of iron and steel workers, and in 1894, with the Pullman strike in Chicago, where federal troops were called in to break up the American Railway Union and dozens of workers were killed. Between 1881 and 1905, there were 36,000 strikes across the United States. Similarly, unsafe labor conditions led to disasters such as the Triangle Shirtwaist Company fire in 1910, in which nearly 150 women died. What Thorstein Veblen in 1899 dubbed "the leisure class" had for years seemed indifferent to such loss of life and the conditions that provoked it.

Workers, however, began to organize for their rights. In the 1880s, the American Federation of Labor emerged as the first unified organization of national unions, providing bargaining power for skilled workers in Congress. The national women's movement also became active in labor legislation, helping secure laws to improve working conditions, housing, sanitation, and educational facilities for the working class. Together women's organizations, labor lobbies, and other reform groups pushed through legislation mandating restrictions on child labor, the eight-hour work day, and prison reform.

137

Naturalism distinguished itself from realism both by its turn to contemporary life in its harshest forms and by its more deterministic attitudes. Feeling the full impact of Charles Darwin's controversial 1859 *The Origin of the Species* and Herbert Spencer's development of Darwin's theories to suggest that in the modern industrial state, as in nature, only the "fittest" should survive, these writers saw little free agency in human action. In Crane's much-heralded *The Red Badge of Courage* (1895), Henry Fleming sees the Civil War and his own engagement in battle through the blinds of romanticism and surrealistic illusions produced by raw fear. At the novel's end, Crane leaves ambiguous whether Fleming has learned anything from his experience, or is capable of such learning. Crane's "Maggie, a Girl of the Streets" (1893) similarly presents Maggie's descent into prostitution and death as something between an accident and the inevitable result of slum upbringing and dysfunctional family life. Beirce's Civil War stories are equally disillusioned in their juxtapositions of heroic or naive perception and gruesome violence, and his *Devil's Dictionary* definitions give a new edge to cynicism. In Dreiser's *Sister Carrie* (1901), Carrie rises to professional success and fortune by chance and despite a complete lack of moral conscience. Jack London's heroes most famously battle the wilds of the Alaskan Klondike—as in "To Build A Fire" (1908) and *The Call of the Wild* (1903)—but he also wrote novels of brutal human competition (*The Sea Wolf*, 1904) and violent socialist rebellion (*The Iron Heel*, 1907), making him among the most popular authors in Russia (and the Soviet Union) for decades. Frank Norris's novels of railroad profiteering (*The Octopus*, 1901) and grain monopoly (*The Pit*, 1903) similarly critique capitalistic exploitation of ordinary workers, as does Upton Sinclair's famous exposé of the Chicago stockyards, *The Jungle* (1906).

As the relation of such literature to social reform and muckraking journalism suggests, many naturalist and realist writers got their start writing for newspapers—for example, Beirce, Cahan, Clemens (under his pseudonym Twain), Crane, Dreiser, Harris, Harte, Howells, London, and Norris. Writers who began with more optimistic views of human agency turned also to bleaker versions of realism as the century drew to a close. Howells's *A Hazard of New Fortunes*, for example, was inspired in part by the Haymarket affair, in which eight radical labor leaders were convicted of killing police officers, and four were hanged. The incident occurred following an ongoing nationwide strike for the eight-hour work day that had begun on May 1, 1886; when several workers were killed in a police action, Chicago labor responded with a peaceful demonstration, during which someone threw a bomb at the police. The Chicago establishment saw the officers' deaths as an opportunity to rid the city of its radical labor leaders and anarchists; it was later proved that all eight men convicted were known at the time to be innocent, and even in 1886 it was clear that their trial was a travesty of justice.

While Clemens did not attribute any specific incidents with triggering the misanthropy of his late fiction, stories such as "The Man that Corrupted Hadleyburg" (1900) and "The United States of Lyncherdom" (1901) reveal how much his confidence in the goodness of the human spirit had been shaken not just by personal losses but by the times. Clemens also wrote a vast literature of protest at U.S. imperialist foreign policy—exemplified by "To the Person Sitting in Darkness" (1901), a savage critique of American missionary activity in China; British conduct during the Boer War in South Africa; and U.S. aggression in the Philippines. Many of these stories and sketches remained unpublished during his lifetime, but others helped to swing public opinion away from missionary and military imperialism. Henry Adams provided a historian's perspective on the disorientation and apparently meaningless chaos of the age in *The Education of Henry Adams* (1907), among the most thoughtful reflections on this era.

The economic and social problems of the nineteenth century eventually gave rise to proportional national preoccupation with reform. By the 1890s, legislation and institutional practices began to improve the living conditions of millions of Americans. Liberal, socialist, and other progressive thinkers made common goals in turning their attention to the country's social crisis, and in making the welfare of ordinary working people into a powerful political cause. The "Gilded Age," then, gave way to the "Progressive Era," which lasted until the beginning of World War I distracted U.S. attention from its domestic policies. Theodore Roosevelt based his two-term presidency (1901–09) on the reform impulse of this era, beginning the effort to curb the giant trusts, promoting labor and social legislation, and originating a policy of natural resource conservation in the form of national parks for the "people." This political mood was spurred by the intolerable conditions described in naturalist literature, but it was also more positively reflected in utopian fictions of the period. Edward Bellamy's *Looking Backward* (1888) was the most famous and successful of these, giving rise to Bellamy Clubs that promoted the nationalization of industry and other reforms depicted in his novel. Other utopias of the period include Howells's *A Traveller from Altruria* (1894) and Charlotte Perkins Gilman's feminist *Herland* (1915).

Color Lines

W.E.B. Du Bois famously wrote in *The Souls of Black Folk* (1903) that "the problem of the Twentieth Century is the problem of the color-line." He might just as accurately have made this remark about the last half of the nineteenth century. As the South became more entrenched in the institution of segregation, as the incidence of lynchings increased, as African Americans became progressively disillusioned with governmental inaction, and as swelling immigration clarified that assimilation into American society was not equally open to all, questions of "race" and color became the focus of heated social and scientific debate. These debates were brought to a head by the 1892 Plessy vs. Ferguson decision of the U.S. Supreme Court, upholding the practice of separate and segregated facilities for "the white and colored races." Eugenics, a pseudo-science claiming to "improve human stock" by promoting the continuation of "the more suitable races or strains of blood" through marital and sexual choice, was becoming increasingly popular; F. Scott Fitzgerald, for example, wrote a song called "Love or Eugenics" for a 1914 Princeton show. Scientists internationally debated the hierarchy of "races," inevitably placing Northern Europeans or Anglo Saxons at the top and Africans near the bottom. Race was assumed to be an attribute of nations and people, loosely defined (the Jewish race, the Swedish race), and believed by many to determine an individual's capacities and qualities.

In this environment, progressive writers of all ancestry sought to counter the prevailing discourse. The two leading African-American theorists and political leaders of the age were Booker T. Washington, founder of the highly successful Tuskegee Institute for vocational education; and Du Bois, a prominent sociologist, a founder of the National Association for the Advancement of Colored People (NAACP), and editor for many years of the NAACP journal, *The Crisis*. Washington supported accommodationist racial compromises, making it a lifelong goal to garner the support of white politicians who were necessary to the continuing growth and influence of his Institute. Hard work and practical, vocational education enabling self-sufficiency would, he believed, lead eventually to white respect for African Americans—as he demonstrated by pointing to his own life story in publications such as *Up from Slavery* (1901). Du Bois, in contrast, argued for the immediate joint responsibility of whites and blacks in addressing the deleterious effects of segregation and racism to both "races." In his view, professional education and national action directed at political and legal reform proved the best hope for progress. By educating the "talented tenth" of their communities to become teachers, doctors, and lawyers, African Americans could educate broader numbers of their people and develop legal and social reforms, serving all black society.

At the beginning of the twentieth century, Washington was the most influential and powerful African American of the nation. Adviser to Presidents McKinley, Roosevelt, and Taft, Washington in fact worked behind the scenes for the full agenda of civil and political rights, even while maintaining a public attitude of compromise. With the publication of Du Bois's *The Souls of Black Folk*, however, the tide began to turn. There Du Bois launched a strong indictment of Washington's philosophy, persuading many African Americans of the limits of Washington's rural and vocational focus. The eloquence and scholarly acumen of his writing also soon made Du Bois internationally renowned for his historical, sociological, cultural, and political commentary on contemporary U.S. society, although the elitism of his notion of a "talented tenth" drew some attack. Du Bois's acute insight into the psychology of racism as creating a "double consciousness" in African Americans—a "sense of always looking at one's self through the eyes of others"—has proved among his most valuable contributions to the production of twentieth century African-American literature.

German immigrant Franz Boas was similarly influential, although in the scientific rather than the cultural realm. Boas pioneered the fields of cultural anthropology, comparative linguistics, and modern folklore. He also wrote extensively against pseudo-scientific arguments promoting racism. For example, in "The Problem of Race," he uses contemporary data to show that neither the functions nor the anatomical traits of a "race" can be defined as hereditary because the variations are so great and environment plays so large a role in introducing changes. "It does not matter from which point of view we consider culture," he argues; "its forms are not dependent upon race."

Anna Julia Cooper's career as an educator, social activist, and writer demonstrates African-American women's introduction of gender into the discourse on race and racial uplift. Educated at Oberlin and eventually earning a doctorate in French from the Sorbonne, Cooper saw the role of women generally and of black women in particular as crucial to the progress of the modern age. "It would be subversive of every human interest that the cry of one-half the human family be stifled," she wrote. Through parenting, education, spiritual guidance, and the strength of nonviolent perseverance, as well as in their more public and activist roles, Cooper believed women could powerfully effect social change. Such attitudes were also the topic of literature of the period—for example, in Frances Ellen Watkins Harper's *Iola Leroy, or Shadows Uplifted* (1893), Pauline Hopkins's *Contending Forces, a Romance Illustrative of Negro Life North and South* (1900), and novels by Amelia Johnson and Emma Dunham Kelly, as well as in poetry and stories by Alice Dunbar-Nelson. In fact, the production of African-American literature was dominated by women at the end of the nineteenth century; between 1890 and 1910, black women published more works of fiction than black men had published in the previous half century. Poetry by Paul Laurence Dunbar and the novels and stories of Charles Chesnutt similarly contributed to the discourse on the lives of African-American women and men.

Race was less prominently an issue of literary focus for Mexican, Asian, and Native Americans, whose differences from dominant Anglo-European America were more often conceived in cultural terms. Perhaps in part for this reason, they did not participate in defining the terms of the theoretical discourse as African Americans did from the late nineteenth century on. There was considerable commentary on cultural conflict, but it typically took the form of life-writing, or remained most expressive in oral forms.

Among the few publications contributing directly to the larger social debate, Sarah Winnemucca Hopkins castigated whites for their un-Christian treatment of the Paiutes in *Life Among the Piutes: Their Wrongs and Claims* (1883), and a Sioux Indian rights activist, Gertrude Bonnin (Zitkala-Sa), published an essay of disillusioned commentary on assimilation called "Why I am a Pagan" (1902). A Ponca chief, Standing Bear, together with Susette and Francis La Flesche, formed the Omaha Ponca Committee to protest Ponca forcible removal from their land and toured the United States giving public lectures. Euro-American poet Helen Hunt Jackson turned late in her life to writing about the Indian peoples of the West, in a bestselling novel, *Ramona* (1884), and in two nonfiction works, *Century of Dishonor: A Sketch of the United States Government's Dealings with Some of the Indian Tribes* (1881) and a *Report on Conditions and Needs of the Mission Indians of California* (1883).

Oral Traditions and Life Writing

The late nineteenth century witnessed the development of anthropology and folklore study as intellectual disciplines, spurred in the United States by Franz Boas, who taught at Columbia University for over forty years. Folklore refers to the verbal, spiritual, and material elements of a culture passed on through oral transmission and by observation and imitation. As Boas and his students, including Margaret Meade, Ruth Benedict, and Zora Neale Hurston, made clear, such material changes over time, and consequently must be understood contextually and historically, not as a universal or timeless record of a "primitive" people. As a part of this interest, many researchers turned to the extremely rich and varied oral traditions of the African- and Native-American populations of the United States, and writers began to develop materials from these traditions into their own literature. Retold or transcribed oral productions became a popular part of the literary market.

As mentioned previously, Harris and Chesnutt were the best-known authors reconstructing African-American folktales and bringing them to popular attention through magazine and book publication. Harris published nearly two hundred animal trickster tales and Chesnutt published several stories that combine magical and spiritual elements. While the sources of the animal tales are largely African, the tales of witchcraft and "goophering" both participate in that trickster tradition and show elements of the transformation of African religious practice in the New World. Like all folk traditions, African-American tales changed according to the times and conditions in which they were told. One of the more remarkable changes was the development around the turn of the century of stories relating a contest of wits between "John" and the "Massa," or slave and slave owner—or, in later versions, generally between black and white men. In such tales, like many of the earlier animal tales in which a small animal outwits a larger or faster or stronger one, the slave outwits the owner. Such tales were first collected and published in the mid-1910s and became extremely popular—for example, in Harlem Renaissance author Zora Neale Hurston's groundbreaking anthropological collection, *Mules and Men* (1935).

Native Americans were also active in this period in preserving the legends, songs, and tales of their oral traditions, as were Euro-American ethnologists collecting Indian lore. In fact, because Native-American culture had such obvious and radical differences from Euro-American culture, the surge of popular interest in collecting Native-American tales was initially greater than that in collecting African-American tales. Charles Eastman, the best-known Native-American writer of his day, published three books of Sioux legends and stories, a book of customs and philosophical commentary called *The Soul of the Indian* (1911), and a collection of short biographies of Indian leaders, as well as a two-part autobiography (all in collaboration with his wife, Elaine Goodale Eastman). Bonnin (Zitkala-Sa) published a volume of Sioux legends and another volume of short stories about the Sioux. Mohawk Pauline Johnson (Tekahionwake) published several volumes containing poems and stories about Indian life, and retelling some legends.

Native-American oral traditions were also changing in the nineteenth century. The most significant change occurred with the rise of the Ghost Dance religion. On January 1, 1889, a Paiute named Wovoka (also known as Quoitze Ow and Jack Wilson) received an apocalyptic vision. This vision foretold that if Indians performed particular dances and songs for five or six nights running; and if they ceased lying, stealing, and fighting against the whites; the whites would disappear, buffalo would reappear, and Indians could return to traditional ways of life. Given the dire circumstances of most Native-American peoples by the 1880s, it was not surprising that the religion was enthusiastically embraced across the West, especially among the young. While Native societies responded variously to the pacifist and moral aspects of Wovoka's vision, the songs and dances were widely adopted and new songs and dances were composed to express Indian spiritual power. Euro-American hysteria arose out of ignorance about what these practices could mean and fear of the newly confident and enthusiastic intertribal gatherings. In response, the Seventh Cavalry rushed to Wounded Knee in December of 1890. Its slaughter of men, women, and children there effectively put an end to large-scale Native-American resistance to the reservation movement and clinched Euro-American domination of the West. Because the spreading of this religion coincided with the early work of anthropologists and ethnomusicologists, many of its songs were recorded, as were more traditional Indian songs, chants, and prayers. Several Native Americans participated in this early anthropological work, including Nez Perce Archie Phinney, Sioux Ella Deloria, Navajo William Morgan, and Seneca Arthur C. Parker.

Almost as popular as collections of Native-American legends and tales were autobiographies. While folklore had some of the appeal of regional writing, these life-writings participated fully in the social realist tradition of unvarnished documentary. Many relate Indian children's forced removal from their homes to be sent to Euro-American–run boarding schools, the schools' oppressively assimilationist practices, and the later pain of having to decide between the obvious advantages of further Euro-American professionalism and return to the traditions of their ancestors. Eastman, Bonnin, Winnemucca, Cherokee John Milton Oskison, and Omaha Francis LeFlesche were among the many who turned to life-writing in this period. It was not until the 1920s and 1930s that Native-American authors turned in any numbers to writing either poetry or novels.

The first life-writing by an Asian-American writer also appears in this period, in Edith Maud (Sui Sin Far) Eaton's publication of *Mrs. Spring Fragrance* (1912), and in other stories and sketches she published in journals and newspapers. Like many of the Native writers of this period, Eaton was of mixed race and writes about the effects of growing up between two worlds. Most of her stories are set in San Francisco or the Northwest and show the daily hurdles of prejudice faced by, but also the ordinary pleasures of, Chinese and mixed race Asians in the United States.

Euro- and African-American life-writing retained the popularity it already enjoyed in this period. Both famous and unknown people published their life stories—from Henry Adams's highly crafted and philosophical *Education*, to Frederick Douglass's second and third rewritings of his life story, to Jane Addams's *Twenty Years at Hull House*, to the privately printed diaries of Henry and William James's sister Alice James (who lived for decades in invalidism and published no other writing). African-American slave narratives were popular before the Civil War and contributed importantly to abolitionism. A number of narratives—many "as told to" friends or scribes—also appeared after the war, adding harrowing tales of life during the war itself and through the Reconstruction period to their narratives of antebellum life. Several of these life-narratives have been recovered in collections published in the late twentieth century, and African-American novelists and poets continue to explore the riches of this tradition in contemporary writing.

In the American Southwest, the *corrido* developed from the Spanish literary ballad as reshaped by both Spanish and indigenous American music, and by local politics. While *corridos* were sung before the Civil War, the period from 1860 to 1920 marked the high point of its development and popularity. These oral narratives frequently focused on Mexican-Anglo rivalry and, like trickster tales, almost inevitably showed the Mexican-American farmer or outlaw to be more clever, more heroic, and often more moral than the

Anglo-American law enforcement representative or powerful landowner. For example, the extremely popular "Ballad of Gregorio Cortez" heroizes a farmer unjustly accused of stealing, whose legal defense became a celebrated political cause in Mexico and the United States. Many *corridos* were also written about Mexican Revolutionary war heroes, particularly those who fought against the U.S. army as well as against Mexican dictators. They also regained widespread popularity during the Chicano/a Rights struggle and national grape boycott led by César Chávez and Dolores Huerta in the late 1960s. Several early *corridos* were printed in Mexico in the early twentieth century and circulated throughout the Southwest as broadsides, as well as orally.

The "New Woman" and the New Century

Middle-class American women enjoyed the most privileged legal, financial, and educational circumstances of any middle-class women in the world at the turn of the century. By mid-century, U.S. state legislatures had begun to overturn the historical rule of coverture adopted from English Common Law that had denied married women property and political rights under the doctrine declaring a wife to be "covered" by the rights of her husband. With the Married Women's Property Laws of New York in 1860 and 1862, married women in that state gained substantial right to control their own wages, property, and inheritance. Similar laws in many other states soon followed, although married women did not enjoy equal legal rights with men in all states until nearly the middle of the twentieth century. Married women's property acts coincided with changes in marital law providing women easier access to divorce. By the turn of the century, both single and married women in most states could hold individual checking accounts, inherit and will property, and dispose of their income independently. In the area of politics, women possessed limited suffrage rights in twenty-five states, full suffrage in four states, and were eligible for local and state offices in most states.

American women also enjoyed broad access to higher education. By the 1870s, there were a number of women's colleges with academic standards modeled after those at prestigious male institutions, as well as many colleges and universities with coeducational student bodies—thanks in particular to the land-grant program signed into law by Abraham Lincoln in 1862, establishing a fully coeducational state university system. While it was still unusual for a woman to choose a college education, a middle-class woman with a public high school education could do so, and many did. The effect of college education on women of this era can hardly be overestimated. In college, a woman was expected to succeed at a wide variety of endeavors utterly divorced from Victorian notions of feminine occupation—not just to study science and history but often to place a career before marriage, to determine her own type and pattern of work, and basically in every way to think for herself. The women graduating in the 1870s and '80s—the first generation to do so in substantial numbers—translated this educational displacement from gender norms into optimistic ambitions for altering national conventions and laws. These women included M. Carey Thomas, president of Bryn Mawr College; Jane Addams, founder of Hull House; Florence Kelley, first factory inspector for the State of Illinois; Alice Hamilton, first woman on the faculty of Harvard Medical School and initiator of the field of industrial medicine; and Grace Abbott, national labor advocate—among many others. Because they were quintessentially American in their usually small-town and bourgeois backgrounds, and because superior education offered them both economic autonomy and secure social status, they did not sacrifice social respect by pioneering new careers and rejecting traditional roles.

Women's rights and suffrage leader Susan B. Anthony summarized the century's gains in 1897: "The close of the nineteenth century finds every trade, vocation, and profession open to women, and every opportunity at their command for preparing themselves to follow these occupations." While Anthony overstates the case, and despite the persisting job discrimination, lower pay for equal work, and traditional patterns of job segregation, the attitudes with which young women viewed the possibilities of their lives in the early twentieth century would indeed have been unrecognizable in 1865. The three decades from 1890 until 1920 (when the women's suffrage amendment was passed) were the most supportive of women's rights, professionalism, and creative expression of any until the 1970s.

Not surprisingly, in the midst of this gender revolution, the question of what was to become of the American woman was on many authors' minds. In two late essays on American women, for example, Henry James responds to anti-feminist diatribes by asserting that the Victorian isolation of the American woman socially and professionally from men definitely impoverished rather than enriched her understanding and perspective: as "[t]he product of an order in which no presence was really so taken for granted as her own, her view of relations was thereby inordinately simplified." This gender segregation was, in his view, yet another manifestation of what he calls, "a civilization addicted to nothing if not to waste"—in this case the waste of women's potential. Many of James's novels take women's moral agency as their primary focus—from the feminists of *The Bostonians* to the painful enlightenment of Maggie Verver about her adulterous husband and best friend in *The Golden Bowl*. Although both realist and naturalist writing are typically seen as dominated by men and by an insistent ideology of masculinity, authors such as Crane, Chesnutt, and Dreiser also chose women's lives as the focus of some of their most important fiction, and much of Hamlin Garland's fiction shows great sympathy and attention to his female

146

characters. Henry Adams also speculates about the "force" of the new American woman in the most famous chapter of his *Education*, "The Virgin and the Dynamo."

More attuned to the range of women's lives and desires, Edith Wharton, Kate Chopin, and Charlotte Perkins Gilman are the writers of their era justly most famous for their explorations of women in an era on the cusp of change but where dominant social and sexual attitudes remained entrenched in earlier conservatism. Wharton frequently portrays high society in "old" New York, but her depiction of impoverished working women in *The House of Mirth* (1905), as also of Lily Barth's painful descent from wealth and confident sexual power to poverty and despair, is sympathetic and chillingly realistic. In other novels and stories, Wharton writes (albeit in veiled terms) about women's sexuality, divorce, infidelity, ambition, and the whole range of psychological experiences of mothers, daughters, sisters, friends, and wives in this era of change. Wharton's female protagonists are never on a pedestal or idealized, and they are not restricted to conventional modes of feeling or perception.

Kate Chopin also dealt with a range of issues facing women in the mixed race communities of the Louisiana bayou and New Orleans, but most famously with women's sexual desire. Edna Pontellier is the most fully drawn and best-known of Chopin's heroines who revel in the sensual pleasures of eating, walking, swimming, and sexual expression. In *The Awakening*, Edna not only chooses to leave husband and children but recognizes that the great love she feels for the man she would currently choose as her lover will only be temporary and that she no more wants to be married to him than to any other man; she wants, heretically for a mother and sexually active woman, to "belong to herself." The release of the novel brought on a torrent of abuse; reviewers called it diseased, sick, and dangerous to the morals of young women, and the book was banned in Chopin's native St. Louis.

Charlotte Perkins Gilman wrote poetry, short stories, and extensive economic and social commentary on gender conventions as they cripple men's and women's—but especially women's—lives. "The Yellow Wallpaper," her best-known story, gives fictional form to the symptoms of neurological disorder that had arisen almost epidemically among Victorian women in the United States and were being treated by the medical profession in repressive and infantilizing fashion. The infamous "rest cure" represented in Gilman's story required that a woman suffering nervous disorder refrain from all intellectual activity—including reading, writing, or talking to friends; she should be fed pablum, forced to spend long hours in bed, and remain strictly under the control of her physician. Gilman, Alice James, and Jane Addams were among the famous women of the late nineteenth century prescribed such treatment. The result of this "cure" in Gilman's story is the insanity of the female narrator, who escapes her doctor-husband at the end only by joining the hundreds of other women she fantasizes as having already left obedience to patriarchy behind. The implied lessons of this story are presented at witty and scholarly length in other of Gilman's publications: *Women and Economics* (1898), *The Home: Its Work and Influence* (1910), and *The Man-Made World* (1911).

Freeman, Jewett, Harper, Hopkins, and multiple other women of the late nineteenth and early twentieth centuries also published fiction portraying the large and small heroisms of women's private lives and critiquing prevailing gender ideologies. Alcott published melodramatic blood and thunder stories with a feminist edge anonymously in small magazines, including the story "Behind a Mask: or, A Woman's Power." Poets such as Dickinson, Sarah Piatt, Ellen Wheeler Wilcox, Adah Isaacs Mencken, Helen Hunt Jackson, and Emma Lazarus also made the iniquities or double standards of gender norms a topic of their verse. While they by and large did not participate in formal organizations promoting women's rights and did not call themselves feminists, such writers addressed many of the concerns to become central to feminist writing of the late twentieth century. The women's movement has, in fact, been the longest-lasting reform movement of U.S. history. It is hardly surprising, then, that nearly all the writers of this period—male and female—saw changing gender norms and particularly the changing shapes of women's lives as key to understanding the realities of the modern world.

MARK TWAIN
[1835–1910]

On October 19, 1865, about one month shy of his thirtieth birthday, Mark Twain wrote to his brother that he had finally, after at least four false starts, decided on a career: "I have had a 'call' to literature, of a low order—i.e., humorous. It is nothing to be proud of, but it is my strongest suit, & if I were to listen to that maxim of stern duty which says that to do right you <u>must</u> multiply the one or the two or the three talents which the Almighty entrust to your keeping, I would long ago have ceased to meddle with things for which I was by nature unfitted & turned my attention to seriously scribbling to excite the <u>laughter</u> of God's creatures." Forty years later, in a passage written for his autobiography, he described his career as a humorist in a different way: "Humor is only a fragrance, a decoration. . . . Humor must not professedly teach, and it must not professedly preach, but it must do both if it would live forever. . . . I have always preached. That is the reason that I have lasted thirty years. If the humor came of its own accord and uninvited, I have allowed it a place in my sermon, but I was not writing the sermon for the sake of the humor. I should have written the sermon just the same, whether any humor applied for admission or not" (July 31, 1906). As befits a man who was known for his exaggerations, both statements stretch the truth, and as equally befits a man who gave himself the pen name Mark Twain, each is essentially true to one of Twain's two main poses. On the one hand, he set himself up as mischievous iconoclast bent on having and provoking fun. In this pose, Twain provided much-needed comic relief from Victorian seriousness. On the other hand, much of his greatest work is profoundly serious, participating in the Victorian obsession with morality and character, chastising hypocrisy wherever he found it—including in himself.

In a sense, Twain's doubleness is a pure product of America, stemming from the variety of experiences a chaotic and turbulent life brought his way. Born Samuel Langhorn Clemens on November 30, 1835, in the recently founded rural hamlet of Florida, Missouri, and raised in the Mississippi riverfront town of Hannibal, Missouri, Twain began his life on the edge of American culture. Though his father was a fairly well-read, free-thinking, self-styled aristocrat, Twain's main social context was the crude culture of the Old Southwest, with its peculiar mix of working-class democracy and slavery, of practical morality and revival religion, of grog shops and temperance movements. The next to last of seven children and one of three to live to adulthood, Samuel Clemens was born into a family of declining fortunes. His family tried to maintain a stance of gentility in the face of adversity, but they could afford no more than a haphazard education for Sam up to the age of twelve, when, a year after his father's death, he was apprenticed to the printing trade.

Printing appealed to the family not simply because it was practical, but also because it was one of few manual trades that had an aura of gentility. With the honorable precedent of Benjamin Franklin to vouch for its value, the print shop was seen by many Americans as an alternative education for ambitious bright young men who could not afford college. And so it served for Clemens. Already an avid reader, he found in the print shop as heterogeneous a mix of written material as any person could hope for. Beyond the usual doses of politics and opinion, which were the bread and butter of early American journalism, a rural Western paper of the day printed fine poetry, doggerel verse, humorous sketches, speeches, travel correspondence, and just about anything else that might interest its audience. The crucial thing was that the copy would be either very cheap or free, and in a day of weak copyright law, that meant that every tiny local newspaper could—and usually did—steal almost any short piece of writing that came across its path.

In this context, Clemens learned both the rough rhythms of vernacular expression and the complex cadences of formal rhetoric. In the rambunctious context of the print shop, he also learned much about practical joking, irreverence, and the spirit of satire. In June of 1853, aged seventeen, he left home to begin life as an itinerant journeyman printer. Over the next four years, he worked in St. Louis, New York City, Philadelphia, Muscatine and Keokuk Iowa, and Cincinnati, and looked for work in Washington, D.C. His letters home suggest that he was hard working, averse to drinking, and devoted to self-cultivation by taking his recreation in the fine libraries established by the printer's guilds in New York and Philadelphia. By twenty-one, Clemens had lived in the East and West, North and South, big city and small town, and had already begun to write travel letters describing his experiences.

In the spring of 1857, tired of printing's long hours and limited prospects, Clemens sought a change. He first planned to go to Brazil to participate in the then legal trade in coca, but on his way down the Mississippi River, changed his mind again. Borrowing money from his brother-in-law in St. Louis to pay for another apprenticeship, he began the onerous process of learning to be a riverboat pilot, described in loving detail in "Old Times on the Mississippi," serialized in the Atlantic Monthly *in 1875. Riverboats were the lifeblood of Western commerce, but the reputation of boatmen was not high. As much as piloting was difficult and lucrative, it was a job suspect in the eyes of the genteel, in part because it brought the boat-worker into contact with gamblers, prostitutes, slave-traders, business sharks, frontiersmen, and various other opportunists who were drawn to this turbulent conduit between frontier and city. From an environment steeped in literature, Clemens stepped into a different world. For the first time in his life, he had money and the prestige money could bring, and began a habit of conspicuous consumption and terrible investments. His interest in cultivating gentility waned, and he learned the rougher accomplishments that his mother had warned him against. Nonetheless, he maintained an interest in writing, publishing occasional satires and travel letters.*

As a man whose livelihood was based on North-South commerce and on an economy based on slavery, Clemens was opposed to the Republican Party and to secessionists. When the Civil War began in 1861, he first hid out so as not to be conscripted as a Union riverboat pilot; when it was clear that river commerce had ceased until war's end, he left his career as a pilot and enlisted in a Missouri militia supporting states' rights, an experience he described later in "A Private History of a Campaign that Failed" (1885). Within weeks, he abandoned military service to travel West with his brother Orion, an ardent abolitionist Republican who had just been appointed by the new Lincoln Administration to serve as secretary to the new Territorial government of Nevada. Like many Americans, Clemens could not reconcile his divided loyalties; he left Missouri in July of 1861 for what he thought would be a brief vacation and some desultory silver mining while the war passed. The war turned out to be more substantial than anyone expected, and Clemens's exile turned out to be longer yet. He spent over five years in Nevada and California, with a trip to Hawaii—described in a rich mix of autobiography and fiction in Roughing It *(1872). In the far West, the former printer and pilot became a professional writer.*

The transition was not an easy one. Bitten with mining fever, Clemens spent himself into debt. Desperate for money, he took an offer from the Virginia City (Nevada) Territorial Enterprise *to work as a reporter. There, he learned much about writing from Joe Goodman, the paper's editor and proprietor, who had Clemens write regular news and gave him free reign for creative work. Goodman was the first in a series of editors and colleagues who understood that Clemens's talents and experiences gave him the unique opportunity to create an important literature in an American vernacular.*

It was in Nevada that Clemens adopted the pen name Mark Twain, which was variously interpreted as the leadsman's call on a riverboat for "two fathoms," or as the number of drinks Clemens habitually added to his bar tab. This second interpretation says much about the kind of life Clemens led out West, where he participated energetically in the rough-and-tumble world of frontier journalism. He made many enemies, but the wit and wildness of his style also won him a wide audience in the West. After leaving his staff position on the Enterprise *in 1864 and after a brief stint as a staff reporter for the San Francisco* Call, *he worked as a traveling corespondent for several newspapers and as a writer for San Francisco's literary journal,* The Golden Era, *publishing literary sketches in magazines and travel correspondence, usually first in newspapers and then collected in books. At about the same time, he developed another of his talents, that of a humorist on the lecture circuit. His stage performances kept him in touch with the spoken quality of American English, preventing him from imitating the British literary forms usually preferred by American writers.*

His life experiences to this point enabled him to see much of the richness and many of the contradictions of American culture. Without usually working too deeply into the substance of those contradictions, his early sketches tend to play on the surface, exploiting incongruities in manners and language. The exception may be the "Jumping Frog" story he published in 1865, which rises to an iconographic level in depicting the development of American culture. Still, Clemens had not yet developed the habit of pushing incongruity to great depth, nor had he conjoined his ability to see through public shams with self-reflection. At this stage in his career, Mark Twain came across as a cocky, ebullient humorist and satirist. At the same time, the serious side of Clemens was far from satisfied with what he saw as the financial, moral, and intellectual shortcomings in his life. As he put it in a letter to his mother when he was on the verge of the first of many trips to Europe:

> Curse the endless delays! They always kill me—they make me neglect every duty & then I have a conscience that tears me like a wild beast. I wish I never had to stop anywhere a month. I do more mean things, the moment I get a chance to fold my hands & sit down than ever I can get forgiveness for. (June 1, 1867)

As much as Clemens mocked the rest of the world in his pose as Mark Twain, he privately reviled his participation in that world.

In running away, he found two things that provided material for his writing and the strength to develop it. While touring Europe and the Middle East, he struck on a typically American refrain about history, suggesting in the letters that would be collected into the extraordinary bestseller The Innocents Abroad *(1869) that Europe is dead, trapped by the burden of its own past. But in seeing America's relationship to that history, he began a lifelong meditation on the power of the past to shape the present. Twain found support to develop these ideas in personal relationships, most importantly that with Olivia Langdon, whom he met in 1867. Olivia Langdon was one of three children of a wealthy Elmira, New York, couple that was politically well connected, had been active abolitionists and members of the Underground Railroad, and who vigorously supported radical Republican efforts to secure equal rights for African Americans. They were also quite religious, strong temperance advocates, and were* among the founders of Elmira College. To Clemens, they represented the respectability he had once been encouraged to pursue but that he had left behind, and they exposed him to social attitudes toward African Americans that were radically different from those of his youth. In almost every way, his connections with the Langdon family stretched him.

After an intense courtship that is well documented in their letters, Olivia Langdon married Samuel Clemens, and thus began a literary collaboration that lasted until her death in 1904. Clemens turned over to his wife the task of "taming" him, suggesting how completely he accepted Victorian attitudes toward gender roles. But over the course of a marriage, their prescribed roles became less rigid. Olivia became Twain's most important literary adviser. She edited his manuscripts and, while she often pushed him toward propriety, she as often pushed him away from ironic bitterness and toward humor. Thus, she encouraged that aspect of Twain's work that was imbued with serious moral purpose, but she also encouraged his more extravagant humor, and encouraged him to use his humor to develop his moral vision.

About the same time that Clemens found his marriage helping him to reconcile two very different sides of his personality, he developed a number of friendships with scholars, writers, and artists. Most important of these was his friendship with William Dean Howells. Along with Olivia Langdon and Joseph Goodman, Howells had the greatest influence on Clemens's career. And like both Goodman and Langdon, Howells shared a deep knowledge of conventional culture with an appreciation for the power and potential depth of Twain's unconventional gifts. In various ways, all three connected the once provincial Twain to a larger world of letters, helped him to discipline himself as a writer and encouraged him to look into himself and his world to create a deep humor. With their advice, guidance, and frequently, editing, Twain learned to turn simple social incongruity into a way of interrogating human ethics. As much as he began his career seeing himself torn between old and new, East and West, gentility and barbarism, his experiences with both sides of those ostensible divides showed commonalities, for both good and evil, and helped him develop a moral sensitivity that turned him into America's conscience by the end of his career. No longer a trivial funny fellow, no longer a self-loathing clown, Twain came to accept the power of humor to find depth and solace.

Beginning in the 1870s, then, came a series of books that drew on Twain's personal experiences and on his continuing study of history. These converged in his most famous books, The Adventures of Tom Sawyer (1876) and Adventures of Huckleberry Finn (1884), both of which address the American experience from personal and historical points of view. The shift in tone between the two—with the first being what Twain called a "hymn to boyhood," and the second a much darker and thematically richer book—suggests something of the serious turn his studies and self-reflection had given his writing. His *sense of humor had become an incisive tool for challenging America's growing nostalgia for the antebellum days. With a broader eye on the English-speaking world, Twain then published* A Connecticut Yankee in King Arthur's Court *(1889) taking late Victorian medievalism on both sides of the Atlantic to task. At the same time, the twisting incongruities Twain's ironic imagination kept uncovering, led him to doubt whether material progress made much difference in human moral development. By this time, his writings presented a counter-voice both to elitist longing for an orderly and hierarchical world and to simplistic American faith in progress. In this way, his humor threatened to turn into a deeply pessimistic irony, and much of Twain's late work has a bitter tone. But as much as many readers have thus drawn the conclusion that Twain's career described a trajectory toward nihilism and despair, many of his later works, most particularly the innovative "Chapters from My Autobiography" (1906–07) show that his humor was equally capable of finding joy out of sorrow.*

In finding through humor a way to bridge his internal divides, Twain became one of America's most influential writers. At first, most Americans held him to be little more than a popular favorite, but influential figures of his own generation, such as Annie Fields, John Hay, and William Dean Howells, supported his work, and many writers of the next generation saw him as a significant model to follow in creating a truly American literature in both form and substance. Substantially because he created new ways of treating American materials through American voices, he provided a model for such widely different kinds of writers as Ernest Hemingway, T. S. Eliot, Ralph Ellison, and Kurt Vonnegut. His work endures in part because it looks at the fundamental paradoxes of American life, and as such, his writings have generated as much antipathy as praise. Indeed, the unease Twain's writings inspires is perhaps more important than the emulation. Toni Morrson, describing the anxiety and pleasure Huck Finn *has given both to her and to today's culture, says, "For a hundred years, the argument about what this novel is has been identified, reidentified, examined, waged, and advanced. What it cannot be is dismissed. It is classic literature, which is to say it heaves, manifests, and lasts." These words could easily apply to any number of Twain's works.*

Gregg Camfield
University of the Pacific

For Further Reading

Primary Works:

The Celebrated Jumping Frog of Calaveras County, and Other Sketches, 1867; *The Innocents Abroad,* 1869; *Roughing It,* 1872; *The Gilded Age* (with Charles Dudley Warner), 1873; *Old Times on the Mississippi,* 1875, 1883; "The Facts Concerning the Recent Carnival of Crime in Connecticut," 1876; *The Adventures of Tom Sawyer,* 1876; *A Tramp Abroad,* 1880; *The Prince and the Pauper,* 1881; *Life on the Mississippi,* 1883; *Adventures of Huckleberry Finn,* 1884; "The Private History of a Campaign that Failed," 1885; *A Connecticut Yankee in King Arthur's Court,* 1889; *Pudd'nhead Wilson,* 1894; "How to Tell a Story," 1895; *Personal Recollections of Joan of Arc,* 1896; *Following the Equator,* 1897; "The Man That Corrupted Hadleyburg," 1899; "To the Person Sitting in Darkness," 1901; "Chapters from My Autobiography," 1906–07; *Mark Twain's Speeches,* 1910; *The Mysterious Stranger and Other Stories,* 1922; *Mark Twain's Autobiography,* ed. A. B. Paine, 1924; *Mark Twain's Notebooks and Journals,* 3 vols., ed. Frederick Anderson, et al., 1975; *Mark Twain's Letters,* 5 vols., ed. Edgar Marquess Branch, 1988–97; *Mark Twain: Collected Tales, Sketches, Speeches, and Essays,* ed. Louis J. Budd, 1992; *Oxford Mark Twain,* 29 vols., series ed. Shelley Fisher Fishkin, 1997.

Secondary Works:

Kenneth Lynn, *Mark Twain and Southwestern Humor,* 1959; Henry Nash Smith, *Mark Twain: The Development of a Writer,* 1962; James M. Cox, *Mark Twain: The Fate of Humor,* 1966; Alan Gribben, *Mark Twain's Library,* 1980; Louis J. Budd, *Our Mark Twain: The Making of His Public Personality,* 1983; Robert Sattelmeyer and J. Donald Crowley, eds., *One Hundred Years of Huckleberry Finn,* 1985; James S Leonard and Thomas A. Tenney, *Satire or Evasion? Black Perspectives on Huckleberry Finn,* 1992; Shelley Fisher Fishkin, *Was Huck Black? Mark Twain and African-American Voices,* 1994; Gregg Camfield, *Sentimental Twain: Samuel Clemens in the Maze of Moral Philosophy,* 1994; Laura Skandera-Trombley, *Mark Twain in the Company of Women,* 1995; Bruce Michelson, *Mark Twain on the Loose,* 1995; Susan K. Harris, *The Courtship of Olivia Langdon and Mark Twain,* 1996; Everett Emerson, *Mark Twain: A Literary Life,* 2000.

The Notorious Jumping Frog
of Calaveras[1] County[◆]

MARK TWAIN

In compliance with the request of a friend of mine, who wrote me from the East, I called on good-natured, garrulous old Simon Wheeler, and inquired after my friend's friend, Leonidas W. Smiley, as requested to do, and I hereunto append the result. I have a lurking suspicion that *Leonidas W.* Smiley is a myth; that my friend never knew such a personage; and that he only conjectured that, if I asked old Wheeler about him, it would remind him of his infamous *Jim* Smiley, and he would go to work and bore me nearly to death with some infernal reminiscence of him as long and tedious as it should be useless to me. If that was the design, it certainly ceeded.

I found Simon Wheeler dozing comfortably by the barroom stove of the dilapidated tavern in the ancient mining camp of Angel's, and I noticed that he was fat and bald-headed, and had an expression of winning gentleness and simplicity upon his tranquil countenance. He roused up, and gave me good-day. I told him a friend of mine had commissioned me to make some inquiries about a cherished companion of his boyhood named *Leonidas W. Smiley—Rev. Leonidas W.* Smiley—a young minister of the Gospel, who he had heard was at one time a resident of Angel's Camp. I added that if Mr. Wheeler could tell me anything about this Rev. Leonidas W. Smiley, I would feel under many obligations to him.

Simon Wheeler backed me into a corner and blockaded me there with his chair, and then sat down and reeled off the monotonous narrative which follows this paragraph. He never smiled, he never frowned, he never changed his voice from the gentle-flowing key to which he tuned his initial sentence, he never betrayed the slightest suspicion of enthusiasm; but all through the interminable narrative there ran a vein of impressive earnestness and sincerity, which showed me plainly that, so far from his imagining that there was

---

[◆]First published in the *New York Saturday Press,* November 1865; the story was revised and reprinted in *The Celebrated Jumping Frog of Calaveras County, and Other Sketches* (1867) and again in *Sketches, New and Old* (1875). In the latter version, the story is called "The 'Jumping Frog' In English. Then in French. Then Clawed back into a Civilized Language Once More, By Patient, Unremunerated Toil" and begins with the version of the text reproduced here.
[1]Twain's note instructs readers that Calaveras is pronounced *Cal-e-vá-ras.*

anything ridiculous or funny about his story, he regarded it as a really important matter, and admired its two heroes as men of transcendent genius in *finesse.* I let him go on in his own way, and never interrupted him once.

Rev. Leonidas W. H'm, Reverend Le—well, there was a feller here once by the name of *Jim* Smiley, in the winter of '49—or maybe it was the spring of '50—I don't recollect exactly, somehow, though what makes me think it was one or the other is because I remember the big flume wasn't finished when he first came to the camp; but any way, he was the curiosest man about always betting on anything that turned up you ever see, if he could get anybody to bet on the other side; and if he couldn't he'd change sides. Any way that suited the other man would suit *him*—any way just so's he got a bet, *he* was satisfied. But still he was lucky, uncommon lucky, he most always come out winner. He was always ready and laying for a chance; there couldn't be no solit'ry thing mentioned but that feller'd offer to bet on it, and take any side you please, as I was just telling you. If there was a horse-race, you'd find him flush or you'd find him busted at the end of it; if there was a dog-fight, he'd bet on it; if there was a cat-fight, he'd bet on it; if there was a chicken-fight, he'd bet on it; why, if there was two birds setting on a fence, he would bet you which one would fly first; or if there was a camp-meeting, he would be there reg'lar to bet on Parson Walker, which he judged to be the best exhorter about here, and so he was, too, and a good man. If he even seen a straddle-bug start to go anywheres, he would bet you how long it would take him to get wherever he was going to, and if you took him up, he would foller that straddle-bug to Mexico but what he would find out where he was bound for and how long he was on the road. Lots of the boys here has seen that Smiley, and can tell you about him. Why, it never made no difference to *him*—he'd bet on *any* thing—the dangdest feller. Parson Walker's wife laid very sick once, for a good while, and it seemed as if they warn't going to save her; but one morning he come in, and Smiley up and asked how she was, and he said she was considerable better—thank the Lord for his inf'nite mercy—and coming on so smart that with the blessing of Prov'dence she'd get well yet; and Smiley, before he thought says, "Well, I'll resk two-and-a-half she don't anyway."

Thish-yer Smiley had a mare—the boys called her the fifteen-minute nag, but that was only in fun, you know, because of course she was faster than that—and he used to win money on that horse, for all she was so slow and always had the asthma, or the distemper, or the consumption, or something of that kind. They used to give her two or three hundred yards start, and then pass her under way; but always at the fag end of the race she'd get excited and desperate-like, and come cavorting and straddling up, and scattering her legs around limber, sometimes in the air, and sometimes out to one side among the fences, and kicking up m-o-r-e dust, and raising m-o-r-e racket with her coughing and sneezing and blowing her nose—and *always* fetch up at the stand just about a neck ahead, as near as you could cipher it down.

And he had a little small bull-pup, that to look at him you'd think he warn't worth a cent but to set around and look ornery and lay for a chance to steal something. But as soon as money was up on him he was a different dog; his under-jaw'd begin to stick out like the fo'castle of a steamboat, and his teeth would uncover and shine like the furnaces. And a dog might tackle him and bully-rag him, and bite him, and throw him over his shoulder two or three times, and Andrew Jackson[2]—which was the name of the pup—Andrew Jackson would never let on but what *he* was satisfied, and hadn't expected nothing else—and the bets being doubled and doubled on the side all the time, till the money was all up; and then all of a sudden he would grab that other dog jest by the j'int of his hind leg and freeze to it—not chaw, you understand, but only jest grip and hang on till they throwed up the sponge, if it was a year. Smiley always come out winner on that pup, till he harnessed a dog once that didn't have no hind legs, because they'd been sawed off by a circular saw, and when the thing had gone along far enough, and the money was all up, and he come to make a snatch for his pet holt, he saw in a minute how he's been imposed on, and how the other dog had him in the door, so to speak, and he 'peared surprised, and then he looked sorter discouraged-like, and didn't try no more to win the fight, and so he got shucked out bad. He give Smiley a look, as much as to say his heart was broke, and it was *his* fault, for putting up a dog that hadn't no hind legs for him to take holt of, which was his main dependence in a fight, and then he limped off a piece and laid down and died. It was a good pup, was that Andrew Jackson, and would have made a name for hisself if he'd lived, for the stuff was in him and he had genius—I know it, because he hadn't had no opportunities to speak of, and it don't stand to reason that a dog could make such a fight as he could under them circumstances if he hadn't no talent. It always makes me feel sorry when I think of that last fight of his'n, and the way it turned out.

Well, thish-yer Smiley had rat-tarriers, and chicken cocks, and tomcats and all them kind of things, till you couldn't rest, and you couldn't fetch nothing for him to bet on but he'd match you. He ketched a frog one day, and took him home, and said he cal'lated to educate him; and so he never done nothing for three months but set in his back yard and learn that frog to jump. And you bet you he *did* learn him, too. He'd give him a little punch behind, and the next minute you'd see that frog whirling in the air like a doughnut—see him turn one summerset, or may be a couple, if got a good start, and come down flat-footed and all right, like a cat. He got him up so in the matter of ketching flies, and kep' him in practice so constant, that he'd nail a fly every time as fur as he could see him. Smiley said all a frog wanted was education, and he could do 'most anything—and I believe him. Why,

[2]Andrew Jackson (1767–1845) was a general who became the seventh president of the United States.

I've seen him set Dan'l Webster[3] down here on this floor—Dan'l Webster was the name of the frog—and sing out, "Flies, Dan'l, flies!" and quicker'n you could wink, he'd spring straight up and snake a fly off'n the counter there, and flop down on the floor again as solid as a gob of mud, and fall to scratching the side of his head with his hind foot as indifferent as if he hadn't no idea he'd been doin' any more'n any frog might do. You never see a frog so modest and straightfor'ard as he was, for all he was so gifted. And when it come to fair and square jumping on a dead level, he could get over more ground at one straddle than any animal of his breed you ever see. Jumping on a dead level was his strong suit, you understand; and when it come to that, Smiley would ante up money on him as long as he had a red. Smiley was monstrous proud of his frog, and well he might be, for fellers that had traveled and been everywheres all said he laid over any frog that ever *they* see.

Well, Smiley kep' the beast in a little lattice box, and he used to fetch him down town sometimes and lay for a bet. One day a feller—a stranger in the camp, he was—come acrost him with his box, and says:

"What might it be that you've got in the box?"

And Smiley says, sorter indifferent-like, "It might be a parrot, or it might be a canary, maybe, but it ain't—it's only just a frog."

And the feller took it, and looked at it careful, and turned it round this way and that, and says, "H'm—so 'tis. Well, what's *he* good for?"

"Well," Smiley says, easy and careless, "he's good enough for *one* thing, I should judge—he can outjump any frog in Calaveras county."

The feller took the box again, and took another long, particular look, and give it back to Smiley, and says, very deliberate, "Well," he says, "I don't see no p'ints about that frog that's any better'n any other frog."

"Maybe you don't," Smiley says. "Maybe you understand frogs and maybe you don't understand 'em; maybe you've had experience, and maybe you ain't only a amature, as it were. Anyways, I've got *my* opinion and I'll resk forty dollars that he can outjump any frog in Calaveras county."

And the feller studied a minute, and then says, kinder sad like, "Well, I'm only a stranger here, and I ain't got no frog; but if I had a frog, I'd bet you."

And then Smiley says, "That's all right—that's all right—if you'll hold my box a minute, I'll go and get you a frog." And so the feller took the box, and put up his forty dollars along with Smiley's, and set down to wait.

So he set there a good while thinking and thinking to hisself, and then he got the frog out and prized his mouth open and took a teaspoon and filled him full of quail shot—filled him pretty near up to his chin—and set him on the floor. Smiley he went to the swamp and slopped around in the mud for a

---

[3]Daniel Webster (1782–1852), senator from Massachusetts and the most famous American orator of the nineteenth century.

long time, and finally he ketched a frog, and fetched him in, and give him to this feller, and says:

"Now, if you're ready, set him alongside of Dan'l, with his forepaws just even with Dan'l's, and I'll give the word." Then he says, "One—two—three—git!" and him and the feller touched up the frogs from behind, and the new frog hopped off lively, but Dan'l give a heave, and hysted up his shoulders—so—like a Frenchman, but it warn't no use—he couldn't budge; he was planted as solid as a church, and he couldn't no more stir than if he was anchored out. Smiley was a good deal surprised, and he was disgusted too, but he didn't have no idea what the matter was, of course.

The feller took the money and started away; and when he was going out at the door, he sorter jerked his thumb over his shoulder—so—at Dan'l, and says again, very deliberate, "Well," he says, "*I* don't see no p'ints about that frog that's any better'n any other frog."

Smiley he stood scratching his head and looking down at Dan'l a long time, and at last he says, "I do wonder what in the nation that frog throw'd off for—I wonder if there ain't something the matter with him—he 'pears to look mighty baggy, somehow." And he ketched Dan'l by the nap of the neck, and hefted him, and says, "Why blame my cats if he don't weigh five pound!" and turned him upside down and he belched out a double handful of shot. And then he see how it was, and he was the maddest man—he set the frog down and took out after that feller, but he never ketched him. And—"

[Here Simon Wheeler heard his name called from the front yard, and got up to see what was wanted.] And turning to me as he moved away, he said: "Just set where you are, stranger, and rest easy—I ain't going to be gone a second."

But, by your leave, I did not think that a continuation of the history of the enterprising vagabond *Jim* Smiley would be likely to afford me much information concerning the *Rev. Leonidas W.* Smiley, and so I started away.

At the door I met the sociable Wheeler returning, and he button-holed me and recommenced:

"Well, thish-yer Smiley had a yaller one-eyed cow that didn't have no tail, only jest a short stump like a bannanner, and—"

However, lacking both time and inclination, I did not wait to hear about the afflicted cow, but took my leave.

[1865, 1867]

Literary Modernisms
Writing in America, 1914–1945

Robin Schulze

Throughout the last three decades of the nineteenth century, the pace of change in American life accelerated dramatically. Roughly one third of the continental United States was transformed from grasslands and prairie into farms and ranches. Hundreds of industrial cities sprang up, seemingly overnight and from nothing, across the country. Millions of immigrants flocked to the nation's shores eager to begin new lives. Trains carried people and goods great distances at great speeds. The railroads came to symbolize the new scale of American enterprise, as gigantic corporations began to dominate American industry. New technologies changed the ways people lived and worked. By the turn of the twentieth century, all of these transformations had placed the country and its people under unprecedented social, economic, and political stress. Some feared, in the apocalyptic spirit of the end of the century, that an overwhelmed America would simply cease to exist.

Where some saw only problems, however, others saw opportunities. The changes in American life, while frightening to many, seemed to herald the possibility of a new age of American progress. Throughout the two decades prior to World War I, a group of white, educated, middle-class Americans set out to control the unruly forces of the twentieth century. They labeled themselves "Progressives." If the frantic new energies loosed upon America might somehow be harnessed and controlled, they believed, then a new and better world would certainly result. Their efforts resulted in one of the great ages of American reform. The general spirit of change that Progressives embraced, their willingness to ask questions about how America might be made better for many, radiated outward into American culture. As then Chicago editor Floyd Dell remembered of the decade before World War I, "the atmosphere was electric" with the prospect of transformation. "Something," he concluded, "was in the air."

The first order of business for American Progressives was the idea of democracy itself. Progressives feared that America was becoming a country controlled by special interests and political machines—a land of corrupt bosses and powerless laborers who might, if they felt entirely disenfranchised, be moved to take matters into their own hands and foment class warfare of the kind brewing in Europe and Russia. In order to save democracy, Progressives reasoned, the country needed to institute some basic economic and political reforms that would help to salvage the Jeffersonian ideal of an educated populace of landed, equally enfranchised citizens. They set out to reform the political process and adapt government by the people, for the people, to the demands of the industrial age.

In order to make America safe for democracy, Progressives such as economists Richard Ely and Albert Shaw; muckraking journalists Lincoln Steffens and Upton Sinclair; social scientists Elsie Parsons and Florence Kelly; politicians Robert La Follette; and most important, "trust-busting" U.S. President, Teddy Roosevelt (1901–09), felt that government needed to assert control over American industry. Throughout the latter half of the nineteenth century, Darwin's theories of evolution by means of natural selection translated, for many economists and businessmen, into the notion of the survival of the fittest as a means of business practice. Big companies gobbled up little ones; large corporations forced small firms out of business. All was fair in the free market. What was good for the market, however, was not always good for democracy. Unchecked competition resulted in grinding poverty and horrible working conditions for laborers, as well as unprecedented labor unrest nationwide. Rather than view the American economy as a jungle filled with creatures vying for dominance that should be left to their own devices, Progressives felt the time had come to step in and control the forces that had run amok. If human beings had the power to understand evolution, Progressives reasoned, then it was their duty to direct the process toward efficient, humane, and egalitarian ends. The tidal wave of American industry and invention that had so rapidly changed the nation could, if properly channeled, bring benefits to all.

As the economic principle of laissez-faire (the principle of letting business operate without interference) lost its luster, Progressives set out to solve social problems such as poverty, crime, and vice with the aid of the laboratory. Economics, political science, sociology, psychology—the data from these new fields would provide the blueprints for modern American progress. For many educated, white, middle-class Americans of the early twentieth century, the scientific expert took the place of the man of faith as the acknowledged font of wisdom. "There is nothing accidental," wrote journalist Walter Lippmann in 1914, "in the fact that democracy in politics is the twin brother of scientific thinking. . . . They had to come together." He asserted: "As absolutism falls, science arises. It *is* self-government. For when the impulse that overthrows kings and priests and unquestioned creeds becomes self-conscious we call it science."

The spirit of investigation that permeated the nation in the decades before World War I led to whole sets of new ideas that challenged, to use Lippmann's label, the country's "unquestioned creeds." One of the first creeds to be challenged concerned the role of women. Throughout the late nineteenth century, white women began to view education as an integral part of female self-development. Eager to move beyond the domestic sphere and join the national task of reform, women entered colleges and professional schools in unprecedented numbers. By and large, the women who blazed feminist trails in the public sphere between 1880 and 1915 argued their place in the world on the basis of the special talents of their gender. If women were the acknowledged "nurturers" of the domestic realm—caregivers for children and guardians of the cleanliness and godliness of the household—then women were best suited to tend to such matters in the public realm as well. The "women's sphere" and the public sphere overlapped. On the basis of such arguments, women became social workers, industrial health specialists, child welfare advocates, doctors, and educators. They pioneered research in the fields of psychology, sociology, and anthropology. They also banded together to form female communities in settlement houses and women's colleges that nurtured and protected those women who followed in their footsteps. These "New Women" of the Progressive era made a lasting impression on America's cultural landscape. The nature and function of the "New Woman" became a hotly debated topic. It remains a testament to their energies that, by the end of World War I, the percentages of professionals, college students, and professors who were women were larger than in 1960.

Another creed that the investigative spirit of the age challenged concerned the workings of the human brain itself. Throughout the late nineteenth century, American biologists, prompted by Darwin's theories, had come to view humans as animals and the human brain as a chemical machine—a collection of switches and wires that when stimulated in certain ways would do certain things. Sensation led to feeling led to willed response. In the decade before World War I, however, scientists began to wonder if such a formulation could truly explain the stranger, more irrational forms of human behavior. The teachings of Sigmund Freud—the New Psychology—introduced scientists worldwide to the notion that human behaviors might not be a matter of conscious decision, but a result of primitive impulses and repressed, regressive drives that percolated below the surface of conscious thought. As Freud's ideas became popular currency in the Unites States in the years leading up to, and during, World War I, Americans began to think of their actions, emotions, and even their most seemingly innocuous words, in terms of the repressed motives they might reveal. Freud's ideas also did the unthinkable in that they connected the workings of the human brain, the font of wisdom, with human sexual instincts. Suddenly, sex was everywhere.

It is a testament to the openness of the Progressive era that most scientifically minded Americans viewed Freud's discoveries as a further opportunity to clear the Victorian air. If, they concluded, human actions and feelings might be better understood, they might be better controlled and directed. Bringing secrets to light, putting repressed motives "on the table," and exposing hypocrisies seemed admirable goals rather than signs of social and moral decline.

The Progressive spirit, however, had distinct limits in America. At its heart American Progressivism was bent on disseminating urban middle-class values. Reformers wished to improve the lives of America's poor and dispossessed as a corollary to wider political and economic changes, but their goals were, for the most part, assimilationist. White, middle-class people wanted to make the poor, particularly the immigrant poor, think and act as they did. They were willing to extend a helping hand to those who seemed most likely to eventually share their values. Those persons whom middle-class white Americans did not wish to assimilate—African Americans in particular—did not figure in the Progressive program. Progressive Americans also had no use for anarchists, communists, international trade unionists, and all those not willing to work within the American democratic system.

The Progressive drive in America, the sense that new solutions had to be found to new social problems, also had its limits when it came to art. Some of the nation's modernist writers grew up in Progressive households well attuned to the scientific spirit of change. Others felt the pull of the city and Progressive energies and, in search of new ideas and opportunities, left small town life behind. As they began to think of themselves as writers, however, they began to sense that America's art in no way reflected the whirl of changes—technological, political, social—that confronted the nation. The scientific Progressive spirit seemed to have no analogue in the realm of culture. As the poet and prose writer Gertrude Stein phrased the problem, "America is the mother of the twentieth century civilization, but she is now early Victorian." Harvard philosopher George Santayana echoed her complaint in 1911: "America is a young country with an old mentality . . . a survival of the beliefs and standards of the father." One half of the American consciousness, he argued, "floated gently in the backwater, while, alongside, in invention and industry and social organization the other half was leaping down a sort of Niagara Rapids." Part of the American brain, he concluded, was "all aggressive enterprise," the other "all genteel tradition." In the decade prior to World War I, young American writers began to attempt to send American culture over the falls. Their efforts set in motion the range of literature that critics now refer to as American literary modernisms.

While no set of generalizations can ever adequately describe the literature of the modernist era in America, it is useful to think of its genesis in terms of the conventions of literary genres. At the beginning of the twentieth century, most members of the American reading public expected that literature would follow certain rules. Poems, for example, would present elevated thoughts in regular patterns of rhyme and meter, and novels would tell fictional stories that mirrored traditional notions of causality and chronology: this happened, then that happened. As the creeds of American culture changed, however, writers began to sense that literature must change as well. In the light of America's rapid urbanization, the discoveries of science, the incursions of the New Woman, the changing conception of the human mind and soul, there seemed to be much to write about—so much that, for many writers, conventional modes of literary representation seemed inadequate. Prompted by the spirit of reform that permeated American life, writers began to abandon the generic literary conventions that seemed empty prescriptions, and rummage the other arts for new forms. Taking cues from the visual arts, writers experimented with the literary equivalents of Post-Impressionist techniques such as collage and the Cubist drive to display an object from a variety of different perspectives. Borrowing from music, writers attempted to create literature that could be polyphonic and poetry that would mimic the movement of the musical phrase rather than the beat of the metronome. Progressive ideas of efficiency and scientific objectivity translated, for some writers, into a hard-edged, unsentimental aesthetic that valued precision over transcendence. For others, the urge to clear the air led to attempts to make literature a less mediated expression of emotions. These writers, too, wanted to arrive at a raw truth, but of feeling.

The energy needed to push American culture out of the backwater came from a variety of places. A few writers simply concluded that, in order to write in a wholly new way to suit the new age, they needed to leave American shores to gain perspective on the gap between the rush of American life and the stodginess of American art. In 1904, Gertrude Stein, after studying psychology at Harvard and medicine at Johns Hopkins, took up permanent residence in Paris. Along with her brother Leo, she began to collect and promote the works of fine artists such as Pablo Picasso, Paul Cézanne, and Henri Matisse—Post-Impressionist painters who rejected the notion that art needed to mirror recognizable natural forms. She also set to work on her literary experiments designed to challenge the notion of proper representation in her own medium, the English language. Disrupting the conventions of English syntax, Stein's poems and prose prompted readers to imagine words themselves as objects that had properties, both visual and musical, apart from their "meaning." Her dizzying and unsettling writing, as well as her acuity in judging the works of other artists, made Stein the center of an international group of avant-garde artists in search of new languages and forms. In 1908, poet Ezra Pound escaped to London where he, like Stein in Paris, put his titanic energies to work tracking down like-minded artists of all nationalities.

He also began his search for alternative models of good verse in the works of medieval troubadour poets such as Bertran De Born (c. 1140–c. 1214) and François Villon (1431–1463). A linguist at heart, Pound, too, focused on the poet's pesky medium of language. His goal, as he put it, was to revise the "doughy mess of third-hand Keats" that American poetry had become, to wipe away the overused images and cliches of the past and make American verse more direct and sincere. In 1911, the poet Hilda (H.D.) Doolittle caught up with Pound in London and together she, Pound, and British poet Richard Aldington, began to translate American notions of efficiency into a stripped-down aesthetic of verse they dubbed "Imagism." As Pound recorded the tenets of Imagist aesthetics in his essay, "A Retrospect," the poet should attempt:

1. Direct treatment of the "thing" whether subjective or objective.
2. To use absolutely no word that does not contribute to the presentation.
3. As regarding rhythm: to compose in the sequence of the musical phrase, not in sequence of a metronome.

The result, Pound and H.D. believed, would be clear, precise verse free of rhetorical bombast. The Imagists further warned poets to "go in fear of abstractions." Rather than rely on large abstract terms to communicate inner thoughts and feelings, such as Love or Peace, poets should create images—concrete pictures painted with words that would always prove more precise representations of complex thoughts and emotions than overused abstractions. From their outposts in Paris and London, Stein, Pound, and H.D. set the artistic world thinking about the power of particular words and how writers might use them in startling and unconventional ways. Americans all, they fostered cosmopolitan and unapologetic attitudes about artistic creation generally. Art, they believed, need not pander to the American backwater consciousness. If the public did not understand or accept their creations, they would share them with a small international community of free-thinkers sympathetic to their discoveries. "All countries are equally damned," Pound declared, "and all great art is born of the metropolis (or in the metropolis): The metropolis is always accused by the peasant of 'being mad after foreign notions.'"

The majority of American writers at work before World War I, however, congregated in American cities. Those raised in the Midwest flocked to Chicago. Removed from the genteel traditions of the urban East, Chicago was, in the decades before World War I, a lively, chaotic industrial center eager to outgrow its reputation as a collection of lumber mills and slaughter houses at the edge of a big lake. It was also the fastest growing city in the world. In 1904, muckraker Lincoln Steffens described Chicago as "First in violence, deepest in dirt; loud, lawless, unlovely, . . . an overgrown gawk of a village; the 'tough' among cities, a spectacle for the nation." The problems that Chicago faced, however, also made it a hotbed of reform activity. Between 1894 and 1904, American educator, philosopher, and social scientist John Dewey taught at the University of Chicago and used the Chicago public schools as a working laboratory for his experiments in progressive education. In Dewey's wake the University of Chicago became the nation's undisputed center of sociological research, the premier think-tank to address the social problems of the industrial city. Social worker Jane Addams struggled to improve the lives of the residents of Chicago's slums from her settlement house, Hull House, and campaigned, along with her many supporters, for child labor laws and adult education for the foreign-born.

As some Progressive Chicagonians lobbied for civic improvements, others, sensing the cultural void that had driven Stein and Pound to Europe, began to argue for the importance of the arts. In 1912, Harriet Monroe, a struggling poet and journalist well-connected with Chicago's civic leaders, started a little magazine called *Poetry: A Magazine of Verse*. Monroe loved her city, but she believed that no city, or country for that matter, could be truly great without art to match its life. Monroe was convinced, like Pound and Stein, that most artworks produced in America around the turn of the century amounted to little more than bad copies of outmoded European models. Her goal was to extend the progressive spirit to the realm of literature and give authors a place to publish new art that would both reflect and ennoble a new age. She reasoned that Chicago, itself a sprawling, unformed mass of humanity, physically and psychologically distant from the Europeanized social rituals of New York, Boston, and Philadelphia, was the perfect venue for an American artistic revolution.

During *Poetry*'s first four years, Monroe introduced the American public to many of the American poets whose works seemed distinctly different from those of their more conservative contemporaries. In 1912, Carl Sandburg came to Chicago to work as a journalist for the *Socialist Chicago Evening World*. After two years amid the urban tumult, he published the first of his *Chicago Poems* in *Poetry*, lyrics of urban life that his peers deemed a breakthrough in American verse. In 1912, Vachel Lindsay began to share his work with the *Poetry* magazine crowd, moving back and forth between Chicago and his home in Springfield, Illinois. In January 1913, Monroe published his "General William Booth Enters into Heaven," a poem set to music and drumbeats that made Lindsay a literary celebrity. In 1912, Hilda Doolittle's and Ezra Pound's free verse Imagist poems first made landfall in American in Monroe's magazine along with the Imagist manifesto that gave American poets new rules for writing. Pound found an ally in Monroe and took up duties as her "foreign correspondent." In 1912, poet Robert Frost made his important dip into literary London where he met Pound and found a British publisher for his first two volumes of verse. Pound, in turn, passed Frost's poems back across the Atlantic to Monroe for publication in Chicago. A friend of Pound's from his early days at the University of Pennsylvania, poet William Carlos Williams first sent his verse to Monroe in 1913. In 1914, Edgar Lee Masters, a Chicago lawyer, began to publish his haunting psychological studies of small town life, the poems of *Spoon River Anthology*, in *Reedy's Mirror* under the pseudonym "Webster Ford." Monroe reprinted a series of the *Spoon River* poems that same year and became one of Masters's biggest champions. In 1915, Monroe gave her American audience its first taste of the unconventional and musical work of T.S. Eliot when she published "The Love Song of J. Alfred Prufrock."

Monroe's progressive experiment in creating a national literary culture on the prairie existed side by side and mixed freely with other experiments. In the years before the American entrance into World War I, Chicago seemed a big enough city to hold them all. Socialist journalist Floyd Dell came to Chicago from Davenport, Iowa, in 1909 to write for the literary review of the *Chicago Evening Post*. Suspicious of links between art and civic improvement, Dell formed the center of a group of artists, including experimental playwright Susan Glaspell, whose goals were often more socially radical than those of Monroe. In 1913, Sherwood Anderson abandoned his business career, his wife, and his family and came to Chicago with a trunk full of manuscripts determined to become a fiction writer. Floyd Dell encouraged his quest. Returning to his Ohio roots, Anderson started to publish sketches of American misfits that expressed his own conflicted sense of small town American life. Collected together in his short story sequence, *Winesburg, Ohio* (1919), Andersons' portraits broke literary ground in their poignant, often brutal, exploration of the blunted interior lives of their subjects. In 1914, Margaret Anderson, the bohemian journalist from the Dell crowd who had escaped to Chicago from Columbus, Indiana, began her assault on traditional notions of gentility in the pages of *The Little Review*. In the years before World War I, Chicago constituted America's literary Niagara Rapids.

Between 1913 and 1917, the lure of Chicago gave way to the pull of bohemian New York City. As the Midwest became more conservative and writers less anxious about succumbing to genteel European influences, artists drifted east to Greenwich Village in the south end of Manhattan, a cosmopolitan hive of activity that they hoped would remain lively in spite of the country's shifting sensibilities. The writers that the Village attracted were, for the most part, more politically and sexually radical than their Midwestern counterparts, a reaction against the limits some authors sensed in middle-class progressivism. Floyd Dell left Chicago for the Village and Max Eastman's magazine, *The Masses*, an openly socialist periodical that blended art and politics. Following Dell's lead, Margaret Anderson moved the *Little Review* to the Village in 1916. Ezra Pound followed the tide and abandoned Monroe's *Poetry* to work with Andersons' *Review* because he felt Monroe was too wedded to the creation of a uniquely American verse to suit his cosmopolitan sense of culture. Susan Glaspell and Jig Cook came to the Village and, inspired by the example of the Chicago Little Theater, started a laboratory theater troupe for the production of new American plays, The Provincetown Players. Together, Glaspell and Cook strove to encourage a uniquely American idiom in the realm of drama. They had a flare for the irreverent and cared nothing about the responses of the commercial theater audience to their work. Playwright Eugene O'Neill joined the Players in 1916, bringing with him the suitcase full of unproduced plays that would launch his career. The group also attracted William Carlos Williams, Edna Saint Vincent Millay, and Alfred Kreymborg. Kreymborg, in turn, started *Others: A Magazine of Verse, Poetry*'s most serious American competitor in the publication of experimental poems. In 1915, Marianne Moore met and befriended Kreymborg during an extended trip to New York City. *Others* provided Moore an important venue for her poems throughout her early career. Journalist, poet, and fiction writer Djuna Barnes moved to the Village that same year. Once ensconced in the Village, artists, intellectuals, and radicals flocked to socialite Mabel Dodge's salon where they read each other's work and traded ideas. Her soirees were made all the more exciting by the presence of avant-garde European artists such as Marcel Duchamp and Francis Picabia who came to New York to escape World War I, bringing with them the vibrant irrationalities of DaDaism.

By 1917, however, Greenwich Village had changed. Over the years, as it became known as a hub of bohemian activity, the Village started to attract those interested only in exploiting the liberal atmosphere rather than contributing to the community. As Guido Bruno, the editor of the little magazine *Bruno's Weekly*, remembered:

> A sort of Coney Island grew up almost overnight; the quiet of the village was disturbed. The sacred peace was broken. Money changers had invaded the holy ground. Slumming parties came nightly to "do the village." The police had to interfere very often with the "high life" in basements and cellars. Artists, writers, and old residents fled as fast as they could. And then we entered the war. More serious business called us.

War Abroad and at Home

Progressivism inspired a general sense of openness in American society. People were willing, for a brief period of time, to discuss radical ideas—political, social, and literary—in formerly conservative forums. The Socialist Party flourished and socialism seemed destined to become a major force in American politics. Trade unions and collective action groups proliferated. Women moved out of the domestic sphere and into the professions and the workplace in record numbers. In such a climate, Harriet Monroe could publish experimental poems in her magazine and still count on receiving the backing of Chicago's more conventional wealthy industrialists. The spirit of change and urban reform that so engaged America's cities in the early years of the twentieth century, however, was short-lived. In the summer of 1914, England, France, and Russia (soon to be joined by Italy) went to war with Germany and Austria-Hungary. World War I changed the nature of American culture and American life.

When the war started, Americans did not pay much attention. Consumed with their own domestic problems, Americans of all races and classes had little desire to join in what they deemed a strictly European conflict. Indeed, in 1914, very few Americans thought of themselves as directly involved in the fate of nations on the other side of the Atlantic. Many Americans had a strong sense of America's cultural and ideological separateness. The problems of an old, corrupt Europe seemed far away and none of the nation's business. Many new Americans, themselves recent immigrants from the countries caught up in the conflict, did not relish the thought of taking up arms against their kin. From the standpoint of American business, the war seemed an opportunity rather than a tragedy. A noncombatant America might grow rich supplying goods and arms to support the destructive folly of nations overseas. As the war began in the summer of 1914 and British generals promised a complete victory by Christmas, most Americans were content to ignore the war news relegated to the back pages of American newspapers.

At first, President Woodrow Wilson, a pacifist at heart, agreed with popular opinion. A political realist, he understood that the country was, at best, divided over the issue of going to war. A dedicated Progressive, Wilson also feared that all of the political and economic reforms of the past fifteen years might be undone by the social, cultural, and economic stress of the conflict. "Every reform we have won will be lost if we go into this war," Wilson declared in 1914. Unwilling to abandon his crusade against "special privilege," Wilson did not wish to switch the country's focus from domestic affairs to foreign matters. Mobilization and liberalism, the conduct of war and the free and open discussion of issues, were not, in Wilson's view, compatible ends. As late as 1916, Wilson won re-election by campaigning on the slogan, "He Kept Us Out of the War." Before he began his second term, however, Wilson had started to rethink his position. Ultimately he concluded that, with Europe at war, there could be no real peace at home. Reluctantly, he began to take tentative steps to mobilize the nation. In April 1917, he asked Congress to declare war on Germany, arguing that "The world must be made safe for democracy."

Wilson's change of heart had a profound effect on the country's Progressives. Those who had voted for Wilson because of his commitment to keep them out of the war felt profoundly betrayed. Like Wilson, they worried that a shift from domestic to foreign affairs would put an end to the country's reform spirit, erode personal freedoms, and, by virtue of the huge industrial push the country needed to wage war, throw the nation back in the hands of the big business and special interests. The more outward-looking members of the movement, on the other hand, supported the war. They viewed it as a chance with the direct intervention of the federal government to build on the reforms they had already won. The war offered opportunities for increased government control of free markets, additional perks for workers, advances in centralization and taxation to redistribute income, and improvements in both gender and race relations. Still others in the Progressive fold approved the war as a way to spread the egalitarian system of democracy throughout the world.

Whatever their reasons for either supporting or decrying the war, Progressives split over the issue of American involvement in ways that shattered the fragile network of coalitions that made extensive liberal reforms possible. In the end, the war proved the realization of Wilson's worst nightmares. As America mobilized, the governmental reform agenda that the more hopeful Progressives had imagined did not come to pass. Rather than assert governmental control over American businesses, Wilson chose a strategy of informal cooperation that resulted in unprecedented windfalls for the nation's companies. Total profits from American business climbed from $4 billion to $10 billion between 1914 and 1917. The war linked business and government more closely, but it also organized and solidified American corporate power. Rather than expand the reach of democracy, the war greatly curtailed civil liberties at home. In 1917, Wilson endorsed the Espionage Act that proscribed severe penalties for those found guilty of interfering with the draft or encouraging disloyalty to the United States. Labor unions opposed to the war, such as the Industrial Workers of the World (IWW), lost power as their members were arrested and jailed. In 1918, Wilson supplemented the Espionage Act with the Sedition Act, which extended penalties to anyone who dared to abuse the government in print. The war also put the benefits of democracy out of reach for those who wished to become American citizens. Between 1914 and 1917, fear of foreigners started the slow closing of America's borders to immigrants. The liberal agenda in the United States received a further blow in 1917 with the advent of the Russian Revolution and the Bolsheviks' rise to power. Disillusioned and anxious, Progressives inclined to distrust more radical forms of Socialism retreated from reform entirely. Those on the other end of the spectrum, angered by Wilson's failures, abandoned Progressivism and Socialism for the more radical promise of Communism. Indeed, between 1919 and 1920, the success of the Bolshevik Revolution and the establishment of two Communist parties in America triggered a full-scale "Red Scare" throughout the nation. As public anxiety grew about the stability of democracy, tolerance for political differences of all kinds decreased. Communism and Socialism became synonymous with violent revolution rather than progressive change.

The country's change of mood during the years of the war had distinct consequences for the authors who had begun their literary experiments before the conflict. Many of America's young men who had just started to think of themselves as writers welcomed the opportunity to experience the war that, as Wilson promised, would "end all wars." Ernest Hemingway, rejected by the U.S. Army because of his bad eyesight, volunteered as a Red Cross ambulance driver and shipped out to Italy in 1918. E.E. Cummings left in 1917 to drive a Red Cross ambulance in France, only to wind up in a French prison for writing letters home to the Unites States that were frankly critical of the Allied High Command. John Dos Passos served in both the French ambulance corps and the U.S. medical corps. F. Scott Fitzgerald enlisted, but the war ended before he was shipped overseas. William Faulkner joined the Royal Canadian Air Force when he did not meet the size requirements for the U.S. Army. Like Fitzgerald, Faulkner trained, but did not see action. T.S. Eliot attempted to enlist while in London, but restrictions on travel made it impossible for him to return to American shores for basic training. His fellow exile, Ezra Pound, was more circumspect. Having lived in London since 1908, Pound was horrified to witness the wholesale slaughter of the English and French artists he had come to view as his allies in the advancement of international art and culture. While other Americans tried desperately to join in the conflict, he penned obituaries and criticized the cultural depravity that had given birth to the horror.

The young American authors who made it to the front witnessed their share of death and mayhem. Perhaps the greatest shocks, however, awaited them on their return to the United States. They country that America's soldier-writers returned to did not much resemble the nation they had left. The war made certain opinions dangerous to hold in America, an uncomfortable prospect for writers who had grown used to the free exchange of radical ideas. Some of the little magazines that had fueled the artistic revolution of the Progressive era, such as *The Egoist* and *Others* had disappeared, (in 1919 and 1920, respectively), killed by the pressures of the war and the changes in public tastes. A few of the more radical organs that criticized the war, such as Max Eastman's *Masses*, had run afoul of the Sedition Act. Some of the survivors, such as the *Little Review*, began to be openly suppressed by societies organized to prevent vice. Those writers who had weathered the war years at home experienced the end of American progressive idealism as a gradual erosion, a sad slow death of national purpose that left them wondering about the true nature of the country and its supposed mission. Throughout the decade that followed, many of America's writers transmuted progressive questions about how the country should work (who should vote, who should hold office, how should those persons be chosen) into questions about America's social and cultural destiny. Who are we? How did we get here? Where are we going? Their answers to these questions formed the basis of a darker and more searching literature different from the exuberant and innovative works that defined America's Progressive moment.

The "New Negro" Movement

Throughout the first two decades of the twentieth century, African Americans struggled within the confines of an openly racist America to both define and enact their own notions of social and political progress. Mainstream American Progressivism was a white, middle-class movement dedicated to solving the economic, political, and social problems created by the country's rapid urban industrial growth. While some white reformers were willing to entertain the notion of improving the lives of African Americans, few were willing to champion African-American civic equality. For many whites, the idea of "reform" included, as the African-American leader W.E.B. Du Bois proclaimed, the removal of African Americans "from political life and consequently from the best chance of earning a living." The spirit of change in the air prompted middle-class African Americans to aggressively pursue reform on their own terms. Questions of African-American self-determination and how best to achieve that end sparked a movement that had profound consequences for modernist art.

At the turn of the twentieth century, the African-American population in America consisted of two distinctly different groups, one Southern, the other Northern. Southern African-American men worked, for the most part, as tenant farmers or unskilled industrial wage laborers. Southern African-American women worked principally as domestics. Blacks in the South existed in perpetual poverty and in constant fear of white violence. Although African-American men had voted in large numbers during the years immediately following the Civil War, by 1900 they were effectively barred from voting in the South by a range of local laws, restrictive tests, and acts of blatant intimidation. Northern blacks faired somewhat better. African-American industrial workers and domestics in the North earned significantly higher wages than their Southern counterparts. The concentration of African Americans in Northern cities created a number of black enclaves that proved havens of mutual support. African-American men in the North voted. Northern blacks had greater access to education than did Southern blacks and, by the turn of the twentieth century, a small but prosperous middle class emerged, led by an educated strata of African American professionals such as ministers, lawyers, doctors, and teachers. Northern blacks were not subjected to the daily humiliations of Southern segregation. White racism, while a ubiquitous fact of Northern life, was more subtle than the explicit political restrictions imposed by whites in the South.

Southern African Americans, however, were not utterly without power. At the turn of the twentieth century, they exercised the one right that Southern whites could not take away in the wake of slavery: They moved North. African-American migration North began as a trickle. By the years of World War I, it had become a flood. As the country geared up to enter the European conflict, jobs increased in Northern factories, coal mines, railroads, and shipyards. Between 1910 and 1920, nearly a million African Americans left the South behind for Northern cities such as Chicago, New York, Philadelphia, and Cleveland. The black author and activist James Weldon Johnson called the Great Migration "tantamount to a general strike" against the South. Those who traveled sent money home to relatives who followed. Restrictions on foreign immigration during World War I made Northern industry even more hungry for workers and willing to hire blacks.

As African Americans moved North, the dynamics of the country's industrial cities began to change. In the decade prior to World War I, two competing principal notions of the path to black equality predominated among the members of the African-American middle class. Some, in the tradition of Booker T. Washington, believed that African-American economic empowerment was the necessary precursor to black political self-determination. Once African Americans had, through mutual assistance, created an economic base indispensable to the nation, Washington's followers argued, then civil and political rights for blacks would inevitably follow. Others, in the tradition of W.E.B. Du Bois and the early National Association for the Advancement of Colored People (NAACP, founded 1909), believed that complete political and civil equality with whites should be the African-American community's immediate goal. Du Bois argued that African Americans should work to secure the education and advancement of the "talented tenth" of African Americans, the intellectual elite who would achieve equality with whites in all things and then work to secure the rights of other blacks.

By the end of World War I, however, the flood of migrants from the South and the upheavals of the war changed the nature of the African-American political conversation in the North, introducing a new, more radical element. A new group of educated, politicized blacks emerged who identified more closely with the lives and cultures of laborers—the black masses who had risked everything to reach the North. Like the followers of Booker T. Washington, they had a strong sense of inter-racial solidarity. Unlike Washington's followers, however, they had little patience with plans that delayed the possibility of first-class American citizenship. Some of these political "New Negroes" (as they dubbed themselves) extended their identification with the black masses into the potentially raceless realm of Socialist and Communist ideologies, where racial hatreds were explained in terms of the economics of class struggle. "Class first" was their motto. Their goal was to bring black and white workers together and promote class consciousness. Others were attracted to Socialist ideas, but argued that the special oppression of blacks could not be couched in purely economic terms. "Race first" was their rallying cry. Still others abandoned Socialism and became followers of Marcus Garvey and his Universal Negro Improvement Association. Garvey was a fervent Pan-African nationalist who dreamed of establishing a colony for African Americans on the African continent. His ultimate vision was that of an African empire, a massive black self-help organization that would extend its protection to African Americans at all points on the globe.

Born of the ferment, mass migrations, and relative urban African-American prosperity of the war years, political New Negroism reached its apex during the years of World War I. The conditions that had created the political realignments, however, were short-lived. In the years after the war, the New Negro movement became primarily a cultural rather than a political phenomenon. As Ernest Allen writes of the shift, "Into this political vacuum rode the cultural New Negro, proclaiming a newly discovered truth that America's racial problems would be resolved through black artistic expression." Like the political New Negroes who preceded them, the cultural New Negroes were a diverse group. One belief, however, held them all together—the notion that African-American art could have a profound impact on America's racial problems.

The aesthetic principles behind New Negro art, however, were always a hotly debated issue within the ranks, particularly in the movement's center, the bustling section of Manhattan above 125th Street known as Harlem. Throughout the years of the Great Migration, Harlem proved a key destination for Southern African Americans seeking a better life. It also beckoned young, educated blacks eager to move beyond the Victorian values of their middle-class precursors. A locus of lively cultural and political exchange, Harlem was the home of the publishing offices of *Opportunity,* the journal of the National Urban League edited by Charles S. Johnson, and *The Crisis,* the journal of the National Association for the Advancement of Colored People edited by W.E.B. Du Bois. Poet and novelist Jessie Fauset assumed the literary editorship of the *Crisis* in 1919. Although ostensibly political organs, these publications functioned under the guiding principle that the development of black art was a key component of black social uplift. Together, they offered African-American writers an unprecedented chance to share their work with a large audience. Although all of the writers involved in the movement agreed about the importance of art to the social advancement of African Americans, however, they did not always concur about just what sorts of art would best do the trick.

Most scholars of the cultural New Negro movement in Harlem describe it as bounded by two competing aesthetic notions of New Negroism that, when examined closely, have more in common than one might think. At one pole they place Du Bois and his ideas about art as a means of African-American social uplift. As members of the "talented tenth," it was the job of artists, Du Bois believed, to articulate the aspirations of an inarticulate race so that whites might hear, take notice, and change things. Du Bois saw no real contradiction between art and propaganda. He consistently urged black artists to paint elevating portraits of black life that would help to undermine white stereotypes. He encouraged African-American writers to make use of vernacular and folk materials as a means of introducing whites to the true beauty and sophistication of black culture. He also actively campaigned against the presentation of images of black "low life" that he found particularly demeaning. If whites could be made to believe in black intellectual and cultural equality, then African-American civic equality would become a possibility.

At the other pole scholars place Alain Locke, an African-American writer and intellectual with a Harvard Ph.D. in philosophy. Unlike Du Bois, Locke believed that African-American art had come of age to the point where it need not always seek to "fight social battles and compensate social wrongs" on the level of its content. In other words, Locke did not agree that art must always present "improving" images of black life. The artist must, he insisted, feel free to present whatever his or her creative impulse demanded. Locke did not abandon the notion, however, that the sheer beauty of African-American art for art's sake could be a powerful weapon in the fight for racial equality. Cultural recognition of the profound skill of black artists by whites could not help but advance the African-American quest for social justice. Nor did Locke excuse black artists of their duty to speak for the inarticulate black masses. "What stirs inarticulately in the masses is already vocal," he insisted, "on the lips of the talented few, and the future listens, however the present may shut its ears." Ultimately, Locke did not abandon many of the expectations of the propagandistic strain of New Negroism.

While the younger writers in the New Negro movement, among them Zora Neal Hurston, Countee Cullen, Jessie Fauset, Claude McKay, Jean Toomer, Sterling Brown, Helene Johnson, and Langston Hughes, happily published their work in Alain Locke's anthology, *The New Negro* (1925), as well as in *Opportunity* and the *Crisis*, they did not necessarily agree with the aesthetic principles that drove such vehicles. Claude McKay, a confirmed Socialist during his Harlem days, resented suggestions that he should "tone down" the political bent of his art for the sake of impressing a bourgeois white audience. His first book of poems, *Harlem Shadows* (1922), might have pleased with its traditional forms (particularly the sonnet), but many of McKay's angry verses directed at white racism made little attempt to offer up innocuous or improving images black life. Countee Cullen was, of course, in favor of improving the conditions of his race, but did not want his lyrical poetry reduced to African-American propaganda. Cullen wished his verse to stand as an example of artistic achievement rather than as an example of black achievement. In Cullen's view, the solution to social unity rested not in proof of African-American cultural accomplishment, but in Christian love. Zora Neale Hurston, a trained anthropologist interested in black folk culture, asserted her right to use "low" images of black life despite Du Bois's objections. Hurston argued her case under the rubric of "art for art's sake," but understood better than many of her colleagues that folk materials—tall tales, horror stories, sly jokes—constituted shared, often subversive, forms of communication that granted African Americans a sense of group identity apart from white culture. She often used her materials to explore the rituals and languages that blacks had made for themselves as a means of survival. The black masses, in Hurston's view, were not inarticulate, but sophisticated in ways that bourgeois readers did not recognize. Langston Hughes believed that if poetry was to be an agent of social change it must appeal to and portray blacks of all classes, not only the upper reaches of the black intelligentsia. Rather than absorb and imitate ideas of culture handed down by whites, African Americans, Hughes believed, needed to claim a culture of their own. Hughes turned to the expressive language of black music—jazz, blues, and spirituals—in order to celebrate and forge a sense of racial identity. Hughes asserted in his book *The Weary Blues* (1926) the right to speak about, and with, the dispossessed—to help others see the beauty, as he put it, of his own people. He also invited his readers of all races to hear and feel the pain behind the songs they found entertaining.

Regardless of tactics, the predominant spirit of the New Negro literary Renaissance was one of racial affirmation. African-American authors inscribed blackness as a source of power and joy. Throughout the literature of the New Negro movement, the desire for political self-determination echoed in a desire for cultural self-determination. Whatever strategies they used, the writers of the cultural New Negro movement made the first real inroads into white mainstream American literary culture in American history. The art that the African-American men and women writers of the age produced stands as testament to their passionate belief that art mattered and could make a difference in how people viewed the world.

The Roar of the Twenties

"The business of America is business"
—Calvin Coolidge, Thirtieth President of the United States (1923–28)

No quote so clearly speaks of the difference between the America of the Progressive era and the America of the 1920s. While Progressives worked to downplay the rapacity of American capitalism, many white middle-class Americans of the 1920s celebrated the power of the new economy. Buoyed by the worldwide need for grain in the wake of World War I and aided by the invention of labor-saving machines, American farmers began the decade with unprecedented wealth. The corporation regained its hold on the American worker and the American psyche. Instead of a country of reformers, America became a land of producers and consumers. Prosperity meant that more Americans than ever before had leisure time and pocket money. Mass advertising became a fact of American life and buying things became a civic duty. In the nation's cities, women shortened their skirts, bobbed their hair, and learned to smoke. Men learned to "get ahead" and make a "good first impression." Americans of all races and classes became addicted to the radio, cinema, and vaudeville. Automobiles, airplanes, telephones, electric lights, and phonographs became important parts of American life.

The glitter of new entertainments, the wonder of new inventions, the hum of new machines were, however, of a piece with the country's growing conservatism. Throughout the 1920s, membership in labor unions declined, as did the number of strikes nationwide. Increased restrictions on immigration to the United States culminated in the National Origins Act of 1924. The law placed a quota on immigration, limiting the annual number of immigrants from a particular nationality to two percent of the population of that group already present in the country. The quotas effectively restricted the political power of America's ethnic communities and changed the shape of ethnic life. Without newcomers to fuel the economies of ethnic enclaves in urban cities, the established inhabitants were forced to assimilate more directly into the American mainstream economy. Throughout the 1920s, African Americans in the South suffered a renewed onslaught of vicious physical violence—whippings, beatings, brandings, and lynchings—at the hands of white supremacists. By 1924, the Ku Klux Klan, active in the South and the North, had an estimated six million members in the United States.

Despite the outward trappings of bobbed hair and hiked skirts, American women, too, suffered a social backlash. In 1920, after two decades of struggle, American women finally won a federal amendment giving women the right to vote. The enfranchisement of females, however, did not translate into a change in cultural attitudes about the proper role of women. In the years before the war, a small but significant proportion of white, middle-class, educated women opted to remain unmarried and pursue lives in the public sphere. By the war years, however, male resistance to such incursions grew as more and more educated women rejected the traditional demands of domesticity. Male anxieties about changing gender roles led to a variety of strategies designed to lure women back to marriage and motherhood. Sociologists argued for a new kind of marriage that pictured men and women as companions and married sex as a form of mutual pleasure. Economists argued the importance of a mother's role as "home manager" and "purchasing agent" of the domestic sphere, granting married women greater responsibility as consumers. Medical experts and sexologists argued the eugenic need for educated women, the country's best "breeding stock," to reproduce. As a corollary to all of these arguments, the woman who chose to forego marriage and children for the sake of a career increasingly came to be seen as "abnormal." In the views of some scholars, young women of the 1920s were more likely than young women of the Progressive era to view sexual fulfillment as an important component of their liberation, an emphasis that many earlier feminists deemed a distraction from the real work of political empowerment. Throughout the 1920s, the number of women in male-dominated professions declined. The number of educated white women who married rose. The workplace and the dance hall became acceptable interludes for single women, but the popular culture of the 1920s insistently portrayed marriage as a woman's proper destination.

American writers responded to the contradictions of American culture — its fun-loving, leisure-oriented liberality coupled with its ruthless demand for conformity — in a variety of ways. Many simply left the country to join the previous generation of American exiles in Europe. America's wealth made it possible for Americans to live in financially depressed European countries on paltry sums sent from home. Others stayed in the United States and attempted to use the financial windfall to promote their artistic and cultural visions. In 1919, the wealthy young eccentric Scofield Thayer and his partner Sibley Watson bought the Chicago journal, *The Dial*, and moved it to New York with the ambitious purpose of making the magazine the premier journal of modernist art and literature in the world. The *Dial*'s deep pockets allowed many artists to finally make a living from the proceeds of their work. Flush times and the American lust for leisure also meant that experimental and established American publishers alike were more willing to take chances on work that seemed radically new. The conservative retrenchment of the nation at large, the booming economy, and the growing acceptance of social liberties that seemed more surface than substance made the literature and verse of the period seem less threatening. In the urban North, modern art began to become a valued commodity — a marker of a style and sensibility that was chic rather than dangerously radical.

In the view of many of America's writers, the situation was ironic. Much of the literature that the Roaring Twenties turned into a commodity viewed the commodification of American life with disgust. By and large, the works that artists penned either at home or abroad during the 1920s were darker and more retrospective than the exuberant, innovative creations of the Progressive era. Having discarded generic conventions and broken through to new forms during the previous decade, artists who had established themselves in the 1910s used their new techniques to reflect on the bewildering collapse of the energies that had made their earlier work possible. In 1920, Ezra Pound published his critique of his own, and London's, pre-war aesthetic failures in *Hugh Selwyn Mauberley*. Throughout the poem, Pound attacked his earlier work as hopelessly and decadently detached from current events. That same year, Edna Saint Vincent Millay published her flippant and mocking lyrics about the joys and failures of Greenwich Village bohemia, *A Few Figs from Thistles*. Many of Millay's poems chided both herself and her contemporaries for choosing pleasure over political action. In 1922, Sinclair Lewis published his scathing account of contemporary American consumerism, *Babbitt*. The lead character of the book became a symbol in the modernist era of shallow middle-class conformity and crass materialism. T.S. Eliot published his great poem about loss of purpose, *The Waste Land*, in which he extended his personal feelings of dislocation and alienation outward to the world at large. Eugene O'Neill released the primal Socialist scream of *The Hairy Ape*. In 1923, William Carlos Williams published *Spring and All*, his experimental integration of poetry and prose in which he attempted to transform images of modern life into symbols of tenuous renewal that could restore Americans to lost sources of vitality. Wallace Stevens published *Harmonium*, a book of poems that argued the absolute necessity of the lost Progressive ideal of change to the artistic process. Elmer Rice published his play *The Adding Machine* about the strange revenge of a corporate drone who, when hearing he is to be replaced by a machine, murders his boss. In 1924, Marianne Moore published *Observations*, a book of poems that questioned the ethical underpinnings of modern life and modern art. In 1925, Robinson Jeffers sadly bore witness to an American settling "in the mould of its vulgarity" in *Roan Stallion, Tamar, and Other Poems*, and Willa Cather speculated grimly on America's collapse into selfish materialism in *The Professor's House*.

Perhaps some of the darkest literature, however, came from the pens of modernists who began their careers in the wake of World War I. Many of these young men and women experienced the false promise of the war and the consequent end of American reform as a fall from grace that signaled the abrupt end of their youth. Having been so eager to get to the battlefront in 1918, novelist Ernest Hemingway ended his war experience in a Milan hospital after he nearly lost a leg (and his life) to an Austrian mortar. He then returned home to an America that had, in his view, lost all its passion and purpose. The double blow made Hemingway a determined critic of soulless American materialism. In 1926, he produced his first novel, *The Sun Also Rises*, in which he compared Spanish culture, steeped in ancient ritual, to America's fast and empty modern life. Leaving the lushness of Victorian prose behind, Hemingway made his mark with a powerful shorthand style that proved the artistic equivalent of the early twentieth century doctrine of efficiency—a modern language for modern times. Traditional critics railed against his repetitive diction and "Dick and Jane" syntax. His writing, they claimed, was better suited to the newsroom than the novel. Hemingway, however, believed that the strength of his writing resided, not in the words he penned, but in the words he held back. "I always try to write on the principle of the iceberg," he declared in a 1958 interview. "There is seven-eighths of it underwater for every part that shows. . . . Anything you know you can eliminate only strengthens your iceberg."

Throughout the second half of the decade, the mood of much of the literature created by younger modernists remained somber. In 1925, novelist F. Scott Fitzgerald immortalized the death of American Progressivism in *The Great Gatsby*. In 1926, Hart Crane published his passionately nostalgic lyrics in *White Buildings*, and Langston Hughes proclaimed both his allegiance to black vernacular traditions and his disgust for the continuing inequities of American life in *The Weary Blues*. In 1929, William Faulkner found his great subjects—the loss of the unique traditions of Southern culture and the decline of the American South into crass and heartless materialism—in the multiple narratives of *The Sound and the Fury*. American prosperity produced an outpouring of American art born of dissatisfaction.

For many artists, the second half of the 1920s only confirmed their sense of national and global decline. Throughout the 1920s, Fascism took hold in Europe. Mussolini came to power in Italy in 1922. In 1923, Hitler and the National Socialist German Worker's Party, a precursor of the Nazis, attempted to overthrow the Bavarian government. Hitler penned his political testament *Mein Kampf* (1925) while in jail for his actions and, upon his release, set about garnering the right-wing support he needed to finally take power of Germany in 1933. The 1920s also proved a worrisome decade for those sympathetic to international Communism. In 1924, Lenin died, leaving a power vacuum, that after years of political turmoil, was ultimately filled by Joseph Stalin in 1929. Stalin ruled by suppressing his political opponents and demanding the total subservience of art and culture to the demands of the state. Throughout the early 1930s, he initiated a series of bloody political purges that, by some estimates, killed one out of every five citizens in the Soviet Union. Americans also learned at mid-decade that their twenty-ninth president, Warren G. Harding (1920–23), had presided over an administration rife with graft and corruption in which several top officials had sold the power of their offices for personal gain. In 1927 Americans witnessed the sad end of the saga of two immigrant workingmen, Nicola Sacco and Bartolomeo Vanzetti. Professed anarchists and labor leaders, the men had, many believed, been charged and convicted of murder solely because of their political beliefs. Attempts to secure a retrial failed, even when a convict confessed to the crime in 1925, and the two men were executed on August 23, 1927. Still, the juggernaut of American prosperity rolled on throughout the late 1920s. By 1928, when President Herbert Hoover was elected the thirty-first president of the United States, record numbers of Americans were sinking their savings into the stock market and speculating on land deals, convinced that they too could strike it rich.

The Great Depression and Its Aftermath

The booming American economy of the late 1920s, however, proved to be a dangerous house of cards. Built on a foundation of bad debt, unchecked speculation, overproduction, and risky banking practices, the teetering edifice collapsed in 1929. In September, stock prices began to slip. By the end of October, leading stocks had lost forty percent of more of their value. Fortunes evaporated and lives were ruined. At first, many Americans who had not invested in the market believed that they would weather the financial storm unharmed. The Crash, however, had far-reaching implications that gradually enveloped the entire nation. Banks across the country began to fail, taking with them the life savings of many Americans. Without disposable income, people could not buy the goods that the nation had been producing at a record pace. American consumerism ground to a halt and businesses failed in record numbers. Those who lost their jobs in turn had no money to spend and the cycle repeated itself again and again. By the spring of 1932, unemployment in the United States had reached 12 million. By 1933, roughly one out of every three people wanting work in America was unemployed. In response to America's economic crisis, European countries, still suffering the economic effects of World War I, spiraled into even deeper depressions as global trade collapsed. The crisis overseas paved the way for the rise of Adolph Hitler's Nazi Party.

As it deepened, the Great Depression spawned an epidemic of fear, poverty, hunger, and social dislocation. People abandoned their homes and neighborhoods and took to the road in search of work. Schools closed. Makeshift towns of cardboard boxes and plywood, dubbed Hoovervilles, sprung up on the outskirts of America's towns and cities. Food riots broke out. The Communist Party, which had lost members during the 1920s, suddenly sprang to life in the United States. Workers began to talk in serious tones about a proletarian revolution in America.

In a sad conjunction of circumstances, the American climate began to fail along with the economy. Starting around 1931, the United States suffered a series of unprecedented droughts that slowly crippled the nation's agriculture. Throughout the 1920s, Midwest farmers had greatly expanded their agricultural production. Caught up in the speculative fever of the boom years, farmers plowed, planted, and harvested as much and as often as they could. Ranchers, too, abused and overgrazed their lands, depleting the soil throughout the West. Bringing agriculture and livestock to marginal lands, however, had its costs. As the Depression hit, farmers cut back on production, leaving already dry fields unplanted and fragile topsoil susceptible to wind erosion. The economic situation, combined with one of the worst sustained droughts in U.S. history (1931–35), destroyed the agricultural base of the country's midsection. Farms literally blew away, forcing farmers to abandon their lands and search for work at a time when jobs were nowhere to be found. Dust storms deposited topsoil on cities as far away as New York and Boston.

American authors, too, suffered with the rest. The Great Depression brought the heyday of the American expatriate experience to a rapid close. Without support from home to buoy their efforts abroad, many writers were forced to return to America. Others chose to leave Europe as the political environment became increasingly repressive and unstable. American publishing went into hibernation between 1931 and 1934 and the number of books produced worldwide dropped dramatically. The publishers that managed to survive were frantic to publish popular books with broad-based appeal. As a result, their tolerance for both new authors and work they considered "experimental" dropped. Americans had little money to spend on reading material and, as a result, writers found themselves without incomes.

A New Deal for America

"The money changers have fled from their high seats in the temple of our civilization. We may now restore that temple to the ancient truths."
—Franklin D. Roosevelt
Thirty-second President of the United States (1932–45)

Throughout his Administration (1928–32), Herbert Hoover consistently refused to violate the principles of self-reliance and rugged individualism that he believed had made the country great. Private charity, he thought, could solve the problems of the Depression. Government had no place in either the daily workings of American business or the daily lives of the American people. The broad reach of human suffering, however, made rugged individualism impossible for many. Men and women who believed as strongly as Hoover in the individualist creeds of American culture made their way to bread lines and soup kitchens, ashamed of themselves and their circumstances. "The cold truth," historian Charles Beard announced in 1931, "is that the individualist creed of everybody for himself and the devil take the hindmost is principally responsible for the distress in which Western civilization finds itself. . . . Whatever merits the creed may have had in days of primitive agriculture and industry, it is not applicable in an age of technology, science, and rationalized economy." As the Depression worsened, Americans grew increasingly frustrated with Hoover's apparent lack of action and with the inflexible notions of self-reliance that underlay his reluctance to intervene.

In 1932, Americans voiced their opinion of Hoover by voting him out of office and voting in Franklin D. Roosevelt, who promised Americans a "New Deal." Roosevelt's New Deal amounted to nothing less than a sweeping reappraisal of the role of government in American life. The programs and policies of the New Deal pushed America closer to Socialism than it had ever ventured before. During the first one hundred days of his presidency, Roosevelt's Administration initiated more legislation than any administration in the country's history. The Federal Relief Administration granted emergency funds to those in need. The Civil Works Administration and the Public Works Administration gave people jobs building roads, schools, bridges, parks, and sewers. The Tennessee Valley Authority gave people employment developing the resources of the Tennessee River Valley and bringing electricity to the South. The Civilian Conservation Corps put people to work in the national forests, parks, and other public lands. The National Recovery Administration attempted to bring prices and wages under federal control. The Agricultural Adjustment Administration provided aid to farmers and regulated crop production. The Social Security Act created America's nest egg. The Wagner Act guaranteed the right of labor unions to bargain collectively through their own representatives.

Where Hoover's policies placed faith in the ideal of individual initiative, Roosevelt's policies were rooted in his belief that it was the job of government to provide the greatest good for the greatest number of Americans. Hoover looked at the country and saw individuals; Roosevelt looked at the country and saw individuals who, for the good of the nation, needed to learn to work as a group. Throughout the 1930s, Americans embraced collective action in a number of forms. Labor unions, which had languished during the 1920s, swelled to record numbers. Auto workers, textile workers, meat packers, dock workers, and seamen took advantage of the protections of the Wagner Act, organized, and made their presence felt. Farmers joined cooperatives and mutual aid societies. Even black sharecroppers, perhaps the most dispossessed group of workers in the country, sought to unionize. Roosevelt tried, through his printed addresses and "fireside chats," to promote the idea that Americans, despite their differences and regional particularities, were the citizens of one nation with common hardships and common dreams.

Roosevelt also put the nation's writers to work. In 1935, he signed legislation that created the Works Progress Administration, a massive jobs program that included the Federal Art Project, the Federal Music Project, the Federal Theater Project, and the Federal Writers Project. At a time in American history when many viewed artists with suspicion and deemed art a frivolous luxury, the government decided to pay artists a living wage for doing what they did best. When queried directly about why he supported such programs, the head of the Works Progress Agency, Harry Hopkins, responded "Hell! They've got to eat just like other people." Throughout the late 1930s, African Americans in particular benefited due to the government's willingness to hire blacks as well as whites. Zora Neal Hurston, Richard Wright, and Sterling Brown all contributed to Federal Projects.

For many of America's authors, the problems wrought by the Great Depression were not only economic, but artistic and cultural. How, writers wondered, should they write in a world so changed? Throughout the 1930s, artists hotly debated questions about the relationship between aesthetics and politics. What was the role of art in desperately hard times? Did artists have a responsibility to anyone but themselves and their creations? The response of America's writers to such questions in the context of the changing public ethos of the period were varied. The Depression inspired some to make clearer connections between the substance of their art and their political beliefs. A number of radicals on the far left argued that art should be used as a weapon of class warfare. Throughout the early 1930s, poet Langston Hughes traveled in the Soviet Union and penned verses in support of proletarian revolution. Critic and author Michael Gold published his Communist literary manifesto, "Towards Proletarian Art," in the *New Masses.* His piece argued that literature should picture the lives of working people, embody social themes, and inspire the revolutionary spirit. Clifford Odets earned his reputation as the foremost proletarian playwright of his day when his plays *Waiting for Lefty* and *Awake and Sing* both enjoyed popular productions in New York in 1935. Deeply affected by the plight of striking textile workers, Sherwood Anderson declared himself a Communist and turned his energies to writing journalistic commentaries in support of laborers. Poet Genevieve Taggard published her most radically political and didactic volume, *Calling Western Union* (1936). Her poems bore witness to the failure of farms, the death of children, and the attempts of striking Vermont quarry workers to gain a decent wage. Richard Wright joined the Communist Party and published his first book, a collection of four novellas titled *Uncle Tom's Children* (1938). His starkly naturalistic approach to fiction granted his readers a politicized vision of the effects of American racism.

Other writers not directly committed to a proletarian agenda were nonetheless effected by the times. In 1935, Wallace Stevens published his ruminations on the proper relationship between the poet's imagination and the stresses of the actual world in the poems of *Ideas of Order*. Between 1933 and 1937, Ernest Hemingway struggled to write his fourth novel, *To Have and Have Not*, in which he attempted to address the economic and social discrepancies between rich and poor in America. Throughout the early 1930s, Marianne Moore wrote a series of poems that T.S. Eliot later dubbed as her "animalies," portraits of her animals that often doubled as lessons in resilience and resistance in the face of hardships and aggression. Novelist Katherine

Anne Porter penned chilling accounts of the consequences of human apathy in "Flowering Judas" and "Noon Wine," and William Faulkner reflected with increasing intensity on the tragic failures of the American South. In 1936, the *San Francisco News* hired John Steinbeck to report on the living conditions of people pouring into California to escape the ravages of the Dust Bowl. His seven-part investigative series outlining the exploitation of the migrant laborers, "The Harvest Gypsies," formed the backdrop for his poignant epic novel, *The Grapes of Wrath* (1939).

By the end of the 1930s, America had almost fully recovered from the ravages of the Depression. The country did not regain complete economic health, however, until Roosevelt began to mobilize the nation for a second, and far more bloody, World War. The cultural stresses of World War II and its aftermath again changed the nation and its art. For those writers who had lived through the first war, the second seemed almost too much to bear. Hemingway watched in horror as his beloved Spain fell under Francisco Franco's Fascist control (with the help of Hitler's war machine) in 1939. By 1941, the Nazi blitz had gobbled up Czechoslovakia, Poland, Norway, Denmark, Belgium, Holland, Greece, Yugoslavia, and France. In December 1941, the Japanese bombed Pearl Harbor, and Roosevelt, who had anticipated the need for America to enter the conflict, declared war on Japan. In turn, Japan's allies, Italy and Germany, declared war on the United States. Before the war finally ended in 1945, America had lost 300,000 citizens. The world had lost, by some estimates, 30 million. The writers who survived the war to write about it had a terrifying new cultural and psychic landscape to draw upon, filled with fire storms, concentration camps, and the atom bomb. The literature they created reflected a new and frightening reality.

Literature of the 20th Century (1900-1945)

The Love Song of J. Alfred Prufrock*

T. S. ELIOT

S'io credessi che mia risposta fosse
a persona che mai tornasse al mondo,
questa fiamma staria senza più scosse.
Ma per ciò che giammai di questo fondo
non tornò vivo alcun, s'i'odo il vero,
senza tema d'infamia ti rispondo.[1]

Let us go then, you and I,
When the evening is spread out against the sky
Like a patient etherised upon a table;
Let us go, through certain half-deserted streets,
The muttering retreats   5
Of restless nights in one-night cheap hotels
And sawdust restaurants with oyster-shells:
Streets that follow like a tedious argument
Of insidious intent
To lead you to an overwhelming question. . .   10
Oh, do not ask, 'What is it?'
Let us go and make our visit.

---

*"The Love Song of J. Alfred Prufrock" first appeared in *Poetry: A Magazine of Verse* in June 1915. Eliot first collected the poem in *Prufrock and Other Observations* (1917).

[1]"If I thought my answer were to one who would ever return to the world, this flame should stay without another movement; but since none ever returned alive from this depth, if what I hear is true, I answer thee without fear of infamy." Eliot's epigraph comes from Canto 27 of Dante's *Inferno,* in which Dante visits the eighth circle of hell reserved for evil counselors. The words are uttered by Count Guido de Montefeltrano, also known in Dante's time as "The Fox." Montefeltrano is condemned to burn in a prison of fire because of his destructive advice to Pope Boniface. A brilliant political and military tactician, Guido, in his youth, led troops against the Papacy and was excommunicated. He then repented his sins and retired to a monastery. The corrupt Pope Boniface, however, lured Guido out of retirement by offering him reinstatement in the church in exchange for his cunning services in suppressing the Pope's enemies. Seduced by the Pope's promises of a ticket to heaven, Guido aided the Pope's corrupt designs, only to find upon his death that he had been double-crossed and sent to hell for his efforts. Dante imagines Guido as a man "taken in by his own craftiness."

In the room the women come and go
Talking of Michelangelo.[2]

The yellow fog that rubs its back upon the window-panes,   15
The yellow smoke that rubs its muzzle on the window-panes,
Licked its tongue into the corners of the evening,
Lingered upon the pools that stand in drains,
Let fall upon its back the soot that falls from chimneys,
Slipped by the terrace, made a sudden leap,   20
And seeing that it was a soft October night,
Curled once about the house, and fell asleep.

And indeed there will be time
For the yellow smoke that slides along the street
Rubbing its back upon the window-panes;   25
There will be time, there will be time
To prepare a face to meet the faces that you meet;
There will be time to murder and create,
And time for all the works and days of hands
That lift and drop a question on your plate;   30
Time for you and time for me,
And time yet for a hundred indecisions,
And for a hundred visions and revisions,
Before the taking of a toast and tea.

In the room the women come and go   35
Talking of Michelangelo.

And indeed there will be time
To wonder, 'Do I dare?' and, 'Do I dare?'
Time to turn back and descend the stair,
With a bald spot in the middle of my hair—   40
(They will say: 'How his hair is growing thin!')
My morning coat, my collar mounting firmly to the chin,
My necktie rich and modest, but asserted by a simple pin—
(They will say: 'But how his arms and legs are thin!')
Do I dare   45
Disturb the universe?
In a minute there is time
For decisions and revisions which a minute will reverse.

---

[2]Michelangelo (1475–1564), the revered Italian sculptor, painter, architect, and poet.

For I have known them all already, known them all—
Have known the evenings, mornings, afternoons,   50
I have measured out my life with coffee spoons;
I know the voices dying with a dying fall
Beneath the music from a farther room.
  So how should I presume?

And I have known the eyes already, known them all—   55
The eyes that fix you in a formulated phrase,
And when I am formulated, sprawling on a pin,
When I am pinned and wriggling on the wall,
Then how should I begin
To spit out all the butt-ends of my days and ways?   60
  And how should I presume?

And I have known the arms already, known them all—
Arms that are braceleted and white and bare
(But in the lamplight, downed with light brown hair!)
Is it perfume from a dress   65
That makes me so digress?
Arms that lie along a table, or wrap about a shawl.
  And should I then presume?
  And how should I begin?

  . . . . .

Shall I say, I have gone at dusk through narrow streets   70
And watched the smoke that rises from the pipes
Of lonely men in shirt-sleeves, leaning out of windows? . . .

I should have been a pair of ragged claws
Scuttling across the floors of silent seas.

  . . . . .

And the afternoon, the evening, sleeps so peacefully!   75
Smoothed by long fingers,
Asleep . . . tired . . . or it malingers,
Stretched on the floor, here beside you and me.
Should I, after tea and cakes and ices,
Have the strength to force the moment to its crisis?   80
But though I have wept and fasted, wept and prayed,

Though I have seen my head (grown slightly bald) brought in
    upon a platter,[3]
I am no prophet—and here's no great matter;
I have seen the moment of my greatness flicker,
And I have seen the eternal Footman hold my coat, and snicker,   85
And in short, I was afraid.

And would it have been worth it, after all,
After the cups, the marmalade, the tea,
Among the porcelain, among some talk of you and me,
Would it have been worth while,   90
To have bitten off the matter with a smile,
To have squeezed the universe into a ball
To roll it towards some overwhelming question,
To say: 'I am Lazarus,[4] come from the dead,
Come back to tell you all, I shall tell you all'—   95
If one, settling a pillow by her head,
    Should say: 'That is not what I meant at all.
    That is not it, at all.'

And would it have been worth it, after all,
Would it have been worth while,   100
After the sunsets and the dooryards and the sprinkled streets,
After the novels, after the teacups, after the skirts that trail along the
    floor—
And this, and so much more?—
It is impossible to say just what I mean!

---

[3]Prufrock's image of his own severed head upon a platter refers to the Biblical story of Salomé and John the Baptist [see Mark VI:17–28]. Salomé was the daughter of Queen Herodias who married King Herod, her former husband's brother. John the Baptist publicly disapproved the marriage and Herod, to please Herodias, had John imprisoned. Herodias hated John for his insults and wanted him dead, but Herod resisted. The daughter of Herodias by her first husband was Salomé. Salomé danced before Herod and so enticed him that he promised to give anything she wished. Prompted by her mother, Salomé asked for the head of John the Baptist on a charger. In Oscar Wilde's scandal-provoking 1894 play on the subject, Salomé lusts after John the Baptist, who refuses her sexual advances and pays with his life. Wilde also portrays John as a prophet who utters omens that neither Herod or Herodias can understand.

[4]Lazarus: Prufrock invokes Jesus' parable of Lazarus and Dives told in Luke XVI:19–31. In the parable, Dives, a rich man, ignores the suffering of a poor man, Lazarus, who begs for crumbs from Dives's table. When Lazarus dies, he goes to heaven. When Dives dies, he goes to hell and suffers horrible torments. Dives implores God to allow Lazarus to return from the dead and warn Dives's relatives to repent. God denies his request on the grounds that Lazarus's errand would be futile: "If they hear not Moses and the prophets, neither will they be persuaded, though one rose from the dead."

But as if a magic lantern[5] threw the nerves in patterns on a screen: 105
Would it have been worth while
If one, settling a pillow or throwing off a shawl,
And turning toward the window, should say:
　'That is not it at all,
　That is not what I meant, at all.'   110

　. . . . .

No! I am not Prince Hamlet,[6] nor was meant to be;
Am an attendant lord, one that will do
To swell a progress, start a scene or two,
Advise the prince; no doubt, an easy tool,
Deferential, glad to be of use,   115
Politic, cautious, and meticulous;
Full of high sentence, but a bit obtuse;
At times, indeed, almost ridiculous—
Almost, at times, the Fool.[7]

I grow old . . . I grow old . . .   120
I shall wear the bottoms of my trousers rolled.

Shall I part my hair behind? Do I dare to eat a peach?
I shall wear white flannel trousers, and walk upon the beach.
I have heard the mermaids singing, each to each.

I do not think that they will sing to me.   125

I have seen them riding seaward on the waves
Combing the white hair of the waves blown back
When the wind blows the water white and black.

We have lingered in the chambers of the sea
By sea-girls wreathed with seaweed red and brown   130
Till human voices wake us, and we drown.

　　　　　　　　　　　　　　　[1915]

---

[5]An early form of optical projector that projected enlarged still pictures from glass slides.

[6]Prince Hamlet: the protagonist of William Shakespeare's tragedy, *Hamlet.* A common interpretation of the play in Eliot's day cast Hamlet as undermined by a central flaw in his character: his crippling indecisiveness.

[7]The Fool, or jester, was a stock character of Elizabethan drama. An entertainer of the wealthy and powerful, the Fool frequently uttered truths under the guise of seemingly incomprehensible gibberish.

[so much depends]*

"The Red Wheelbarrow"

WILLIAM CARLOS WILLIAMS

---

so much depends
upon

a red wheel
barrow

glazed with rain   5
water

beside the white
chickens

[1923]

---

*[so much depends] first appeared in Williams's book *Spring and All* (1923). The book constituted an avant-garde melding of prose and poetry. Williams organized his thoughts into fanciful "chapters" that contained both exuberant essayistic paragraphs and untitled verses identified with roman numerals. [so much depends] appeared immediately before the prose statements below:

The fixed categories into which life is divided must always hold. These things are normal—essential to every activity. But they exist—but not as dead dissections.

The curriculum of knowledge cannot but be divided into the sciences, the thousand and one groups of data, scientific, philosophic or whatnot—as many as there exist in Shakespeare—things that make his appear the university of all ages.

But this is not the thing. In the galvanic category of—The same things exist, but in a different condition when energized by imagination.

The whole field of education is affected—There is no end of detail that is without significance.

Education would begin by placing in the mind of the student the nature of knowledge—in the dead state and the nature of the force which may energize it.

This would clarify his field at once—He would then see the use of data

But at present knowledge is placed before a man as if it were a stair at the top of which a DEGREE is obtained which is superlative.

nothing could be more ridiculous. To data there is no end. There is proficiency in dissection and a knowledge of parts but in the use of knowledge—

It is the imagination that—

When Williams collected the poems from the volume later in his career, he titled [so much depends] "The Red Wheelbarrow."

[anyone lived in a pretty how town]♦

E. E. CUMMINGS

anyone lived in a pretty how town
(with up so floating many bells down)
spring summer autumn winter
he sang his didn't he danced his did.

Women and men(both little and small)   5
cared for anyone not at all
they sowed their isn't they reaped their same
sun moon stars rain

children guessed(but only a few
and down they forgot as up they grew   10
autumn winter spring summer)
that noone loved him more by more

when by now and tree by leaf
she laughed his joy she cried his grief
bird by snow and stir by still   15
anyone's any was all to her

someones married their everyones
laughed their cryings and did their dance
(sleep wake hope and then)they
said their nevers they slept their dream   20

stars rain sun moon
(and only the snow can begin to explain
how children are apt to forget to remember
with up so floating many bells down)

one day anyone died i guess   25
(and noone stooped to kiss his face)
busy folk buried them side by side
little by little and was by was

all by all and deep by deep
and more by more they dream their sleep   30
noone and anyone earth by april
wish by spirit and if by yes.

Women and men(both dong and ding)
summer autumn winter spring
reaped their sowing and went their came   35
sun moon stars rain

[1940]

Big Two-Hearted River: Parts I and II[♦][1]

ERNEST HEMINGWAY

Part I

The train went on up the track out of sight, around one of the hills of burnt timber. Nick sat down on the bundle of canvas and bedding the baggage man had pitched out of the door of the baggage car. There was no town, nothing but the rails and the burned-over country. The thirteen saloons that had lined the one street of Seney had not left a trace. The foundations of the Mansion House hotel stuck up above the ground. The stone was chipped and split by the fire. It was all that was left of the town of Seney.[2] Even the surface had been burned off the ground.

Nick looked at the burned-out stretch of hillside, where he had expected to find the scattered houses of the town and then walked down the railroad track to the bridge over the river. The river was there. It swirled against the log spiles of the bridge. Nick looked down into the clear, brown water, colored from the pebbly bottom, and watched the trout keeping themselves steady in the current with wavering fins. As he watched them they changed their positions by quick angles, only to hold steady in the fast water again. Nick watched them a long time.

He watched them holding themselves with their noses into the current, many trout in deep, fast moving water, slightly distorted as he watched far down through the glassy convex surface of the pool, its surface pushing and swelling smooth against the resistance of the log-driven piles of the bridge. At the bottom of the pool were the big trout. Nick did not see them at first. Then he saw them at the bottom of the pool, big trout looking to hold themselves

---

Reprinted with permission of Scribner, a Division of Simon & Shuster, from *In Our Time* by Ernest Hemingway. Copyright © 1925 by Charles Scribner's Sons. Copyright renewed 1953 by Ernest Hemingway.

[♦]"Big Two-Hearted River: Part I" and "Big Two-Hearted River: Part II" first appeared in *This Quarter* in Spring 1925. Hemingway first collected the stories in the trade version of *In Our Time* (1925).

[1]The Two-Hearted River runs parallel to Lake Superior across the northern edge of Michigan's Upper Peninsula.

[2]The town of Seney still exists. Its present-day location is seven miles southeast of Manistique Lake on Michigan's Upper Peninsula.

on the gravel bottom in a varying mist of gravel and sand, raised in spurts by the current.

Nick looked down into the pool from the bridge. It was a hot day. A kingfisher flew up the stream. It was a long time since Nick had looked into a stream and seen trout. They were very satisfactory. As the shadow of the kingfisher moved up the stream, a big trout shot upstream in a long angle, only his shadow marking the angle, then lost his shadow as he came through the surface of the water, caught the sun, and then, as he went back into the stream under the surface, his shadow seemed to float down the stream with the current, unresisting, to his post under the bridge where he tightened facing up into the current.

Nick's heart tightened as the trout moved. He felt all the old feeling.

He turned and looked down the stream. It stretched away, pebbly-bottomed with shallows and big boulders and a deep pool as it curved away around the foot of a bluff.

Nick walked back up the ties to where his pack lay in the cinders beside the railway track. He was happy. He adjusted the pack harness around the bundle, pulling straps tight, slung the pack on his back, got his arms through the shoulder straps and took some of the pull off his shoulders by leaning his forehead against the wide band of the tump-line. Still, it was too heavy. It was much too heavy. He had his leather rod-case in his hand and leaning forward to keep the weight of the pack high on his shoulders he walked along the road that paralleled the railway track, leaving the burned town behind in the heat, and then turned off around a hill with a high, fire-scarred hill on either side onto a road that went back into the country. He walked along the road feeling the ache from the pull of the heavy pack. The road climbed steadily. It was hard work walking up-hill. His muscles ached and the day was hot, but Nick felt happy. He felt he had left everything behind, the need for thinking, the need to write, other needs. It was all back of him.

From the time he had gotten down off the train and the baggage man had thrown his pack out of the open car door things had been different. Seney was burned, the country was burned over and changed, but it did not matter. It could not all be burned. He knew that. He hiked along the road, sweating in the sun, climbing to cross the range of hills that separated the railway from the pine plains.

The road ran on, dipping occasionally, but always climbing. Nick went on up. Finally the road after going parallel to the burnt hillside reached the top. Nick leaned back against a stump and slipped out of the pack harness. Ahead of him, as far as he could see, was the pine plain. The burned country stopped off at the left with the range of hills. On ahead islands of dark pine trees rose out of the plain. Far off to the left was the line of the river. Nick followed it with his eye and caught glints of the water in the sun.

There was nothing but the pine plain ahead of him, until the far blue hills that marked the Lake Superior height of land. He could hardly see them, faint and far away in the heat-light over the plain. If he looked too steadily they were gone. But if he only half-looked they were there, the far-off hills of the height of land.

Nick sat down against the charred stump and smoked a cigarette. His pack balanced on the top of the stump, harness holding ready, a hollow molded in it from his back. Nick sat smoking, looking out over the country. He did not need to get his map out. He knew where he was from the position of the river.

As he smoked, his legs stretched out in front of him, he noticed a grasshopper walk along the ground and up onto his woolen sock. The grasshopper was black. As he had walked along the road, climbing, he had started many grasshoppers from the dust. They were all black. They were not the big grasshoppers with yellow and black or red and black wings whirring out from their black wing sheathing as they fly up. These were just ordinary hoppers, but all a sooty black in color. Nick had wondered about them as he walked, without really thinking about them. Now, as he watched the black hopper that was nibbling at the wool of his sock with its fourway lip, he realized that they had all turned black from living in the burned-over land. He realized that the fire must have come the year before, but the grasshoppers were all black now. He wondered how long they would stay that way.

Carefully he reached his hand down and took hold of the hopper by the wings. He turned him up, all his legs walking in the air, and looked at his jointed belly. Yes, it was black too, iridescent where the back and head were dusty.

"Go on, hopper," Nick said, speaking out loud for the first time. "Fly away somewhere."

He tossed the grasshopper up into the air and watched him sail away to a charcoal stump across the road.

Nick stood up. He leaned his back against the weight of his pack where it rested upright on the stump and got his arms through the shoulder straps. He stood with the pack on his back on the brow of the hill looking out across the country, toward the distant river and then struck down the hillside away from the road. Underfoot the ground was good walking. Two hundred yards down the hillside the fire line stopped. Then it was sweet fern, growing ankle high, to walk through, and clumps of jack pines; a long undulating country with frequent rises and descents, sandy underfoot and the country alive again.

Nick kept his direction by the sun. He knew where he wanted to strike the river and he kept on through the pine plain, mounting small rises to see other rises ahead of him and sometimes from the top of a rise a great solid island of pines off to his right or his left. He broke off some sprigs of the heathery sweet fern, and put them under his pack straps. The chafing crushed it and he smelled it as he walked.

He was tired and very hot, walking across the uneven, shadeless pine plain. At any time he knew he could strike the river by turning off to his left. It could not be more than a mile away. But he kept on toward the north to hit the river as far upstream as he could go in one day's walking.

For some time as he walked Nick had been in sight of one of the big islands of pine standing out above the rolling high ground he was crossing. He dipped down and then as he came slowly up to the crest of the bridge he turned and made toward the pine trees.

There was no underbrush in the island of pine trees. The trunks of the trees went straight up or slanted toward each other. The trunks were straight and brown without branches. The branches were high above. Some interlocked to make a solid shadow on the brown forest floor. Around the grove of trees was a bare space. It was brown and soft underfoot as Nick walked on it. This was the over-lapping of the pine needle floor, extending out beyond the width of the high branches. The trees had grown tall and the branches moved high, leaving in the sun this bare space they had once covered with shadow. Sharp at the edge of this extension of the forest floor commenced the sweet fern.

Nick slipped off his pack and lay down in the shade. He lay on his back and looked up into the pine trees. His neck and back and the small of his back rested as he stretched. The earth felt good against his back. He looked up at the sky, through the branches, and then shut his eyes. He opened them and looked up again. There was a wind high up in the branches. He shut his eyes again and went to sleep.

Nick woke stiff and cramped. The sun was nearly down. His pack was heavy and the straps painful as he lifted it on. He leaned over with the pack on and picked up the leather rod-case and started out from the pine trees across the sweet fern swale, toward the river. He knew it could not be more than a mile.

He came down a hillside covered with stumps into a meadow. At the edge of the meadow flowed the river. Nick was glad to get to the river. He walked upstream through the meadow. His trousers were soaked with the dew as he walked. After the hot day, the dew had come quickly and heavily. The river made no sound. It was too fast and smooth. At the edge of the meadow, before he mounted to a piece of high ground to make camp, Nick looked down the river at the trout rising. They were rising to insects come from the swamp on the other side of the stream when the sun went down. The trout jumped out of water to take them. While Nick walked through the little stretch of meadow alongside the stream, trout had jumped high out of the water. Now as he looked down the river, the insects must be settling on the surface, for the trout were feeding steadily all down the stream. As far down the long stretch as he could see, the trout were rising, making circles all down the surface of the water, as though it were starting to rain.

The ground rose, wooded and sandy, to overlook the meadow, the stretch of river and the swamp. Nick dropped his pack and rod-case and looked for a level piece of ground. He was very hungry and he wanted to make his camp before he cooked. Between two jack pines, the ground was quite level. He took the ax out of the pack and chopped out two projecting roots. That leveled a piece of ground large enough to sleep on. He smoothed out the sandy soil with his hand and pulled all the sweet fern bushes by their roots. His hands smelled good from the sweet fern. He smoothed the up-rooted earth. He did not want anything making lumps under the blankets. When he had the ground smooth, he spread his three blankets. One he folded double, next to the ground. The other two he spread on top.

With the ax he slit off a bright slab of pine from one of the stumps and split it into pegs for the tent. He wanted them long and solid to hold in the ground. With the tent unpacked and spread on the ground, the pack, leaning against a jackpine, looked much smaller. Nick tied the rope that served the tent for a ridge-pole to the trunk of one of the pine trees and pulled the tent up off the ground with the other end of the rope and tied it to the other pine. The tent hung on the rope like a canvas blanket on a clothesline. Nick poked a pole he had cut up under the back peak of the canvas and then made it a tent by pegging out the sides. He pegged the sides out taut and drove the pegs deep, hitting them down into the ground with the flat of the ax until the rope loops were buried and the canvas was drum tight.

Across the open mouth of the tent Nick fixed cheesecloth to keep out mosquitoes. He crawled inside under the mosquito bar with various things from the pack to put at the head of the bed under the slant of the canvas. Inside the tent the light came through the brown canvas. It smelled pleasantly of canvas. Already there was something mysterious and homelike. Nick was happy as he crawled inside the tent. He had not been unhappy all day. This was different though. Now things were done. There had been this to do. Now it was done. It had been a hard trip. He was very tired. That was done. He had made his camp. He was settled. Nothing could touch him. It was a good place to camp. He was there, in the good place. He was in his home where he had made it. Now he was hungry.

He came out, crawling under the cheesecloth. It was quite dark outside. It was lighter in the tent.

Nick went over to the pack and found, with his fingers, a long nail in a paper sack of nails, in the bottom of the pack. He drove it into the pine tree, holding it close and hitting it gently with the flat of the ax. He hung the pack up on the nail. All his supplies were in the pack. They were off the ground and sheltered now.

Nick was hungry. He did not believe he had ever been hungrier. He opened and emptied a can of pork and beans and a can of spaghetti into the frying pan.

"I've got a right to eat this kind of stuff, if I'm willing to carry it," Nick said. His voice sounded strange in the darkening woods. He did not speak again.

He started a fire with some chunks of pine he got with the ax from a stump. Over the fire he stuck a wire grill, pushing the four legs down into the ground with his boot. Nick put the frying pan on the grill over the flames. He was hungrier. The beans and spaghetti warmed. Nick stirred them and mixed them together. They began to bubble, making little bubbles that rose with difficulty to the surface. There was a good smell. Nick got out a bottle of tomato catchup and cut four slices of bread. The little bubbles were coming faster now. Nick sat down beside the fire and lifted the frying pan off. He poured about half the contents out into the tin plate. It spread slowly on the plate. Nick knew it was too hot. He poured on some tomato catchup. He knew the beans and spaghetti were still too hot. He looked at the fire, then at the tent, he was not going to spoil it all by burning his tongue. For years he had never enjoyed fried bananas because he had never been able to wait for them to cool. His tongue was very sensitive. He was very hungry. Across the river in the swamp, in the almost dark, he saw a mist rising. He looked at the tent once more. All right. He took a full spoonful from the plate.

"Chrise," Nick said, "Geezus Chrise," he said happily.

He ate the whole plateful before he remembered the bread. Nick finished the second plateful with the bread, mopping the plate shiny. He had not eaten since a cup of coffee and a ham sandwich in the station restaurant at St. Ignace. It had been a very fine experience. He had been that hungry before, but had not been able to satisfy it. He could have made camp hours before if he had wanted to. There were plenty of good places to camp on the river. But this was good.

Nick tucked two big chips of pine under the grill. The fire flared up. He had forgotten to get water for the coffee. Out of the pack he got a folding canvas bucket and walked down the hill, across the edge of the meadow, to the stream. The other bank was in the white mist. The grass was wet and cold as he knelt on the bank and dipped the canvas bucket into the stream. It bellied and pulled hard in the current. The water was ice cold. Nick rinsed the bucket and carried it full up to the camp. Up away from the stream it was not so cold.

Nick drove another big nail and hung up the bucket full of water. He dipped the coffee pot half full, put some more chips under the grill onto the fire and put the pot on. He could not remember which way he made coffee. He could remember an argument about it with Hopkins, but not which side he had taken. He decided to bring it to a boil. He remembered now that was Hopkins's way. He had once argued about everything with Hopkins. While he waited for the coffee to boil, he opened a small can of apricots. He liked to open cans. He emptied the can of apricots out into a tin cup. While he watched the coffee on the fire, he drank the juice syrup of the apricots, carefully at first to keep from spilling, then meditatively, sucking the apricots down. They were better than fresh apricots.

The coffee boiled as he watched. The lid came up and coffee and grounds ran down the side of the pot. Nick took it off the grill. It was a triumph for Hopkins. He put sugar in the empty apricot cup and poured some of the coffee out to cool. It was too hot to pour and he used his hat to hold the handle of the coffee pot. He would not let it steep in the pot at all. Not the first cup. It should be straight Hopkins all the way. Hop deserved that. He was a very serious coffee drinker. He was the most serious man Nick had ever known. Not heavy, serious. That was a long time ago. Hopkins spoke without moving his lips. He had played polo. He made millions of dollars in Texas. He had borrowed carfare to go to Chicago, when the wire came that his first big well had come in. He could have wired for money. That would have been too slow. They called Hop's girl the Blonde Venus. Hop did not mind because she was not his real girl. Hopkins said very confidently that none of them would make fun of his real girl. He was right. Hopkins went away when the telegram came. That was on the Black River. It took eight days for the telegram to reach him. Hopkins gave away his .22 caliber Colt automatic pistol to Nick. He gave his camera to Bill. It was to remember him always by. They were all going fishing again next summer. The Hop Head was rich. He would get a yacht and they would all cruise along the north shore of Lake Superior. He was excited but serious. They said good-bye and all felt bad. It broke up the trip. They never saw Hopkins again. That was a long time ago on the Black River.[3]

Nick drank the coffee, the coffee according to Hopkins. The coffee was bitter. Nick laughed. It made a good ending to the story. His mind was starting to work. He knew he could choke it because he was tired enough. He spilled the coffee out of the pot and shook the grounds loose into the fire. He lit a cigarette and went inside the tent. He took off his shoes and trousers, sitting on the blankets, rolled the shoes up inside the trousers for a pillow and got in between the blankets.

Out through the front of the tent he watched the glow of the fire, when the night wind blew on it. It was a quiet night. The swamp was perfectly quiet. Nick stretched under the blanket comfortably. A mosquito hummed close to his ear. Nick sat up and lit a match. The mosquito was on the canvas, over his head. Nick moved the match quickly up to it. The mosquito made a satisfactory hiss in the flame. The match went out. Nick lay down again under the blanket. He turned on his side and shut his eyes. He was sleepy. He felt sleep coming. He curled up under the blanket and went to sleep.

---

[3]A river in northern mainland Michigan that empties into Lake Huron at Cheboygan.

Part II

In the morning the sun was up and the tent was starting to get hot. Nick crawled out under the mosquito netting stretched across the mouth of the tent, to look at the morning. The grass was wet on his hands as he came out. He held his trousers and his shoes in his hands. The sun was just up over the hill. There was the meadow, the river and the swamp. There were birch trees in the green of the swamp on the other side of the river.

The river was clear and smoothly fast in the early morning. Down about two hundred yards were three logs all the way across the stream. They made the water smooth and deep above them. As Nick watched, a mink crossed the river on the logs and went into the swamp. Nick was excited. He was excited by the early morning and the river. He was really too hurried to eat breakfast, but he knew he must. He built a little fire and put on the coffee pot.

While the water was heating in the pot he took an empty bottle and went down over the edge of the high ground to the meadow. The meadow was wet with dew and Nick wanted to catch grasshoppers for bait before the sun dried the grass. He found plenty of good grasshoppers. They were at the base of the grass stems. Sometimes they clung to a grass stem. They were cold and wet with the dew, and could not jump until the sun warmed them. Nick picked them up, taking only the medium-sized brown ones, and put them into the bottle. He turned over a log and just under the shelter of the edge were several hundred hoppers. It was a grasshopper lodging house. Nick put about fifty of the medium browns into the bottle. While he was picking up the hoppers the others warmed in the sun and commenced to hop away. They flew when they hopped. At first they made one flight and stayed stiff when they landed, as though they were dead.

Nick knew that by the time he was through with breakfast they would be as lively as ever. Without dew in the grass it would take him all day to catch a bottle full of good grasshoppers and he would have to crush many of them, slamming at them with his hat. He washed his hands at the stream. He was excited to be near it. Then he walked up to the tent. The hoppers were already jumping stiffly in the grass. In the bottle, warmed by the sun, they were jumping in a mass. Nick put in a pine stick as a cork. It plugged the mouth of the bottle enough, so the hoppers could not get out and left plenty of air passage.

He had rolled the log back and knew he could get grasshoppers there every morning.

Nick laid the bottle full of jumping grasshoppers against a pine trunk. Rapidly he mixed some buckwheat flour with water and stirred it smooth, one cup of flour, one cup of water. He put a handful of coffee in the pot and dipped a lump of grease out of a can and slid it sputtering across the hot skillet. On the smoking skillet he poured smoothly the buckwheat batter. It spread like lava, the grease spitting sharply. Around the edges the buckwheat cake began to firm, then brown, then crisp. The surface was bubbling slowly to porousness. Nick pushed under the browned under surface with a fresh pine chip. He shook the skillet sideways and the cake was loose on the surface. I won't try and flop it, he thought. He slid the chip of clean wood all the way under the cake, and flopped it over onto its face. It sputtered in the pan.

When it was cooked Nick regreased the skillet. He used all the batter. It made another big flapjack and one smaller one.

Nick ate a big flapjack and a smaller one, covered with apple butter. He put apple butter on the third cake, folded it over twice, wrapped it in oiled paper and put it in his shirt pocket. He put the apple butter jar back in the pack and cut bread for two sandwiches.

In the pack he found a big onion. He sliced it in two and peeled the silky outer skin. Then he cut one half into slices and made onion sandwiches. He wrapped them in oiled paper and buttoned them in the other pocket of his khaki shirt. He turned the skillet upside down on the grill, drank the coffee, sweetened and yellow brown with the condensed milk in it, and tidied up the camp. It was a good camp.

Nick took his fly rod out of the leather rod-case, jointed it, and shoved the rod-case back into the tent. He put on the reel and threaded the line through the guides. He had to hold it from hand to hand, as he threaded it, or it would slip back through its own weight. It was a heavy, double tapered fly line. Nick had paid eight dollars for it a long time ago. It was made heavy to lift back in the air and come forward flat and heavy and straight to make it possible to cast a fly which has no weight. Nick opened the aluminum leader box. The leaders were coiled between the damp flannel pads. Nick had wet the pads at the water cooler on the train up to St. Ignace. In the damp pads the gut leaders had softened and Nick unrolled one and tied it by a loop at the end on the heavy fly line. He fastened a hook on the end of the leader. It was a small hook; very thin and springy.

Nick took it from his hook book, sitting with the rod across his lap. He tested the knot and the spring of the rod by pulling the line taut. It was a good feeling. He was careful not to let the hook bite into his finger.

He started down to the stream, holding his rod, the bottle of grasshoppers hung from his neck by a thong tied in half hitches around the neck of the bottle. His landing net hung by a hook from his belt. Over his shoulder was a long flour sack tied at each corner into an ear. The cord went over his shoulder. The sack flapped against his legs.

Nick felt awkward and professionally happy with all his equipment hanging from him. The grasshopper bottle swung against his chest. In his shirt the breast pockets bulged against him with the lunch and his fly book.

He stepped into the stream. It was a shock. His trousers clung tight to his legs. His shoes felt the gravel. The water was a rising cold shock.

Rushing, the current sucked against his legs. Where he stepped in, the water was over his knees. He waded with the current. The gravel slid under his shoes. He looked down at the swirl of water below each leg and tipped up the bottle to get a grasshopper.

The first grasshopper gave a jump in the neck of the bottle and went out into the water. He was sucked under in the whirl by Nick's right leg and came to the surface a little way down stream. He floated rapidly, kicking. In a quick circle, breaking the smooth surface of the water, he disappeared. A trout had taken him.

Another hopper poked his face out of the bottle. His antennae wavered. He was getting his front legs out of the bottle to jump. Nick took him by the head and held him while he threaded the slim hook under his chin, down through his thorax and into the last segments of his abdomen. The grasshopper took told of the hook with his front feet, spitting tobacco juice on it. Nick dropped him into the water.

Holding the rod in his right hand he let out line against the pull of the grasshopper in the current. He stripped off line from the reel with his left hand and let it run free. He could see the hopper in the little waves of the current. It went out of sight.

There was a tug on the line. Nick pulled against the taut line. It was his first strike. Holding the now living rod across the current, he brought in the line with his left hand. The rod bent in jerks, the trout pumping against the current. Nick knew it was a small one. He lifted the rod straight up in the air. It bowed with the pull.

He saw the trout in the water jerking with his head and body against the shifting tangent of the line in the stream.

Nick took the line in his left hand and pulled the trout, thumping tiredly against the current, to the surface. His back was mottled the clear, water-over-gravel color, his side flashing in the sun. The rod under his right arm, Nick stooped, dipping his right hand into the current. He held the trout, never still, with his moist right hand, while he unhooked the barb from his mouth, then dropped him back into the stream.

He hung unsteadily in the current, then settled to the bottom beside a stone. Nick reached down his hand to touch him, his arm to the elbow under water. The trout was steady in the moving stream, resting on the gravel, beside a stone. As Nick's fingers touched him, touched his smooth, cool, underwater feeling he was gone, gone in a shadow across the bottom of the stream.

He's all right, Nick thought. He was only tired.

He had wet his hand before he touched the trout, so he would not disturb the delicate mucus that covered him. If a trout was touched with a dry hand, a white fungus attacked the unprotected spot. Years before when he had fished crowded streams, with fly fishermen ahead of him and behind him, Nick had again and again come on dead trout, furry with white fungus, drifted against a rock, or floating belly up in some pool. Nick did not like to fish with other men on the river. Unless they were of your party, they spoiled it.

He wallowed down the stream, above his knees in the current, through the fifty yards of shallow water above the pile of logs that crossed the stream. He did not rebait his hook and held it in his hand as he waded. He was certain he could catch small trout in the shallows, but he did not want them. There would be no big trout in the shallows this time of day.

Now the water deepened up his thighs sharply and coldly. Ahead was the smooth dammed-back flood of water above the logs. The water was smooth and dark; on the left, the lower edge of the meadow; on the right the swamp.

Nick leaned back against the current and took a hopper from the bottle. He threaded the hopper on the hook and spat on him for good luck. Then he pulled several yards of line from the reel and tossed the hopper out ahead onto the fast, dark water. It floated down towards the logs, then the weight of the line pulled the bait under the surface. Nick held the rod in his right hand, letting the line run out through his fingers.

There was a long tug. Nick struck and the rod came alive and dangerous, bent double, the line tightening, coming out of water, tightening, all in a heavy, dangerous, steady pull. Nick felt the moment when the leader would break if the strain increased and let the line go.

The reel ratcheted into a mechanical shriek as the line went out in a rush. Too fast. Nick could not check it, the line rushing out, the reel note rising as the line ran out.

With the core of the reel showing, his heart feeling stopped with the excitement, leaning back against the current that mounted icily his thighs, Nick thumbed the reel hard with his left hand. It was awkward getting his thumb inside the fly reel frame.

As he put on pressure the line tightened into sudden hardness and beyond the logs a huge trout went high out of the water. As he jumped, Nick lowered the tip of the rod. But he felt, as he dropped the tip to ease the strain, the moment when the strain was too great; the hardness too tight. Of course, the leader had broken. There was no mistaking the feeling when all spring left the line and it became dry and hard. Then it went slack.

His mouth dry, his heart down, Nick reeled in. He had never seen so big a trout. There was a heaviness, a power not to be held, and then the bulk of him, as he jumped. He looked as broad as a salmon.

Nick's hand was shaky. He reeled in slowly. The thrill had been too much. He felt, vaguely, a little sick, as though it would be better to sit down.

The leader had broken where the hook was tied to it. Nick took it in his hand. He thought of the trout somewhere on the bottom, holding himself steady over the gravel, far down below the light, under the logs, with the hook in his jaw. Nick knew the trout's teeth would cut through the snell of the hook. The hook would imbed itself in his jaw. He'd bet the trout was angry. Anything that size would be angry. That was a trout. He had been solidly hooked. Solid as a rock. He felt like a rock, too, before he started off. By God, he was a big one. By God, he was the biggest one I ever heard of.

Nick climbed out onto the meadow and stood, water running down his trousers and out of his shoes, his shoes squlchy. He went over and sat on the logs. He did not want to rush his sensations any.

He wriggled his toes in the water, in his shoes, and got out a cigarette from his breast pocket. He lit it and tossed the match into the fast water below the logs. A tiny trout rose at the match, as it swung around in the fast current. Nick laughed. He would finish the cigarette.

He sat on the logs, smoking, drying in the sun, the sun warm on his back, the river shallow ahead entering the woods, curving into the woods, shallows, light glittering, big watersmooth rocks, cedars along the bank and white birches, the logs warm in the sun, smooth to sit on, without bark, gray to the touch; slowly the feeling of disappointment left him. It went away slowly, the feeling of disappointment that came sharply after the thrill that made his shoulders ache. It was all right now. His rod lying out on the logs. Nick tied a new hook on the leader, pulling the gut tight until it grimped into itself in a hard knot.

He baited up, then picked up the rod and walked to the far end of the logs to get into the water, where it was not too deep. Under and beyond the logs was a deep pool. Nick walked around the shallow shelf near the swamp shore until he came out on the shallow bed of the stream.

On the left, where the meadow ended and the woods began, a great elm tree was uprooted. Gone over in a storm, it lay back into the woods, its roots clotted with dirt, grass growing in them, rising a solid bank beside the stream. The river cut to the edge of the uprooted tree. From where Nick stood he could see deep channels, like ruts, cut in the shallow bed of the stream by the flow of the current. Pebbly where he stood and pebbly and full of boulders beyond; where it curved near the tree roots, the bed of the stream was marly and between the ruts of deep water green weed fronds swung in the current.

Nick swung the rod back over his shoulder and forward, and the line, curving forward, laid the grasshopper down on one of the deep channels in the weeds. A trout struck and Nick hooked him.

Holding the rod far out toward the uprooted tree and sloshing backward in the current, Nick worked the trout, plunging, the rod bending alive, out of the danger of the weeds into the open river. Holding the rod, pumping alive against the current, Nick brought the trout in. He rushed, but always came, the spring of the rod yielding to the rushes, sometimes jerking under water, but always bringing him in. Nick eased downstream with the rushes. The rod above his head he led the trout over the net, then lifted.

The trout hung heavy in the net, mottled trout back and silver sides in the meshes. Nick unhooked him; heavy sides, good to hold, big undershot jaw, and slipped him, heaving and big sliding, into the long sack that hung from his shoulders in the water.

Nick spread the mouth of the sack against the current and it filled, heavy with water. He held it up, the bottom in the stream, and the water poured out through the sides. Inside at the bottom was the big trout, alive in the water.

Nick moved downstream. The sack out ahead of him sunk heavy in the water, pulling from his shoulders. It was getting hot, the sun hot on the back of his neck.

Nick had one good trout. He did not care about getting many trout. Now the stream was shallow and wide. There were trees along both banks. The trees of the left bank made short shadows on the current in the forenoon sun. Nick knew there were trout in each shadow. In the afternoon, after the sun had crossed toward the hills, the trout would be in the cool shadows on the other side of the stream.

The very biggest ones would lie up close to the bank. You could always pick them up there on the Black. When the sun was down they all moved out into the current. Just when the sun made the water blinding in the glare before it went down, you were liable to strike a big trout anywhere in the current. It was almost impossible to fish then, the surface of the water was blinding as a mirror in the sun. Of course, you could fish upstream, but in a stream like the Black, or this, you had to wallow against the current and in a deep place, the water piled up on you. It was no fun to fish upstream with this much current.

Nick moved along through the shallow stretch watching the banks for deep holes. A beech tree grew close beside the river, so that the branches hung down into the water. The stream went back in under the leaves. There were always trout in a place like that.

Nick did not care about fishing that hole. He was sure he would get hooked in the branches.

It looked deep though. He dropped the grasshopper so the current took it under water, back in under the overhanging branch. The line pulled hard and Nick struck. The trout threshed heavily, half out of water in the leaves and branches. The line was caught. Nick pulled hard and the trout was off. He reeled in and holding the hook in his hand, walked down the stream.

Ahead, close to the left bank, was a big log. Nick saw it was hollow; pointing up river the current entered it smoothly, only a little ripple spread each side of the log. The water was deepening. The top of the hollow log was gray and dry. It was partly in shadow.

Nick took the cork out of the grasshopper bottle and a hopper clung to it. He picked him off, hooked him and tossed him out. He held the rod far out so that the hopper on the water moved into the current flowing into the hollow log. Nick lowered the rod and the hopper floated in. There was a heavy strike. Nick swung the rod against the pull. It felt as though he were hooked into the log itself, except for the live feeling.

He tried to force the fish out into the current. It came, heavily.

The line went slack and Nick thought the trout was gone. Then he saw him, very near, in the current, shaking his head, trying to get the hook out. His mouth was clamped shut. He was fighting the hook in the clear flowing current.

Looping in the line with his left hand, Nick swung the rod to make the line taut and tried to lead the trout toward the net, but he was gone, out of sight, the line pumping. Nick fought him against the current, letting him thump in the water against the spring of the rod. He shifted the rod to his left hand, worked the trout upstream, holding his weight, fighting on the rod, and then let him down into the net. He lifted him clear of the water, a heavy half circle in the net, the net dripping, unhooked him and slid him into the sack.

He spread the mouth of the sack and looked down in at the two big trout alive in the water.

Through the deepening water, Nick waded over to the hollow log. He took the sack off, over his head, the trout flopping as it came out of water, and hung it so the trout were deep in the water. Then he pulled himself up on the log and sat, the water from his trouser and boots running down into the stream. He laid his rod down, moved along to the shady end of the log and took the sandwiches out of his pocket. He dipped the sandwiches in the cold water. The current carried away the crumbs. He ate the sandwiches and dipped his hat full of water to drink, the water running out through his hat just ahead of his drinking.

It was cool in the shade, sitting on the log. He took a cigarette out and struck a match to light it. The match sunk into the gray wood, making a tiny furrow. Nick leaned over the side of the log, found a hard place and lit the match. He sat smoking and watching the river.

Ahead the river narrowed and went into a swamp. The river became smooth and deep and the swamp looked solid with cedar trees, their trunks close together, their branches solid. It would not be possible to walk through a swamp like that. The branches grew so low. You would have to keep almost level with the ground to move at all. You could not crash through the branches. That must be why the animals that lived in swamps were built the way they were, Nick thought.

He wished he had brought something to read. He felt like reading. He did not feel like going on into the swamp. He looked down the river. A big cedar slanted all the way across the stream. Beyond that the river went into the swamp.

Nick did not want to go in there now. He felt a reaction against deep wading with the water deepening up under his armpits, to hook big trout in places impossible to land them. In the swamp the banks were bare, the big cedars came together overhead, the sun did not come through, except in patches; in the fast deep water, in the half light, the fishing would be tragic. In the swamp fishing was a tragic adventure. Nick did not want it. He did not want to go down the stream any further today.

He took out his knife, opened it and stuck it in the log. Then he pulled up the sack, reached into it and brought out one of the trout. Holding him near the tail, hard to hold, alive, in his hand, he whacked him against the log. The trout quivered, rigid. Nick laid him on the log in the shade and broke the neck of the other fish the same way. He laid them side by side on the log. They were fine trout.

Nick cleaned them, slitting them from the vent to the tip of the jaw. All the insides and the gills and tongue came out in one piece. They were both males; long gray-white strips of milt, smooth and clean. All the insides clean and compact, coming out all together. Nick tossed the offal ashore for the minks to find.

He washed the trout in the stream. When he held them back up in the water they looked like live fish. Their color was not gone yet. He washed his hands and dried them on the log. Then he laid the trout on the sack spread out on the log, rolled them up in it, tied the bundle and put it in the landing net. His knife was still standing, blade stuck in the log. He cleaned it on the wood and put it in his pocket.

Nick stood up on the log, holding his rod, the landing net hanging heavy, then stepped into the water and splashed ashore. He climbed the bank and cut up into the woods, toward the high ground. He was going back to camp. He looked back. The river just showed through the trees. There were plenty of days coming when he could fish the swamp.

[1925]

Neighbour Rosicky[*]

WILLA CATHER

I

When Doctor Burleigh told neighbour Rosicky he had a bad heart, Rosicky protested.

"So? No, I guess my heart was always pretty good. I got a little asthma, maybe. Just a awful short breath when I was pitchin' hay last summer, dat's all."

"Well now, Rosicky, if you know more about it than I do, what did you come to me for? It's your heart that makes you short of breath, I tell you. You're sixty-five years old, and you've always worked hard, and your heart's tired. You've got to be careful from now on, and you can't do heavy work any more. You've got five boys at home to do it for you."

The old farmer looked up at the Doctor with a gleam of amusement in his queer triangular-shaped eyes. His eyes were large and lively, but the lids were caught up in the middle in a curious way, so that they formed a triangle. He did not look like a sick man. His brown face was creased but not wrinkled, he had a ruddy colour in his smooth-shaven cheeks and in his lips, under his long brown moustache. His hair was thin and ragged around his ears, but very little grey. His forehead, naturally high and crossed by deep parallel lines, now ran all the way up to his pointed crown. Rosicky's face had the habit of looking interested,—suggested a contented disposition and a reflective quality that was gay rather than grave. This gave him a certain detachment, the easy manner of an onlooker and observer.

"Well, I guess you ain't got no pills fur a bad heart, Doctor Ed. I guess the only thing is fur me to git me a new one."

Doctor Burleigh swung round in his desk-chair and frowned at the old farmer. "I think if I were you I'd take a little care of the old one, Rosicky."

Rosicky shrugged. "Maybe I don't know how. I expect you mean fur me not to drink my coffee no more."

"I wouldn't, in your place. But you'll do as you choose about that. I've never yet been able to separate a Bohemian from his coffee or his pipe. I've

[*]"Neighbor Rosicky" first appeared serialized in the April and May 1930 issues of *Woman's Home Companion.* Cather first collected the story in *Obscure Destinies* (1932).

quit trying. But the sure thing is you've got to cut out farm work. You can feed the stock and do chores about the barn, but you can't do anything in the fields that makes you short of breath."

"How about shelling corn?"

"Of course not!"

Rosicky considered with puckered brows.

"I can't make my heart go no longer'n it wants to, can I, Doctor Ed?"

"I think it's good for five or six years yet, maybe more, if you'll take the strain off it. Sit around the house and help Mary. If I had a good wife like yours, I'd want to stay around the house."

His patient chuckled. "It ain't no place fur a man. I don't like no old man hanging round the kitchen too much. An' my wife, she's a awful hard worker her own self."

"That's it; you can help her a little. My Lord, Rosicky, you are one of the few men I know who has a family he can get some comfort out of; happy dispositions, never quarrel among themselves, and they treat you right. I want to see you live a few years and enjoy them."

"Oh, they're good kids, all right," Rosicky assented.

The Doctor wrote him a prescription and asked him how his oldest son, Rudolph, who had married in the spring, was getting on. Rudolph had struck out for himself, on rented land. "And how's Polly? I was afraid Mary mightn't like an American daughter-in-law, but it seems to be working out all right."

"Yes, she's a fine girl. Dat widder woman bring her daughters up very nice. Polly got lots of spunk, an' she got some style, too. Da's nice, for young folks to have some style." Rosicky inclined his head gallantly. His voice and his twinkly smile were an affectionate compliment to his daughter-in-law.

"It looks like a storm, and you'd better be getting home before it comes. In town in the car?" Doctor Burleigh rose.

"No, I'm in de wagon. When you got five boys, you ain't got much chance to ride round in de Ford. I ain't much for cars, noway."

'Well, it's a good road out to your place; but I don't want you bumping around in a wagon much. And never again on a hay-rake, remember!"

Rosicky placed the Doctor's fee delicately behind the desk-telephone, looking the other way, as if this were an absent-minded gesture. He put on his plush cap and his corduroy jacket with a sheepskin collar, and went out.

The Doctor picked up his stethoscope and frowned at it as if he were seriously annoyed with the instrument. He wished it had been telling tales about some other man's heart, some old man who didn't look the Doctor in the eye so knowingly, or hold out such a warm brown hand when he said good-bye. Doctor Burleigh had been a poor boy in the country before he went away to medical school; he had known Rosicky almost ever since he could remember, and he had a deep affection for Mrs. Rosicky.

Only last winter he had had such a good breakfast at Rosicky's, and that when he needed it. He had been out all night on a long, hard confinement case at Tom Marshall's,—a big rich farm where there was plenty of stock and plenty of feed and a great deal of expensive farm machinery of the newest model, and no comfort whatever. The woman had too many children and too much work, and she was no manager. When the baby was born at last, and handed over to the assisting neighbour woman, and the mother was properly attended to, Burleigh refused any breakfast in that slovenly house, and drove his buggy—the snow was too deep for a car—eight miles to Anton Rosicky's place. He didn't know another farm-house where a man could get such a warm welcome, and such good strong coffee with rich cream. No wonder the old chap didn't want to give up his coffee!

He had driven in just when the boys had come back from the barn and were washing up for breakfast. The long table, covered with a bright oilcloth, was set out with dishes waiting for them, and the warm kitchen was full of the smell of coffee and hot biscuit and sausage. Five big handsome boys, running from twenty to twelve, all with what Burleigh called natural good manners,—they hadn't a bit of the painful self-consciousness he himself had to struggle with when he was a lad. One ran to put his horse away, another helped him off with his fur coat and hung it up, and Josephine, the youngest child and the only daughter, quickly set another place under her mother's direction.

With Mary, to feed creatures was the natural expression of affection,—her chickens, the calves, her big hungry boys. It was a rare pleasure to feed a young man whom she seldom saw and of whom she was as proud as if he belonged to her. Some country housekeepers would have stopped to spread a white cloth over the oilcloth, to change the thick cups and plates for their best china, and the wooden-handled knives for plated ones. But not Mary.

"You must take us as you find us, Doctor Ed. I'd be glad to put out my good things for you if you was expected, but I'm glad to get you any way at all."

He knew she was glad,—she threw back her head and spoke out as if she were announcing him to the whole prairie. Rosicky hadn't said anything at all; he merely smiled his twinkling smile, put some more coal on the fire, and went into his own room to pour the Doctor a little drink in a medicine glass. When they were all seated, he watched his wife's face from his end of the table and spoke to her in Czech. Then, with the instinct of politeness which seldom failed him, he turned to the Doctor and said slyly: "I was just tellin' her not to ask you no questions about Mrs. Marshall till you eat some breakfast. My wife, she's terrible fur to ask questions."

The boys laughed, and so did Mary. She watched the Doctor devour her biscuit and sausage, too much excited to eat anything herself. She drank her coffee and sat taking in everything about her visitor. She had known him when he was a poor country boy, and was boastfully proud of his success, always saying: "What do people go to Omaha for, to see a doctor, when we got the best one in the State right here?" If Mary liked people at all, she felt physical pleasure in the sight of them, personal exultation in any good fortune that came to them. Burleigh didn't know many women like that, but he knew she was like that.

When his hunger was satisfied, he did, of course, have to tell them about Mrs. Marshall, and he noticed what a friendly interest the boys took in the matter.

Rudolph, the oldest one (he was still living at home then), said: "The last time I was over there, she was lifting them big heavy milk-cans, and I knew she oughtn't to be doing it."

"Yes, Rudolph told me about that when he come home, and I said it wasn't right," Mary put in warmly. "It was all right for me to do them things up to the last, for I was terrible strong, but that woman's weakly. And do you think she'll be able to nurse it, Ed?" She sometimes forgot to give him the title she was so proud of. "And to think of your being up all night and then not able to get a decent breakfast! I don't know what's the matter with such people."

"Why, Mother," said one of the boys, "if Doctor Ed had got breakfast there, we wouldn't have him here. So you ought to be glad."

"He knows I'm glad to have him, John, any time. But I'm sorry for that poor woman, how bad she'll feel the Doctor had to go away in the cold without his breakfast."

"I wish I'd been in practice when these were getting born." The Doctor looked down the row of close-clipped heads. "I missed some good breakfasts by not being."

The boys began to laugh at their mother because she flushed so red, but she stood her ground and threw up her head. "I don't care, you wouldn't have got away from this house without breakfast. No doctor ever did. I'd have had something ready fixed that Anton could warm up for you."

The boys laughed harder than ever, and exclaimed at her: "I'll bet you would!" "She would, that!"

"Father, did you get breakfast for the doctor when we were born?"

"Yes, and he used to bring me my breakfast, too, mighty nice. I was always awful hungry!" Mary admitted with a guilty laugh.

While the boys were getting the Doctor's horse, he went to the window to examine the house plants. "What do you do to your geraniums to keep them blooming all winter, Mary? I never pass this house that from the road I don't see your windows full of flowers."

She snapped off a dark red one, and a ruffled new green leaf, and put them in his buttonhole. "There, that looks better. You look too solemn for a young man, Ed. Why don't you git married? I'm worried about you. Settin' at breakfast, I looked at you real hard, and I seen you've got some grey hairs already."

"Oh, yes! They're coming. Maybe they'd come faster if I married."

"Don't talk so. You'll ruin your health eating at the hotel. I could send your wife a nice loaf of nut bread, if you only had one. I don't like to see a young man getting grey. I'll tell you something, Ed; you make some strong black tea and keep it handy in a bowl, and every morning just brush it into your hair, an' it'll keep the grey from showin' much. That's the way I do!"

Sometimes the Doctor heard the gossipers in the drug-store wondering why Rosicky didn't get on faster. He was industrious, and so were his boys, but they were rather free and easy, weren't pushers, and they didn't always show good judgment. They were comfortable, they were out of debt, but they didn't get much ahead. Maybe, Doctor Burleigh reflected, people as generous and warm-hearted and affectionate as the Rosickys never got ahead much; maybe you couldn't enjoy your life and put it into the bank, too.

II

When Rosicky left Doctor Burleigh's office he went into the farm-implement store to light his pipe and put on his glasses and read over the list Mary had given him. Then he went into the general merchandise place next door and stood about until the pretty girl with the plucked eyebrows, who always waited on him, was free. Those eyebrows, two thin India-ink strokes, amused him, because he remembered how they used to be. Rosicky always prolonged his shopping by a little joking; the girl knew the old fellow admired her, and she liked to chaff with him.

"Seems to me about every other week you buy ticking,[1] Mr. Rosicky, and always the best quality," she remarked as she measured off the heavy bolt with red stripes.

"You see, my wife is always makin' goose-fedder pillows, an' de thin stuff don't hold in dem little down-fedders."

"You must have lots of pillows at your house."

"Sure. She makes quilts of dem, too. We sleeps easy. Now she's makin' a fedder quilt for my son's wife. You know Polly, that married my Rudolph. How much my bill, Miss Pearl?"

"Eight eighty-five."

"Chust make it nine, and put in some candy fur de women."

"As usual. I never did see a man buy so much candy for his wife. First thing you know, she'll be getting too fat."

---

[1] a strong linen or cotton fabric used for upholstering.

"I'd like dat. I ain't much fur all dem slim women like what de style is now."

"That's one for me, I suppose, Mr. Bohunk!"[2] Pearl sniffed and elevated her India-ink strokes.

When Rosicky went out to his wagon, it was beginning to snow,—the first snow of the season, and he was glad to see it. He rattled out of town and along the highway through a wonderfully rich stretch of country, the finest farms in the county. He admired this High Prairie, as it was called, and always liked to drive through it. His own place lay in a rougher territory, where there was some clay in the soil and it was not so productive. When he bought his land, he hadn't the money to buy on High Prairie; so he told his boys, when they grumbled, that if their land hadn't some clay in it, they wouldn't own it at all. All the same, he enjoyed looking at these fine farms, as he enjoyed looking at a prize bull.

After he had gone eight miles, he came to the graveyard, which lay just at the edge of his own hay-land. There he stopped his horses and sat still on his wagon seat, looking about at the snowfall. Over yonder on the hill he could see his own house, crouching low, with the clump of orchard behind and the windmill before, and all down the gentle hill-slope the rows of pale gold cornstalks stood out against the white field. The snow was falling over the cornfield and the pasture and the hay-land, steadily, with very little wind,—a nice dry snow. The graveyard had only a light wire fence about it and was all overgrown with long red grass. The fine snow, settling into this red grass and upon the few little evergreens and the headstones, looked very pretty.

It was a nice graveyard, Rosicky reflected, sort of snug and homelike, not cramped or mournful,—a big sweep all round it. A man could lie down in the long grass and see the complete arch of the sky over him, hear the wagons go by; in summer the mowing-machine rattled right up to the wire fence. And it was so near home. Over there across the cornstalks his own roof and windmill looked so good to him that he promised himself to mind the Doctor and take care of himself. He was awful fond of his place, he admitted. He wasn't anxious to leave it. And it was a comfort to think that he would never have to go farther than the edge of his own hayfield. The snow, falling over his barnyard and the graveyard, seemed to draw things together like. And they were all old neighbours in the graveyard, most of them friends; there was nothing to feel awkward or embarrassed about. Embarrassment was the most disagreeable feeling Rosicky knew. He didn't often have it,—only with certain people whom he didn't understand at all.

Well, it was a nice snowstorm; a fine sight to see the snow falling so quietly and graciously over so much open country. On his cap and shoulders, on the horses' backs and manes, light, delicate, mysterious it fell; and with it a dry cool fragrance was released into the air. It meant rest for vegetation and

---

[2]slang for a laborer from east-central Europe; Bo(hemian) + alteration of Hung(arian).

men and beasts, for the ground itself; a season of long nights for sleep, leisurely breakfasts, peace by the fire. This and much more went through Rosicky's mind, but he merely told himself that winter was coming, clucked to his horses, and drove on.

When he reached home, John, the youngest boy, ran out to put away his team for him, and he met Mary coming up from the outside cellar with her apron full of carrots. They went into the house together. On the table, covered with oilcloth figured with clusters of blue grapes, a place was set, and he smelled hot coffee-cake of some kind. Anton never lunched in town; he thought that extravagant, and anyhow he didn't like the food. So Mary always had something ready for him when he got home.

After he was settled in his chair, stirring his coffee in a big cup, Mary took out of the oven a pan of *kolache*[3] stuffed with apricots, examined them anxiously to see whether they had got too dry, put them beside his plate, and then sat down opposite him.

Rosicky asked her in Czech if she wasn't going to have any coffee.

She replied in English, as being somehow the right language for transacting business: "Now what did Doctor Ed say, Anton? You tell me just what."

"He said I was to tell you some compliments, but I forgot 'em." Rosicky's eyes twinkled.

"About you, I mean. What did he say about your asthma?"

"He says I ain't got no asthma." Rosicky took one of the little rolls in his broad brown fingers. The thickened nail of his right thumb told the story of his past.

"Well, what is the matter? And don't try to put me off."

"He don't say nothing much, only I'm a little older, and my heart ain't so good like it used to be."

Mary started and brushed her hair back from her temples with both hands as if she were a little out of her mind. From the way she glared, she might have been in a rage with him.

"He says there's something the matter with your heart? Doctor Ed says so?"

"Now don't yell at me like I was a hog in de garden, Mary. You know I always did like to hear a woman talk soft. He didn't say anything de matter wid my heart, only it ain't so young like it used to be, an' he tell me not to pitch hay or run de corn-sheller."

Mary wanted to jump up, but she sat still. She admired the way he never under any circumstances raised his voice or spoke roughly. He was city-bred, and she was country-bred; she often said she wanted her boys to have their papa's nice ways.

---

[3] a traditional Czech pastry filled with fruit.

"You never have no pain there, do you? It's your breathing and your stomach that's been wrong. I wouldn't believe nobody but Doctor Ed about it. I guess I'll go see him myself. Didn't he give you no advice?"

"Chust to take it easy like, an' stay round de house dis winter. I guess you got some carpenter work for me to do. I kin make some new shelves for you, and I want dis long time to build a closet in de boys' room and make dem two little fellers keep dere clo'es hung up."

Rosicky drank his coffee from time to time, while he considered. His moustache was of the soft long variety and came down over his mouth like the teeth of a buggy-rake over a bundle of hay. Each time he put down his cup, he ran his blue handkerchief over his lips. When he took a drink of water, he managed very neatly with the back of his hand.

Mary sat watching him intently, trying to find any change in his face. It is hard to see anyone who has become like your own body to you. Yes, his hair had got thin, and his high forehead had deep lines running from left to right. But his neck, always clean shaved except in the busiest seasons, was not loose or baggy. It was burned a dark reddish brown, and there were deep creases in it, but it looked firm and full of blood. His cheeks had a good colour. On either side of his mouth there was a half-moon down the length of his cheek, not wrinkles, but two lines that had come there from his habitual expression. He was shorter and broader than when she married him; his back had grown broad and curved, a good deal like the shell of an old turtle, and his arms and legs were short.

He was fifteen years older than Mary, but she had hardly ever thought about it before. He was her man, and the kind of man she liked. She was rough, and he was gentle,—city-bred, as she always said. They had been shipmates on a rough voyage and had stood by each other in trying times. Life had gone well with them because, at bottom, they had the same ideas about life. They agreed, without discussion, as to what was most important and what was secondary. They didn't often exchange opinions, even in Czech,—it was as if they had thought the same thought together. A good deal had to be sacrificed and thrown overboard in a hard life like theirs, and they had never disagreed as to the things that could go. It had been a hard life, and a soft life, too. There wasn't anything brutal in the short, broad-backed man with the three-cornered eyes and the forehead that went on to the top of his skull. He was a city man, a gentle man, and though he had married a rough farm girl, he had never touched her without gentleness.

They had been at one accord not to hurry through life, not to be always skimping and saving. They saw their neighbours buy more land and feed more stock than they did, without discontent. Once when the creamery agent came to the Rosickys to persuade them to sell him their cream, he told them how much money the Fasslers, their nearest neighbours, had made on their cream last year.

"Yes," said Mary, "and look at them Fassler children! Pale, pinched little things, they look like skimmed milk. I'd rather put some colour into my children's faces than put money into the bank."

The agent shrugged and turned to Anton.

"I guess we'll do like she says," said Rosicky.

III

Mary very soon got into town to see Doctor Ed, and then she had a talk with her boys and set a guard over Rosicky. Even John, the youngest, had his father on his mind. If Rosicky went to throw hay down from the loft, one of the boys ran up the ladder and took the fork from him. He sometimes complained that though he was getting to be an old man, he wasn't an old woman yet.

That winter he stayed in the house in the afternoons and carpentered, or sat in the chair between the window full of plants and the wooden bench where the two pails of drinking-water stood. This spot was called "Father's corner," though it was not a corner at all. He had a shelf there, where he kept his Bohemian papers and his pipes and tobacco, and his shears and needles and thread and tailor's thimble. Having been a tailor in his youth, he couldn't bear to see a woman patching at his clothes, or at the boys'. He liked tailoring, and always patched all the overalls and jackets and work shirts. Occasionally he made over a pair of pants one of the older boys had outgrown, for the little fellow.

While he sewed, he let his mind run back over his life. He had a good deal to remember, really; life in three countries. The only part of his youth he didn't like to remember was the two years he had spent in London, in Cheapside, working for a German tailor who was wretchedly poor. Those days, when he was nearly always hungry, when his clothes were dropping off him for dirt, and the sound of a strange language kept him in continual bewilderment, had left a sore spot in his mind that wouldn't bear touching.

He was twenty when he landed at Castle Garden in New York, and he had a protector who got him work in a tailor shop in Vesey Street, down near the Washington Market. He looked upon that part of his life as very happy. He became a good workman, he was industrious, and his wages were increased from time to time. He minded his own business and envied nobody's good fortune. He went to night school and learned to read English. He often did overtime work and was well paid for it, but somehow he never saved anything. He couldn't refuse a loan to a friend, and he was self-indulgent. He liked a good dinner, and a little went for beer, a little for tobacco; a good deal went to the girls. He often stood through an opera on Saturday nights; he could get standing-room for a dollar. Those were the great days of opera in New York, and it gave a fellow something to think about for the rest of the week. Rosicky had a quick ear, and a childish love of all the stage splendour; the scenery, the costumes, the ballet. He usually went with a chum, and after the performance they had beer and maybe some oysters somewhere. It was a fine life; for the first five years or so it satisfied him completely. He was never hungry or cold or dirty, and everything amused him: a fire, a dog fight, a parade, a storm, a ferry ride. He thought New York the finest, richest, friendliest city in the world.

Moreover, he had what he called a happy home life. Very near the tailor shop was a small furniture-factory, where an old Austrian, Loeffler, employed a few skilled men and made unusual furniture, most of it to order, for the rich German housewives up-town. The top floor of Loeffler's five-storey factory was a loft, where he kept his choice lumber and stored the odd pieces of furniture left on his hands. One of the young workmen he employed was a Czech, and he and Rosicky became fast friends. They persuaded Loeffler to let them have a sleeping-room in one corner of the loft. They bought good beds and bedding and had their pick of the furniture kept up there. The loft was low-pitched, but light and airy, full of windows, and good-smelling by reason of the fine lumber put up there to season. Old Loeffler used to go down to the docks and buy wood from South America and the East from the sea captains. The young men were as foolish about their house as a bridal pair. Zichec, the young cabinet-maker, devised every sort of convenience, and Rosicky kept their clothes in order. At night and on Sundays, when the quiver of machinery underneath was still, it was the quietest place in the world, and on summer nights all the sea winds blew in. Zichec often practised on his flute in the evening. They were both fond of music and went to the opera together. Rosicky thought he wanted to live like that for ever.

But as the years passed, all alike, he began to get a little restless. When spring came round, he would begin to feel fretted, and he got to drinking. He was likely to drink too much of a Saturday night. On Sunday he was languid and heavy, getting over his spree. On Monday he plunged into work again. So he never had time to figure out what ailed him, though he knew something did. When the grass turned green in Park Place, and the lilac hedge at the back of Trinity churchyard put out its blossoms, he was tormented by a longing to run away. That was why he drank too much; to get a temporary illusion of freedom and wide horizons.

Rosicky, the old Rosicky, could remember as if it were yesterday the day when the young Rosicky found out what was the matter with him. It was on a Fourth of July afternoon, and he was sitting in Park Place in the sun. The lower part of New York was empty. Wall Street, Liberty Street, Broadway, all empty. So much stone and asphalt with nothing going on, so many empty windows. The emptiness was intense, like the stillness in a great factory when the machinery stops and the belts and bands cease running. It was too great a change, it took all the strength out of one. Those blank buildings, without the stream of life pouring through them, were like empty jails. It struck young Rosicky that this was the trouble with big cities; they built you in from the earth itself, cemented you away from any contact with the ground. You lived in an unnatural world, like the fish in an aquarium, who were probably much more comfortable than they ever were in the sea.

On that very day he began to think seriously about the articles he had read in the Bohemian papers, describing prosperous Czech farming communities in the West. He believed he would like to go out there as a farm hand; it was hardly possible that he could ever have land of his own. His people had always been workmen; his father and grandfather had worked in shops. His mother's parents had lived in the country, but they rented their farm and had a hard time to get along. Nobody in his family had ever owned any land,— that belonged to a different station of life altogether. Anton's mother died when he was little, and he was sent into the country to her parents. He stayed with them until he was twelve, and formed those ties with the earth and the farm animals and growing things which are never made at all unless they are made early. After his grandfather died, he went back to live with his father and stepmother, but she was very hard on him, and his father helped him to get passage to London.

After that Fourth of July day in Park Place, the desire to return to the country never left him. To work on another man's farm would be all he asked; to see the sun rise and set and to plant things and watch them grow. He was a very simple man. He was like a tree that has not many roots, but one tap-root that goes down deep. He subscribed for a Bohemian paper printed in Chicago, then for one printed in Omaha. His mind got farther and farther west. He began to save a little money to buy his liberty. When he was thirty-five, there was a great meeting in New York of Bohemian athletic societies, and Rosicky left the tailor shop and went home with the Omaha delegates to try his fortune in another part of the world.

IV

Perhaps the fact that his own youth was well over before he began to have a family was one reason why Rosicky was so fond of his boys. He had almost a grandfather's indulgence for them. He had never had to worry about any of them—except, just now, a little about Rudolph.

On Saturday night the boys always piled into the Ford, took little Josephine, and went to town to the moving-picture show. One Saturday morning they were talking at the breakfast table about starting early that evening, so that they would have an hour or so to see the Christmas things in the stores before the show began. Rosicky looked down the table.

"I hope you boys ain't disappointed, but I want you to let me have de car tonight. Maybe some of you can go in with de neighbours."

Their faces fell. They worked hard all week, and they were still like children. A new jack-knife or a box of candy pleased the older one as much as the little fellow.

"If you and Mother are going to town," Frank said, "maybe you could take a couple of us along with you, anyway."

"No, I want to take de car down to Rudolph's, and let him an' Polly go in to de show. She don't git into town enough, an' I'm afraid she's gettin' lonesome, an' he can't afford no car yet."

That settled it. The boys were a good deal dashed. Their father took another piece of apple-cake and went on: "Maybe next Saturday night de two little fellers can go along wid dem. "

"Oh, is Rudolph going to have the car every Saturday night?"

Rosicky did not reply at once; then he began to speak seriously: "Listen, boys; Polly ain't lookin' so good. I don't like to see nobody lookin' sad. It comes hard fur a town girl to be a farmer's wife. I don't want no trouble to start in Rudolph's family. When it starts, it ain't so easy to stop. An American girl don't git used to our ways all at once. I like to tell Polly she and Rudolph can have the car every Saturday night till after New Year's, if it's all right with you boys."

"Sure it's all right, Papa," Mary cut in. "And it's good you thought about that. Town girls is used to more than country girls. I lay awake nights, scared she'll make Rudolph discontented with the farm."

The boys put as good a face on it as they could. They surely looked forward to their Saturday nights in town. That evening Rosicky drove the car the half-mile down to Rudolph's new, bare little house.

Polly was in a short-sleeved gingham dress, clearing away the supper dishes. She was a trim, slim little thing, with blue eyes and shingled yellow hair, and her eyebrows were reduced to a mere brush-stroke, like Miss Pearl's.

"Good evening, Mr. Rosicky. Rudolph's at the barn, I guess." She never called him father, or Mary mother. She was sensitive about having married a foreigner. She never in the world would have done it if Rudolph hadn't been such a handsome, persuasive fellow and such a gallant lover. He had graduated in her class in the high school in town, and their friendship began in the ninth grade.

Rosicky went in, though he wasn't exactly asked. "My boys ain't goin' to town tonight, an' I brought de car over fur you two to go in to de picture show."

Polly, carrying dishes to the sink, looked over her shoulder at him. "Thank you. But I'm late with my work tonight, and pretty tired. Maybe Rudolph would like to go in with you."

"Oh, I don't go to de shows! I'm too old-fashioned. You won't feel so tired after you ride in de air a ways. It's a nice clear night, an' it ain't cold. You go an' fix yourself up, Polly, an' I'll wash de dishes an' leave everything nice fur you."

Polly blushed and tossed her bob. "I couldn't let you do that, Mr. Rosicky. I wouldn't think of it."

Rosicky said nothing. He found a bib apron on a nail behind the kitchen door. He slipped it over his head and then took Polly by her two elbows and pushed her gently toward the door of her own room. "I washed up de kitchen many times for my wife, when de babies was sick or somethin'. You go an' make yourself look nice. I like you to look prettier'n any of dem town girls when you go in. De young folks must have some fun, an' I'm goin' to look out fur you, Polly."

That kind, reassuring grip on her elbows, the old man's funny bright eyes, made Polly want to drop her head on his shoulder for a second. She restrained herself, but she lingered in his grasp at the door of her room, murmuring tearfully: "You always lived in the city when you were young, didn't you? Don't you ever get lonesome out here?"

As she turned round to him, her hand fell naturally into his, and he stood holding it and smiling into her face with his peculiar, knowing, indulgent smile without a shadow of reproach in it. "Dem big cities is all right fur de rich, but dey is terrible hard fur de poor."

"I don't know. Sometimes I think I'd like to take a chance. You lived in New York, didn't you?"

"An' London. Da's bigger still. I learned my trade dere. Here's Rudolph comin', you better hurry."

"Will you tell me about London some time?"

"Maybe. Only I ain't no talker, Polly. Run an' dress yourself up."

The bedroom door closed behind her, and Rudolph came in from the outside, looking anxious. He had seen the car and was sorry any of his family should come just then. Supper hadn't been a very pleasant occasion. Halting in the doorway, he saw his father in a kitchen apron, carrying dishes to the sink. He flushed crimson and something flashed in his eye. Rosicky held up a warning finger.

"I brought de car over fur you an' Polly to go to de picture show, an' I made her let me finish here so you won't be late. You go put on a clean shirt, quick!"

"But don't the boys want the car, Father?"

"Not tonight dey don't." Rosicky fumbled under his apron and found his pants pocket. He took out a silver dollar and said in a hurried whisper: "You go an' buy dat girl some ice cream an' candy tonight, like you was courtin'. She's awful good friends wid me."

Rudolph was very short of cash, but he took the money as if it hurt him. There had been a crop failure all over the county. He had more than once been sorry he'd married this year.

In a few minutes the young people came out, looking clean and a little stiff. Rosicky hurried them off, and then he took his own time with the dishes. He scoured the pots and pans and put away the milk and swept the kitchen. He put some coal in the stove and shut off the draughts, so the place would be warm for them when they got home late at night. Then he sat down and had a pipe and listened to the clock tick.

Generally speaking, marrying an American girl was certainly a risk. A Czech should marry a Czech. It was lucky that Polly was the daughter of a poor widow woman; Rudolph was proud, and if she had a prosperous family to throw up at him, they could never make it go. Polly was one of four sisters, and they all worked; one was book-keeper in the bank, one taught music, and Polly and her younger sister had been clerks, like Miss Pearl. All four of them were musical, had pretty voices, and sang in the Methodist choir, which the eldest sister directed.

Polly missed the sociability of a store position. She missed the choir, and the company of her sisters. She didn't dislike housework, but she disliked so much of it. Rosicky was a little anxious about this pair. He was afraid Polly would grow so discontented that Rudy would quit the farm and take a factory job in Omaha. He had worked for a winter up there, two years ago, to get money to marry on. He had done very well, and they would always take him back at the stockyards. But to Rosicky that meant the end of everything for his son. To be a landless man was to be a wage-earner, a slave, all your life; to have nothing, to be nothing.

Rosicky thought he would come over and do a little carpentering for Polly after the New Year. He guessed she needed jollying. Rudolph was a serious sort of chap, serious in love and serious about his work.

Rosicky shook out his pipe and walked home across the fields. Ahead of him the lamplight shone from his kitchen windows. Suppose he were still in a tailor shop on Vesey Street, with a bunch of pale, narrow-chested sons working on machines, all coming home tired and sullen to eat supper in a kitchen that was a parlour also; with another crowded, angry family quarrelling just across the dumb-waiter shaft, and squeaking pulleys at the windows where dirty washings hung on dirty lines above a court full of old brooms and mops and ash-cans. . . .

He stopped by the windmill to look up at the frosty winter stars and draw a long breath before he went inside. That kitchen with the shining windows was dear to him; but the sleeping fields and bright stars and the noble darkness were dearer still.

V

On the day before Christmas the weather set in very cold; no snow, but a bitter, biting wind that whistled and sang over the flat land and lashed one's face

like fine wires. There was baking going on in the Rosicky kitchen all day, and
Rosicky sat inside, making over a coat that Albert had outgrown into an overcoat for John. Mary had a big red geranium in bloom for Christmas, and a
row of Jerusalem cherry trees, full of berries. It was the first year she had ever
grown these; Doctor Ed brought her the seeds from Omaha when he went to
some medical convention. They reminded Rosicky of plants he had seen in
England; and all afternoon, as he stitched, he sat thinking about those two
years in London, which his mind usually shrank from even after all this while.

He was a lad of eighteen when he dropped down into London, with no
money and no connexions except the address of a cousin who was supposed
to be working at a confectioner's. When he went to the pastry shop, however,
he found that the cousin had gone to America. Anton tramped the streets for
several days, sleeping in doorways and on the Embankment, until he was in
utter despair. He knew no English, and the sound of the strange language all
about him confused him. By chance he met a poor German tailor who had
learned his trade in Vienna, and could speak a little Czech. This tailor, Lifschnitz, kept a repair shop in a Cheapside basement, underneath a cobbler.
He didn't much need an apprentice, but he was sorry for the boy and took
him in for no wages but his keep and what he could pick up. The pickings
were supposed to be coppers given you when you took work home to a cus-
tomer. But most of the customers called for their clothes themselves, and the
coppers that came Anton's way were very few. He had, however, a place to
sleep. The tailor's family lived upstairs in three rooms; a kitchen, a bedroom,
where Lifschnitz and his wife and five children slept, and a living-room. Two
corners of this living-room were curtained off for lodgers; in one Rosicky
slept on an old horsehair sofa, with a feather quilt to wrap himself in. The
other corner was rented to a wretched, dirty boy, who was studying the violin. He actually practised there. Rosicky was dirty, too. There was no way to
be anything else. Mrs. Lifschnitz got the water she cooked and washed with
from a pump in a brick court, four flights down. There were bugs in the
place, and multitudes of fleas, though the poor woman did the best she could.
Rosicky knew she often went empty to give another potato or a spoonful of
dripping to the two hungry, sad-eyed boys who lodged with her. He used to
think he would never get out of there, never get a clean shirt to his back
again. What would he do, he wondered, when his clothes actually dropped to
pieces and the worn cloth wouldn't hold patches any longer?

It was still early when the old farmer put aside his sewing and his recollections. The sky had been a dark grey all day, with not a gleam of sun, and the
light failed at four o'clock. He went to shave and change his shirt while the
turkey was roasting. Rudolph and Polly were coming over for supper.

After supper they sat round in the kitchen, and the younger boys were
saying how sorry they were it hadn't snowed. Everybody was sorry. They

wanted a deep snow that would lie long and keep the wheat warm, and leave the ground soaked when it melted.

"Yes, sir!" Rudolph broke out fiercely; "if we have another dry year like last year, there's going to be hard times in this country."

Rosicky filled his pipe. "You boys don't know what hard times is. You don't owe nobody, you got plenty to eat an' keep warm, an' plenty water to keep clean. When you got them, you can't have it very hard."

Rudolph frowned, opened and shut his big right hand, and dropped it clenched upon his knee. "I've got to have a good deal more than that, Father, or I'll quit this farming gamble. I can always make good wages railroading, or at the packing house, and be sure of my money."

"Maybe so," his father answered dryly.

Mary, who had just come in from the pantry and was wiping her hands on the roller towel, thought Rudy and his father were getting too serious. She brought her darning-basket and sat down in the middle of the group.

"I ain't much afraid of hard times, Rudy," she said heartily. 'We've had a plenty, but we've always come through. Your father wouldn't never take nothing very hard, not even hard times. I got a mind to tell you a story on him. Maybe you boys can't hardly remember the year we had that terrible hot wind, that burned everything up on the Fourth of July? All the corn an' the gardens. An' that was in the days when we didn't have alfalfa yet,—I guess it wasn't invented.

"Well, that very day your father was out cultivatin' corn, and I was here in the kitchen makin' plum preserves. We had bushels of plums that year. I noticed it was terrible hot, but it's always hot in the kitchen when you're pre-servin', an' I was too busy with my plums to mind. Anton come in from the field about three o'clock, an' I asked him what was the matter.

"'Nothin',' he says, 'but it's pretty hot, an' I think I won't work no more today.' He stood round for a few minutes, an' then he says: 'Ain't you near through? I want you should git up a nice supper for us tonight. It's Fourth of July.'

"I told him to git along, that I was right in the middle of preservin', but the plums would taste good on hot biscuit. 'I'm goin' to have fried chicken, too,' he says, and he went off an' killed a couple. You three oldest boys was little fellers, playin' round outside, real hot an' sweaty, an' your father took you to the horse tank down by the windmill an' took off your clothes an' put you in. Them two box-elder trees was little then, but they made shade over the tank. Then he took off all his own clothes, an' got in with you. While he was playin' in the water with you, the Methodist preacher drove into our place to say how all the neighbours was goin' to meet at the schoolhouse that night, to pray for rain. He drove right to the windmill, of course, and there was your father and you three with no clothes on. I was in the kitchen door, an' I had to laugh, for the preacher acted like he ain't never seen a naked man before. He surely was embarrassed, an' your father couldn't git to his clothes; they was all hangin' up on the windmill to let the sweat dry out of 'em. So he laid in the tank where he was, an' put one of you boys on top of him to cover him up a little, an' talked to the preacher.

"When you got through playin' in the water, he put clean clothes on you and a clean shirt on himself, an' by that time I'd begun to get supper. He says: 'It's too hot in here to eat comfortable. Let's have a picnic in the orchard. We'll eat our supper behind the mulberry hedge, under them linden trees.'

"So he carried our supper down, an' a bottle of my wild-grape wine, an' everything tasted good, I can tell you. The wind got cooler as the sun was goin' down, and it turned out pleasant, only I noticed how the leaves was curled up on the linden trees. That made me think, an' I asked your father if that hot wind all day hadn't been terrible hard on the gardens an' the corn.

"'Corn,' he says, 'there ain't no corn.'

"'What you talkin' about?' I said. 'Ain't we got forty acres?'

"'We ain't got an ear,' he says, 'nor nobody else ain't got none. All the corn in this country was cooked by three o'clock today, like you'd roasted it in an oven.'

"'You mean you won't get no crop at all?' I asked him. I couldn't believe it, after he'd worked so hard.

"'No crop this year,' he says. 'That's why we're havin' a picnic. We might as well enjoy what we got.'

"An' that's how your father behaved, when all the neighbours was so discouraged they couldn't look you in the face. An' we enjoyed ourselves that year, poor as we was, an' our neighbours wasn't a bit better off for bein' miserable. Some of 'em grieved till they got poor digestions and couldn't relish what they did have."

The younger boys said they thought their father had the best of it. But Rudolph was thinking that, all the same, the neighbours had managed to get ahead more, in the fifteen years since that time. There must be something wrong about his father's way of doing things. He wished he knew what was going on in the back of Polly's mind. He knew she liked his father, but he knew, too, that she was afraid of something. When his mother sent over coffee-cake or prune tarts or a loaf of fresh bread, Polly seemed to regard them with a certain suspicion. When she observed to him that his brothers had nice manners, her tone implied that it was remarkable they should have. With his mother she was stiff and on her guard. Mary's hearty frankness and gusts of good humour irritated her. Polly was afraid of being unusual or conspicuous in any way, of being "ordinary," as she said!

When Mary had finished her story, Rosicky laid aside his pipe.

"You boys like me to tell you about some of dem hard times I been through in London?" Warmly encouraged, he sat rubbing his forehead along the deep creases. It was bothersome to tell a long story in English (he nearly always talked to the boys in Czech), but he wanted Polly to hear this one.

"Well, you know about dat tailor shop I worked in in London? I had one Christmas dere I ain't never forgot. Times was awful bad before Christmas; de boss ain't got much work, an' have it awful hard to pay his rent. It ain't so much fun, bein' poor in a big city like London, I'll say! All de windows is full of good t'ings to eat, an' all de pushcarts in de streets is full, an' you smell 'em all de time, an' you ain't got no money,—not a damn bit. I didn't mind de cold so much, though I didn't have no overcoat, chust a short jacket I'd out-grown so it wouldn't meet on me, an' my hands was chapped raw. But I always had a good appetite, like you all know, an' de sight of dem pork pies in de windows was awful fur me!

"Day before Christmas was terrible foggy dat year, an' dat fog gits into your bones and makes you all damp like. Mrs. Lifschnitz didn't give us nothin' but a little bread an' drippin' for supper, because she was savin' to try for to give us a good dinner on Christmas Day. After supper de boss say I can go an' enjoy myself, so I went into de streets to listen to de Christmas singers. Dey sing old songs an' make very nice music, an' I run round after dem a good ways, till I got awful hungry. I t'ink maybe if I go home, I can sleep till morning an' forget my belly.

"I went into my corner real quiet, and roll up in my fedder quilt. But I ain't got my head down, till I smell somet'ing good. Seem like it git stronger an' stronger, an' I can't git to sleep noway. I can't understand dat smell. Dere was a gas light in a hall across de court, dat always shine in at my window a little. I got up an' look round. I got a little wooden box in my corner fur a stool, 'cause I ain't got no chair. I picks up dat box, and under it dere is a roast goose on a platter! I can't believe my eyes. I carry it to de window where de light comes in, an' touch it and smell it to find out, an' den I taste it to be sure. I say, I will eat chust one little bite of dat goose, so I can go to sleep, and tomorrow I won't eat none at all. But I tell you, boys, when I stop, one half of dat goose was gone!"

The narrator bowed his head, and the boys shouted. But little Josephine slipped behind his chair and kissed him on the neck beneath his ear.

"Poor little Papa, I don't want him to be hungry!"

"Da's long ago, child. I ain't never been hungry since I had your mudder to cook fur me."

"Go on and tell us the rest, please," said Polly.

"Well, when I come to realize what I done, of course, I felt terrible. I felt better in de stomach, but very bad in de heart. I set on my bed wid dat platter on my knees, an' it all come to me; how hard dat poor woman save to buy dat goose, and how she get some neighbour to cook it dat got more fire, an' how she put it in my corner to keep it away from dem hungry children. Dere was a old carpet hung up to shut my corner off, an' de children wasn't allowed to go in dere. An' I know she put it in my corner because she trust me more'n she did de violin boy. I can't stand it to face her after I spoil de Christmas. So I put on my shoes and go out into de city. I tell myself I better throw myself in de river; but I guess I ain't dat kind of a boy.

"It was after twelve o'clock, an' terrible cold, an' I start out to walk about London all night. I walk along de river awhile, but dere was lots of drunks all along; men, and women too. I chust move along to keep away from de police. I git onto de Strand, an' den over to New Oxford Street, where dere was a big German restaurant on de ground floor, wid big windows all fixed up fine, an' I could see de people havin' parties inside. While I was lookin' in, two men and two ladies come out, laughin' and talkin' and feelin' happy about all dey been eatin' an' drinkin', and dey was speakin' Czech,—not like de Austrians, but like de home folks talk it.

"I guess I went crazy, an' I done what I ain't never done before nor since. I went right up to dem gay people an' begun to beg dem: 'Fellow-countrymen, for God's sake give me money enough to buy a goose!'

"Dey laugh, of course, but de ladies speak awful kind to me, an' dey take me back into de restaurant and give me hot coffee and cakes, an' make me tell all about how I happened to come to London, an' what I was doin' dere. Dey take my name and where I work down on paper, an' both of dem ladies give me ten shillings.

"De big market at Covent Garden ain't very far away, an' by dat time it was open. I go dere an' buy a big goose an' some pork pies, an' potatoes and onions, an' cakes an' oranges fur de children,—all I could carry! When I git home, everybody is still asleep. I pile all I bought on de kitchen table, an' go in an' lay down on my bed, an' I ain't waken up till I hear dat woman scream when she come out into her kitchen. My goodness, but she was surprise! She laugh an' cry at de same time, an' hug me and waken all de children. She ain't stop fur no breakfast; she git de Christmas dinner ready dat morning, and we all sit down an' eat all we can hold. I ain't never seen dat violin boy have all he can hold before.

"Two three days after dat, de two men come to hunt me up, an' dey ask my boss, and he give me a good report an' tell dem I was a steady boy all right. One of dem Bohemians was very smart an' run a Bohemian newspaper in New York, an' de odder was a rich man, in de importing business, an' dey been travelling togedder. Dey told me how t'ings was easier in New York, an' offered to pay my passage when dey was goin' home soon on a boat. My boss say to me: 'You go. You ain't got no chance here, an' I like to see you git ahead, fur you always been a good boy to my woman, and fur dat fine Christmas dinner you give us all.' An' da's how I got to New York."

That night when Rudolph and Polly, arm in arm, were running home across the fields with the bitter wind at their backs, his heart leaped for joy when she said she thought they might have his family come over for supper on New Year's Eve. "Let's get up a nice supper, and not let your mother help at all; make her be company for once."

"That would be lovely of you, Polly," he said humbly. He was a very simple, modest boy, and he, too, felt vaguely that Polly and her sisters were more experienced and worldly than his people.

VI

The winter turned out badly for farmers. It was bitterly cold, and after the first light snows before Christmas there was no snow at all,—and no rain. March was as bitter as February. On those days when the wind fairly punished the country, Rosicky sat by his window. In the fall he and the boys had put in a big wheat planting, and now the seed had frozen in the ground. All that land would have to be ploughed up and planted over again, planted in corn. It had happened before, but he was younger then, and he never worried about what had to be. He was sure of himself and of Mary; he knew they could bear what they had to bear, that they would always pull through somehow. But he was not so sure about the young ones, and he felt troubled because Rudolph and Polly were having such a hard start.

Sitting beside his flowering window while the panes rattled and the wind blew in under the door, Rosicky gave himself to reflection as he had not done since those Sundays in the loft of the furniture-factory in New York, long ago. Then he was trying to find what he wanted in life for himself; now he was trying to find what he wanted for his boys, and why it was he so hungered to feel sure they would be here, working this very land, after he was gone.

They would have to work hard on the farm, and probably they would never do much more than make a living. But if he could think of them as staying here on the land, he wouldn't have to fear any great unkindness for them. Hardships, certainly; it was a hardship to have the wheat freeze in the ground when seed was so high; and to have to sell your stock because you had no feed. But there would be other years when everything came along right, and you caught up. And what you had was your own. You didn't have to choose between bosses and strikers, and go wrong either way. You didn't have to do with dishonest and cruel people. They were the only things in his experience he had found terrifying and horrible; the look in the eyes of a dishonest and crafty man, of a scheming and rapacious woman.

In the country, if you had a mean neighbour, you could keep off his land and make him keep off yours. But in the city, all the foulness and misery and brutality of your neighbours was part of your life. The worst things he had come upon in his journey through the world were human,—depraved and poisonous specimens of man. To this day he could recall certain terrible faces in the London streets. There were mean people everywhere, to be sure, even in their own country town here. But they weren't tempered, hardened, sharpened, like the treacherous people in cities who live by grinding or cheating or poisoning their fellow-men. He had helped to bury two of his fellow-workmen in the tailoring trade, and he was distrustful of the organized industries that see one out of the world in big cities. Here, if you were sick, you had Doctor Ed to look after you; and if you died, fat Mr. Haycock, the kindest man in the world, buried you.

It seemed to Rosicky that for good, honest boys like his, the worst they could do on the farm was better than the best they would be likely to do in the city. If he'd had a mean boy, now, one who was crooked and sharp and tried to put anything over on his brothers, then town would be the place for him. But he had no such boy. As for Rudolph, the discontented one, he would give the shirt off his back to anyone who touched his heart. What Rosicky really hoped for his boys was that they could get through the world without ever knowing much about the cruelty of human beings. "Their mother and me ain't prepared them for that," he sometimes said to himself.

These thoughts brought him back to a grateful consideration of his own case. What an escape he had had, to be sure! He, too, in his time, had had to take money for repair work from the hand of a hungry child who let it go so wistfully; because it was money due his boss. And now, in all these years, he had never had to take a cent from anyone in bitter need,—never had to look at the face of a woman become like a wolf's from struggle and famine. When he thought of these things, Rosicky would put on his cap and jacket and slip down to the barn and give his work-horses a little extra oats, letting them eat it out of his hand in their slobbery fashion. It was his way of expressing what he felt, and made him chuckle with pleasure.

The spring came warm, with blue skies,—but dry, dry as a bone. The boys began ploughing up the wheat-fields to plant them over in corn. Rosicky would stand at the fence corner and watch them, and the earth was so dry it blew up in clouds of brown dust that hid the horses and the sulky plough and the driver. It was a bad outlook.

The big alfalfa-field that lay between the home place and Rudolph's came up green, but Rosicky was worried because during that open windy winter a great many Russian thistle plants had blown in there and lodged. He kept asking the boys to rake them out; he was afraid their seed would root and "take the alfalfa." Rudolph said that was nonsense. The boys were working so hard planting corn, their father felt he couldn't insist about the thistles, but he set great store by that big alfalfa-field. It was a feed you could depend on,—and there was some deeper reason, vague, but strong. The peculiar green of that clover woke early memories in old Rosicky, went back to something in his childhood in the old world. When he was a little boy, he had played in fields of that strong blue-green colour.

One morning, when Rudolph had gone to town in the car, leaving a work-team idle in his barn, Rosicky went over to his son's place, put the horses to the buggy-rake, and set about quietly raking up those thistles. He behaved with guilty caution, and rather enjoyed stealing a march on Doctor Ed, who was just then taking his first vacation in seven years of practice and was attending a clinic in Chicago. Rosicky got the thistles raked up, but did not stop to burn them. That would take some time, and his breath was pretty short, so he thought he had better get the horses back to the barn.

He got them into the barn and to their stalls, but the pain had come on so sharp in his chest that he didn't try to take the harness off. He started for the house, bending lower with every step. The cramp in his chest was shutting him up like a jack-knife. When he reached the windmill, he swayed and caught at the ladder. He saw Polly coming down the hill, running with the swiftness of a slim greyhound. In a flash she had her shoulder under his armpit.

"Lean on me, Father, hard! Don't be afraid. We can get to the house all right."

Somehow they did, though Rosicky became blind with pain; he could keep on his legs, but he couldn't steer his course. The next thing he was conscious of was lying on Polly's bed, and Polly bending over him wringing out bath towels in hot water and putting them on his chest. She stopped only to throw coal into the stove, and she kept the tea-kettle and the black pot going. She put these hot applications on him for nearly an hour, she told him afterwards, and all that time he was drawn up stiff and blue, with the sweat pouring off him.

As the pain gradually loosed its grip, the stiffness went out of his jaws, the black circles round his eyes disappeared, and a little of his natural colour came back. When his daughter-in-law buttoned his shirt over his chest at last, he sighed.

"Da's fine, de way I feel now, Polly. It was a awful bad spell, an' I was so sorry it all come on you like it did."

Polly was flushed and excited. "Is the pain really gone? Can I leave you long enough to telephone over to your place?"

Rosicky's eyelids fluttered. "Don't telephone, Polly. It ain't no use to scare my wife. It's nice and quiet here, an' if I ain't too much trouble to you, just let me lay still till I feel like myself. I ain't got no pain now. It's nice here."

Polly bent over him and wiped the moisture from his face. "Oh, I'm so glad it's over!" she broke out impulsively. "It just broke my heart to see you suffer so, Father."

Rosicky motioned her to sit down on the chair where the tea-kettle had been, and looked up at her with that lively affectionate gleam in his eyes. "You was awful good to me, I won't never forgit dat. I hate it to be sick on you like dis. Down at de barn I say to myself, dat young girl ain't had much experience in sickness, I don't want to scare her, an' maybe she's got a baby comin' or somet'ing."

Polly took his hand. He was looking at her so intently and affectionately and confidingly; his eyes seemed to caress her face, to regard it with pleasure. She frowned with her funny streaks of eyebrows, and then smiled back at him.

"I guess maybe there is something of that kind going to happen. But I haven't told anyone yet, not my mother or Rudolph. You'll be the first to know."

His hand pressed hers. She noticed that it was warm again. The twinkle in his yellow-brown eyes seemed to come nearer.

"I like mighty well to see dat little child, Polly," was all he said. Then he closed his eyes and lay half-smiling. But Polly sat still, thinking hard. She had a sudden feeling that nobody in the world, not her mother, not Rudolph, or anyone, really loved her as much as old Rosicky did. It perplexed her. She sat frowning and trying to puzzle it out. It was as if Rosicky had a special gift for loving people, something that was like an ear for music or an eye for colour. It was quiet, unobtrusive; it was merely there. You saw it in his eyes,—perhaps that was why they were merry. You felt it in his hands, too. After he dropped off to sleep, she sat holding his warm, broad, flexible brown hand. She had never seen another in the least like it. She wondered if it wasn't a kind of gypsy hand, it was so alive and quick and light in its communications,—very strange in a farmer. Nearly all the farmers she knew had huge lumps of fists, like mauls, or they were knotty and bony and uncomfortable-looking, with stiff fingers. But Rosicky's was like quicksilver, flexible, muscular, about the colour of a pale cigar, with deep, deep creases across the palm. It wasn't nervous, it wasn't a stupid lump; it was a warm brown human hand, with some cleverness in it, a great deal of generosity, and something else which Polly could only call "gypsy-like,"—something nimble and lively and sure, in the way that animals are.

Polly remembered that hour long afterwards; it had been like an awakening to her. It seemed to her that she had never learned so much about life from anything as from old Rosicky's hand. It brought her to herself; it communicated some direct and untranslatable message.

When she heard Rudolph coming in the car, she ran out to meet him.

"Oh, Rudy, your father's been awful sick! He raked up those thistles he's been worrying about, and afterwards he could hardly get to the house. He suffered so I was afraid he was going to die."

Rudolph jumped to the ground. "Where is he now?"

"On the bed. He's asleep. I was terribly scared, because, you know, I'm so fond of your father." She slipped her arm through his and they went into the house. That afternoon they took Rosicky home and put him to bed, though he protested that he was quite well again.

The next morning he got up and dressed and sat down to breakfast with his family. He told Mary that his coffee tasted better than usual to him, and he warned the boys not to bear any tales to Doctor Ed when he got home. After breakfast he sat down by his window to do some patching and asked Mary to thread several needles for him before she went to feed her chickens,—her eyes were better than his, and her hands steadier. He lit his pipe and took up John's overalls. Mary had been watching him anxiously all morning, and as she went out of the door with her bucket of scraps, she saw that he was smiling. He was thinking, indeed, about Polly, and how he might never have known what a tender heart she had if he hadn't got sick over there. Girls nowadays didn't wear their heart on their sleeve. But now he knew Polly would make a fine woman after the foolishness wore off. Either a woman had that sweetness at her heart or she hadn't. You couldn't always tell by the look of them; but if they had that, everything came out right in the end.

After he had taken a few stitches, the cramp began in his chest, like yesterday. He put his pipe cautiously down on the window-sill and bent over to ease the pull. No use,—he had better try to get to his bed if he could. He rose and groped his way across the familiar floor, which was rising and falling like the deck of a ship. At the door he fell. When Mary came in, she found him lying there, and the moment she touched him she knew that he was gone.

Doctor Ed was away when Rosicky died, and for the first few weeks after he got home he was hard driven. Every day he said to himself that he must get out to see that family that had lost their father. One soft, warm moonlight night in early summer he started for the farm. His mind was on other things, and not until his road ran by the graveyard did he realize that Rosicky wasn't over there on the hill where the red lamplight shone, but here, in the moonlight. He stopped his car, shut off the engine, and sat there for a while.

A sudden hush had fallen on his soul. Everything here seemed strangely moving and significant, though signifying what, he did not know. Close by the wire fence stood Rosicky's mowing-machine, where one of the boys had been cutting hay that afternoon; his own work-horses had been going up and down there. The new-cut hay perfumed all the night air. The moonlight silvered the long, billowy grass that grew over the graves and hid the fence; the few little evergreens stood out black in it, like shadows in a pool. The sky was very blue and soft, the stars rather faint because the moon was full.

For the first time it struck Doctor Ed that this was really a beautiful graveyard. He thought of city cemeteries; acres of shrubbery and heavy stone, so arranged and lonely and unlike anything in the living world. Cities of the dead, indeed; cities of the forgotten, of the "put away." But this was open and free, this little square of long grass which the wind for ever stirred. Nothing but the sky overhead, and the many-coloured fields running on until they met that sky. The horses worked here in summer; the neighbours passed on their way to town; and over yonder, in the cornfield, Rosicky's own cattle would be eating fodder as winter came on. Nothing could be more undeathlike than this place; nothing could be more right for a man who had helped to do the work of great cities and had always longed for the open country and had got to it at last. Rosicky's life seemed to him complete and beautiful.

[New York, 1928]

The Road Not Taken[1]

ROBERT FROST

Two roads diverged in a yellow wood,
And sorry I could not travel both
And be one traveler, long I stood
And looked down one as far as I could
To where it bent in the undergrowth;   5

Then took the other, as just as fair,
And having perhaps the better claim,
Because it was grassy and wanted wear;
Though as for that the passing there
Had worn them really about the same,   10

And both that morning equally lay
In leaves no step had trodden black.
Oh, I kept the first for another day!
Yet knowing how way leads on to way,
I doubted if I should ever come back.   15

I shall be telling this with a sigh
Somewhere ages and ages hence:
Two roads diverged in a wood, and I—
I took the one less traveled by,
And that has made all the difference.   20

[1915]

---

[1]"The Road Not Taken" first appeared in the *Atlantic Monthly* in August 1915. Frost first collected the poem in *Mountain Interval* (1916).

Stopping by Woods on a Snowy Evening[*]

ROBERT FROST

Whose woods these are I think I know.
His house is in the village though;
He will not see me stopping here
To watch his woods fill up with snow.

My little horse must think it queer   5
To stop without a farmhouse near
Between the woods and frozen lake
The darkest evening of the year.

He gives his harness bells a shake
To ask if there is some mistake.   10
The only other sound's the sweep
Of easy wind and downy flake.

The woods are lovely, dark and deep,
But I have promises to keep,
And miles to go before I sleep,   15
And miles to go before I sleep.

[1923]

[*]"Stopping by Woods on a Snowy Evening" first appeared in the *New Republic* in March 1923.
Frost first collected the poem in his fourth volume, *New Hampshire* (1923).

The Negro Speaks of Rivers

LANGSTON HUGHES

———————————

I've known rivers:
I've known rivers ancient as the world and older than the
    flow of human blood in human veins.

My soul has grown deep like the rivers.

I bathed in the Euphrates when dawns were young.   5
I built my hut near the Congo and it lulled me to sleep.
I looked upon the Nile and raised the pyramids above it.
I heard the singing of the Mississippi when Abe Lincoln
    went down to New Orleans, and I've seen its muddy
    bosom turn all golden in the sunset.   10

I've known rivers:
Ancient, dusky rivers.

My soul has grown deep like the rivers.

[1921]

"The Negro Speaks of Rivers" first appeared in the *Crisis* in June 1921. In his collection *The Weary Blues*, the poem bears the dedication "To W. E. B. Du Bois," the first editor of the *Crisis*.

Literature of the 20th Century (1945-Present)

The Glass Menagerie

TENNESSEE WILLIAMS

Nobody, not even the rain, has such small hands.[1]
e.e. cummings

Scene: An Alley in St. Louis

Part I.   *Preparation for a Gentleman Caller.*
Part II.   *The Gentleman calls.*

Time: *Now and the Past.*

The Characters

Amanda Wingfield (the mother): A little woman of great but confused vitality clinging frantically to another time and place. Her characterization must be carefully created, not copied from type. She is not paranoiac, but her life is paranoia. There is much to admire in Amanda, and as much to love and pity as there is to laugh at. Certainly she has endurance and a kind of heroism, and though her foolishness makes her unwittingly cruel at times, there is tenderness in her slight person.

Laura Wingfield (her daughter): Amanda, having failed to establish contact with reality, continues to live vitally in her illusions, but Laura's situation is even graver. A childhood illness has left her crippled, one leg slightly shorter than the other, and held in a brace. This defect need not be more than suggested on the stage. Stemming from this, Laura's separation increases till she is like a piece of her own glass collection, too exquisitely fragile to move from the shelf.

Tom Wingfield (her son): And the narrator of the play. A poet with a job in a warehouse. His nature is not remorseless, but to escape from a trap he has to act without pity.

Jim O'Connor (the gentleman caller): A nice, ordinary, young man.

---

[1]the last line of an e.e. cummings poem: "Somewhere i have never travelled, gladly beyond."

Scene One

*The Wingfield apartment is in the rear of the building, one of those vast hive-like con-
glomerations of cellular living-units that flower as warty growths in overcrowded
urban centers of lower middle-class population and are symptomatic of the impulse of
this largest and fundamentally enslaved section of American society to avoid fluidity
and differentiation and to exist and function as one interfused automatism.*

*The apartment faces an alley and is entered by a fire escape, a structure whose name
is a touch of accidental poetic truth, for all of these huge buildings are always burning
with the slow and implacable fires of human desperation. The fire escape is part of
what we see—that is, the landing of it and steps descending from it.*

*The scene is memory and is therefore nonrealistic. Memory takes a lot of poetic
license. It omits some details; others are exaggerated, according to the emotional value
of the articles it touches, for memory is seated predominantly in the heart. The interior
is therefore rather dim and poetic.*

*At the rise of the curtain, the audience is faced with the dark, grim rear wall of the
Wingfield tenement. This building is flanked on both sides by dark, narrow alleys
which run into murky canyons of tangled clotheslines, garbage cans, and the sinister
latticework of neighboring fire escapes. It is up and down these side alleys that exterior
entrances and exits are made during the play. At the end of Tom's opening commentary, the dark tenement wall slowly becomes transparent and reveals the interior of
the ground-floor Wingfield apartment.*

*Nearest the audience is the living room, which also serves as a sleeping room for
Laura, the sofa unfolding to make her bed. Just beyond, separated from the living
room by a wide arch or second proscenium with transparent faded portieres (or second
curtain), is the dining room. In an old-fashioned whatnot in the living room are seen
scores of transparent glass animals. A blown-up photograph of the father hangs on the
wall of the living room, to the left of the archway. It is the face of a very handsome
young man in a doughboy's First World War cap. He is gallantly smiling, ineluctably
smiling, as if to say "I will be smiling forever."*

*Also hanging on the wall, near the photograph, are a typewriter keyboard chart
and a Gregg shorthand diagram. An upright typewriter on a small table stands
beneath the charts.*

*The audience hears and sees the opening scene in the dining room through both the
transparent fourth wall of the building and the transparent gauze portieres of the
dining-room arch. It is during this revealing scene that the fourth wall slowly ascends,
out of sight. This transparent exterior wall is not brought down again until the very
end of the play, during Tom's final speech.*

*The narrator is an undisguised convention of the play. He takes whatever license
with dramatic convention is convenient to his purposes.*

*Tom enters, dressed as a merchant sailor, and strolls across to the fire escape. There
he stops and lights a cigarette. He addresses the audience.*

Tom.   Yes, I have tricks in my pocket, I have things up my sleeve. But I am
the opposite of a stage magician. He gives you illusion the appearance of
truth. I give you truth in the pleasant disguise of illusion.

To begin with, I turn back time. I reverse it to that quaint period, the thirties, when the huge middle class of America was matriculating in a school for the blind. Their eyes had failed them, or they had failed their eyes, and so they were having their fingers pressed forcibly down on the fiery Braille alphabet of a dissolving economy.

In Spain there was a revolution Here there was only shouting and confusion. In Spain there was Guernica.[2] Here there were disturbances of labor, sometimes pretty violent, in otherwise peaceful cities such as Chicago, Cleveland, Saint Louis . . .

This is the social background of the play.

(Music begins to play)

The play is memory. Being a memory play, it is dimly lighted, it is sentimental, it is not realistic. In memory everything seems to happen to music. That explains the fiddle in the wings.

I am the narrator of the play, and also a character in it. The other characters are my mother, Amanda, my sister, Laura, and a gentleman caller who appears in the final scenes. He is the most realistic character in the play, being an emissary from a world of reality that we were somehow set apart from. But since I have a poet's weakness for symbols, I am using this character also as a symbol; he is the long-delayed but always expected something that we live for. There is a fifth character in the play who doesn't appear except in this larger-than-life-size photograph over the mantel. This is our father who left us a long time ago. He was a telephone man who fell in love with long distances; he gave up his job with the telephone company and skipped the light fantastic out of town . . .

The last we heard of him was a picture postcard from Mazatlan, on the Pacific coast of Mexico, containing a message of two words: "Hello—Goodbye!" and no address.

I think the rest of the play will explain itself. . . .

(Amanda's voice becomes audible through the portieres.)

(Legend on screen: "Ou sont les neiges d'antan?")[3]

(Tom divides the portieres and enters the dining room. Amanda and Laura are seated at a drop-leaf table. Eating is indicated by gestures without food or utensils. Amanda faces the audience. Tom and Laura are seated in Profile. The interior is lit up softly and through the scrim we see Amanda and Laura seated at the table.)

---

[2]town in northern Spain, bombed on April 26, 1937, during the Spanish Civil War.
[3]French: "Where are the snows of yesteryear?" A refrain from "Ballade of the Ladies of Bygone Times" (1462), by François Villon (1431–1463?).

241

Amanda (calling). Tom?

Tom. Yes, Mother.

Amanda. We can't say grace until you come to the table!

Tom. Coming, Mother. (*He bows slightly and withdraws, reappearing a few moments later in his place at the table.*)

Amanda (to her son). Honey, don't *push* with your *fingers*. If you have to push with something, the thing to push with is a crust of bread. And chew—chew! Animals have secretions in their stomachs which enable them to digest food without mastication, but human beings are supposed to chew their food before they swallow it down. Eat food leisurely, son, and really enjoy it. A well-cooked meal has lots of delicate flavors that have to be held in the mouth for appreciation. So chew your food and give your salivary glands a chance to function!

(*Tom deliberately lays his imaginary fork down and pushes his chair back from the table.*)

Tom. I haven't enjoyed one bite of this dinner because of your constant directions on how to eat it. It's you that make me rush through meals with your hawklike attention to every bite I take. Sickening—spoils my appetite—all this discussion of—animals' secretion—salivary glands—mastication!

Amanda (lightly). Temperament like a Metropolitan star!

(*Tom rises and walks toward the living room.*)

You're not excused from the table.

Tom. I'm getting a cigarette.

Amanda. You smoke too much.

(*Laura rises.*)

Laura. I'll bring in the blanc mange.

(*Tom remains standing with his cigarette by the portieres.*)

Amanda (rising). No, sister, no, sister—you be the lady this time and I'll be the darky.

Laura. I'm already up.

Amanda. Resume your seat, little sister—I want you to stay fresh and pretty—for gentlemen callers!

Laura (sitting down). I'm not expecting any gentlemen callers.

Amanda (crossing out to the kitchenette, airily). Sometimes they come when they are least expected! Why, I remember one Sunday afternoon in Blue Mountain—

(She enters the kitchenette.)

Tom.   I know what's coming!
Laura.   Yes. But let her tell it.
Tom.   Again?
Laura.   She loves to tell it.

(Amanda returns with a bowl of dessert.)

Amanda.   One Sunday afternoon in Blue Mountain—your mother received—
seventeen!—gentlemen callers! Why, sometimes there weren't chairs enough to accommodate them all. We had to send the nigger over to bring in folding chairs from the parish house.
Tom (remaining at the portieres). How did you entertain those gentlemen callers?
Amanda.   I understood the art of conversation!
Tom.   I bet you could talk.
Amanda.   Girls in those days *knew* how to talk, I can tell you.
Tom.   Yes?

(Image on screen: Amanda as a girl on a porch, greeting callers.)

Amanda.   They knew how to entertain their gentlemen callers. It wasn't enough for a girl to be possessed of a pretty face and a graceful figure—although I wasn't slighted in either respect. She also needed to have nimble wit and a tongue to meet all occasions.
Tom.   What did you talk about?
Amanda.   Things of importance going on in the world! Never anything coarse or common or vulgar.

(She addresses Tom as though he were seated in the vacant chair at the table though he remains by the portieres. He plays this scene as though reading from a script.)

My callers were gentlemen—all! Among my callers were some of the most prominent young planters of the Mississippi Delta—planters and sons of planters!

(Tom motions for music and a spot of light on Amanda. Her eyes lift, her face glows, her voice becomes rich and elegiac.)
(Screen legend: "Ou sont les neiges d'antan?")

There was young Champ Laughlin who later became vice-president of the Delta Planters Bank. Hadley Stevenson who was drowned in Moon Lake and left his widow one hundred and fifty thousand in Government bonds. There were the Cutrere brothers, Wesley and Bates. Bates was one of my bright particular beaux! He got in a quarrel with that wild Wainwright boy. They shot it out on the floor of Moon Lake Casino. Bates was shot through the stomach. Died in the ambulance on his way to Memphis. His widow was also well provided-for, came into eight or ten thousand acres, that's all. She married him on the rebound—never loved her—carried my picture on him the night he died! And there was that boy that every girl in the Delta had set her cap for! That beautiful, brilliant young Fitzhugh boy from Greene County!

Tom.   What did he leave his widow?

Amanda.   He never married! Gracious, you talk as though all of my old admirers had turned up their toes to the daisies!

Tom.   Isn't this the first you've mentioned that still survives?

Amanda.   That Fitzhugh boy went North and made a fortune—came to be known as the Wolf of Wall Street! He had the Midas touch, whatever he touched turned to gold! And I could have been Mrs. Duncan J. Fitzhugh, mind you! But—I picked your *father*!

Laura (rising). Mother, let me clear the table.

Amanda.   No, dear, you go in front and study your typewriter chart. Or practice your shorthand a little. Stay fresh and pretty!—It's almost time for our gentlemen callers to start arriving. (*She flounces girlishly toward the kitchenette*) How many do you suppose we're going to entertain this afternoon?

(*Tom throws down the paper and jumps up with a groan.*)

Laura (alone in the dining room). I don't believe we're going to receive any, Mother.

Amanda (reappearing, airily). What? No one—not one? You must be joking!

(*Laura nervously echoes her laugh. She slips in a fugitive manner through the half-open portieres and draws them gently behind her A shaft of very clear light is thrown on her face against the faded tapestry of the curtains. Faintly the music of "The Glass Menagerie" is heard as she continues, lightly:*)

Not one gentleman caller? It can't be true! There must be a flood, there must have been a tornado!

Laura.   It isn't a flood, it's not a tornado, Mother. I'm just not popular like you were in Blue Mountain. . . .

(*Tom utters another groan. Laura glances at him with a faint, apologetic smile. Her voice catches a little:*)

Mother's afraid I'm going to be an old maid.

(*The scene dims out with the "Glass Menagerie" music.*)

Scene Two

On the dark stage the screen is lighted with the image of blue roses. Gradually Laura's figure becomes apparent and the screen goes out. The music subsides.

Laura is seated in the delicate ivory chair at the small claw-foot table. She wears a dress of soft violet material for a kimono — her hair is tied back from her forehead with a ribbon. She is washing and polishing her collection of glass. Amanda appears on the fire escape steps. At the sound of her ascent, Laura catches her breath, thrusts the bowl of ornaments away, and sets herself stiffly before the diagram of the typewriter keyboard as though it held her spellbound. Something has happened to Amanda. It is written in her face as she climbs to the landing: a look that is grim and hopeless and a little absurd. She has on one of those cheap or imitation velvety-looking cloth coats with imitation fur collar. Her hat is five or six years old, one of those dreadful cloche hats that were worn in the late Twenties, and she is clutching an enormous black patent-leather pocketbook with nickel clasps and initials. This is her full-dress outfit, the one she usually wears to the D.A.R.[4] Before entering she looks through the door. She purses her lips, opens her eyes very wide, rolls them upward and shakes her head. Then she slowly lets herself in the door. Seeing her mother's expression Laura touches her lips with a nervous gesture.

Laura. Hello, Mother, I was — *(She makes a nervous gesture toward the chart on the wall. Amanda leans against the shut door and stares at Laura with a martyred look.)*
Amanda. Deception? Deception? *(She slowly removes her hat and gloves, continuing the sweet suffering stare. She lets the hat and gloves fall on the floor — a bit of acting.)*
Laura (shakily). How was the D.A.R. meeting?

(Amanda slowly opens her purse and removes a dainty white handkerchief which she shakes out delicately and delicately touches to her lips and nostrils.)

Didn't you go to the D.A.R. meeting, Mother?
Amanda (faintly, almost inaudibly). — No. — No. *(then more forcibly:)* I did not have the strength — to go to the D.A.R. In fact, I did not have the courage! I wanted to find a hole in the ground and hide myself in it forever! *(She crosses slowly to the wall and removes the diagram of the typewriter keyboard. She holds it in front of her for a second, staring at it sweetly and sorrowfully — then bites her lips and tears it in two pieces.)*
Laura (faintly). Why did you do that, Mother?

(Amanda repeats the same procedure with the chart of the Gregg Alphabet.)

---

[4]Daughters of the American Revolution, a patriotic society dedicated to perpetuating the "memory and spirit of the men and women who achieved American independence."

Why are you—

Amanda.   Why? Why? How old are you, Laura?

Laura.   Mother, you know my age.

Amanda.   I thought that you were an adult; it seems that I was mistaken. (*She crosses slowly to the sofa and sinks down and stares at Laura.*)

Laura.   Please don't stare at me, Mother.

(*Amanda closes her eyes and lowers her head. There is a ten-second pause.*)

Amanda.   What are we going to do, what is going to become of us, what is the future?

(*There is another pause.*)

Laura.   Has something happened, Mother?

(*Amanda draws a long breath, takes out the handkerchief again, goes through the dabbing process.*)

Mother, has—something happened?

Amanda.   I'll be all right in a minute, I'm just bewildered—(*She hesitates.*)—by life. . . .

Laura.   Mother, I wish that you would tell me what's happened!

Amanda.   As you know, I was supposed to be inducted into my office at the D.A.R. this afternoon.

(*Screen image: A swarm of typewriters.*)

But I stopped off at Rubicam's Business College to speak to your teachers about your having a cold and ask them what progress they thought you were making down there.

Laura.   Oh . . . .

Amanda.   I went to the typing instructor and introduced myself as your mother. She didn't know who you were. "Wingfield," she said, "We don't have any such student enrolled at the school!"

I assured her she did, that you had been going to classes since early in January. "I wonder," she said, "if you could be talking about that terribly shy little girl who dropped out of school after only a few days' attendance?"

"No," I said, "Laura, my daughter, has been going to school every day for the past six weeks!"

"Excuse me," she said. She took the attendance book out and there was your name, unmistakably printed, and all the dates you were absent until they decided you had dropped out of school.

I still said, "No, there must have been some mistake! There must have been some mix-up in the records!"

And she said, "No—I remember her perfectly now. Her hands shook so that she couldn't hit the right keys! The first time we gave a speed test, she broke down completely—was sick at the stomach and almost had to be carried into the wash room! After that morning she never showed up any more. We phoned the house but never got any answer"—While I was working at Famous-Barr, I suppose, demonstrating those—

(She indicates a brassiere with her hands.)

Oh! I felt so weak I could barely keep on my feet! I had to sit down while they got me a glass of water! Fifty dollars' tuition, all of our plans—my hopes and ambitions for you—just gone up the spout, just gone up the spout like that.

(Laura draws a long breath and gets awkwardly to her feet. She crosses to the Victrola and winds it up.)

What are you doing?
Laura.   Oh! *(She releases the handle and returns to her seat.)*
Amanda.   Laura, where have you been going when you've gone out pretending that you were going to business college?
Laura.   I've just been going out walking.
Amanda.   That's not true.
Laura.   It is. I just went walking.
Amanda.   Walking? Walking? In winter? Deliberately courting pneumonia in that light coat? Where did you walk to, Laura?
Laura.   All sorts of places—mostly in the park.
Amanda.   Even after you'd started catching that cold?
Laura.   It was the lesser of two evils, Mother.

(Screen image: Winter scene in a park.*)*

I couldn't go back there. I—threw up—on the floor!
Amanda.   From half past seven till after five every day you mean to tell me you walked around in the park, because you wanted to make me think that you were still going to Rubicam's Business College?
Laura.   It wasn't as bad as it sounds. I went inside places to get warmed up.
Amanda.   Inside where?
Laura.   I went in the art museum and the bird houses at the Zoo. I visited the penguins every day! Sometimes I did without lunch and went to the movies. Lately I've been spending most of my afternoons in the Jewel Box, that big glass house where they raise tropical flowers.

Amanda.   You did all this to deceive me, just for deception?

(Laura looks down.)

Why?

Laura.   Mother, when you're disappointed, you get that awful suffering look on your face, like the picture of Jesus' mother in the museum!

Amanda.   Hush!

Laura.   I couldn't face it.

(There is a pause. A whisper of strings is heard. Legend on screen: "The Crust of Humility.")

Amanda (hopelessly fingering the huge pocketbook). So what are we going to do the rest of our lives? Stay home and watch the parades go by? Amuse ourselves with the glass menagerie, darling? Eternally play those worn-out phonograph records your father left as a painful reminder of him? We won't have a business career—we've given that up because it gave us nervous indigestion! *(She laughs wearily.)* What is there left but dependency all our lives? I know so well what becomes of unmarried women who aren't prepared to occupy a position. I've seen such pitiful cases in the South—barely tolerated spinsters living upon the grudging patronage of sister's husband or brother's wife!—stuck away in some little mousetrap of a room—encouraged by one in-law to visit another—little birdlike women without any nest—eating the crust of humility all their life! Is that the future that we've mapped out for ourselves? I swear it's the only alternative I can think of! *(She pauses.)* It isn't a very pleasant alternative, is it? *(She pauses again.)* Of course—some girls *do marry.*

(Laura twists her hands nervously.)

Haven't you ever liked some boy?

Laura.   Yes. I liked one once. *(She rises.)* I came across his picture a while ago.

Amanda (with some interest). He gave you his picture?

Laura.   No, it's in the yearbook.

Amanda (disappointed). Oh—a high school boy.

(Screen image: Jim as the high school hero bearing a silver cup.)

Laura.   Yes. His name was Jim. *(She lifts the heavy annual from the claw-foot table.)* Here he is in *The Pirates of Penzance.*

Amanda (absently). The what?

Laura.   The operetta the senior class put on. He had a wonderful voice and we sat across the aisle from each other Mondays, Wednesdays and Fridays in the Aud. Here he is with the silver cup for debating! See his grin?

Amanda (absently). He must have had a jolly disposition.
Laura. He used to call me—Blue Roses.

(Screen image: Blue roses.)

Amanda. Why did he call you such a name as that?
Laura. When I had that attack of pleurosis—he asked me what was the matter when I came back. I said pleurosis—he thought I said Blue Roses! So that's what he always called me after that. Whenever he saw me, he'd holler, "Hello, Blue Roses!" I didn't care for the girl that he went out with. Emily Meisenbach. Emily was the best-dressed girl at Soldan. She never struck me, though, as being sincere . . . It says in the Personal Section—they're engaged. That's—six years ago! They must be married by now.
Amanda. Girls that aren't cut out for business careers usually wind up married to some nice man. *(She gets up with a spark of revival.)* Sister, that's what you'll do!

(Laura utters a startled, doubtful laugh. She reaches quickly for a piece of glass.)

Laura. But, Mother—
Amanda. Yes? (*She goes over to the phonograph.)*
Laura (in a tone of frightened apology). I'm—crippled!
Amanda. Nonsense! Laura, I've told you never, never to use that word. Why, you're not crippled, you just have a little defect—hardly noticeable, even! When people have some slight disadvantage like that, they cultivate other things to make up for it—develop charm—and vivacity—and—charm! That's all you have to do! *(She turns again to the phonograph.)* One thing your father had *plenty of*—was *charm*!

(The scene fades out with music.)

Scene Three

Legend on screen: "After the fiasco—"

(Tom speaks from the fire escape landing.)

Tom. After the fiasco at Rubicam's Business College, the idea of getting a gentleman caller for Laura began to play a more and more important part in Mother's calculations. It became an obsession. Like some archetype of the universal unconscious, the image of the gentleman caller haunted our small apartment. . . .

(Screen image: A young man at the door of a house with flowers.)

An evening at home rarely passed without some allusion to this image, this specter, this hope. . . . Even when he wasn't mentioned, his presence hung in Mother's preoccupied look and in my sister's frightened, apologetic manner—hung like a sentence passed upon the Wingfields!

Mother was a woman of action as well as words. She began to take logical steps in the planned direction. Late that winter and in the early spring—realizing that extra money would be needed to properly feather the nest and plume the bird—she conducted a vigorous campaign on the telephone, roping in subscribers to one of those magazines for matrons called *The Homemaker's Companion,* the type of journal that features the socialized sublimations of ladies of letters who think in terms of delicate cuplike breasts, slim, tapering waists, rich, creamy thighs, eyes like wood smoke in autumn, fingers that soothe and caress like strains of music, bodies as powerful as Etruscan sculpture.

(Screen image: The cover of a glamor magazine.*)*

(Amanda enters with the telephone on a long extension cord. She is spotlighted in the dim stage.)

Amanda.   Ida Scott? This is Amanda Wingfield! We *missed* you at the D.A.R. last Monday! I said to myself: She's probably suffering with that sinus condition! How is that sinus condition?

Horrors! Heaven have mercy!—You're a Christian martyr, yes, that's what you are, a Christian martyr!

Well, I just now happened to notice that your subscription to the *Companion*'s about to expire! Yes, it expires with the next issue, honey!—just when that wonderful new serial by Bessie Mae Hopper is getting off to such an exciting start. Oh, honey, it's something that you can't miss! You remember how *Gone with the Wind* took everybody by storm? You simply couldn't go out if you hadn't read it. All everybody *talked* was Scarlett O'Hara. Well, this is a book that critics already compare to *Gone with the Wind.* It's the *Gone with the Wind* of the post–World-War generation!— What?—Burning?—Oh, honey, don't let them burn, go take a look in the oven and I'll hold the wire! Heavens—I think she's hung up!

(The scene dims out.)

(Legend on screen: "You think I'm in love with Continental Shoemakers?"*)*
(Before the lights come up again, the violent voices of Tom and Amanda are heard. They are quarrelling behind the portieres. In front of them stands Laura with clenched hands and panicky expression. A clear pool of light is on her figure throughout this scene.)

Tom.   What in Christ's name am I—

Amanda (shrilly). Don't you use that—
Tom. —supposed to do!
Amanda. —expression! Not in my—
Tom. Ohhh!
Amanda. —presence! Have you gone out of your senses?
Tom. I have, that's true, *driven* out!
Amanda. What is the matter with you, you—big—big—IDIOT!
Tom. Look!—I've got *no thing*, no single thing—
Amanda. Lower your voice!
Tom. —in my life here that I can call my OWN! Everything is—
Amanda. Stop that shouting!
Tom. Yesterday you confiscated my books! You had the nerve to—
Amanda. I took that horrible novel back to the library—yes! That hideous book by that insane Mr. Lawrence.

(Tom laughs wildly,)

I cannot control the output of diseased minds or people who cater to them—

(Tom laughs still more wildly.)

BUT I WON'T ALLOW SUCH FILTH BROUGHT INTO MY HOUSE! No, no, no, no, no!
Tom. House, house! Who pays rent on it, who makes a slave of himself to—
Amanda (fairly screeching). Don't you DARE to—
Tom. No, no, *I* mustn't say things! *I've* got to just—
Amanda. Let me tell you—
Tom. I don't want to hear any more!

(He tears the portieres open. The dining-room area is lit with a turgid smoky red glow. Now we see Amanda; her hair is in metal curlers and she is wearing a very old bathrobe, much too large for her slight figure, a relic of the faithless Mr. Wingfield. The upright typewriter now stands on the drop-leaf table, along with a wild disarray of manuscripts. The quarrel was probably precipitated by Amanda's interruption of Tom's creative labor. A chair lies overthrown on the floor. Their gesticulating shadows are cast on the ceiling by the fiery glow.)

Amanda. You *will* hear more, you—
Tom. No, I won't hear more, I'm going out!
Amanda. You come right back in—

Tom. Out, out, out! Because I'm—

Amanda. Come back here, Tom Wingfield! I'm not through talking to you!

Tom. Oh, go—

Laura (desperately). —Tom!

Amanda. You're going to listen, and no more insolence from you! I'm at the end of my patience!

(He comes back toward her)

Tom. What do you think I'm at? Aren't I supposed to have any patience to reach the end of, Mother? I know, I know. It seems unimportant to you, what I'm *doing*—what I *want* to do—having a little *difference* between them! You don't think that—

Amanda. I think you've been doing things that you're ashamed of. That's why you act like this. I don't believe that you go every night to the movies. Nobody goes to the movies night after night. Nobody in their right minds goes to the movies as often as you pretend to. People don't go to the movies at nearly midnight, and movies don't let out at two A.M.: Come in stumbling. Muttering to yourself like a maniac! You get three hours' sleep and then go to work. Oh, I can picture the way you're doing down there. Moping, doping, because you're in no condition.

Tom (wildly). No, I'm in no condition!

Amanda. What right have you got to jeopardize your job? Jeopardize the security of us all? How do you think we'd manage if you were—

Tom. Listen! You think I'm crazy about the *warehouse*? *(He bends fiercely toward her slight figure.)* You think I'm in love with the Continental Shoemakers? You think I want to spend fifty-five *years* down there in that—*celotex interior!* with—*fluorescent—tubes!* I'd rather somebody picked up a crowbar and battered out my brains—than go back mornings! I *go!* Every time you come in yelling that Goddamn *"Rise and Shine!"* *"Rise and Shine!"* I say to myself. "How *lucky dead* people are!" But I get up. I *go!* For sixty-five dollars a month I give up all that I dream of doing and being *ever!* And you say self—*self's* all I ever think of. Why, listen, if self is what I thought of, Mother, I'd be where he is—GONE! *(He points to his father's picture.)* As far as the system of transportation reaches! *(He starts past her. She grabs his arm.)* Don't grab at me, Mother!

Amanda. Where are you going?

Tom. I'm going to the *movies*!

Amanda. I don't believe that lie!

(Tom crouches toward her, overtowering her tiny figure. She backs away, gasping.)

Tom. I'm going to opium dens! Yes, opium dens, dens of vice and criminals' hangouts, Mother. I've joined the Hogan Gang, I'm a hired assassin, I carry a tommy gun in a violin case! I run a string of cat houses in the Valley! They call me Killer, Killer Wingfield, I'm leading a double-life, a simple, honest warehouse worker by day, by night a dynamic *czar* of the *underworld, Mother.* I go to gambling casinos, I spin away fortunes on the roulette table! I wear a patch over one eye and a false mustache, sometimes I put on green whiskers. On those occasions they call me—*El Diablo!*[5] Oh, I could tell you many things to make you sleepless! My enemies plan to dynamite this place. They're going to blow us all sky-high some night! I'll be glad, very happy, and so will you! You'll go up, up on a broomstick, over Blue Mountain with seventeen gentlemen callers! You ugly—babbling old—*witch.* . . .

(He goes through a series of violent, clumsy movements, seizing his overcoat, lunging to the door, pulling it fiercely open. The women watch him, aghast. His arm catches in the sleeve of the coat as he struggles to pull it on. For a moment he is pinioned by the bulky garment. With an outraged groan he tears the coat off again, splitting the shoulder of it, and hurls it across the room. It strikes against the shelf of Laura's glass collection, and there is a tinkle of shattering glass. Laura cries out as if wounded.)

(Music.)

(Screen legend: "The Glass Menagerie."*)*

Laura *(shrilly).* My glass!—menagerie. . . . *(She covers her face and turns away.)*

(But Amanda is still stunned and stupefied by the "ugly witch" so that she barely notices this occurrence. Now she recovers her speech.)

Amanda *(in an awful voice).* I won't speak to you—until you apologize!

(She crosses through the portieres and draws them together behind her. Tom is left with Laura. Laura clings weakly to the mantel with her face averted. Tom stares at her stupidly for a moment. Then he crosses to the shelf. He drops awkwardly on his knees to collect the fallen glass, glancing at Laura as if he would speak but couldn't.)

("The Glass Menagerie" music steals in as the scene dims out.)

Scene Four

The interior of the apartment is dark. There is a faint light in the alley. A deep-voiced bell in a church is tolling the hour of five.

Tom appears at the top of the alley. After each solemn boom of the bell in the tower, he shakes a little noisemaker or rattle as if to express the tiny spasm of man in contrast

---

[5]Spanish: The Devil!

to the sustained power and dignity of the Almighty. This and the unsteadiness of his advance make it evident that he has been drinking. As he climbs the few steps to the fire escape landing light steals up inside. Laura appears in the front room in a night-dress. She notices that Tom's bed is empty. Tom fishes in his pockets for his door key, removing a motley assortment of articles in his search, including a shower of movie ticket stubs and an empty bottle. At last he finds the key, but just as he is about to insert it, it slips from his fingers. He strikes a match and crouches below the door.

Tom (bitterly). One crack—and it falls through!

(Laura opens the door.)

Laura. Tom! Tom, what are you doing?
Tom. Looking for a door key.
Laura. Where have you been all this time?
Tom. I have been to the movies.
Laura. All this time at the movies?
Tom. There was a very long program. There was a Garbo picture and a Mickey Mouse and a travelogue and a newsreel and a preview of coming attractions. And there was an organ solo and a collection for the Milk Fund—simultaneously—which ended up in a terrible fight between a fat lady and an usher!
Laura (innocently). Did you have to stay through everything?
Tom. Of course! And, oh, I forgot! There was a big stage show! The head-liner on this stage show was Malvolio the Magician. He performed wonderful tricks, many of them, such as pouring water back and forth between pitchers. First it turned to wine and then it turned to beer and then it turned to whisky. I know it was whisky it finally turned into because he needed somebody to come up out of the audience to help him, and I came up—both shows! It was Kentucky Straight Bourbon. A very generous fellow, he gave souvenirs. *(He pulls from his back pocket a shimmering rainbow-colored scarf.)* He gave me this. This is his magic scarf. You can have it, Laura. You wave it over a canary cage and you get a bowl of goldfish. You wave it over the goldfish bowl and they fly away canaries. . . . But the wonderfullest trick of all was the coffin trick. We nailed him into a coffin and he got out of the coffin without removing one nail. *(He has come inside.)* There is a trick that would come in handy for me—get me out of this two-by-four situation! *(He flops on the bed and starts removing his shoes.)*
Laura. Tom—shhh!
Tom. What're you shushing me for?
Laura. You'll wake up Mother.
Tom. Goody, goody! Pay 'er back for all those "Rise an' Shines." *(He lies down, groaning.)* You know it don't take much intelligence to get yourself

into a nailed-up coffin, Laura. But who the hell ever got himself out of one without removing one nail?

(As if in answer, the father's grinning photograph lights up. The scene dims out.) (Immediately following, the church bell is heard striking six. At the sixth stroke the alarm clock goes off in Amanda's room, and after a few moments we hear her calling: "Rise and Shine! Rise and Shine! Laura, go tell your brother to rise and shine!")

Tom (sitting up slowly). I'll rise—but I won't shine.

(The light increases.)

Amanda. Laura, tell your brother his coffee is ready.

(Laura slips into the front room.)

Laura. Tom!—It's nearly seven. Don't make Mother nervous.

(He stares at her stupidly.)

(beseechingly:) Tom, speak to Mother this morning. Make up with her, apologize, speak to her!
Tom. She won't to me. It's her that started not speaking.
Laura. If you just say you're sorry she'll start speaking.
Tom. Her not speaking—is that such a tragedy?
Laura. Please—please!
Amanda (calling from the kitchenette). Laura, are you going to do what I asked you to do, or do I have to get dressed and go out myself?
Laura. Going, going—soon as I get on my coat!

(She pulls on a shapeless felt hat with a nervous, jerky movement, pleadingly glancing at Tom. She rushes awkwardly for her coat. The coat is one of Amanda's inaccurately made-over, the sleeves too short for Laura.)

Butter and what else?
Amanda (entering from the kitchenette). Just butter. Tell them to charge it.
Laura. Mother, they make such faces when I do that.
Amanda. Sticks and stones can break our bones, but the expression on Mr. Garfinkel's face won't harm us! Tell your brother his coffee is getting cold.
Laura (at the door). Do what I asked you, will you, will you, Tom?

(He looks sullenly away.)

Amanda. Laura, go now or just don't go at all!
Laura (rushing out). Going—going!

(A second later she cries out. Tom springs up and crosses to the door. Tom opens the door.)

Tom. Laura?

Laura. I'm all right. I slipped, but I'm all right.

Amanda (peering anxiously after her). If anyone breaks a leg on those fire-escape steps, the landlord ought to be sued for every cent he possesses! *(She shuts the door. Now she remembers she isn't speaking to Tom and returns to the other room.)*

(As Tom comes listlessly for his coffee, she turns her back to him and stands rigidly facing the window on the gloomy gray vault of the areaway. Its light on her face with its aged but childish features is cruelly sharp, satirical as a Daumier[6] print.)

(The music of "Ave Maria" is heard softly.)

(Tom glances sheepishly but sullenly at her averted figure and slumps at the table. The coffee is scalding hot; he sips it and gasps and spits it back in the cup. At his gasp, Amanda catches her breath and half turns. Then she catches herself and turns back to the window. Tom blows on his coffee, glancing side-wise at his mother She clears her throat. Tom clears his. He starts to rise, sinks back down again, scratches his head, clears his throat again. Amanda coughs. Tom raises his cup in both hands to blow on it, his eyes staring over the rim of it at his mother for several moments. Then he slowly sets the cup down and awkwardly and hesitantly rises from the chair.)

Tom (hoarsely). Mother. I—I apologize, Mother.

(Amanda draws a quick, shuddering breath. Her face works grotesquely. She breaks into childlike tears.)

I'm sorry for what I said, for everything that I said, I didn't mean it.

Amanda (sobbingly). My devotion has made me a witch and so I make myself hateful to my children!

Tom. No, you *don't.*

Amanda. I worry so much, don't sleep, it makes me nervous!

Tom (gently). I understand that.

Amanda. I've had to put up a solitary battle all these years. But you're my right-hand bower! Don't fall down, don't fail!

Tom (gently). I try, Mother.

Amanda (with great enthusiasm). Try and you will *succeed!* *(The notion makes her breathless.)* Why, you—you're just *full* of natural endowments! Both of my children—they're *unusual* children! Don't you think I know it? I'm so—*proud!* Happy and—feel I've—so much to be thankful for but—promise me one thing, son!

---

[6]Honoré Daumier (1808–1879). French caricaturist, painter, and sculptor.

Tom.   What, Mother?

Amanda.   Promise, son, you'll—never be a drunkard!

Tom (turns to her grinning). I will never be a drunkard, Mother.

Amanda.   That's what frightened me so, that you'd be drinking! Eat a bowl of Purina!

Tom.   Just coffee, Mother.

Amanda.   Shredded wheat biscuit?

Tom.   No. No, Mother, just coffee.

Amanda.   You can't put in a day's work on an empty stomach. You've got ten minutes—don't gulp! Drinking too-hot liquids makes cancer of the stomach. . . . Put cream in.

Tom.   No, thank you.

Amanda.   To cool it.

Tom.   No! No, thank you, I want it black.

Amanda.   I know, but it's not good for you. We have to do all that we can to build ourselves up. In these trying times we live in, all that we have to cling to is—each other. . . . That's why it's important to—Tom, I—I sent out your sister so I could discuss something with you. If you hadn't spoken I would have spoken to you. *(She sits down.)*

Tom (gently). What is it, Mother, that you want to discuss?

Amanda.   *Laura!*

(Tom puts his cup down slowly.)

(Legend on screen: "Laura." Music: "The Glass Menagerie.")

Tom.   —Oh.—Laura . . .

Amanda (touching his sleeve). You know how Laura is. So quiet but—still water runs deep! She notices things and I think she—broods about them.

(Tom looks up.)

A few days ago I came in and she was crying.

Tom.   What about?

Amanda.   You.

Tom.   Me?

Amanda.   She has an idea that you're not happy here.

Tom.   What gave her that idea?

Amanda.   What gives her any idea? However, you do act strangely. I—I'm not criticizing, understand *that*! I know your ambitions do not lie in the warehouse, that like everybody in the whole wide world—you've had to—make sacrifices, but—Tom—Tom—life's not easy, it calls for—Spartan endurance! There's so many things in my heart that I cannot describe to you! I've never told you but I—*loved* your father. . . .

Tom (gently). I know that, Mother.

Amanda. And you—when I see you taking after his ways! Staying out late—and—well, you *had* been drinking the night you were in that—terrifying condition! Laura says that you hate the apartment and that you go out nights to get away from it! Is that true, Tom?

Tom. No. You say there's so much in your heart that you can't describe to me. That's true of me, too. There's so much in my heart that I can't describe to *you*! So let's respect each other's—

Amanda. But, why—*why*, Tom—are you always so *restless*? Where do you *go* to, nights?

Tom. I—go to the movies.

Amanda. Why do you go to the movies so much, Tom?

Tom. I go to the movies because—I like adventure. Adventure is something I don't have much of at work, so I go to the movies.

Amanda. But, Tom, you go to the movies *entirely* too *much*!

Tom. I like a lot of adventure.

(Amanda looks baffled, then hurt. As the familiar inquisition resumes, Tom becomes hard and impatient again. Amanda slips back into her querulous attitude toward him.)

(Image on screen: A sailing vessel with Jolly Roger.)

Amanda. Most young men find adventure in their careers.

Tom. Then most young men are not employed in a warehouse.

Amanda. The world is full of young men employed in warehouses and offices and factories.

Tom. Do all of them find adventure in their careers?

Amanda. They do or they do without it! Not everybody has a craze for adventure.

Tom. Man is by instinct a lover, a hunter, a fighter, and none of those instincts are given much play at the warehouse!

Amanda. Man is by instinct! Don't quote instinct to me! Instinct is something that people have got away from! It belongs to animals! Christian adults don't want it!

Tom. What do Christian adults want, then, Mother?

Amanda. Superior things! Things of the mind and the spirit! Only animals have to satisfy instincts! Surely your aims are somewhat higher than theirs! Than monkeys—pigs—

Tom. I reckon they're not.

Amanda. You're joking. However, that isn't what I wanted to discuss.

Tom (rising). I haven't much time.

Amanda (pushing his shoulders). Sit down.

Tom. You want me to punch in red at the warehouse, Mother?

Amanda. You have five minutes. I want to talk about Laura.

(Screen legend: "Plans and Provisions.")

Tom. All right! What about Laura?

Amanda. We have to be making some plans and provisions for her. She's older than you, two years, and nothing has happened. She just drifts along doing nothing. It frightens me terribly how she just drifts along.

Tom. I guess she's the type that people call home girls.

Amanda. There's no such type, and if there is, it's a pity! That is unless the home is hers, with a husband!

Tom. What?

Amanda. Oh, I can see the handwriting on the wall as plain as I see the nose in front of my face! It's terrifying! More and more you remind me of your father! He was out all hours without explanation!—Then *left!* *Goodbye!* And me with the bag to hold. I saw that letter you got from the Merchant Marine. I know what you're dreaming of. I'm not standing here blindfolded. *(She pauses.)* Very well, then. Then *do* it! But not till there's somebody to take your place.

Tom. What do you mean?

Amanda. I mean that as soon as Laura has got somebody to take care of her, married, a home of her own, independent—why, then you'll be free to go wherever you please, on land, on sea, whichever way the wind blows you! But until that time you've got to look out for your sister. I don't say me because I'm old and don't matter! I say for your sister because she's young and dependent.

I put her in business college—a dismal failure! Frightened her so it made her sick at the stomach. I took her over to the Young People's League at the church. Another fiasco. She spoke to nobody, nobody spoke to her. Now all she does is fool with those pieces of glass and play those worn-out records. What kind of a life is that for a girl to lead?

Tom. What can I do about it?

Amanda. Overcome selfishness! Self, self, self is all that you ever think of!

(Tom springs up and crosses to get his coat. It is ugly and bulky. He pulls on a cap with earmuffs.)

Where is your muffler? Put your wool muffler on!

(He snatches it angrily from the closet, tosses it around his neck and pulls both ends tight.)

Tom! I haven't said what I had in mind to ask you.

Tom. I'm too late to—

Amanda (catching his arm—very importunately; then shyly). Down at the
  warehouse, aren't there some—nice young men?
Tom.   No!
Amanda.   There *must* be—*some* . . .
Tom.   Mother—*(He gestures.)*
Amanda.   Find out one that's clean-living—doesn't drink and ask him out
  for sister!
Tom.   What?
Amanda.   For *sister*! To *meet*! Get *acquainted*!
Tom (stamping to the door). Oh, my go-osh!
Amanda.   Will you?

(He opens the door. She says, imploringly:)

  Will you?

(He starts down the fire escape.)

  Will you? *Will* you, dear?
Tom (calling back). Yes!

*(Amanda closes the door hesitantly and with a troubled but faintly hopeful
expression.)*

(Screen image: The cover of a glamor magazine.)

(The spotlight picks up Amanda at the phone.)

Amanda.   Ella Cartwright? This is Amanda Wingfield!
  How are you, honey?
  How is that kidney condition?

(There is a five-second pause.)

  Horrors!

(There is another pause.)

You're a Christian martyr, yes, honey, that's what you are, a Christian martyr! Well, I just now happened to notice in my little red book that your
subscription to the *Companion* has just run out! I knew that you wouldn't
want to miss out on the wonderful serial starting in this new issue. It's by
Bessie Mae Hopper, the first thing she's written since *Honeymoon for*

Three. Wasn't that a strange and interesting story? Well, this one is even lovelier, I believe. It has a sophisticated, society background. It's all about the horsey set on Long Island!

(The light fades out.)

Scene Five

Legend on the screen: "Annunciation."
Music is heard as the light slowly comes on.

It is early dusk of a spring evening. Supper has just been finished in the Wingfield apartment. Amanda and Laura, in light-colored dresses, are removing dishes from the table in the dining room, which is shadowy, their movements formalized almost as a dance or ritual, their moving forms as pale and silent as moths. Tom, in white shirt and trousers, rises from the table and crosses toward the fire escape.

Amanda (as he passes her). Son, will you do me a favor?
Tom. What?
Amanda. Comb your hair! You look so pretty when your hair is combed!

(Tom slouches on the sofa with the evening paper. Its enormous headline reads: "Franco Triumphs.")[7]

There is only one respect in which I would like you to emulate your father.
Tom. What respect is that?
Amanda. The care he always took of his appearance. He never allowed himself to look untidy.

(He throws down the paper and crosses to the fire escape.)

Where are you going?
Tom. I'm going out to smoke.
Amanda. You smoke too much. A pack a day at fifteen cents a pack. How much would that amount to in a month? Thirty times fifteen is how much Tom? Figure it out and you will be astounded at what you could save. Enough to give you a night-school course in accounting at Washington U.! Just think what a wonderful thing that would be for you, son!

---

[7]Francisco Franco Bahamonde (1892–1975), general and leader of the nationalist forces that overthrew the Spanish democratic republic in the Spanish Civil War.

(Tom is unmoved by the thought.)

Tom.   I'd rather smoke. *(He steps out on the landing, letting the screen door slam.)*

Amanda (sharply). I know! That's the tragedy of it. . . . *(Alone, she turns to look at her husband's picture.)*

(Dance music: "The World Is Waiting for the Sunrise!")

Tom (to the audience). Across the alley from us was the Paradise Dance Hall. On evenings in spring the windows and doors were open and the music came outdoors. Sometimes the lights were turned out except for a large glass sphere that hung from the ceiling. It would turn slowly about and filter the dusk with delicate rainbow colors. Then the orchestra played a waltz or a tango, something that had a slow and sensuous rhythm. Couples would come outside, to the relative privacy of the alley. You could see them kissing behind ash pits and telephone poles. This was the compensation for lives that passed like mine, without any change or adventure. Adventure and change were imminent in this year. They were waiting around the corner for all these kids. Suspended in the midst over Berchtesgaden, caught in the folds of Chamberlain's umbrella.[8] In Spain there was Guernica! But here there was only hot swing music and liquor, dance halls, bars, and movies, and sex that hung in the gloom like a chandelier and flooded the world with brief, deceptive rainbows. . . . All the world was waiting for bombardments!

(Amanda turns from the picture and comes outside.)

Amanda (sighing). A fire escape landing's a poor excuse for a porch. *(She spreads a newspaper on a step and sits down, gracefully and demurely as if she were settling into a swing on a Mississippi veranda.)* What are you looking at?

Tom.   The moon.

Amanda.   Is there a moon this evening?

Tom.   It's rising over Garfinkel's Delicatessen.

Amanda.   So it is! A little silver slipper of a moon. Have you made a wish on it yet?

Tom.   Um-hum.

Amanda.   What did you wish for?

---

[8]Arthur Neville Chamberlain (1869–1940), British Prime Minister (1937–40), tried to negotiate peace with Hitler through a policy of appeasement. Accused of gullibility, Neville and his trademark black umbrella became symbols of the folly of trying to strike a deal with evil.

Tom. That's a secret.

Amanda. A secret, huh? Well, I won't tell mine either. I will be just as mysterious as you.

Tom. I bet I can guess what yours is.

Amanda. Is my head so transparent?

Tom. You're not a sphinx.

Amanda. No, I don't have secrets. I'll tell you what I wished for on the moon. Success and happiness for my precious children! I wish for that whenever there's a moon, and when there isn't a moon, I wish for it, too.

Tom. I thought perhaps you wished for a gentleman caller.

Amanda. Why do you say that?

Tom. Don't you remember asking me to fetch one?

Amanda. I remember suggesting that it would be nice for your sister if you brought home some nice young man from the warehouse. I think that I've made that suggestion more than once.

Tom. Yes, you have made it repeatedly.

Amanda. Well?

Tom. We are going to have one.

Amanda. *What?*

Tom. A gentleman caller!

(The annunciation is celebrated with music.)

(Amanda rises.)

(Image on screen: A caller with a bouquet.)

Amanda. You mean you have asked some nice young man to come over?

Tom. Yep. I've asked him to dinner.

Amanda. You really did?

Tom. I did!

Amanda. You did, and did he—*accept?*

Tom. He did!

Amanda. Well, well—well, well! That's—lovely!

Tom. I thought that you would be pleased.

Amanda. It's definite then?

Tom. Very definite.

Amanda. Soon?

Tom. Very soon.

Amanda. For heaven's sake, stop putting on and tell me some things, will you?

Tom. What things do you want me to tell you?

Amanda. *Naturally* I would like to know when he's *coming!*

Tom. He's coming tomorrow.

Amanda. *Tomorrow?*

Tom. Yep. Tomorrow.

Amanda. But, Tom!

Tom. Yes, Mother?

Amanda. Tomorrow gives me no time!

Tom. Time for what?

Amanda. Preparations! Why didn't you phone me at once, as soon as you asked him, the minute that he accepted? Then, don't you see, I could have been getting ready!

Tom. You don't have to make any fuss.

Amanda. Oh, Tom, Tom, Tom, of course I have to make a fuss! I want things nice, not sloppy! Not thrown together. I'll certainly have to do some fast thinking, won't I?

Tom. I don't see why you have to think at all.

Amanda. You just don't know. We can't have a gentleman caller in a pigsty! All my wedding silver has to be polished, the monogrammed table linen ought to be laundered! The windows have to be washed and fresh curtains put up. And how about clothes? We have to *wear* something, don't we?

Tom. Mother, this boy is no one to make a fuss over!

Amanda. Do you realize he's the first young man we've introduced to your sister? It's terrible, dreadful, disgraceful that poor little sister has never received a single gentleman caller! Tom, come inside!

(She opens the screen door.)

Tom. What for?

Amanda. I want to ask you some things.

Tom. If you're going to make such a fuss, I'll call it off, I'll tell him not to come!

Amanda. You certainly won't do anything of the kind. Nothing offends people worse than broken engagements. It simply means I'll have to work like a Turk! We won't be brilliant, but we will pass inspection. Come on inside.

(Tom follows her inside, groaning.)

Sit down.

Tom. Any particular place you would like me to sit?

Amanda. Thank heavens I've got that new sofa! I'm also making payments on a floor lamp I'll have sent out! And put the chintz covers on, they'll brighten things up! Of course I'd hoped to have these walls re-papered. . . . What is the young man's name?

Tom. His name is O'Connor.

Amanda. That, of course, means fish—tomorrow is Friday! I'll have that salmon loaf—with Durkee's dressing! What does he do? He works at the warehouse?

Tom.   Of course! How else would I—

Amanda.   Tom, he—doesn't drink?

Tom.   Why do you ask me that?

Amanda.   Your father *did*!

Tom.   Don't get started on that!

Amanda.   He *does* drink, then?

Tom.   Not that I know of!

Amanda.   Make sure, be certain! The last thing I want for my daughter's a boy who drinks!

Tom.   Aren't you being a little bit premature? Mr. O'Connor has not yet appeared on the scene!

Amanda.   But will tomorrow. To meet your sister, and what do I know about his character? Nothing! Old maids are better off than wives of drunkards!

Tom.   Oh, my God!

Amanda.   Be still!

Tom (leaning forward to whisper).   Lots of fellows meet girls whom they don't marry!

Amanda.   Oh, talk sensibly, Tom—and don't be sarcastic! *(She has gotten a hairbrush.)*

Tom.   What are you doing?

Amanda.   I'm brushing that cowlick down! *(She attacks his hair with the brush.)* What is this young man's position at the warehouse?

Tom (submitting grimly to the brush and the interrogation).   This young man's position is that of a shipping clerk, Mother.

Amanda.   Sounds to me like a fairly responsible job, the sort of a job you would be in if you just had more *get-up.* What is his salary? Have you any idea?

Tom.   I would judge it to be approximately eighty-five dollars a month.

Amanda.   Well—not princely, but—

Tom.   Twenty more than I make.

Amanda.   Yes, how well I know! But for a family man, eighty-five dollars a month is not much more than you can just get by on. . . .

Tom.   Yes, but Mr. O'Connor is not a family man.

Amanda.   He might be, mightn't he? Some time in the future?

Tom.   I see. Plans and provisions.

Amanda.   You are the only young man that I know of who ignores the fact that the future becomes the present, the present the past, and the past turns into everlasting regret if you don't plan for it!

Tom.   I will think that over and see what I can make of it.

Amanda.   Don't be supercilious with your mother! Tell me some more about this—what do you call him?

Tom.   James D. O'Connor. The D. is for Delaney.

Amanda.   Irish on *both* sides! *Gracious!* And doesn't drink?

Tom.   Shall I call him up and ask him right this minute?

Amanda.   The only way to find out about those things is to make discreet inquiries at the proper moment. When I was a girl in Blue Mountain and it was suspected that a young man drank, the girl whose attentions he had been receiving, if any girl *was,* would sometimes speak to the minister of his church, or rather her father would if her father was living, and sort of feel him out on the young man's character. That is the way such things are discreetly handled to keep a young woman from making a tragic mistake!

Tom.   Then how did you happen to make a tragic mistake?

Amanda.   That innocent look of your father's had everyone fooled! He *smiled*—the world was *enchanted*! No girl can do worse than put herself at the mercy of a handsome appearance! I hope that Mr. O'Connor is not too good-looking.

Tom.   No, he's not too good-looking. He's covered with freckles and hasn't too much of a nose.

Amanda.   He's not right-down homely, though?

Tom.   Not right-down homely. Just medium homely, I'd say.

Amanda.   Character's what to look for in a man.

Tom.   That's what I've always said, Mother.

Amanda.   You've never said anything of the kind and I suspect you would never give it a thought.

Tom.   Don't be so suspicious of me.

Amanda.   At least I hope he's the type that's up and coming.

Tom.   I think he really goes in for self-improvement.

Amanda.   What reason have you to think so?

Tom.   He goes to night school.

Amanda (beaming). Splendid! What does he do, I mean study?

Tom.   Radio engineering and public speaking!

Amanda.   Then he has visions of being advanced in the world! Any young man who studies public speaking is aiming to have an executive job some day! And radio engineering! A thing for the future! Both of these facts are very illuminating. Those are the sort of things that a mother should know concerning any young man who comes to call on her daughter. Seriously or—not.

Tom.   One little warning. He doesn't know about Laura. I didn't let on that we had dark ulterior motives. I just said, why don't you come and have dinner with us? He said okay and that was the whole conversation.

Amanda.   I bet it was! You're eloquent as an oyster. However, he'll know about Laura when he gets here. When he sees how lovely and sweet and pretty she is, he'll thank his lucky stars he was asked to dinner.

Tom.   Mother, you mustn't expect too much of Laura.

Amanda.   What do you mean?

Tom. Laura seems all those things to you and me because she's ours and we love her. We don't even notice she's crippled any more.

Amanda. Don't say crippled! You know that I never allow that word to be used!

Tom. But face facts, Mother. She is and—that's not all—

Amanda. What do you mean "not all"?

Tom. Laura is very different from other girls.

Amanda. I think the difference is to her advantage.

Tom. Not quite all—in the eyes of others—strangers—she's terribly shy and lives in a world of her own and those things make her seem a little peculiar to people outside the house.

Amanda. Don't say peculiar.

Tom. Face the facts. She is.

(The dance hall music changes to a tango that has a minor and somewhat ominous tone.)

Amanda. In what way is she peculiar—may I ask?

Tom (gently). She lives in a world of her own—a world of little glass ornaments, Mother. . . .

(He gets up. Amanda remains holding the brush, looking at him, troubled.)

She plays old phonograph records and—that's about all—*(He glances at himself in the mirror and crosses to the door.)*

Amanda (sharply). Where are you going?

Tom. I'm going to the movies. *(He goes out the screen door.)*

Amanda. Not to the movies, every night to the movies! *(She follows quickly to the screen door.)* I don't believe you always go to the movies!

(He is gone. Amanda looks worriedly after him for a moment. Then vitality and optimism return and she turns from the door, crossing the portieres.)

Laura! Laura!

(Laura answers from the kitchenette.)

Laura. Yes, Mother.

Amanda. Let those dishes go and come in front!

(Laura appears with a dish towel. Amanda speaks to her gaily.)

Laura, come here and make a wish on the moon!

(Screen image: The Moon.*)*

Laura (entering). Moon—moon?
Amanda.   A little silver slipper of a moon. Look over your left shoulder, Laura, and make a wish!

(Laura looks faintly puzzled as if called out of sleep. Amanda seizes her shoulders and turns her at an angle by the door.)

Now! Now, darling, *wish!*
Laura.   What shall I wish for, Mother?
Amanda (her voice trembling and her eyes suddenly filling with tears). Happiness! Good fortune!

(The sound of the violin rises and the stage dims out.)

Scene Six

The light comes up on the fire escape landing. Tom is leaning against the grill, smoking.

(Screen image: The high school hero.*)*

Tom.   And so the following evening I brought Jim home to dinner. I had known Jim slightly in high school. In high school Jim was a hero. He had tremendous Irish good nature and vitality with the scrubbed and polished look of white chinaware. He seemed to move in a continual spotlight. He was a star in basketball, captain of the debating club, president of the senior class and the glee club and he sang the lead in the annual light operas. He was always running or bounding, never just walking. He seemed always at the point of defeating the law of gravity. He was shooting with such velocity through his adolescence that you would logically expect him to arrive at nothing short of the White House by the time he was thirty. But Jim apparently ran into more interference after his graduation from Soldan. His speed had definitely slowed. Six years after he left high school he was holding a job that wasn't much better than mine.

(Screen image: The Clerk.*)*

He was the only one at the warehouse with whom I was on friendly terms. I was valuable to him as someone who could remember his former glory, who had seen him win basketball games and the silver cup in debating. He knew of my secret practice of retiring to a cabinet of the washroom to work on poems when business was slack in the warehouse. He called me Shakespeare. And while the other boys in the warehouse regarded me with suspicious hostility, Jim took a humorous attitude toward me. Gradually his attitude affected the others, their hostility wore off and they also began to smile at me as people smile at an oddly fashioned dog who trots across their path at some distance.

I knew that Jim and Laura had known each other at Soldan, and I had heard Laura speak admiringly of his voice. I didn't know if Jim remembered her or not. In high school Laura had been as unobtrusive as Jim had been astonishing. If he did remember Laura, it was not as my sister, for when I asked him to dinner, he grinned and said, "You know, Shakespeare, I never thought of you as having folks!"

He was about to discover that I did. . . .

(Legend on screen: "The accent of a coming foot.")

(The light dims out on Tom and comes up in the Wingfield living room — a delicate lemony light. It is about five on a Friday evening of late spring which comes "scattering poems in the sky.")

(Amanda has worked like a Turk in preparation for the gentleman caller. The results are astonishing, The new floor lamp with its rose silk shade is in place, a colored paper lantern conceals the broken light fixture in the ceiling, new billowing white curtains are at the windows, chintz covers are on the chairs and sofa, a pair of new sofa pillows make their initial appearance. Open boxes and tissue paper are scattered on the floor.)

(Laura stands in the middle of the room with lifted arms while Amanda crouches before her, adjusting the hem of a new dress, devout and ritualistic. The dress is colored and designed by memory. The arrangement of Laura's hair is changed; it is softer and more becoming. A fragile, unearthly prettiness has come out in Laura: she is like a piece of translucent glass touched by light, given a momentary radiance, not actual, not lasting.)

Amanda (impatiently). Why are you trembling?

Laura.   Mother, you've made me so nervous!

Amanda.   How have I made you nervous?

Laura.   By all this fuss! You make it seem so important!

Amanda.   I don't understand you, Laura. You couldn't be satisfied with just sitting home, and yet whenever I try to arrange something for you, you seem to resist it. *(She gets up.)* Now take a look at yourself. No, wait! Wait just a moment — I have an idea!

Laura.   What is it now?

(Amanda produces two powder puffs which she wraps in handkerchiefs and stuffs in Laura's bosom.)

Laura.   Mother, what are you doing?

Amanda. They call them "Gay Deceivers"!

Laura. I won't wear them!

Amanda. You will!

Laura. Why should I?

Amanda. Because, to be painfully honest, your chest is flat.

Laura. You make it seem like we were setting a trap.

Amanda. All pretty girls are a trap, a pretty trap, and men expect them to be.

(Legend on screen: "A pretty trap.")

Now look at yourself, young lady. This is the prettiest you will ever be! *(She stands back to admire Laura.)* I've got to fly now! You're going to be surprised by your mother's appearance!

(Amanda crosses through the portieres, humming gaily. Laura moves slowly to the long mirror and stares solemnly at herself. A wind blows the white curtains inward in a slow, graceful motion and with a faint, sorrowful sighing.)

Amanda (from somewhere behind the portieres). It isn't dark enough yet.

(Laura turns slowly before the mirror with a troubled look.)

(Legend on screen: "This is my sister: Celebrate her with strings!" Music plays.)

Amanda (laughing, still not visible). I'm going to show you something. I'm going to make a spectacular appearance!

Laura. What is it, Mother?

Amanda. Possess your soul in patience—you will see! Something I've resurrected from that old trunk! Styles haven't changed so terribly much after all. . . . *(She parts the portieres.)* Now just look at your mother! *(She wears a girlish frock of yellowed voile with a blue silk sash. She carries a bunch of jonquils—the legend of her youth is nearly revived. Now she speaks feverishly.)* This is the dress in which I led the cotillion. Won the cakewalk twice at Sunset Hill, wore one Spring to the Governor's Ball in Jackson! See how I sashayed around the ballroom, Laura? *(She raises her skirt and does a mincing step around the room.)* I wore it on Sundays for my gentlemen callers! I had it on the day I met your father. . . . I had malaria fever all that Spring. The change of climate from East Tennessee to the Delta—weakened resistance. I had a little temperature all the time— not enough to be serious—just enough to make me restless and giddy! Invitations poured in—parties all over the Delta! "Stay in bed," said Mother, "you have a fever!"—but I just wouldn't. I took quinine but kept on going, going! Evenings, dances! Afternoons, long, long rides! Picnics—lovely! So lovely, that country in May—all lacy with dogwood, literally flooded with jonquils! That was the spring I had the craze for jonquils. Jonquils became an absolute obsession. Mother said, "Honey, there's no more room for jonquils." And still I kept on bringing in more jonquils. Whenever, wherever I saw them, I'd say, "Stop! Stop! I see jonquils!" I made the young men help me gather the jonquils! It was a joke, Amanda and her jonquils. Finally there were no more vases to hold them, every available space was filled with jonquils. No vases to hold them? All right, I'll hold them myself! And then I—*(She stops in front of the picture. Music plays.)* met your father! Malaria fever and jonquils and then—this—boy.... *(She switches on the rose-colored lamp.)* I hope they get here before it starts to rain. *(She crosses the room and places the jonquils in a bowl on the table.)* I gave your brother a little extra change so he and Mr. O'Connor could take the service car home.

Laura (with an altered look). What did you say his name was?
Amanda.   O'Connor.
Laura.   What is his first name?
Amanda.   I don't remember. Oh, yes, I do. It was—Jim!

(Laura sways slightly and catches hold of a chair.)

(Legend on screen: "Not, Jim!")

Laura (faintly). Not—Jim!
Amanda.   Yes, that was it, it was Jim! I've never known a Jim that wasn't nice! *(The music becomes ominous.)*
Laura.   Are you sure his name is Jim O'Connor?
Amanda.   Yes. Why?
Laura.   Is he the one that Tom used to know in high school?
Amanda.   He didn't say so. I think he just got to know him at the warehouse.
Laura.   There was a Jim O'Connor we both knew in high school—*(then, with effort)* If that is the one that Tom is bringing to dinner—you'll have to excuse me, I won't come to the table.
Amanda.   What sort of nonsense is this?
Laura.   You asked me once if I'd ever liked a boy. Don't you remember I showed you this boy's picture?
Amanda.   You mean the boy you showed me in the year-book?
Laura.   Yes, that boy.
Amanda.   Laura, Laura, were you in love with that boy?
Laura.   I don't know, Mother. All I know is I couldn't sit at the table if it was him!
Amanda.   It won't be him! It isn't the least bit likely. But whether it is or not, you will come to the table. You will not be excused.

Laura. I'll have to be, Mother.

Amanda. I don't intend to humor your silliness, Laura. I've had too much from you and your brother, both! So just sit down and compose yourself till they come. Tom has forgotten his key so you'll have to let them in, when they arrive.

Laura (panicky). Oh, Mother—*you* answer the door!

Amanda (lightly). I'll be in the kitchen—busy!

Laura. Oh, Mother, please answer the door, don't make me do it!

Amanda (crossing into the kitchenette). I've got to fix the dressing for the salmon. Fuss, fuss—silliness!—over a gentleman caller!

(The door swings shut. Laura is left alone.)

(Legend on screen: "Terror!")

(She utters a low moan and turns off the lamp—sits stiffly on the edge of the sofa, knotting her fingers together.)

(Legend on screen: "The Opening of a Door!")

(Tom and Jim appear on the fire escape steps and climb to the landing. Hearing their approach, Laura rises with a panicky gesture. She retreats to the portieres. The doorbell rings. Laura catches her breath and touches her throat. Low drums sound.)

Amanda (calling). Laura, sweetheart! The door!

(Laura stares at it without moving.)

Jim. I think we just beat the rain.

Tom. Uh-huh. *(He rings again, nervously. Jim whistles and fishes for a cigarette.)*

Amanda (very, very gaily). Laura, that is your brother and Mr. O'Connor! Will you let them in, darling!

(Laura crosses toward the kitchenette door.)

Laura (breathlessly). Mother—you go to the door!

(Amanda steps out of the kitchenette and stares furiously at Laura. She points imperiously at the door)

Laura. Please, please!

Amanda (in fierce whisper). What is the matter with you, you silly thing?

Laura (desperately). Please, you answer it, *please*!

Amanda. I told you I wasn't going to humor you, Laura. Why have you chosen this moment to lose your mind?

Laura. Please, please, please, you go!

Amanda. You'll have to go to the door because I can't!

Laura (despairingly). I can't either!

Amanda. *Why?*

Laura. I'm *sick!*

Amanda. I'm sick, too—of your nonsense! Why can't you and your brother be normal people? Fantastic whims and behavior!

(Tom gives a long ring.)

Preposterous goings on! Can you give me one reason—*(She calls out lyrically.) Coming! Just one second!*—why should you be afraid to open a door? Now you answer it, Laura!

Laura. Oh, oh, oh . . . *(She returns through the portieres, darts to the Victrola, winds it frantically and turns it on.)*

Amanda. Laura Wingfield, you march right to that door!

Laura. Yes—yes, Mother!

(A faraway, scratchy rendition of "Dardanella" softens the air and gives her strength to move through it. She slips to the door and draws it cautiously open. Tom enters with the caller, Jim O'Connor.)

Tom. Laura, this is Jim. Jim, this is my sister, Laura.

Jim (stepping inside). I didn't know that Shakespeare had a sister!

Laura (retreating, stiff and trembling, from the door). How—how do you do?

Jim (heartily, extending his hand). Okay!

(Laura touches it hesitantly with hers.)

Jim. Your hand's *cold,* Laura!

Laura. Yes, well—I've been playing the Victrola. . . .

Jim. Must have been playing classical music on it! You ought to play a little hot swing music to warm you up!

Laura. Excuse me—I haven't finished playing the Victrola. . . . *(She awkwardly hurries into the front room. She pauses a second by the Victrola. Then she catches her breath and darts through the portieres like a frightened deer.)*

Jim (grinning). What was the matter?

Tom. Oh—with Laura? Laura is—terribly shy.

Jim. Shy, huh? It's unusual to meet a shy girl nowadays. I don't believe you ever mentioned you had a sister.

Tom. Well, now you know. I have one. Here is the *Post Dispatch.* You want a piece of it?

Jim.   Uh-huh.

Tom.   What piece? The comics?

Jim.   Sports! *(He glances at it.)* Ole Dizzy Dean is on his bad behavior.

Tom (uninterested). Yeah? *(He lights a cigarette and goes over to the fire-escape door.)*

Jim.   Where are *you* going?

Tom.   I'm going out on the terrace.

Jim (going after him). You know, Shakespeare—I'm going to sell you a bill of goods!

Tom.   What goods?

Jim.   A course I'm taking.

Tom.   Huh?

Jim.   In public speaking! You and me, we're not the warehouse type.

Tom.   Thanks—that's good news. But what has public speaking got to do with it?

Jim.   It fits you for—executive positions!

Tom.   Awww.

Jim.   I tell you it's done a helluva lot for me.

(Image on screen: Executive at his desk.)

Tom.   In what respect?

Jim.   In every! Ask yourself what is the difference between you an' me and men in the office down front? Brains?—No!—Ability?—No! Then what? Just one little thing—

Tom.   What is that one little thing?

Jim.   Primarily it amounts to—social poise! Being able to square up to people and hold your own on any social level!

Amanda (from the kitchenette). Tom?

Tom.   Yes, Mother?

Amanda.   Is that you and Mr. O'Connor?

Tom.   Yes, Mother.

Amanda.   Well, you just make yourselves comfortable in there.

Tom.   Yes, Mother.

Amanda.   Ask Mr. O'Connor if he would like to wash his hands.

Jim.   Aw, no—no—thank you—I took care of that at the warehouse. Tom—

Tom.   Yes?

Jim.   Mr. Mendoza was speaking to me about you.

Tom.   Favorably?

Jim.   What do you think?

Tom.   Well—

Jim.   You're going to be out of a job if you don't wake up.

Tom.   I am waking up—
Jim.   You show no signs.
Tom.   The signs are interior.

(Image on screen: The sailing vessel with the Jolly Roger again.*)*

Tom.   I'm planning to change. *(He leans over the fire-escape rail, speaking with quiet exhilaration. The incandescent marquees and signs of the first-run movie houses light his face from across the alley. He looks like a voyager.)* I'm right at the point of committing myself to a future that doesn't include the warehouse and Mr. Mendoza or even a night-school course in public speaking.
Jim.   What are you gassing about?
Tom.   I'm tired of the movies.
Jim.   Movies!
Tom.   Yes, movies! Look at them—*(a wave toward the marvels of Grand Avenue)* All of those glamorous people—having adventures—hogging it all, gobbling the whole thing up! You know what happens? People go to the *movies* instead of *moving*! Hollywood characters are supposed to have all the adventures for everybody in America, while everybody in America sits in a dark room and watches them have them! Yes, until there's a war. That's when adventure becomes available to the masses! *Everyone's* dish, not only Gable's! Then the people in the dark room come out of the dark room to have some adventures themselves—goody, goody! It's our turn now, to go to the South Sea Island—to make a safari—to be exotic, far-off! But I'm not patient. I don't want to wait till then. I'm tired of the *movies* and I am *about* to *move*!
Jim (incredulously). Move?
Tom.   Yes.
Jim.   When?
Tom.   Soon!
Jim.   Where? When?

(The music seems to answer the question, while Tom thinks it over. He searches in his pockets.)

Tom.   I'm starting to boil inside. I know I seem dreamy, but inside—well, I'm boiling! Whenever I pick up a shoe, I shudder a little thinking how short life is and what I am doing! Whatever that means, I know it doesn't mean shoes—except as something to wear on a traveler's feet! *(He finds what he has been searching for in his pockets and holds out a paper to Jim.)* Look—
Jim.   What?
Tom.   I'm a member.

Jim (reading). The Union of Merchant Seamen.

Tom. I paid my dues this month, instead of the light bill.

Jim. You will regret it when they turn the lights off.

Tom. I won't be here.

Jim. How about your mother?

Tom. I'm like my father. The bastard son of a bastard! Did you notice how he's grinning in his picture in there? And he's been absent going on sixteen years!

Jim. You're just talking, you drip. How does your mother feel about it?

Tom. Shhh! Here comes Mother! Mother is not acquainted with my plans!

Amanda (coming through the poitieres). Where are you all?

Tom. On the terrace, Mother,

(They start inside. She advances to them. Tom is distinctly shocked at her appearance. Even Jim blinks a little. He is making his first contact with girlish Southern vivacity and in spite of the night-school course in public speaking is somewhat thrown off the beam by the unexpected outlay of social charm. Certain responses are attempted by Jim but are swept aside by Amanda's gay laughter and chatter. Tom is embarrassed but after the first shock Jim reacts very warmly. He grins and chuckles, is altogether won over.)

(Image on screen: Amanda as a girl.)

Amanda (coyly smiling, shaking her girlish ringlets). Well, well, well, so this is Mr. O'Connor. Introductions entirely unnecessary. I've heard so much about you from my boy. I finally said to him, Tom—good gracious!— why don't you bring this paragon to supper? I'd like to meet this nice young man at the warehouse!—instead of just hearing him sing your praises so much! I don't know why my son is so stand-offish—that's not Southern behavior!

Let's sit down and—I think we could stand a little more air in here! Tom, leave the door open. I felt a nice fresh breeze a moment ago. Where has it gone to? Mmm, so warm already! And not quite summer, even. We're going to burn up when summer really gets started. However, we're having—we're having a very light supper. I think light things are better fo' this time of year. The same as light clothes are. Light clothes an' light food are what warm weather calls fo'. You know our blood gets so thick during th' winter—it takes a while fo' us to *adjust* ou'selves—when the season changes . . . It's come so quick this year. I wasn't prepared. All of a sud-den—heavens! Already summer! I ran to the trunk an' pulled out this light dress—terribly old! Historical almost! But feels so good—so good an' co-ol, y' know. . . .

Tom. Mother—

Amanda. Yes, honey?

Tom. How about—supper?

Amanda. Honey, you go ask Sister if supper is ready! You know that Sister is in full charge of supper! Tell her you hungry boys are waiting for it. *(to Jim)* Have you met Laura?

Jim. She—

Amanda. Let you in? Oh, good, you've met already! It's rare for a girl as sweet an' pretty as Laura to be domestic! But Laura is, thank heavens, not only pretty but also very domestic. I'm not at all. I never was a bit. I never could make a thing but angel-food cake. Well, in the South we had so many servants. Gone, gone, gone. All vestiges of gracious living! Gone completely! I wasn't prepared for what the future brought me. All of my gentlemen callers were sons of planters and so of course I assumed that I would be married to one and raise my family on a large piece of land with plenty of servants. But man proposes—and woman accepts the proposal! To vary that old, old saying a little bit—I married no planter! I married a man who worked for the telephone company! That gallantly smiling gentleman over there! *(She points to the picture.)* A telephone man who—fell in love with long-distance! Now he travels and I don't even know where! But what am I going on for about my—tribulations? Tell me yours—I hope you don't have any! Tom?

Tom (returning). Yes, Mother?

Amanda. Is supper nearly ready?

Tom. It looks to me like supper is on the table.

Amanda. Let me look—*(She rises prettily and looks through the portieres.)* Oh, lovely! But where is Sister?

Tom. Laura is not feeling well and says that she thinks she'd better not come to the table.

Amanda. What? Nonsense! Laura? Oh, Laura!

Laura (from the kitchenette, faintly). Yes, Mother.

Amanda. You really must come to the table. We won't be seated until you come to the table! Come in, Mr. O'Connor. You sit over there, and I'll. . . . Laura? Laura Wingfield! You're keeping us waiting, honey! We can't say grace until you come to the table!

(The kitchenette door is pushed weakly open and Laura comes in. She is obviously quite faint, her lips trembling, her eyes wide and staring. She moves unsteadily toward the table.)

(Screen legend: "Terror!")

(Outside a summer storm is coming on abruptly. The white curtains billow inward at the windows and there is a sorrowful murmur from the deep blue dusk.)

(Laura suddenly stumbles; she catches at a chair with a faint moan.)

Tom. Laura!
Amanda. Laura!

(There is a clap of thunder)

(Screen legend: "Ah!")

(despairingly) Why, Laura, you *are* ill, darling! Tom, help your sister into the living room, dear! Sit in the living room, Laura—rest on the sofa. Well! *(to Jim as Tom helps his sister to the sofa in the living room)* Standing over the hot stove made her ill! I told her that it was just too warm this evening, but—

(Tom comes back to the table.)

Is Laura all right now?
Tom. Yes.
Amanda. What *is* that? Rain? A nice cool rain has come up! *(She gives Jim a frightened look.)* I think we may—have grace—now . . .
(Tom looks at her stupidly.) Tom, honey—you say grace!
Tom. Oh . . . "For these and all thy mercies—"

(They bow their heads, Amanda stealing a nervous glance at Jim. In the living room Laura, stretched on the sofa, clenches her hand to her lips, to hold back a shuddering sob.)

God's Holy Name be praised—

(The scene dims out.)

Scene Seven

It is half an hour later. Dinner is just being finished in the dining room. Laura is still huddled upon the sofa, her feet drawn under her, her head resting on a pale blue pillow, her eyes wide and mysteriously watchful. The new floor lamp with its shade of rose-colored silk gives a soft, becoming light to her face, bringing out the fragile, unearthly prettiness which usually escapes attention. From outside there is a steady murmur of rain, but it is slackening and soon stops; the air outside becomes pale and luminous as the moon breaks through the clouds. A moment after the curtain rises, the lights in both rooms flicker and go out.

Jim. Hey, there, Mr. Light Bulb!

(Amanda laughs nervously.)

(Legend on screen: "Suspension of public service.")

Amanda. Where was Moses when the lights went out? Ha-ha. Do you know the answer to that one, Mr. O'Connor?

Jim. No, Ma'am, what's the answer?

Amanda. In the dark!

(Jim laughs appreciatively.)

Everybody sit still. I'll light the candles. Isn't it lucky we have them on the table? Where's a match? Which of you gentlemen can provide a match?

Jim. Here.

Amanda. Thank you, Sir.

Jim. Not at all, Ma'am!

Amanda (as she lights the candles). I guess the fuse has burnt out. Mr. O'Connor, can you tell a burnt-out fuse? I know I can't and Tom is a total loss when it comes to mechanics.

(They rise from the table and go into the kitchenette, from where their voices are heard.)

Oh, be careful you don't bump into something. We don't want our gentleman caller to break his neck. Now wouldn't that be a fine howdy-do?

Jim. Ha-ha! Where is the fuse-box?

Amanda. Right here next to the stove. Can you see anything?

Jim. Just a minute.

Amanda. Isn't electricity a mysterious thing? Wasn't it Benjamin Franklin who tied a key to a kite? We live in such a mysterious universe, don't we? Some people say that science clears up all the mysteries for us. In my opinion it only creates more! Have you found it yet?

Jim. No, Ma'am. All these fuses look okay to me.

Amanda. Tom!

Tom. Yes, Mother?

Amanda. That light bill I gave you several days ago. The one I told you we got the notices about?

(Legend on screen: "Ha!")

Tom. Oh—yeah.

Amanda. You didn't neglect to pay it by any chance?

Tom. Why, I—

Amanda. Didn't! I might have known it!

Jim. Shakespeare probably wrote a poem on that light bill, Mrs. Wingfield.

Amanda. I might have known better than to trust him with it! There's such a high price for negligence in this world!

Jim. Maybe the poem will win a ten-dollar prize!

Amanda. We'll just have to spend the remainder of the evening in the nineteenth century, before Mr. Edison made the Mazda lamp!

Jim. Candlelight is my favorite kind of light.

Amanda. That shows you're romantic! But that's no excuse for Tom. Well, we got through dinner. Very considerate of them to let us get through dinner before they plunged us into everlasting darkness, wasn't it, Mr. O'Connor?

Jim. Ha-ha!

Amanda. Tom, as a penalty for your carelessness you can help me with the dishes.

Jim. Let me give you a hand.

Amanda. Indeed you will not!

Jim. I ought to be good for something.

Amanda. Good for something? (*Her tone is rhapsodic.*) Why, Mr. O'Connor, nobody, *nobody's* given me this much entertainment in years—as you have!

Jim. Aw, now, Mrs. Wingfield!

Amanda. I'm not exaggerating, not one bit! But Sister is all by her lonesome. You go keep her company in the parlor! I'll give you this lovely old candelabrum that used to be on the altar at the Church of the Heavenly Rest. It was melted a little out of shape when the church burnt down. Lightning struck it one spring. Gypsy Jones was holding a revival at the time and he intimated that the church was destroyed because the Episcopalians gave card parties.

Jim. Ha-ha.

Amanda. And how about you coaxing Sister to drink a little wine? I think it would be good for her! Can you carry both at once?

Jim. Sure. I'm Superman!

Amanda. Now, Thomas, get into this apron!

(*Jim comes into the dining room, carrying the candelabrum, its candles lighted, in one hand and a glass of wine in the other. The door of the kitchenette swings closed on Amanda's gay laughter; the flickering light approaches the portieres. Laura sits up nervously as Jim enters. She can hardly speak from the almost intolerable strain of being alone with a stranger*)

(*Screen legend:* "I don't suppose you remember me at all!")

(*At first, before Jim's warmth overcomes her paralyzing shyness, Laura's voice is thin and breathless, as though she had just run up a steep flight of stairs. Jim's attitude is gently humorous. While the incident is apparently unimportant, it is to Laura the climax of her secret life.*)

Jim. Hello there, Laura.

Laura (faintly). Hello.

(She clears her throat.)

Jim.   How are you feeling now? Better?

Laura.   Yes. Yes, thank you.

Jim.   This is for you. A little dandelion wine. *(He extends the glass toward her with extravagant gallantry.)*

Laura.   Thank you.

Jim.   Drink it—but don't get drunk!

(He laughs heartily. Laura takes the glass uncertainly; she laughs shyly.)

Where shall I set the candles?

Laura.   Oh—oh, anywhere . . .

Jim.   How about here on the floor? Any objections?

Laura.   No.

Jim.   I'll spread a newspaper under to catch the drippings. I like to sit on the floor. Mind if I do?

Laura.   Oh, no.

Jim.   Give me a pillow?

Laura.   What?

Jim.   A pillow!

Laura.   Oh . . . *(She hands him one quickly.)*

Jim.   How about you? Don't you like to sit on the floor?

Laura.   Oh—yes.

Jim.   Why don't you, then?

Laura.   I—will.

Jim.   Take a pillow!

(Laura does. She sits on the floor on the other side of the candelabrum. Jim crosses his legs and smiles engagingly at her.)

I can't hardly see you sitting way over there.

Laura.   I can—see you.

Jim.   I know, but that's not fair, I'm in the limelight.

(Laura moves her pillow closer.)

Good! Now I can see you! Comfortable?

Laura.   Yes.

Jim.   So am I. Comfortable as a cow! Will you have some gum?

Laura.   No thank you.

Jim.   I think that I will indulge, with your permission. *(He musingly unwraps a stick of gum and holds it up.)* Think of the fortune made by the guy that invented the first piece of chewing gum. Amazing, huh? The Wrigley Building is one of the sights of Chicago—I saw it when I went up to the Century of Progress. Did you take in the Century of Progress?

Laura. No, I didn't.

Jim. Well, it was quite a wonderful exposition. What impressed me most was the Hall of Science. Gives you an idea of what the future will be in America, even more wonderful than the present time is! *(There is a pause. Jim smiles at her.)* Your brother tells me you're shy. Is that right, Laura?

Laura. I—don't know.

Jim. I judge you to be an old-fashioned type of girl. Well, I think that's a pretty good type to be. Hope you don't think I'm being too personal—do you?

Laura (hastily, out of embarrassment). I believe I *will* take a piece of gum, if you—don't mind. *(clearing her throat)* Mr. O'Connor, have you—kept up with your singing?

Jim. Singing? Me?

Laura. Yes. I remember what a beautiful voice you had.

Jim. When did you hear me sing?

(Laura does not answer, and in the long pause which follows a man's voice is heard singing offstage.)

> VOICE:
> O blow, ye winds, heigh-ho,
> A-roving I will go!
> I'm off to my love
> With a boxing glove—
> Ten thousand miles away!

Jim. You say you've heard me sing?

Laura. Oh, yes! Yes, very often . . . I—don't suppose—you remember me—at all?

Jim (smiling doubtfully). You know I have an idea I've seen you before. I had that idea as soon as you opened the door. It seemed almost like I was about to remember your name. But the name that I started to call you—wasn't a name! And so I stopped myself before I said it.

Laura. Wasn't it—Blue Roses?

Jim (springing up, grinning). Blue Roses! My gosh, yes—Blue Roses! That's what I had on my tongue when you opened the door! Isn't it funny what tricks your memory plays? I didn't connect you with high school somehow or other. But that's where it was; it was high school. I didn't even know you were Shakespeare's sister! Gosh, I'm sorry.

Laura. I didn't expect you to. You—barely knew me!

Jim. But we did have a speaking acquaintance, huh?

Laura. Yes, we—spoke to each other.

Jim. When did you recognize me?

Laura. Oh, right away!

Jim. Soon as I came in the door?

Laura. When I heard your name I thought it was probably you. I knew that Tom used to know you a little in high school. So when you came in the door—well, then I was—sure.

Jim. Why didn't you *say* something, then?

Laura (breathlessly). I didn't know what to say, I was—too surprised!

Jim. For goodness sakes! You know, this sure is funny!

Laura. Yes! Yes, isn't it, though . . .

Jim. Didn't we have a class in something together?

Laura. Yes, we did.

Jim. What class was that?

Laura. It was—singing—chorus!

Jim. Aw!

Laura. I sat across the aisle from you in the Aud.

Jim. Aw.

Laura. Mondays, Wednesdays, and Fridays.

Jim. Now I remember—you always came in late.

Laura. Yes, it was so hard for me, getting upstairs. I had that brace on my leg—it clumped so loud!

Jim. I never heard any clumping.

Laura (wincing at the recollection). To me it sounded like—thunder!

Jim. Well, well, well, I never even noticed.

Laura. And everybody was seated before I came in. I had to walk in front of all those people. My seat was in the back row. I had to go clumping all the way up the aisle with everyone watching!

Jim. You shouldn't have been self-conscious.

Laura. I know, but I was. It was always such a relief when the singing started.

Jim. Aw, yes, I've placed you now! I used to call you Blue Roses. How was it that I got started calling you that?

Laura. I was out of school a little with pleurosis. When I came back you asked me what was the matter. I said I had pleurosis—you thought I said *Blue Roses.* That's what you always called me after that!

Jim. I hope you didn't mind.

Laura. Oh, no—I liked it. You see, I wasn't acquainted with many—people. . . .

Jim. As I remember you sort of stuck by yourself.

Laura. I—I—never have had much luck at—making friends.

Jim. I don't see why you wouldn't.

Laura. Well, I—started out badly.

Jim. You mean being—

Laura. Yes, it sort of—stood between me—

Jim. You shouldn't have let it!

Laura.   I know, but it did, and—
Jim.   You were shy with people!
Laura.   I tried not to be but never could—
Jim.   Overcome it?
Laura.   No, I—I never could!
Jim.   I guess being shy is something you have to work out of kind of gradually.
Laura (sorrowfully). Yes—I guess it—
Jim.   Takes time!
Laura.   Yes—
Jim.   People are not so dreadful when you know them. That's what you have to remember! And everybody has problems, not just you, but practically everybody has got some problems. You think of yourself as having the only problems, as being the only one who is disappointed. But just look around you and you will see lots of people as disappointed as you are. For instance, I hoped when I was going to high school that I would be further along at this time, six years later, than I am now. You remember that wonderful write-up I had in *The Torch*?
Laura.   Yes! *(She rises and crosses to the table.)*
Jim.   It said I was bound to succeed in anything I went into!

(Laura returns with the high school yearbook.)

   Holy Jeez! *The Torch!*

(He accepts it reverently. They smile across the book with mutual wonder. Laura crouches beside him and they begin to turn the pages. Laura's shyness is dissolving in his warmth.)

Laura.   Here you are in *The Pirates of Penzance*!
Jim (wistfully). I sang the baritone lead in that operetta.
Laura (raptly). So—*beautifully*!
Jim (protesting). Aw—
Laura.   Yes, yes—beautifully—beautifully!
Jim.   You heard me?
Laura.   All three times!
Jim.   No!
Laura.   Yes!
Jim.   All three performances?
Laura (looking down). Yes.
Jim.   Why?
Laura.   I—wanted to ask you to—autograph my program.

(She takes the program from the back of the yearbook and shows it to him.)

Jim.   Why didn't you ask me to?

Laura.   You were always surrounded by your own friends so much that I never had a chance to.

Jim.   You should have just—

Laura.   Well, I—thought you might think I was—

Jim.   Thought I might think you was—what?

Laura.   Oh—

Jim (with reflective relish). I was beleaguered by females in those days.

Laura.   You were terribly popular!

Jim.   Yeah—

Laura.   You had such a—friendly way—

Jim.   I was spoiled in high school.

Laura.   Everybody—liked you!

Jim.   Including you?

Laura.   I—yes, I—did, too—*(She gently closes the book in her lap.)*

Jim.   Well, well, well! Give me that program, Laura.

(She hands it to him. He signs it with a flourish.)

There you are—better late than never!

Laura.   Oh, I—what a—surprise!

Jim.   My signature isn't worth very much right now. But some day—maybe—it will increase in value! Being disappointed is one thing and being discouraged is something else. I am disappointed but I am not discouraged. I'm twenty-three years old. How old are you?

Laura.   I'll be twenty-four in June.

Jim.   That's not old age!

Laura.   No, but—

Jim.   You finished high school?

Laura (with difficulty). I didn't go back.

Jim.   You mean you dropped out?

Laura.   I made bad grades in my final examinations. *(She rises and replaces the book and the program on the table. Her voice is strained.)* How is— Emily Meisenbach getting along?

Jim.   Oh, that kraut-head!

Laura.   Why do you call her that?

Jim.   That's what she was.

Laura.   You're not still—going with her?

Jim.   I never see her.

Laura.   It said in the "Personal" section that you were—engaged!

Jim.   I know, but I wasn't impressed by that—propaganda!

Laura.   It wasn't—the truth?

Jim.   Only in Emily's optimistic opinion!

Laura. Oh—

Legend: "What have you done since high school?")
(Jim lights a cigarette and leans indolently back on his elbows smiling at Laura with a warmth and charm which lights her inwardly with altar candles. She remains by the table, picks up a piece from the glass menagerie collection, and turns it in her hands to cover her tumult.)

Jim (after several reflective puffs on his cigarette). What have you done since high school?

(She seems not to hear him.)

  Huh?

(Laura looks up.)

  I said what have you done since high school, Laura?
Laura. Nothing much.
Jim. You must have been doing something these six long years.
Laura. Yes.
Jim. Well, then, such as what?
Laura. I took a business course at business college—
Jim. How did that work out?
Laura. Well, not very—well—I had to drop out, it gave me—indigestion—

(Jim laughs gently.)

Jim. What are you doing now?
Laura. I don't do anything—much. Oh, please don't think I sit around doing nothing! My glass collection takes up a good deal of time. Glass is something you have to take good care of.
Jim. What did you say—about glass?
Laura. Collection I said—I have one—*(She clears her throat and turns away again, acutely shy.)*
Jim (abruptly). You know what I judge to be the trouble with you? Inferiority complex! Know what that is? That's what they call it when someone low-rates himself! I understand it because I had it, too. Although my case was not so aggravated as yours seems to be. I had it until I took up public speaking, developed my voice, and learned that I had an aptitude for science. Before that time I never thought of myself as being outstanding in any way whatsoever! Now I've never made a regular study of it, but I have a friend who says I can analyze people better than doctors that make a profession of it. I don't claim that to be necessarily true, but I can sure guess a person's psychology, Laura! *(He takes out his gum.)* Excuse me,

Laura. I always take it out when the flavor is gone. I'll use this scrap of paper to wrap it in. I know how it is to get it stuck on a shoe. *(He wraps the gum in paper and puts it in his pocket.)* Yep—that's what I judge to be your principal trouble. A lack of confidence in yourself as a person. You don't have the proper amount of faith in yourself. I'm basing that fact on a number of your remarks and also on certain observations I've made. For instance that clumping you thought was so awful in high school. You say that you even dreaded to walk into class. You see what you did? You dropped out of school, you gave up an education because of a clump, which as far as I know was practically nonexistent! A little physical defect is what you have. Hardly noticeable even! Magnified thousands of times by imagination! You know what my strong advice to you is? Think of yourself as *superior* in some way!

Laura.   In what way would I think?

Jim.   Why, man alive, Laura! just look about you a little. What do you see? A world full of common people! All of 'em born and all of 'em going to die! Which of them has one-tenth of your good points! Or mine! Or anyone else's, as far as that goes—gosh! Everybody excels in some one thing. Some in many! *(He unconsciously glances at himself in the mirror.)* All you've got to do is to discover in what! Take me, for instance. *(He adjusts his tie at the mirror.)* My interest happens to lie in electro-dynamics. I'm taking a course in radio engineering at night school, Laura, on top of a fairly responsible job at the warehouse. I'm taking that course and studying public speaking.

Laura.   Ohhhh.

Jim.   Because I believe in the future of television! *(turning his back to her.)* I wish to be ready to go up right along with it. Therefore I'm planning to get in on the ground floor. In fact I've already made the right connections and all that remains is for the industry itself to get under way! Full steam—*(His eyes are starry.) Knowledge*—Zzzzzp! *Money*—Zzzzzzp!— *Power!* That's the cycle democracy is built on!

(His attitude is convincingly dynamic. Laura stares at him, even her shyness eclipsed in her absolute wonder. He suddenly grins.)

I guess you think I think a lot of myself?

Laura.   No—o-o-o, I—

Jim.   Now how about you? Isn't there something you take more interest in than anything else?

Laura.   Well, I do—as I said—have my—glass collection—

(A peal of girlish laughter rings from the kitchenette.)

Jim.   I'm not right sure I know what you're talking about. What kind of glass is it?

Laura. Little articles of it, they're ornaments mostly! Most of them are little animals made out of glass, the tiniest little animals in the world. Mother calls them the glass menagerie! Here's an example of one, if you'd like to see it! This one is one of the oldest. It's nearly thirteen.

(Music: "The Glass Menagerie.")

Oh, be careful—if you breathe, it breaks!

Jim. I'd better not take it. I'm pretty clumsy with things.

Laura. Go on, I trust you with him! *(She places the piece in his palm.)* There now—you're holding him gently! Hold him over the light, he loves the light! You see how the light shines through him?

Jim. It sure does shine!

Laura. I shouldn't be partial, but he is my favorite one.

Jim. What kind of a thing is this one supposed to be?

Laura. Haven't you noticed the single horn on his forehead?

Jim. A unicorn, huh?

Laura. Mmmm—hmmm!

Jim. Unicorns—aren't they extinct in the modern world?

Laura. I know!

Jim. Poor little fellow, he must feel sort of lonesome.

Laura (smiling). Well, if he does, he doesn't complain about it. He stays on a shelf with some horses that don't have horns and all of them seem to get along nicely together.

Jim. How do you know?

Laura (lightly). I haven't heard any arguments among them!

Jim (grinning). No arguments, huh? Well, that's a pretty good sign! Where shall I set him!

Laura. Put him on the table. They all like a change of scenery once in a while!

Jim. Well, well, well, well—*(He places the glass piece on the table, then raises his arm and stretches.)* Look how big my shadow is when I stretch!

Laura. Oh, oh, yes—it stretches across the ceiling!

Jim (crossing to the door). I think it's stopped raining. *(He opens the fire-escape door and the background music changes to a dance tune.)* Where does the music come from?

Laura. From the Paradise Dance Hall across the alley.

Jim. How about cutting the rug a little, Miss Wingfield?

Laura. Oh, I—

Jim. Or is your program filled up? Let me have a look at it. *(He grasps an imaginary card.)* Why, every dance is taken! I'll just have to scratch some out.

(Waltz music: "La Golondrina.")

Ahhh, a waltz! *(He executes some sweeping turns by himself, then holds his arms toward Laura.*

Laura (breathlessly). I—can't dance!

Jim.   There you go, that inferiority stuff!

Laura.   I've never danced in my life!

Jim.   Come on, try!

Laura.   Oh, but I'd step on you!

Jim.   I'm not made out of glass.

Laura.   How—how—how do we start?

Jim.   Just leave it to me. You hold your arms out a little.

Laura.   Like this?

Jim (taking her in his arms). A little bit higher. Right. Now don't tighten up, that's the main thing about it—relax.

Laura (laughing breathlessly). It's hard not to.

Jim.   Okay.

Laura.   I'm afraid you can't budge me.

Jim.   What do you bet I can't? *(He swings her into motion.)*

Laura.   Goodness, yes, you can!

Jim.   Let yourself go, now, Laura, just let yourself go.

Laura.   I'm—

Jim.   Come on!

Laura.   —trying!

Jim.   Not so stiff—easy does it!

Laura.   I know but I'm—

Jim.   Loosen th' backbone! There now, that's a lot better.

Laura.   Am I?

Jim.   Lots, lots better! *(He moves her about the room in a clumsy waltz.)*

Laura.   Oh, my!

Jim.   Ha-ha!

Laura.   Oh, my goodness!

Jim.   Ha-ha-ha!

(They suddenly bump into the table, and the glass piece on it falls to the floor. Jim stops the dance.)

What did we hit on?

Laura.   Table.

Jim.   Did something fall off it? I think—

Laura.   Yes.

Jim.   I hope that it wasn't the little glass horse with the horn!

Laura.   Yes. *(She stoops to pick it up.)*

Jim.   Aw, aw, aw. It is broken?

Laura.   Now it is just like all the other horses.

Jim. It's lost its—
Laura. Horn! It doesn't matter. Maybe it's a blessing in disguise.
Jim. You'll never forgive me. I bet that that was your favorite piece of glass.
Laura. I don't have favorites much. It's no tragedy, Freckles. Glass breaks so easily. No matter how careful you are. The traffic jars the shelves and things fall off them.
Jim. Still I'm awfully sorry that I was the cause.
Laura (smiling). I'll just imagine he had an operation. The horn was removed to make him feel less—freakish!

(They both laugh.)

Now he will feel more at home with the other horses, the ones that don't have horns.
Jim. Ha-ha, that's very funny! *(Suddenly he is serious.)* I'm glad to see that you have a sense of humor. You know—you're—well—very different! Surprisingly different from anyone else I know! *(His voice becomes soft and hesitant with a genuine feeling.)* Do you mind me telling you that?

(Laura is abashed beyond speech.)

I mean it in a nice way—

(Laura nods shyly, looking away.)

You make me feel sort of—I don't know how to put it! I'm usually pretty good at expressing things, but—this is something that I don't know how to say!

(Laura touches her throat and clears it—turns the broken unicorn in her hands. His voice becomes softer.)

Has anyone ever told you that you were pretty?

(There is a pause, and the music rises slightly. Laura looks up slowly, with wonder and shakes her head.)

Well, you are! In a very different way from anyone else. And all the nicer because of the difference, too.

(His voice becomes low and husky, Laura turns away, nearly faint with the novelty of her emotions.)

I wish that you were my sister. I'd teach you to have some confidence in yourself. The different people are not like other people, but being different is nothing to be ashamed of. Because other people are not such wonderful people. They're one hundred times one thousand. You're one times one! They walk all over the earth. You just stay here. They're common as—weeds, but—you—well, you're—*Blue Roses!*

(Image on screen: Blue Roses.*)*

(The music changes.)

Laura.   But blue is wrong for—roses. . . .
Jim.   It's right for you! You're—pretty!
Laura.   In what respect am I pretty?
Jim.   In all respects—believe me! Your eyes—your hair—are pretty! Your hands are pretty! *(He catches hold of her hand.)* You think I'm making this up because I'm invited to dinner and have to be nice. Oh, I could do that! I could put on an act for you, Laura, and say lots of things without being very sincere. But this time I am. I'm talking to you sincerely. I happened to notice you had this inferiority complex that keeps you from feeling comfortable with people. Somebody needs to build your confidence up and make you proud instead of shy and turning away and—blushing. Somebody—ought to—*kiss* you, Laura!

(His hand slips slowly up her arm to her shoulder as the music swells tumultuously. He suddenly turns her about and kisses her on the lips. When he releases her, Laura sinks on the sofa with a bright, dazed look. Jim backs away and fishes in his pocket for a cigarette.)

(Legend on screen: "A souvenir.")

Stumblejohn!

(He lights the cigarette, avoiding her look. There is a peal of girlish laughter from Amanda in the kitchenette. Laura slowly raises and opens her hand. It still contains the little broken glass animal. She looks at it with a tender, bewildered expression.)

Stumblejohn! I shouldn't have done that—that was way off the beam. You don't smoke, do you?

(She looks up, smiling, not hearing the question. He sits beside her rather gingerly. She looks at him speechlessly—waiting. He coughs decorously and moves a little farther aside as he considers the situation and senses her feelings, dimly, with perturbation. He speaks gently.)

Would you—care for a—mint?

(She doesn't seem to hear him but her look grows brighter even.)

Peppermint? Life Saver? My pocket's a regular drugstore—wherever I go. . . . *(He pops a mint in his mouth. Then he gulps and decides to make a clean breast of it. He speaks slowly and gingerly.)* Laura, you know, if I had a sister like you, I'd do the same thing as Tom. I'd bring out fellows and—introduce her to them. The right type of boys—of a type to—appreciate her. Only—well—he made a mistake about me. Maybe I've got no call to be saying this. That may not have been the idea in having me over. But what if it was? There's nothing wrong about that. The only trouble is that in my case—I'm not in a situation to—do the right thing. I can't take down your number and say I'll phone. I can't call up next week and—ask for a date. I thought I had better explain the situation in case you—misunderstood it and—I hurt your feelings. . . .

(There is a pause. Slowly, very slowly, Laura's look changes, her eyes returning slowly from his to the glass figure in her palm. Amanda utters another gay laugh in the kitchenette.)

Laura *(faintly)*. You—won't—call again?
Jim.   No, Laura, I can't. *(He rises from the sofa.)* As I was just explaining, I've—got strings on me. Laura, I've—been going steady! I go out all the time with a girl named Betty. She's a home-girl like you, and Catholic, and Irish, and in a great many ways we—get along fine. I met her last summer on a moonlight boat trip up the river to Alton, on the Majestic. Well—right away from the start it was—love!

(Legend: Love!*)*

(Laura sways slightly forward and grips the arm of the sofa. He fails to notice, now enrapt in his own comfortable being.)

Being in love has made a new man of me!

(Leaning stiffly forward, clutching the arm of the sofa, Laura struggles visibly with her storm. But Jim is oblivious; she is a long way off.)

The power of love is really pretty tremendous! Love is something that changes the whole world, Laura!

(The storm abates a little and Laura leans back. He notices her again.)

It happened that Betty's aunt took sick, she got a wire and had to go to Centralia. So Tom—when he asked me to dinner—I naturally just accepted the invitation, not knowing that you—that he—that I—*(He stops awkwardly.)* Huh—I'm a stumblejohn!

(He flops back on the sofa. The holy candles on the altar of Laura's face have been snuffed out. There is a look of almost infinite desolation. Jim glances at her uneasily.)

I wish that you would—say something.

(She bites her lip which was trembling and then bravely smiles. She opens her hand again on the broken glass figure. Then she gently takes his hand and raises it level with her own. She carefully places the unicorn in the palm of his hand, then pushes his fingers closed upon it.)

What are you—doing that for? You want me to have him? Laura?

(She nods.)

What for?
Laura. A—souvenir. . . .

(She rises unsteadily and crouches beside the Victrola to wind it up.)

(Legend on screen: "Things have a way of turning out so badly!" Or image: "Gentleman caller waving goodbye—gaily.")

(At this moment Amanda rushes brightly back into the living room. She bears a pitcher of fruit punch in an old-fashioned cut-glass pitcher, and a plate of macaroons. The plate has a gold border and poppies painted on it.)

Amanda. Well, well, well! Isn't the air delightful after the shower! I've made you children a little liquid refreshment. *(She turns gaily to Jim.)* Jim, do you know that song about lemonade?

> "Lemonade, lemonade
> Made in the shade and stirred with a spade—
> Good enough for any old maid!"

Jim (uneasily). Ha-ha! No—I never heard it.
Amanda. Why, Laura! You look so serious!
Jim. We were having a serious conversation.
Amanda. Good! Now you're better acquainted!
Jim (uncertainly). Ha-ha! Yes.
Amanda. You modern young people are much more serious-minded than my generation. I was so gay as a girl!
Jim. You haven't changed, Mrs. Wingfield.
Amanda. Tonight I'm rejuvenated! The gaiety of the occasion, Mr. O'Connor! *(She tosses her head with a peal of laughter, spilling some lemonade.)* Oooo! I'm baptizing myself!

Jim. Here—let me—

Amanda (setting the pitcher down). There now. I discovered we had some maraschino cherries. I dumped them in, juice and all!

Jim. You shouldn't have gone to that trouble, Mrs. Wingfield.

Amanda. Trouble, trouble? Why, it was loads of fun! Didn't you hear me cutting up in the kitchen? I bet your ears were burning! I told Tom how outdone with him I was for keeping you to himself so long a time! He should have brought you over much, much sooner! Well, now that you've found your way, I want you to be a very frequent caller! Not just occasional but all the time. Oh, we're going to have a lot of gay times together! I see them coming! Mmm, just breathe that air! So fresh, and the moon's so pretty! I'll skip back out—I know where my place is when young folks are having a—serious conversation!

Jim. Oh, don't go out, Mrs. Wingfield. The fact of the matter is I've got to be going.

Amanda. Going, now? You're joking! Why, it's only the shank of the evening, Mr. O'Connor.

Jim. Well, you know how it is.

Amanda. You mean you're a young workingman and have to keep work-ingmen's hours. We'll let you off early tonight. But only on the condition that next time you stay later. What's the best night for you? Isn't Saturday night the best night for you workingmen?

Jim. I have a couple of time-clocks to punch, Mrs. Wingfield. One at morn-ing, another one at night!

Amanda. My, but you *are* ambitious! You work at night, too?

Jim. No, Ma'am, not work but—Betty!

(He crosses deliberately to pick up his hat. The band at the Paradise Dance Hall goes into a tender waltz.)

Amanda. Betty? Betty? Who's—Betty!

(There is an ominous cracking sound in the sky.)

Jim. Oh, just a girl. The girl I go steady with!

(He smiles charmingly. The sky falls.)

(Legend: "The Sky Falls.")

Amanda (a long-drawn exhalation). Ohhhh . . . Is it a serious romance, Mr. O'Connor?

Jim. We're going to be married the second Sunday in June.

Amanda. Ohhhh—how nice! Tom didn't mention that you were engaged to be married.

Jim. The cat's not out of the bag at the warehouse yet. You know how they are. They call you Romeo and stuff like that. *(He stops at the oval mirror to put on his hat. He carefully shapes the brim and the crown to give a discreetly dashing effect.)* It's been a wonderful evening, Mrs. Wingfield. I guess this is what they mean by Southern hospitality.

Amanda. It really wasn't anything at all.

Jim. I hope it don't seem like I'm rushing off. But I promised Betty I'd pick her up at the Wabash depot, an' by the time I get my jalopy down there her train'll be in. Some women are pretty upset if you keep 'em waiting.

Amanda. Yes, I know—the tyranny of women! *(She extends her hand.)* Goodbye, Mr. O'Connor. I wish you luck—and happiness—and success! All three of them, and so does Laura! Don't you, Laura?

Laura. Yes!

Jim (taking Laura's hand). Goodbye, Laura. I'm certainly going to treasure that souvenir. And don't you forget the good advice I gave you. *(He raises his voice to a cheery shout.)* So long, Shakespeare! Thanks again, ladies. Good night!

(He grins and ducks jauntily out. Still barely grimacing, Amanda closes the door on the gentleman caller. Then she turns back to the room with a puzzled expression. She and Laura don't dare to face each other. Laura crouches beside the Victrola to wind it.)

Amanda (faintly). Things have a way of turning out so badly. I don't believe that I would play the Victrola. Well, well—well! Our gentleman caller was engaged to be married! *(She raises her voice.)* Tom!

Tom (from the kitchenette). Yes, Mother?

Amanda. Come in here a minute. I want to tell you something awfully funny.

Tom (entering with a macaroon and a glass of the lemonade). Has the gentleman caller gotten away already?

Amanda. The gentleman caller has made an early departure. What a wonderful joke you played on us!

Tom. How do you mean?

Amanda. You didn't mention that he was engaged to be married.

Tom. Jim? Engaged?

Amanda. That's what he just informed us.

Tom. I'll be jiggered! I didn't know about that.

Amanda. That seems very peculiar.

Tom. What's peculiar about it?

Amanda. Didn't you call him your best friend down at the warehouse?

Tom. He is, but how did I know?

Amanda. It seems extremely peculiar that you wouldn't know your best friend was going to be married!

Tom. The warehouse is where I work, not where I know things about people!

Amanda. You don't know things anywhere! You live in a dream; you manufacture illusions!

(He crosses to the door.)

Where are you going?

Tom. I'm going to the movies.

Amanda. That's right, now that you've had us make such fools of ourselves. The effort, the preparations, all the expense! The new floor lamp, the rug, the clothes for Laura! All for what? To entertain some other girl's fiancé! Go to the movies, go! Don't think about us, a mother deserted, an unmarried sister who's crippled and has no job! Don't let anything interfere with your selfish pleasure! Just go, go, go—to the movies!

Tom. All right, I will! The more you shout about my selfishness to me the quicker I'll go, and I won't go to the movies!

Amanda. Go, then! Go to the moon—you selfish dreamer!

(Tom smashes his glass on the floor. He plunges out on the fire escape, slamming the door. Laura screams in fright. The dance-hall music becomes louder. Tom stands on the fire escape, gripping the rail. The moon breaks through the storm clouds, illuminating his face.)

(Legend on screen: "And so goodbye . . .")

(Tom's closing speech is timed with what is happening inside the house. We see, as though through soundproof glass, that Amanda appears to be making a comforting speech to Laura, who is huddled upon the sofa. Now that we cannot hear the mother's speech, her silliness is gone and she has dignity and tragic beauty. Laura's hair hides her face until, at the end of the speech, she lifts her head to smile at her mother. Amanda's gestures are slow and graceful, almost dancelike, as she comforts her daughter. At the end of her speech she glances a moment at the father's picture—then withdraws through the portieres. At the close of Tom's speech, Laura blows out the candles, ending the play.)

Tom. I didn't go to the moon, I went much further—for time is the longest distance between two places. Not long after that I was fired for writing a poem on the lid of a shoe-box. I left Saint Louis. I descended the steps of this fire escape for a last time and followed, from then on, in my father's footsteps, attempting to find in motion what was lost in space. I traveled around a great deal. The cities swept about me like dead leaves, leaves that were brightly colored but torn away from the branches. I would have stopped, but I was pursued by something. It always came upon me unawares, taking me altogether by surprise. Perhaps it was a familiar bit of music. Perhaps it was only a piece of transparent glass. Perhaps I am walking along a street at night, in some strange city, before I have found companions. I pass the lighted window of a shop where perfume is sold. The window is filled with pieces of colored glass, tiny transparent bottles in delicate colors, like bits of a shattered rainbow. Then all at once my sister touches my shoulder. I turn around and look into her eyes. Oh, Laura, Laura, I tried to leave you behind me, but I am more faithful than I intended to be! I reach for a cigarette, I cross the street, I run into the movies or a bar, I buy a drink, I speak to the nearest stranger—anything that can blow your candles out!

(Laura bends over the candles.)

For nowadays the world is lit by lightning! Blow out your candles, Laura—and so goodbye . . . .

(She blows the candles out.)

[1945]

Half and Half
From *The Joy Luck Club*

AMY TAN

———

As proof of her faith, my mother used to carry a small leatherette Bible when she went to the First Chinese Baptist Church every Sunday. But later, after my mother lost her faith in God, that leatherette Bible wound up wedged under a too-short table leg, a way for her to correct the imbalances of life. It's been there for over twenty years.

My mother pretends that Bible isn't there. Whenever anyone asks her what it's doing there, she says, a little too loudly, "Oh this? I forgot." But I know she sees it. My mother is not the best housekeeper in the world, and after all these years that Bible is still clean white.

Tonight I'm watching my mother sweep under the same kitchen table, something she does every night after dinner. She gently pokes her broom around the table leg propped up by the Bible. I watch her, sweep after sweep, waiting for the right moment to tell her about Ted and me, that we're getting divorced. When I tell her, I know she's going to say, "This cannot be."

And when I say that it is certainly true, that our marriage is over, I know what else she will say: "Then you must save it."

And even though I know it's hopeless—there's absolutely nothing left to save—I'm afraid that if I tell her that, she'll still persuade me to try.

I think it's ironic that my mother wants me to fight the divorce. Seventeen years ago she was chagrined when I started dating Ted. My oldest sisters had dated only Chinese boys from church before getting married.

Ted and I met in a politics of ecology class when he leaned over and offered to pay me two dollars for the last week's notes. I refused the money and accepted a cup of coffee instead. This was during my second semester at UC Berkeley, where I had enrolled as a liberal arts major and later changed to fine arts. Ted was in his third year in pre-med, his choice, he told me, ever since he dissected a fetal pig in the sixth grade.

I have to admit that what I initially found attractive in Ted were precisely the things that made him different from my brothers and the Chinese boys I had dated; his brashness; the assuredness in which he asked for things and expected to get them; his opinionated manner; his angular face and lanky body; the thickness of his arms; the fact that his parents immigrated from Tarrytown, New York, not Tientsin, China.

My mother must have noticed these same differences after Ted picked me up one evening at my parents' house. When I returned home, my mother was still up, watching television.

"He is American," warned my mother, as if I had been too blind to notice. "A *waiguoren*."[1]

"I'm American too," I said, "And it's not as if I'm going to marry him or something."

Mrs. Jordan also had a few words to say. Ted had casually invited me to a family picnic, the annual clan reunion held by the polo fields in Golden Gate Park. Although we had dated only a few times in the last month—and certainly had never slept together, since both of us lived at home—Ted introduced me to all his relatives as his girlfriend, which, until then, I didn't know I was.

Later, when Ted and his father went off to play volleyball with the others, his mother took my hand, and we started walking along the grass, away from the crowd. She squeezed my palm warmly but never seemed to look at me.

"I'm so glad to meet you *finally*," Mrs. Jordan said. I wanted to tell her I wasn't really Ted's girlfriend, but she went on. "I think it's nice that you and Ted are having such a lot of fun together. So I hope you won't misunderstand what I have to say."

And then she spoke quietly about Ted's future, his need to concentrate on his medical studies, why it would be years before he could even think about marriage. She assured me she had nothing whatsoever against minorities; she and her husband, who owned a chain of office-supply stores, personally knew many fine people who were Oriental, Spanish, and even black. But Ted was going to be in one of those professions where he would be judged by a different standard, by patients and other doctors who might not be as understanding as the Jordans were. She said it was so unfortunate the way the rest of the world was, how unpopular the Vietnam War was.

"Mrs. Jordan, I am not Vietnamese," I said softly, even though I was on the verge of shouting. "And I have no intention of marrying your son."

When Ted drove me home that day, I told him I couldn't see him anymore. When he asked me why, I shrugged. When he pressed me, I told him what his mother had said, verbatim, without comment.

"And you're just going to sit there! Let my mother decide what's right?" he shouted, as if I were a co-conspirator who had turned traitor. I was touched that Ted was so upset.

---

[1]Chinese: foreigner.

"What should we do?" I asked, and I had a pained feeling I thought was the beginning of love.

In those early months, we clung to each other with a rather silly desperation, because, in spite of anything my mother or Mrs. Jordan could say, there was nothing that really prevented us from seeing one another. With imagined tragedy hovering over us, we became inseparable, two halves creating the whole: yin and yang.[2] I was victim to his hero. I was always in danger and he was always rescuing me. I would fall and he would lift me up. It was exhilarating and draining. The emotional effect of saving and being saved was addicting to both of us. And that, as much as anything we ever did in bed, was how we made love to each other: conjoined where my weaknesses needed protection.

"What should we do?" I continued to ask him. And within a year of our first meeting we were living together. The month before Ted started medical school at UCSF[3] we were married in the Episcopal church, and Mrs. Jordan sat in the front pew, crying as was expected of the groom's mother. When Ted finished his residency in dermatology, we bought a run-down three-story Victorian with a large garden in Ashbury Heights. Ted helped me set up a studio downstairs so I could take in work as a free-lance production assistant for graphic artists.

Over the years, Ted decided where we went on vacation. He decided what new furniture we should buy. He decided we should wait until we moved into a better neighborhood before having children. We used to discuss some of these matters, but we both knew the question would boil down to my saying, "Ted, you decide." After a while, there were no more discussions. Ted simply decided. And I never thought of objecting. I preferred to ignore the world around me, obsessing only over what was in front of me: my T-square, my X-acto knife, my blue pencil.

But last year Ted's feelings about what he called "decision and responsibility" changed. A new patient had come to him asking what she could do about the spidery veins on her cheeks. And when he told her he could suck the red veins out and make her beautiful again, she believed him. But instead, he accidentally sucked a nerve out, and the left side of her smile fell down and she sued him.

After he lost the malpractice lawsuit—his first, and a big shock to him I now realize—he started pushing me to make decisions. Did I think we should buy an American car or a Japanese car? Should we change from whole-life to term insurance? What did I think about that candidate who supported the contras? What about a family?

---

[2]Chinese philosophical principle of opposites, whose union and interactions shape the destiny of all things.

[3] University of California at San Francisco.

I thought about things, the pros and the cons. But in the end I would be so confused, because I never believed there was ever any one right answer, yet there were many wrong ones. So whenever I said, "You decide," or "I don't care," or "Either way is fine with me," Ted would say in his impatient voice, "No, *you* decide. You can't have it both ways, none of the responsibility, none of the blame."

I could feel things changing between us. A protective veil had been lifted and Ted now started pushing me about everything. He asked me to decide on the most trivial matters, as if he were baiting me. Italian food or Thai. One appetizer or two. Which appetizer. Credit card or cash. Visa or MasterCard.

Last month, when he was leaving for a two-day dermatology course in Los Angeles, he asked if I wanted to come along and then quickly, before I could say anything, he added, "Never mind, I'd rather go alone."

"More time to study," I agreed.

"No, because you can never make up your mind about anything," he said.

And I protested, "But it's only with things that aren't important."

"Nothing is important to you, then," he said in a tone of disgust.

"Ted, if you want me to go, I'll go."

And it was as if something snapped in him. "How the hell did we ever get married? Did you just say 'I do' because the minister said 'repeat after me'? What would you have done with your life if I had never married you? Did it ever occur to you?"

This was such a big leap in logic, between what I said and what he said, that I thought we were like two people standing apart on separate mountain peaks, recklessly leaning forward to throw stones at one another, unaware of the dangerous chasm that separated us.

But now I realize Ted knew what he was saying all along. He wanted to show me the rift. Because later that evening he called from Los Angeles and said he wanted a divorce.

Ever since Ted's been gone, I've been thinking, even if I had expected it, even if I had known what I was going to do with my life, it still would have knocked the wind out of me.

When something that violent hits you, you can't help but lose your balance and fall. And after you pick yourself up, you realize you can't trust anybody to save you—not your husband, not your mother, not God. So what can you do to stop yourself from tilting and falling all over again?

My mother believed in God's will for many years. It was as if she had turned on a celestial faucet and goodness kept pouring out. She said it was faith that kept all these good things coming our way, only *I* thought she said "fate," because she couldn't pronounce that "th" sound in "faith."

And later, I discovered that maybe it was fate all along, that faith was just an illusion that somehow you're in control. I found out the most I could have was hope, and with that I was not denying any possibility, good or bad. I was just saying, If there is a choice, dear God or whatever you are, here's where the odds should be placed.

I remember the day I started thinking this, it was such a revelation to me. It was the day my mother lost her faith in God. She found that things of unquestioned certainty could never be trusted again.

We had gone to the beach, to a secluded spot south of the city near Devil's Slide. My father had read in *Sunset* magazine that this was a good place to catch ocean perch. And although my father was not a fisherman but a pharmacist's assistant who had once been a doctor in China, he believed in his *nengkan,* his ability to do anything he put his mind to. My mother believed she had *nengkan* to cook anything my father had a mind to catch. It was this belief in their *nengkan* that had brought my parents to America. It had enabled them to have seven children and buy a house in the Sunset district with very little money. It had given them the confidence to believe their luck would never run out, that God was on their side, that the house gods had only benevolent things to report and our ancestors were pleased, that lifetime warranties meant our lucky streak would never break, that all the elements were in balance, the right amount of wind and water.

So there we were, the nine of us: my father, my mother, my two sisters, four brothers, and myself, so confident as we walked along our first beach. We marched in single file across the cool gray sand, from oldest to youngest. I was in the middle, fourteen years old. We would have made quite a sight, if anyone else had been watching, nine pairs of bare feet trudging, nine pairs of shoes in hand, nine black-haired heads turned toward the water to watch the waves tumbling in.

The wind was whipping the cotton trousers around my legs and I looked for some place where the sand wouldn't kick into my eyes. I saw we were standing in the hollow of a cove. It was like a giant bowl, cracked in half, the other half washed out to sea. My mother walked toward the right, where the beach was clean, and we all followed. On this side, the wall of the cove curved around and protected the beach from both the rough surf and the wind. And along this wall, in its shadow, was a reef ledge that started at the edge of the beach and continued out past the cove where the waters became rough. It seemed as though a person could walk out to sea on this reef, although it looked very rocky and slippery. On the other side of the cove, the wall was more jagged, eaten away by the water. It was pitted with crevices, so when the waves crashed against the wall, the water spewed out of these holes like white gulleys.

Thinking back, I remember that this beach cove was a terrible place, full of wet shadows that chilled us and invisible specks that flew into our eyes and made it hard for us to see the dangers. We were all blind with the newness of this experience: a Chinese family trying to act like a typical American family at the beach.

My mother spread out an old striped bedspread, which flapped in the wind until nine pairs of shoes weighed it down. My father assembled his long bamboo fishing pole, a pole he had made with his own two hands, remembering its design from his childhood in China. And we children sat huddled shoulder to shoulder on the blanket, reaching into the grocery sack full of bologna sandwiches, which we hungrily ate salted with sand from our fingers.

Then my father stood up and admired his fishing pole, its grace, its strength. Satisfied, he picked up his shoes and walked to the edge of the beach and then onto the reef to the point just before it was wet. My two older sisters, Janice and Ruth, jumped up from the blanket and slapped their thighs to get the sand off. Then they slapped each other's back and raced off down the beach shrieking. I was about to get up and chase them, but my mother nodded toward my four brothers and reminded me: *"Dangsying tamende shenti,"* which means "Take care of them," or literally, "Watch out for their bodies." These bodies were the anchors of my life: Matthew, Mark, Luke, and Bing. I fell back onto the sand, groaning as my throat grew tight, as I made the same lament: "Why?" Why did I have to care for them?

And she gave me the same answer: *"Yiding."*

I must. Because they were my brothers. My sisters had once taken care of me. How else could I learn responsibility? How else could I appreciate what my parents had done for me?

Matthew, Mark, and Luke were twelve, ten, and nine, old enough to keep themselves loudly amused. They had already buried Luke in a shallow grave of sand so that only his head stuck out. Now they were starting to pat together the outlines of a sand-castle wall on top of him.

But Bing was only four, easily excitable and easily bored and irritable. He didn't want to play with the other brothers because they had pushed him off to the side, admonishing him, "No, Bing, you'll just wreck it."

So Bing wandered down the beach, walking stiffly like an ousted emperor, picking up shards of rock and chunks of driftwood and flinging them with all his might into the surf. I trailed behind, imagining tidal waves and wondering what I would do if one appeared. I called to Bing every now and then, "Don't go too close to the water. You'll get your feet wet." And I thought how much I seemed like my mother, always worried beyond reason inside, but at the same time talking about the danger as if it were less than it really was. The worry surrounded me, like the wall of the cove, and it made me feel everything had been considered and was now safe.

My mother had a superstition, in fact, that children were predisposed to certain dangers on certain days, all depending on their Chinese birthdate. It was explained in a little Chinese book called *The Twenty-Six Malignant Gates.* There, on each page, was an illustration of some terrible danger that awaited young innocent children. In the corners was a description written in Chinese, and since I couldn't read the characters, I could only see what the picture meant.

The same little boy appeared in each picture: climbing a broken tree limb, standing by a falling gate, slipping in a wooden tub, being carried away by a snapping dog, fleeing from a bolt of lightening. And in each of these pictures stood a man who looked as if he were wearing a lizard costume. He had a big crease in his forehead, or maybe it was actually that he had two round horns. In one picture, the lizard man was standing on a curved bridge, laughing as he watched the little boy flying forward over the bridge rail, his slippered feet already in the air.

It would have been enough to think that even one of these dangers could befall a child. And even though the birthdates corresponded to only one danger, my mother worried about them all. This was because she couldn't figure out how the Chinese dates, based on the lunar calendar, translated into American dates. So by taking them all into account, she had absolute faith she could prevent every one of them.

The sun had shifted and moved over the other side of the cove wall. Everything had settled into place. My mother was busy keeping sand from blowing onto the blanket, then shaking sand out of shoes, and tacking corners of blankets back down again with the now clean shoes. My father was still standing at the end of the reef, patiently casting out, waiting for *nengkan* to manifest itself as a fish. I could see small figures farther down on the beach, and I could tell they were my sisters by their two dark heads and yellow pants. My brothers' shrieks were mixed with those of seagulls. Bing had found an empty soda bottle and was using this to dig sand next to the dark cove wall. And I sat on the sand, just where the shadows ended and the sunny part began.

Bing was pounding the soda bottle against the rock, so I called to him, "Don't dig so hard. You'll bust a hole in the wall and fall all the way to China." And I laughed when he looked at me as though he thought what I said was true. He stood up and started walking toward the water. He put one foot tentatively on the reef, and I warned him, "Bing."

"I'm gonna see Daddy," he protested.

"Stay close to the wall, then, away from the water," I said. "Stay away from the mean fish."

And I watched as he inched his way along the reef, his back hugging the bumpy cove wall. I still see him, so clearly that I almost feel I can make him stay there forever.

I see him standing by the wall, safe, calling to my father, who looks over his shoulder toward Bing. How glad I am that my father is going to watch him for a while! Bing starts to walk over and then something tugs on my father's line and he's reeling as fast as he can.

Shouts erupt. Someone has thrown sand in Luke's face and he's jumped out of his sand grave and thrown himself on top of Mark, thrashing and kicking. My mother shouts for me to stop them. And right after I pull Luke off Mark, I look up and see Bing walking alone to the edge of the reef. In the confusion of the fight, nobody notices. I am the only one who sees what Bing is doing.

Bing walks one, two, three steps. His little body is moving so quickly, as if he spotted something wonderful by the water's edge. And I think, *He's going to fall in.* I'm expecting it. And just as I think this, his feet are already in the air, in a moment of balance, before he splashes into the sea and disappears without leaving so much as a ripple in the water.

I sank to my knees watching that spot where he disappeared, not moving, not saying anything. I couldn't make sense of it. I was thinking, Should I run to the water and try to pull him out? Should I shout to my father? Can I rise on my legs fast enough? Can I take it all back and forbid Bing from joining my father on the ledge?

And then my sisters were back, and one of them said, "Where's Bing?" There was silence for a few seconds and then shouts and sand flying as everyone rushed past me toward the water's edge. I stood there unable to move as my sisters looked by the cove wall, as my brothers scrambled to see what lay behind pieces of driftwood. My mother and father were trying to part the waves with their hands.

We were there for many hours. I remember the search boats and the sunset when dusk came. I had never seen a sunset like that: a bright orange flame touching the water's edge and then fanning out, warming the sea. When it became dark, the boats turned their yellow orbs on and bounced up and down on the dark shiny water.

As I look back, it seems unnatural to think about the colors of the sunset and boats at a time like that. But we all had strange thoughts. My father was calculating minutes, estimating the temperature of the water, readjusting his estimate of when Bing fell. My sisters were calling, "Bing! Bing!" as if he were hiding in some bushes high above the beach cliffs. My brothers sat in the car, quietly reading comic books. And when the boats turned off their yellow orbs, my mother went for a swim. She had never swum a stroke in her life, but her faith in her own *nengkan* convinced her that what these Americans couldn't do, she could. She could find Bing.

And when the rescue people finally pulled her out of the water, she still had her *nengkan* intact. Her hair, her clothes, they were all heavy with the cold water, but she stood quietly, calm and regal as a mermaid queen who had just arrived out of the sea. The police called off the search, put us all in our car, and sent us home to grieve.

• • •

I had expected to be beaten to death, by my father, by my mother, by my sisters and brothers. I knew it was my fault. I hadn't watched him closely enough, and yet I saw him. But as we sat in the dark living room, I heard them, one by one whispering their regrets.

"I was selfish to want to go fishing," said my father.

"We shouldn't have gone for a walk," said Janice, while Ruth blew her nose yet another time.

"Why'd you have to throw sand in my face?" moaned Luke. "Why'd you have to make me start a fight?"

And my mother quietly admitted to me, "I told you to stop their fight. I told you to take your eyes off him."

If I had had any time at all to feel a sense of relief, it would have quickly evaporated, because my mother also said, "So now I am telling you, we must go and find him, quickly, tomorrow morning." And everybody's eyes looked down. But I saw it as my punishment: to go out with my mother, back to the beach, to help her find Bing's body.

Nothing prepared me for what my mother did the next day. When I woke up, it was still dark and she was already dressed. On the kitchen table was a thermos, a teacup, the white leatherette Bible, and the car keys.

"Is Daddy ready?" I asked.

"Daddy's not coming," she said.

"Then how will we get there? Who will drive us?"

She picked up the keys and I followed her out the door to the car. I wondered the whole time as we drove to the beach how she had learned to drive overnight. She used no map. She drove smoothly ahead, turning down Geary, then the Great Highway, signaling at all the right times, getting on the Coast Highway and easily winding the car around the sharp curves that often led inexperienced drivers off and over the cliffs.

When we arrived at the beach, she walked immediately down the dirt path and over to the end of the reef ledge, where I had seen Bing disappear. She held in her hand the white Bible. And looking out over the water, she called to God, her small voice carried up by the gulls to heaven. It began with "Dear God" and ended with "Amen," and in between she spoke in Chinese.

"I have always believed in your blessings," she praised God in that same tone she used for exaggerated Chinese compliments. "We knew they would come. We did not question them. Your decisions were our decisions. You rewarded us for our faith.

"In return we have always tried to show our deepest respect. We went to your house. We brought you money. We sang your songs. You gave us more blessings. And now we have misplaced one of them. We were careless. This is true. We had so many good things, we couldn't keep them in our mind all the time.

"So maybe you hid him from us to teach us a lesson, to be more careful with your gifts in the future. I have learned this. I have put it in my memory. And now I have come to take Bing back."

I listened quietly as my mother said these words, horrified. And I began to cry when she added, "Forgive us for his bad manners. My daughter, this one standing here, will be sure to teach him better lessons of obedience before he visits you again."

After her prayer, her faith was so great that she saw him, three times, waving to her from just beyond the first wave. "*Nale!*"—There! And she would stand straight as a sentinel, until three times her eyesight failed her and Bing turned into a dark spot of churning seaweed.

My mother did not let her chin fall down. She walked back to the beach and put the Bible down. She picked up the thermos and teacup and walked to the water's edge. Then she told me that the night before she had reached back into her life, back when she was a girl in China, and this is what she had found.

"I remember a boy who lost his hand in a firecracker accident," she said. "I saw the shreds of this boy's arm, his tears, and then I heard his mother's claim that he would grow back another hand, better than the last. This mother said she would pay back an ancestral debt ten times over. She would use a water treatment to soothe the wrath of Chu Jung, the three-eyed god of fire. And true enough, the next week this boy was riding a bicycle, both hands steering a straight course past my astonished eyes!"

And then my mother became very quiet. She poke again in a thoughtful, respectful manner.

"An ancestor of ours once stole water from a sacred well. Now the water is trying to steal back. We must sweeten the temper of the Coiling Dragon who lives in the sea. And then we must make him loosen his coils from Bing by giving him another treasure he can hide."

My mother poured out tea sweetened with sugar into the teacup, and threw this into the sea. And then she opened her fist. In her palm was a ring of watery blue sapphire, a gift from her mother, who had died many years before. This ring, she told me, drew coveting stares from women and made them inattentive to the children they guarded so jealously. This would make the Coiling Dragon forgetful of Bing. She threw the ring into the water.

But even with this, Bing did not appear right away. For an hour or so, all we saw was seaweed drifting by. And then I saw her clasp her hands to her chest, and she said in a wondrous voice, "See, it's because we were watching the wrong direction." And I too saw Bing trudging wearily at the far end of the beach, his shoes hanging in his hand, his dark head bent over in exhaustion. I could feel what my mother felt. The hunger in our hearts was instantly filled. And then the two of us, before we could even get to our feet, saw him light a cigarette, grow tall, and become a stranger.

"Ma, let's go," I said as softly as possible.

"He's there," she said firmly. She pointed to the jagged wall across the water. "I see him. He is in a cave, sitting on a little step above the water. He is hungry and a little cold, but he has learned now not to complain too much."

And then she stood up and started walking across the sandy beach as though it were a solid paved path, and I was trying to follow behind, struggling and stumbling in the soft mounds. She marched up the steep path to where the car was parked, and she wasn't even breathing hard as she pulled a large inner tube from the trunk. To this lifesaver, she tied the fishing line from my father's bamboo pole. She walked back and threw the tube into the sea, holding onto the pole.

"This will go where Bing is. I will bring him back," she said fiercely. I had never heard so much *nengkan* in my mother's voice.

The tube followed her mind. It drifted out, toward the other side of the cove where it was caught by stronger waves. The line became taut and she strained to hold on tight. But the line snapped and then spiraled into the water.

We both climbed toward the end of the reef to watch. The tube had now reached the other side of the cove. A big wave smashed it into the wall. The bloated tube leapt up and then it was sucked in, under the wall and into a cavern. It popped out. Over and over again, it disappeared, emerged, glistening black, faithfully reporting it had seen Bing and was going back to try to pluck him from the cave. Over and over again, it dove and popped back up again, empty but still hopeful. And then, after a dozen or so times, it was sucked into the dark recess, and when it came out, it was torn and lifeless.

At that moment, and not until that moment, did she give up. My mother had a look on her face that I'll never forget. It was one of complete despair and horror, for losing Bing, for being so foolish as to think she could use faith to change fate. And it made me angry—so blindingly angry—that everything had failed us.

I know now that I had never expected to find Bing, just as I know now I will never find a way to save my marriage. My mother tells me, though, that I should still try.

"What's the point?" I say. "There's no hope. There's no reason to keep trying."

"Because you must," she says, "This is not hope. Not reason. This is your fate. This is your life, what you must do."

"So what can I do?"

And my mother says, "You must think for yourself, what you must do. If someone tells you, then you are not trying." And then she walks out of the kitchen to let me think about this.

I think about Bing, how I knew he was in danger, how I let it happen. I think about my marriage, how I had seen the signs, really I had. But I just let it happen. And I think now that fate is shaped half by expectation, half by inattention. But somehow, when you lose something you love, faith takes over. You have to pay attention to what you lost. You have to undo the expectation.

My mother, she still pays attention to it. That Bible under the table, I know she sees it. I remember seeing her write in it before she wedged it under.

I lift the table and slide the Bible out. I put the Bible on the table, flipping quickly through the pages, because I know it's there. On the page before the New Testament begins, there's a section called "Deaths," and that's where she wrote "Bing Hsu" lightly, in erasable pencil.

[1989]

From *Woman Hollering Creek*

SANDRA CISNEROS

Mercians

We're waiting for the awful grandmother who is inside dropping pesos into *la ofrenda*[1] box before the altar to La Divina Providencia.[2] Lighting votive candles and genuflecting. Blessing herself and kissing her thumb. Running a crystal rosary between her fingers. Mumbling, mumbling, mumbling.

There are so many prayers and promises and thanks-be-to-God to be given in the name of the husband and the sons and the only daughter who never attend mass. It doesn't matter. Like La Virgen de Guadalupe,[3] the awful grandmother intercedes on their behalf. For the grandfather who hasn't believed in anything since the first PRI[4] elections. For my father, El Periquin,[5] so skinny he needs his sleep. For Auntie Light-skin, who only a few hours before was breakfasting on brain and goat tacos after dancing all night in the pink zone.[6] For Uncle Fat-face, the blackest of the black sheep—*Always remember your Uncle Fat-face in your prayers.* And Uncle Baby—*You go for me, Mamá—God listens to you.*

The awful grandmother has been gone a long time. She disappeared behind the heavy leather outer curtain and the dusty velvet inner. We must stay near the church entrance. We must not wander over to the balloon and punch-ball vendors. We cannot spend our allowance on fried cookies or Familia Burron comic books or those clear cone-shaped suckers that make everything look like a rainbow when you look through them. We cannot run off and have our picture taken on the wooden ponies. We must not climb the steps up the hill behind the church and chase each other through the cemetery. We have promised to stay right where the awful grandmother left us until she returns.

[1]Spanish: the Church offering.

[2]Spanish: the Divine Providence.

[3]Spanish: the Virgin of Guadalupe. Religious pilgrims visit her shrine in Mexico City as an act of piety or as an act of penance.

[4]The Institutional Revolutionary Party, Mexico's governing political party founded in 1946 following the dissolution of the PNR, the National Revolutionary Party.

[5]The tiny parakeet.

[6]Red Zone: district in Mexico City where there are hotels, bars, brothels, and shops.

There are those walking to church on their knees. Some with fat rags tied around their legs and others with pillows, one to kneel on, and one to flop ahead. There are women with black shawls crossing and uncrossing themselves. There are armies of penitents carrying banners and flowered arches while musicians play tinny trumpets and tinny drums.

La Virgen de Guadalupe is waiting inside behind a plate of thick glass. There's also a gold crucifix bent crooked as a mesquite tree when someone once threw a bomb. La Virgen de Guadalupe on the main alter because she's a big miracle, the crooked crucifix on a side altar because that's a little miracle.

But we're outside in the sun. My big brother Junior hunkered against the wall with his eyes shut. My little brother Keeks running around in circles.

Maybe and most probably my little brother is imagining he's a flying feather dancer,[7] like the ones we saw swinging high up from a pole on the Virgin's birthday. I want to be a flying feather dancer too, but when he circles past me he shouts, I'm a B-Fifty-two bomber, you're a German," and shoots me with an invisible machine gun. I'd rather play flying feather dancers, but if I tell my brother this, he might not play with me at all.

"*Girl.* We can't play with a *girl.*" Girl. It's my brothers' favorite insult now instead of "sissy." "You *girl,*" they yell at each other. "You throw that ball like a *girl.*"

I've already made up my mind to be a German when Keeks swoops past again, this time yelling, "I'm Flash Gordon. You're Ming the Merciless and the Mud People." I don't mind being Ming the Merciless, but I don't like being the Mud People. Something wants to come out of the corners of my eyes, but I don't let it. Crying is what *girls* do.

I leave Keeks running around in circles—"I'm the Lone Ranger, you're Tonto." I leave Junior squatting on his ankles and go look for the awful grandmother.

Why do churches smell like the inside of an ear? Like incense and the dark and candles in blue glass? And why does holy water smell of tears? The awful grandmother makes me kneel and fold my hands. The ceiling high and everyone's prayers bumping up there like balloons.

If I stare at the eyes of the saints long enough, they move and wink at me, which makes me a sort of saint too. When I get tired of winking saints, I count the awful grandmother's mustache hairs while she prays for Uncle Old, sick from the worm, and Auntie Cuca, suffering from a life of troubles that left half her face crooked and the other half sad.

There must be a long, long list of relatives who haven't gone to church. The awful grandmother knits the names of the dead and the living into one

---

[7]Mexican acrobats who dress in featherhead costumes and perform while suspended in air by a rope attached to their feet and a tall pole.

long prayer fringed with the grandchildren born in that barbaric country with its barbarian ways.

I put my weight on one knee, then the other, and when they both grow fat as a mattress of pins, I slap them each awake. *Micaela, you may wait outside with Alfredito and Enrique.* The awful grandmother says it all in Spanish, which I understand when I'm paying attention. "What?" I say, though it's neither proper nor polite. "What?" which the awful grandmother hears as "¿*Güat?*" But she only gives me a look and shoves me toward the door.

After all that dust and dark, the light from the plaza makes me squinch my eyes like if I just came out of the movies. My brother Keeks is drawing squiggly lines on the concrete with a wedge of glass and the heel of his shoe. My brother Junior squatting against the entrance, talking to a lady and man.

They're not from here. Ladies don't come to church dressed in pants. And everybody knows men aren't supposed to wear shorts.

"¿*Quieres chicle?*"[8] the lady asks in a Spanish too big for her mouth. "*Gracias,*" The lady gives him a whole handful of gum for free, little cellophane cubes of Chiclets, cinnamon and aqua and the white ones that don't taste like anything but are good for pretend buck teeth.

"*Por favor,*" says the lady. "¿*Un foto?*" pointing to her camera.

"*Sí.*"

She's so busy taking Junior's picture, she doesn't notice me and Keeks.

"Hey, Michele, Keeks. You guys want gum?"

"But you speak English!"

"Yeah," my brother says, "we're Mericans."

We're Mericans, we're Mericans, and inside the awful grandmother prays.

[1991]

---

[8]Spanish: "Do you want gum?"

Everyday Use

ALICE M. WALKER

For Your Grandmama

I will wait for her in the yard that Maggie and I made so clean and wavy yesterday afternoon. A yard like this is more comfortable than most people know. It is not just a yard. It is like an extended living room. When the hard clay is swept clean as a floor and the fine sand around the edges lined with tiny, irregular grooves, anyone can come and sit and look up into the elm tree and wait for the breezes that never come inside the house.

Maggie will be nervous until after her sister goes: she will stand hopelessly in corners, homely and ashamed of the burn scars down her arms and legs, eyeing her sister with a mixture of envy and awe. She thinks her sister has held life always in the palm of one hand, that "no" is a word the world never learned to say to her.

You've no doubt seen those TV shows where the child who has "made it" is confronted, as a surprise, by her own mother and father, tottering in weakly from backstage. (A pleasant surprise, of course: What would they do if parent and child came on the show only to curse out and insult each other?) On TV mother and child embrace and smile into each other's faces. Sometimes the mother and father weep, the child wraps them in her arms and leans across the table to tell how she would not have made it without their help. I have seen these programs.

Sometimes I dream a dream in which Dee and I are suddenly brought together on a TV program of this sort. Out of a dark and soft-seated limousine I am ushered into a bright room filled with many people. There I meet a smiling, gray, sporty man like Johnny Carson who shakes my hand and tells me what a fine girl I have. Then we are on the stage and Dee is embracing me with tears in her eyes. She pins on my dress a large orchid, even though she has told me once that she thinks orchids are tacky flowers.

In real life I am a large, big-boned woman with rough, man-working hands. In the winter I wear flannel nightgowns to bed and overalls during the day. I can kill and clean a hog as mercilessly as a man. My fat keeps me hot in zero weather. I can work outside all day, breaking ice to get water for washing; I can eat pork liver cooked over the open fire minutes after it comes steaming from the hog. One winter I knocked a bull calf straight in the brain between the eyes with a sledge hammer and had the meat hung up to chill before nightfall. But of course all this does not show on television. I am the way my daughter would want me to be: a hundred pounds lighter, my skin like an uncooked barley pancake. My hair glistens in the hot bright lights. Johnny Carson has much to do to keep up with my quick and witty tongue.

But that is a mistake. I know even before I wake up. Who ever knew a Johnson with a quick tongue? Who can even imagine me looking a strange white man in the eye? It seems to me I have talked to them always with one foot raised in flight, with my head turned in whichever way is farthest from them. Dee, though. She would always look anyone in the eye. Hesitation was no part of her nature.

"How do I look, Mama?" Maggie says, showing just enough of her thin body enveloped in pink skirt and red blouse for me to know she's there, almost hidden by the door.

"Come out into the yard," I say.

Have you ever seen a lame animal, perhaps a dog run over by some care-less person rich enough to own a car, sidle up to someone who is ignorant enough to be kind to them? That is the way my Maggie walks. She has been like this, chin on chest, eyes on ground, feet in shuffle, ever since the fire that burned the other house to the ground.

Dee is lighter than Maggie, with nicer hair and a fuller figure. She's a woman now, though sometimes I forget. How long ago was it that the other house burned? Ten, twelve years? Sometimes I can still hear the flames and feel Maggie's arms sticking to me, her hair smoking and her dress falling off her in little black papery flakes. Her eyes seemed stretched open, blazed open by the flames reflected in them. And Dee. I see her standing off under the sweet gum tree she used to dig gum out of; a look of concentration on her face as she watched the last dingy gray board of the house fall in toward the red-hot brick chimney. Why don't you do a dance around the ashes? I'd wanted to ask her. She had hated the house that much.

I used to think she hated Maggie, too. But that was before we raised the money, the church and me, to send her to Augusta to school. She used to read to us without pity; forcing words, lies, other folks' habits, whole lives upon us two, sitting trapped and ignorant underneath her voice. She washed us in a river of make-believe, burned us with a lot of knowledge we didn't necessar-ily need to know. Pressed us to her with the serious way she read, to shove us away at just the moment, like dimwits, we seemed about to understand.

Dee wanted nice things. A yellow organdy dress to wear to her graduation from high school; black pumps to match a green suit she'd made from an old suit somebody gave me. She was determined to stare down any disaster in her efforts. Her eyelids would not flicker for minutes at a time. Often I fought off the temptation to shake her. At sixteen she had a style of her own: and knew what style was.

I never had an education myself. After second grade the school was closed down. Don't ask me why: in 1927 colored asked fewer questions than they do now. Sometimes Maggie reads to me. She stumbles along good-naturedly but can't see well. She knows she is not bright. Like good looks and money, quickness passed her by. She will marry John Thomas (who has mossy teeth in an earnest face) and then I'll be free to sit here and I guess just sing church songs to myself. Although I never was a good singer. Never could carry a tune. I was always better at a man's job. I used to love to milk till I was hooked in the side in '49. Cows are soothing and slow and don't bother you, unless you try to milk them the wrong way.

I have deliberately turned my back on the house. It is three rooms, just like the one that burned, except the roof is tin; they don't make shingle roofs any more. There are no real windows, just some holes cut in the sides, like the portholes in a ship, but not round and not square, with rawhide holding the shutters up on the outside. This house is in a pasture, too, like the other one. No doubt when Dee sees it she will want to tear it down. She wrote me once that no matter where we "choose" to live, she will manage to come see us. But she will never bring her friends. Maggie and I thought about this and Maggie asked me, "Mama, when did Dee ever *have* any friends?"

She had a few. Furtive boys in pink shirts hanging about on washday after school. Nervous girls who never laughed. Impressed with her they worshiped the well-turned phrase, the cute shape, the scalding humor that erupted like bubbles in lye. She read to them.

When she was courting Jimmy T she didn't have much time to pay to us, but turned all her faultfinding power on him. He *flew* to marry a cheap city girl from a family of ignorant flashy people. She hardly had time to recompose herself.

When she comes I will meet—but there they are!

Maggie attempts to make a dash for the house, in her shuffling way, but I stay her with my hand. "Come back here," I say. And she stops and tries to dig a well in the sand with her toe.

It is hard to see them clearly through the strong sun. But even the first glimpse of leg out of the car tells me it is Dee. Her feet were always neat-looking, as if God himself had shaped them with a certain style. From the other side of the car comes a short, stocky man. Hair is all over his head a foot long and hanging from his chin like a kinky mule tail. I hear Maggie suck in her breath. "Uhnnnh," is what it sounds like. Like when you see the wriggling end of a snake just in front of your foot on the road. "Uhnnnh."

Dee next. A dress down to the ground, in this hot weather. A dress so loud it hurts my eyes. There are yellows and oranges enough to throw back the light of the sun. I feel my whole face warming from the heat waves it throws out. Earrings gold, too, and hanging down to her shoulders. Bracelets dangling and making noises when she moves her arm up to shake the folds of the dress out of her armpits. The dress is loose and flows, and as she walks closer, I like it. I hear Maggie go "Uhnnnh" again. It is her sister's hair. It stands straight up like the wool on a sheep. It is black as night and around the edges are two long pigtails that rope about like small lizards disappearing behind her ears.

"Wa-su-zo-Tean-o!" she says, coming on in that gliding way the dress makes her move. The short stocky fellow with the hair to his navel is all grinning and he follows up with "Asalamalakim, my mother and sister!" He moves to hug Maggie but she falls back, right up against the back of my chair. I feel her trembling there and when I look up I see the perspiration falling off her chin.

"Don't get up," says Dee. Since I am stout it takes something of a push. You can see me trying to move a second or two before I make it. She turns, showing white heels through her sandals, and goes back to the car. Out she peeks next with a Polaroid. She stoops down quickly and lines up picture after picture of me sitting there in front of the house with Maggie cowering behind me. She never takes a shot without making sure the house is included. When a cow comes nibbling around the edge of the yard she snaps it and me and Maggie *and* the house. Then she puts the Polaroid in the back seat of the car, and comes up and kisses me on the forehead.

Meanwhile Asalamalakim is going through motions with Maggie's hand. Maggie's hand is as limp as a fish, and probably as cold, despite the sweat, and she keeps trying to pull it back. It looks like Asalamalakim wants to shake hands but wants to do it fancy. Or maybe he don't know how people shake hands. Anyhow, he soon gives up on Maggie.

"Well," I say. "Dee."

"No, Mama," she says. "Not 'Dee,' Wangero Leewanika Kemanjo!"

"What happened to 'Dee'?" I wanted to know.

"She's dead," Wangero said. "I couldn't bear it any long, being named after the people who oppress me."

"You know as well as me you was named after your aunt Dicie," I said. Dicie is my sister. She named Dee. We called her "Big Dee" after Dee was born.

"But who was *she* named after?" asked Wangero.

"I guess after Grandma Dee," I said.

"And who was she named after?" asked Wangero.

"Her mother," I said, and saw Wangero was getting tired. "That's about as far back as I can trace it," I said. Though, in fact, I probably could have carried it back beyond the Civil War through the branches.

"Well," said Asalamalakim, "there you are."

"Uhnnnh," I heard Maggie say.

"There I was not," I said, "before 'Dicie' cropped up in our family, so why should I try to trace it that far back?"

He just stood there grinning, looking down on me like somebody inspecting a Model A car. Every once in a while he and Wangero sent eye signals over my head.

"How do you pronounce this name?" I asked.

"You don't have to call me by it if you don't want to," said Wangero.

"Why shouldn't I?" I asked. "If that's what you want us to call you, we'll call you."

"I know it might sound awkward at first," said Wangero.

"I'll get used to it," I said. "Ream it out again."

Well, soon we got the name out of the way. Asalamalakim had a name twice as long and three times as hard. After I tripped over it two or three times he told me to just call him Hakim-a-barber. I wanted to ask him was he a barber, but I didn't really think he was, so I didn't ask.

"You must belong to those beef-cattle peoples down the road," I said. They said "Asalamalakim" when they met you, too, but they didn't shake hands. Always too busy: feeding the cattle, fixing the fences, putting up salt-lick shelters, throwing down hay. When the white folks poisoned some of the herd the men stayed up all night with rifles in their hands. I walked a mile and a half just to see the sight.

Hakim-a-barber said, "I accept some of their doctrines, but farming and raising cattle is not my style." (They didn't tell me, and I didn't ask, whether Wangero (Dee) had really gone and married him.)

We sat down to eat and right away he said he didn't eat collards and pork was unclean. Wangero, though, went on through the chitlins and corn bread, the greens and everything else. She talked a blue streak over the sweet potatoes. Everything delighted her. Even the fact that we still used the benches her daddy made for the table when we wouldn't afford to buy chairs.

"Oh, Mama!" she cried. Then turned to Hakim-a-barber. "I never knew how lovely these benches are. You can feel the rump prints," she said, running her hands underneath her and along the bench. Then she gave a sigh and her hand closed over Grandma Dee's butter dish. "That's it!" she said. "I knew there was something I wanted to ask you if I could have." She jumped up from the table and went over to the corner where the churn stood, the milk in it clabber by now. She looked at the churn and looked at it.

"This churn top is what I need," she said. "Didn't Uncle Buddy whittle it out of a tree you all used to have?"

"Yes," I said.

"Uh huh," she said happily. "And I want the dasher, too."

"Uncle Buddy whittle that, too?" asked the barber.

Dee (Wangero) looked up at me.

"Aunt Dee's first husband whittled the dash," said Maggie so low you almost couldn't hear her. "His name was Henry, but they called him Stash."

"Maggie's brain is like an elephant's," Wangero said, laughing. "I can use the churn top as a centerpiece for the alcove table," she said, sliding a plate over the churn, "and I'll think of something artistic to do with the dasher."

When she finished wrapping the dasher the handle stuck out. I took it for a moment in my hands. You didn't even have to look close to see where hands pushing the dasher up and down to make butter had left a kind of sink in the wood. In fact, there were a lot of small sinks; you could see where thumbs and fingers had sunk into the wood. It was beautiful light yellow wood, from a tree that grew in the yard where Big Dee and Stash had lived.

After dinner Dee (Wangero) went to the trunk at the foot of my bed and started rifling through it. Maggie hung back in the kitchen over the dishpan. Out came Wangero with two quilts. They had been pieced by Grandma Dee and then Big Dee and me had hung them on the quilt frames on the front porch and quilted them. One was in the Lone Star pattern. The other was Walk Around the Mountain. In both of them were scraps of dresses Grandma Dee had worn fifty and more years ago. Bits and pieces of Grandpa Jarrell's Paisley shirts. And one teeny faded blue piece, about the size of a penny matchbox, that was from Great Grandpa Ezra's uniform that he wore in the Civil War.

"Mama," Wangero said sweet as a bird. "Can I have these old quilts?"

I heard something fall in the kitchen, and a minute later the kitchen door slammed.

"Why don't you take one or two of the others?" I asked. "These old things were just done by me and Big Dee from some tops your grandma pieced before she died."

"No," said Wangero. "I don't want those. They are stitched around the borders by machine."

"That'll make them last better," I said.

"That's not the point," said Wangero. "These are all pieces of dresses Grandma used to wear. She did all this stitching by hand. Imagine!" She held the quilts securely in her arms, stroking them.

"Some of the pieces, like those lavender ones, come from old clothes her mother handed down to her," I said, moving up to touch the quilts. Dee (Wangero) moved back just enough so that I couldn't reach the quilts. They already belong to her.

"Imagine!" she breathed again, clutching them closely to her bosom.

"The truth is," I said, "I promised to give them quilts to Maggie, for when she marries John Thomas."

She gasped like a bee had stung her.

"Maggie can't appreciate these quilts!" she said. "She'd probably be backward enough to put them to everyday use."

"I reckon she would," I said. "God knows I been saving 'em for long enough for nobody using 'em. I hope she will!" I didn't want to bring up how I had offered Dee (Wangero) a quilt when she went away to college. Then she told me they were old-fashioned, out of style.

"But they're *priceless*!" she was saying now, furiously; for she has a temper. "Maggie would put them on the bed and in five years they'd be rags. Less than that!"

"She can always make some more," I said. "Maggie knows how to quilt."

Dee (Wangero) looked at me with hatred. "You just will not understand. The point is these quilts, *these* quilts!"

"Well," I said, stumped. "What would *you* do with them?"

"Hang them," she said. As if that was the only thing you *could* do with quilts.

Maggie by now was standing on the door. I could almost hear the sound her feet made as they scraped over each other.

"She can have them, Mama," she said, like somebody used to never winning anything, or having anything reserved for her. "I can 'member Grandma Dee without the quilts."

I looked at her hard. She had filled her bottom lip with checkerberry snuff and it gave her a face a kind of dopey, hangdog look. It was Grandma Dee and Big Dee who taught her how to quilt herself. She stood there with her scarred hands hidden in the folds of her skirt. She looked at her sister with something like fear but she wasn't mad at her. This was Maggie's portion. This was the way she knew God to work.

When I looked at her like that something hit me in the top of my head and ran down to the soles of my feet. Just like when I'm in church and the spirit of God touches me and I get happy and shout. I did something I never had done before: hugged Maggie to me, then dragged her on into the room, snatched the quilts out of Miss Wangero's hands and dumped them into Maggie's lap. Maggie just sat there on my bed with her mouth open.

"Take one or two of the others," I said to Dee.

But she turned without a word and went out to Hakim-a-barber.

"You just don't understand," she said, as Maggie and I came out to the car.

"What don't I understand?" I wanted to know.

"Your heritage," she said. And then she turned to Maggie, kissed her, and said, "You ought to try to make something of yourself, too, Maggie. It's really a new day for us. But from the way you and Mama still live you'd never know it."

She put on some sunglasses that hid everything above the tip of her nose and her chin.

Maggie smiled; maybe at the sunglasses. But a real smile, not scared. After we watched the car dust settle I asked Maggie to bring me a dip of snuff. And then the two of us sat there just enjoying, until it was time to go in the house and go to bed.

[1973]

The Conversion of the Jews

PHILIP ROTH

"You're a real one for opening your mouth in the first place," Itzie said. "What do you open your mouth all the time for?"

"I didn't bring it up, Itz, I didn't," Ozzie said.

"What do you care about Jesus Christ for anyway?"

"I didn't bring up Jesus Christ. He did. I didn't even know what he was talking about. Jesus is historical, he kept saying. Jesus is historical."[1] Ozzie mimicked the monumental voice of Rabbi Binder.

"Jesus was a person that lived like you and me," Ozzie continued. "That's what Binder said—"

"Yeah?... So what! What do I give two cents whether he lived or not. And what do you gotta open your mouth!" Itzie Lieberman favored closed-mouthedness, especially when it came to Ozzie Freedman's questions. Mrs. Freedman had to see Rabbi Binder twice before about Ozzie's questions and this Wednesday at four-thirty would be the third time. Itzie preferred to keep *his* mother in the kitchen; he settled for behind-the-back subtleties such as gestures, faces, snarls and other less delicate barnyard noises.

"He was a real person, Jesus, but he wasn't like God, and we don't believe he is God." Slowly, Ozzie was explaining Rabbi Binder's position to Itzie, who had been absent from Hebrew School the previous afternoon.[2]

"The Catholics," Itzie said helpfully, "they believe in Jesus Christ, that he's God." Itzie Lieberman used "the Catholics" in its broadest sense—to include the Protestants.

Ozzie received Itzie's remark with a tiny head bob, as though it were a footnote, and went on. "His mother was Mary, and his father probably was Joseph," Ozzie said. "But the New Testament says his real father was God."[3]

---

[1]"Jesus is historical," a rephrasing of the academic notion of "historical Jesus," refers to the focus of twentieth century scholarship on what can be known (or inferred) about the individual man who may have been Jesus.

[2]"Hebrew School the previous afternoon": Jews in the United States who decide not to send their children to a yeshiva or Jewish private day school may send their children to an after-school program, as Ozzie's mother apparently has. Such hour- or two-hour programs occurred at synagogues one or more days of the week.

[3]Mark 1:1

"His *real* father?"

"Yeah," Ozzie said, "that's the big thing, his father's supposed to be God."

"Bull."

"That's what Rabbi Binder says, that it's impossible—"

"Sure it's impossible. That stuff's all bull. To have a baby you gotta get laid," Itzie theologized. "Mary hadda get laid."

"That's what Binder says: 'The only way a woman can have a baby is to have intercourse with a man.'"

"He said *that*, Ozz?" For a moment it appeared that Itzie had put the theological question aside. "He said that, intercourse?" A little curled smile shaped itself in the lower half of Itzie's face like a pink mustache. "What you guys do, Ozz, you laugh or something?"

"I raised my hand."

"Yeah? Whatja say?"

"That's when I asked the question."

Itzie's face lit up. "Whatja ask about—intercourse?"

"No, I asked the question about God, how if He could create the heaven and earth in six days, and make all the animals and the fish and the light in six days—the light especially, that's what always gets me, that He could make the light. Making fish and animals, that's pretty good—"[4]

"That's damn good." Itzie's appreciation was honest but unimaginative: it was as though God had just pitched a one-hitter.

"But making light . . . I mean when you think about it, it's really something," Ozzie said. "Anyway, I asked Binder if He could make all that in six days, and He could *pick* the six days he wanted right out of nowhere, why couldn't He let a woman have a baby without having intercourse."

"You said intercourse, Ozz, to Binder?"

"Yeah."

"Right in class?"

"Yeah."

Itzie smacked the side of his head.

"I mean, no kidding around," Ozzie said, "that'd really be nothing. After all that other stuff, that'd practically be nothing."

Itzie considered a moment. "What'd Binder say?"

"He started all over again explaining how Jesus was historical and how he lived like you and me but he wasn't God. So I said I under*stood* that. What I wanted to know was different."

What Ozzie wanted to know was always different. The first time he had wanted to know how Rabbi Binder could call the Jews "The Chosen

---

[4]Genesis 1

People"[5] if the Declaration of Independence claimed all men to be created equal. Rabbi Binder tried to distinguish for him between political equality and spiritual legitimacy, but what Ozzie wanted to know, he insisted vehemently, was different. That was the first time his mother had to come.

Then there was the plane crash. Fifty-eight people had been killed in a plane crash at La Guardia. In studying a casualty list in the newspaper his mother had discovered among the list of those dead eight Jewish names (his grandmother had nine but she counted Miller as a Jewish name); because of the eight she said the plane crash was "a tragedy." During free-discussion time on Wednesday Ozzie had brought to Rabbi Binder's attention this matter of "some of his relations" always picking out the Jewish names. Rabbi Binder had begun to explain cultural unity and some other things when Ozzie stood up at his seat and said that what he wanted to know was different. Rabbi Binder insisted that he sit down and it was then that Ozzie shouted that he wished all fifty-eight were Jews. That was the second time his mother came.

"And he kept explaining about Jesus being historical, and so I kept asking him. No kidding, Itz, he was trying to make me look stupid."

"So what he finally do?"

"Finally he starts screaming that I was deliberately simple-minded and a wise guy, and that my mother had to come, and this was the last time. And that I'd never get bar-mitzvahed,[6] if he could help it. Then, Itz, then he starts talking in that voice like a statue, real slow and deep, and he says that I better think over what I said about the Lord. He told me to go to his office and think it over." Ozzie leaned his body towards Itzie. "Itz, I thought it over for a solid hour, and now I'm convinced God could do it."

Ozzie had planned to confess his latest transgression to his mother as soon as she came home from work. But it was a Friday night in November and already dark, and when Mrs. Freedman came through the door she tossed off her coat, kissed Ozzie quickly on the face, and went to the kitchen table to light the three yellow candles, two for the Sabbath and one for Ozzie's father.

When his mother lit the candles she would move her two arms slowly towards her[7] dragging them through the air, as though persuading people

---

[5]The notion of "Chosen People" emanates from God's selection, as recorded in the Hebrew Bible, of the Jewish people to promote their monotheistic vision of God. This idea has proven a source of controversy for Judaism, Christianity, and Islam, all of which have claimed for themselves or disputed at various times and in various ways the mantle of "chosenness."

[6]A "bar mitzvah" is an initiation ceremony for Jewish boys of thirteen to their adult religious duties. It usually takes the form of training to chant (more accurately "cantillate") verses from the Hebrew Bible.

[7]After the two Sabbath candles are lit, Jews (usually the oldest female in the household, such as Ozzie's mother) sing the Sabbath prayers for candle-lighting. Before praying, Mrs. Freedman performs the traditional gesture described here, which actually concludes with covering her eyes with her hands before singing the prayer for lighting candles.

whose minds were half made up. And her eyes would get glassy with tears. Even when his father was alive Ozzie remembered that her eyes had gotten glassy, so it didn't have anything to do with his dying. It had something to do with lighting the candles.

As she touched the flaming match to the unlit wick of a Sabbath candle, the phone rang, and Ozzie, standing only a foot from it, plucked it off the receiver and held it muffled to his chest.[8] When his mother lit candles Ozzie felt there should be no noise; even breathing, if you could manage it, should be softened. Ozzie pressed the phone to his breast and watched his mother dragging whatever she was dragging, and he felt his own eyes get glassy. His mother was a round, tired, gray-haired penguin of a woman whose gray skin had begun to feel the tug of gravity and the weight of her own history. Even when she was dressed up she looked like a chosen person. But when she lit candles she looked like something better; like a woman who knew momentarily that God could do anything.

After a few mysterious minutes she was finished. Ozzie hung up the phone and walked to the kitchen table where she was beginning to lay the two places for the four-course Sabbath meal. He told her that she would have to see Rabbi Binder next Wednesday at four-thirty, and then he told her why. For the first time in their life together she hit Ozzie across the face with her hand.

All through the chopped liver and chicken soup parts of the dinner Ozzie cried; he didn't have any appetite for the rest.

On Wednesday, in the largest of the three basement classrooms of the synagogue, Rabbi Marvin Binder, a tall, handsome, broad-shouldered man of thirty with thick strong-fibered black hair, removed his watch from his pocket and saw that it was four o'clock. At the rear of the room Yakov Blotnik, the seventy-one-year-old custodian, slowly polished the large window, mumbling to himself, unaware that it was four o'clock or six o'clock, Monday or Wednesday. To most of the students Yakov Blotnik's mumbling, along with his brown curly beard, scythe nose, and two heel-trailing black cats, made him an object of wonder, a foreigner, a relic, towards whom they were alternately fearful and disrespectful. To Ozzie the mumbling had always seemed a monotonous, curious prayer; what made it curious was that old Blotnik had been mumbling so steadily for so many years, Ozzie suspected he had memorized the prayers and forgotten all about God.

"It is now free-discussion time," Rabbi Binder said. "Feel free to talk about any Jewish matter at all—religion, family, politics, sports—"

There was silence. It was a gusty, clouded November afternoon and it did not seem as though there ever was or could be a thing called baseball. So

---

[8]Since the Jewish Sabbath is a day of rest, all forms of work are prohibited. This commonly includes not answering the phone, which explains why Ozzie, after picking it up, hangs up without having spoken a word to the caller.

nobody this week said a word about that hero from the past, Hank Green-berg[9]—which limited free discussion considerably.

And the soul-battering Ozzie Freedman had just received from Rabbi Binder had imposed its limitation. When it was Ozzie's turn to read aloud from the Hebrew book the rabbi had asked him petulantly why he didn't read more rapidly. He was showing no progress. Ozzie said he could read faster but that if he did he was sure not to understand what he was reading. Nevertheless, at the rabbi's repeated suggestion Ozzie tried, and showed a great talent, but in the midst of a long passage he stopped short and said he didn't understand a word he was reading, and started in again at a drag-footed pace. Then came the soul-battering.

Consequently when free-discussion time rolled around none of the students felt too free. The rabbi's invitation was answered only by the mumbling of feeble old Blotnik.

"Isn't there anything at all you would like to discuss?" Rabbi Binder asked again, looking at his watch. "No questions or comments?"

There was a small grumble from the third row. The rabbi requested that Ozzie rise and give the rest of the class the advantage of his thought.

Ozzie rose. "I forget it now," he said, and sat down in his place.

Rabbi Binder advanced a seat towards Ozzie and poised himself on the edge of the desk. It was Itzie's desk and the rabbi's frame only a dagger's-length away from his face snapped him to sitting attention.

"Stand up again, Oscar," Rabbi Binder said calmly, "and try to assemble your thoughts."

Ozzie stood up. All his classmates turned in their seats and watched as he gave an unconvincing scratch to his forehead.

"I can't assemble any," he announced, and plunked himself down.

"Stand up!" Rabbi Binder advanced from Itzie's desk to the one directly in front of Ozzie; when the rabbinical back was turned Itzie gave it five-fingers off the tip of his nose, causing a small titter in the room. Rabbi Binder was too absorbed in squelching Ozzie's nonsense once and for all to bother with titters. "Stand up, Oscar. What's your question about?"

Ozzie pulled a word out of the air. It was the handiest word. "Religion."

"Oh, now you remember?"

"Yes."

"What is it?"

Trapped, Ozzie blurted the first thing that came to him. "Why can't He make anything He wants to make!"

As Rabbi Binder prepared an answer, a final answer, Itzie, ten feet behind him, raised one finger on his left hand, gestured it meaningfully towards the rabbi's back, and brought the house down.

---

[9]Hank Greenberg (1911–1986) gained a reputation as a prominent Jewish baseball player.

Binder twisted quickly to see what had happened and in the midst of the commotion Ozzie shouted into the rabbi's back what he couldn't have shouted to his face. It was a loud, toneless sound that had the timbre of something stored inside for about six days.

"You don't know! You don't know anything about God!"

The rabbi spun back towards Ozzie. "What?"

"You don't know—you don't—"

"Apologize, Oscar, apologize!" It was a threat.

"You don't—"

Rabbi Binder's hand flicked out at Ozzie's cheek. Perhaps it had only been meant to clamp the boy's mouth shut, but Ozzie ducked and the palm caught him squarely on the nose.

The blood came in a short, red spurt on to Ozzie's shirt front.

The next moment was all confusion. Ozzie screamed, "You bastard, you bastard!" and broke for the classroom door. Rabbi Binder lurched a step backwards, as though his own blood had started flowing violently in the opposite direction, then gave a clumsy lurch forward and bolted out the door after Ozzie. The class followed after the rabbi's huge blue-suited back, and before old Blotnik could turn from his window, the room was empty and everyone was headed full speed up the three flights leading to the roof.

If one should compare the light of day to the life of man: sunrise to birth; sunset—the dropping down over the edge—to death; then as Ozzie Freedman wiggled through the trapdoor of the synagogue roof, his feet kicking backwards bronco-style at Rabbi Binder's outstretched arms—at that moment the day was fifty years old. As a rule, fifty or fifty-five reflects accurately the age of late afternoons in November, for it is in that month, during those hours, that one's awareness of light seems no longer a matter of seeing, but of hearing: light begins clicking away. In fact, as Ozzie locked shut the trapdoor in the rabbi's face, the sharp click of the bolt into the lock might momentarily have been mistaken for the sound of the heavier gray that had just throbbed through the sky.

With all his weight Ozzie kneeled on the locked door; any instant he was certain that Rabbi Binder's shoulder would fling it open, splintering the wood into shrapnel and catapulting his body into the sky. But the door did not move and below him he heard only the rumble of feet, first loud then dim, like thunder rolling away.

A question shot through his brain. "Can this be *me*?" For a thirteen-year-old who had just labeled his religious leader a bastard, twice, it was not an improper question. Louder and louder the question came to him—"Is it me? Is it me?"—until he discovered himself no longer kneeling, but racing crazily towards the edge of the roof, his eyes crying, his throat screaming, and his arms flying every-whichway as though not his own.

"Is it me? Is it me ME ME ME ME! It has to be me—but is it!"

It is the question a thief must ask himself the night he jimmies open his first window, and it is said to be the question with which bridegrooms quiz themselves before the altar.

In the few wild seconds it took Ozzie's body to propel him to the edge of the roof, his self-examination began to grow fuzzy. Gazing down at the street, he became confused as to the problem beneath the question: was it, is-it-me-who-called-Binder-a-bastard? or, is-it-me-prancing-around-on-the-roof? However, the scene below settled all, for there is an instant in any action when whether it is you or somebody else is academic. The thief crams the money in his pockets and scoots out the window. The bridegroom signs the hotel register for two. And the boy on the roof finds a streetful of people gaping at him, necks stretched backwards, faces up, as though he were the ceiling of the Hayden Planetarium.[10] Suddenly you know it's you.

"Oscar! Oscar Freedman!" A voice rose from the center of the crowd, a voice that, could it have been seen, would have looked like the writing on scroll. "Oscar Freedman, get down from there. Immediately!" Rabbi Binder was pointing one arm stiffly up at him; and at the end of that arm, one finger aimed menacingly. It was the attitude of a dictator, but one—the eyes confessed all—whose personal valet had spit neatly in his face.

Ozzie didn't answer. Only for a blink's length did he look towards Rabbi Binder. Instead his eyes began to fit together the world beneath him, to sort out people from places, friends from enemies, participants from spectators. In little jagged starlike clusters his friends stood around Rabbi Binder, who was still pointing. The topmost point on a star compounded not of angels but of five adolescent boys was Itzie. What a world it was, with those stars below, Rabbi Binder below . . . Ozzie, who a moment earlier hadn't been able to control his own body, started to feel the meaning of the word control: he felt Peace and he felt Power.

"Oscar Freedman, I'll give you three to come down."

Few dictators give their subjects three to do anything; but, as always, Rabbi Binder only looked dictatorial.

"Are you ready, Oscar?"

Ozzie nodded his head yes, although he had no intention in the world—the lower one of the celestial one he'd just entered—of coming down even if Rabbi Binder should give him a million.

"All right then," said Rabbi Binder. He ran a hand through his black Samson hair[11] as though it were the gesture prescribed for uttering the first digit.

---

[10]The Hayden Planetarium, part of the American Museum of Natural History in New York City, is famous for its astronomical projection shows on the domed ceiling of the building.

[11]Rabbi Binder's "black Samson hair" is a reference to the biblical strongman Samson, whose great physical strength was lost when his hair was cut. See Judges 16:17.

Then, with his other hand cutting a circle out of the small piece of sky around him, he spoke. "One!"

There was no thunder. On the contrary, at that moment, as though "one" was the cue for which he had been waiting, the world's least thunderous person appeared on the synagogue steps. He did not so much come out the synagogue door as lean out, onto the darkening air. He clutched at the doorknob with one hand and looked up at the roof.

"Oy!"

Yakov Blotnik's old mind hobbled slowly, as if on crutches, and though he couldn't decide precisely what the boy was doing on the roof, he knew it wasn't good—that is, it wasn't-good-for-the-Jews. For Yakov Blotnik life had fractionated itself simply: things were either good-for-the-Jews or no-good-for-the-Jews.

He smacked his free hand to his in-sucked cheek, gently. "Oy, Gut!" And then quickly as he was able, he jacked down his head and surveyed the street. There was Rabbi Binder (like a man at an auction with only three dollars in his pocket, he had just delivered a shaky "Two!"); there were the students, and that was all. So far it-wasn't-so-bad-for-the-Jews. But the boy had to come down immediately, before anybody saw. The problem: how to get the boy off the roof?

Anybody who has ever had a cat on the roof knows how to get him down. You call the fire department. Or first you call the operator and you ask her for the fire department. And the next thing there is great jamming of brakes and clanging of bells and shouting of instructions. And then the cat is off the roof. You do the same thing to get a boy off the roof.

That is, you do the same thing if you are Yakov Blotnik and you once had a cat on the roof.

When the engines, all four of them, arrived, Rabbi Binder had four times given Ozzie the count of three. The big hook-and-ladder swung around the corner and one of the firemen leaped from it, plunging headlong towards the yellow fire hydrant in front of the synagogue. With a huge wrench he began to unscrew the top nozzle. Rabbi Binder raced over to him and pulled at his shoulder.

"There's no fire . . ."

The fireman mumbled back over his shoulder and, heatedly, continued working at the nozzle.

"But there's no fire, there's no fire . . ." Binder shouted. When the fireman mumbled again, the rabbi grasped his face with both hands and pointed it up at the roof.

To Ozzie it looked as though Rabbi Binder was trying to tug the fireman's head out of his body, like a cork from a bottle. He had to giggle at the picture they made: it was a family portrait—rabbi in black skullcap, fireman in red fire hat, and the little yellow hydrant squatting beside like a kid brother, bareheaded. From the edge of the roof Ozzie waved at the portrait, a one-handed, flapping, mocking wave; in doing it his right foot slipped from under him. Rabbi Binder covered his eyes with his hands.

Firemen work fast. Before Ozzie had even regained his balance, a big, round, yellowed net was being held on the synagogue lawn. The firemen who held it looked up at Ozzie with stern, feelingless faces.

One of the firemen turned his head toward Rabbi Binder. "What, is the kid nuts or something?"

Rabbi Binder unpeeled his hands from his eyes, slowly, painfully, as if they were tape. Then he checked: nothing on the sidewalk, no dents in the net.

"Is he gonna jump, or what?" the fireman shouted.

In a voice not at all like a statue, Rabbi Binder finally answered. "Yes. Yes, I think so . . . He's been threatening to . . ."

Threatening to? Why, the reason he was on the roof, Ozzie remembered, was to get away; he hadn't even thought about jumping. He had just run to get away, and the truth was that he hadn't really headed for the roof as much as he'd been chased there.

"What's his name, the kid?"

"Freedman," Rabbi Binder answered. "Oscar Freedman."

The fireman looked up at Ozzie. "What is it with you, Oscar? You gonna jump, or what?"

Ozzie did not answer. Frankly, the question had just arisen.

"Look, Oscar, if you're gonna jump, jump—and if you're not gonna jump, don't jump. But don't waste out time, willya?"

Ozzie looked at the fireman and then at Rabbi Binder. He wanted to see Rabbi Binder cover his eyes one more time.

"I'm going to jump."

And then he scampered around the edge of the roof to the corner, where there was no net below, and he flapped his arms at his sides, swishing the air and smacking his palms to his trousers on the downbeat. He began screaming like some kind of engine, "Wheeeee . . . wheeeeee," and leaning way out over the edge with the upper half of his body. The firemen whipped around to cover the ground with the net. Rabbi Binder mumbled a few words to somebody and covered his eyes. Everything happened quickly, jerkily, as in a silent movie. The crowd, which had arrived with the fire engines, gave out a long, Fourth-of-July fireworks oooh-aahhh. In the excitement no one had paid the crowd much heed, except, of course, Yakov Blotnik, who swung from the doorknob counting heads. "Fier und tsvansik . . . finf und tsvantsik[12] . . . Oy, Gut!" It wasn't like this with the cat.

---

[12]Yiddish for twenty-four, twenty-five.

Rabbi Binder peeked through his fingers, checked the sidewalk and net. Empty. But there was Ozzie racing to the other corner. The firemen raced with him but were unable to keep up. Whenever Ozzie wanted to he might jump and splatter himself on the sidewalk, and by the time the firemen scooted to the spot all they could do with their net would be to cover the mess.

"Wheeeee . . . wheeeee . . ."

"Hey, Oscar," the winded fireman yelled. "What the hell is this, a game or something?"

"Wheeeee . . . wheeeee . . ."

"Hey, Oscar—"

But he was off now to the other corner, flapping his wings fiercely. Rabbi Binder couldn't take it any longer—the fire engines from nowhere, the screaming suicidal boy, the net. He fell to his knees, exhausted, and with his hands curled together in front of his chest like a little dome, he pleaded, "Oscar, stop it, Oscar. Don't jump, Oscar. Please come down . . . Please don't jump."

And further back in the crowd a single voice, a single young voice, shouted a lone word to the boy on the roof.

"Jump!"

It was Itzie. Ozzie momentarily stopped flapping.

"Go head, Ozz—jump!" Itzie broke off his point of the star and courageously, with the inspiration not of a wise-guy but of a disciple, stood alone. "Jump, Ozz, jump!"

Still on his knees, his hands still curled, Rabbi Binder twisted his body back. He looked at Itzie, then agonizingly, back to Ozzie.

"OSCAR, DON'T JUMP! PLEASE, DON'T JUMP . . . please please . . ."

"Jump!" This time it wasn't Itzie but another point of the star. By the time Mrs. Freedman arrived to keep her four-thirty appointment with Rabbi Binder, the whole little upside down heaven was shouting and pleading for Ozzie to jump, and Rabbi Binder no longer was pleading with him not to jump, but was crying into the dome of his hands.

Understandably Mrs. Freedman couldn't figure out what her son was doing on the roof. So she asked.

"Ozzie, my Ozzie, what are you doing? My Ozzie, what is it?"

Ozzie stopped wheeeeeing and slowed his arms down to a cruising flap, the kind birds use in soft winds, but he did not answer. He stood against the low, clouded, darkening sky—light clicked down swiftly now, as on a small gear—flapping softly and gazing down at the small bundle of a woman who was his mother.

"What are you doing, Ozzie?" She turned towards the kneeling Rabbi Binder and rushed so close that only a paper-thickness of dusk lay between her stomach and his shoulders.

"What is my baby doing?"

Rabbi Binder gaped at her but he too was mute. All that moved was the dome of his hands; it shook back and forth like a weak pulse.

"Rabbi, get him down! He'll kill himself. Get him down, my only baby . . ."

"I can't," Rabbi Binder said, "I can't . . ." and he turned his handsome head towards the crowd of boys behind him. "It's them. Listen to them."

And for the first time Mrs. Freedman saw the crowd of boys, and she heard what they were yelling.

"He's doing it for them. He won't listen to me. It's them." Rabbi Binder spoke like one in a trance.

"For them?"

"Yes."

"Why for them?"

"They want him to . . ."

Mrs. Freedman raised her two arms upward as though she were conducting the sky. "For them he's doing it!" And then in a gesture older than pyramids, older than prophets and floods, her arms came slapping down to her sides. "A martyr I have. Look!" She tilted her head to the roof. Ozzie was still flapping softly. "My martyr."

"Oscar, come down, *please*," Rabbi Binder groaned.

In a startling even voice Mrs. Freedman called to the boy on the roof. "Ozzie, come down, Ozzie. Don't be a martyr."

"Gawhead, Ozz—*be* a Martin!" It was Itzie. "Be a Martin, be a Martin," and all the voices joined in singing for Martindom, whatever *it* was. "Be a Martin, be a Martin . . ."

Somehow when you're on a roof the darker it gets the less you can hear. All Ozzie knew was that two groups wanted two new things: his friends were spirited and musical about what they wanted; his mother and the rabbi were even-toned, chanting, about what they didn't want. The rabbi's voice was without tears now and so was his mother's.

The big net stared up at Ozzie like a sightless eye. The big, clouded sky pushed down. From beneath it looked like a gray corrugated board. Suddenly, looking up into that unsympathetic sky, Ozzie realized all the strangeness of what these people, his friends, were asking: they wanted him to jump, to kill himself; they were singing about it now—it made them that happy. And there was an even greater strangeness: Rabbi Binder was on his knees, trembling. If there was a question to be asked now it was not "Is it me?" but rather "Is it us? . . . Is it us?"

Being on the roof, it turned out, was a serious thing. If he jumped would the singing become dancing? Would it? What would jumping stop? Yearningly, Ozzie wished he could rip open the sky, plunge his hands through, and pull out the sun; and on the sun, like a coin, would be stamped Jump or Don't Jump.

Ozzie's knees rocked and sagged a little under him as though they were setting him for a dive. His arms tightened, stiffened, froze, from shoulders to fingernails. He felt as if each part of his body were going to vote as to whether he should kill himself or not—and each part as though it were independent of *him*.

The light took an unexpected click down and the new darkness, like a gag, hushed the friends singing for this and the mother and rabbi chanting for that.

Ozzie stopped counting votes, and in a curiously high voice, like one who wasn't prepared for speech, he spoke.

"Mamma?"

"Yes, Oscar."

"Mamma, get down on your knees, like Rabbi Binder."

"Oscar—"

"Get down on your knees," he said, "or I'll jump."

Ozzie heard a whimper, then a quick rustling, and when he looked down where his mother had stood he saw the top of a head beneath that circle of dress. She was kneeling beside Rabbi Binder.

He spoke again. "Everybody kneel." There was the sound of everybody kneeling.

Ozzie looked around. With one hand he pointed towards the synagogue entrance. "Make *him* kneel."

There was a noise, not of kneeling, but of body-and-cloth stretching. Ozzie could hear Rabbi Binder saying in a gruff whisper, "... or he'll *kill* himself," and when next he looked there was Yakov Blotnik off the doorknob and for the first time in his life upon his knees in the Gentile posture of prayer.

As for the firemen—it is not as difficult as one might imagine to hold a net taut while you are kneeling.

Ozzie looked around again; and then he called to Rabbi Binder.

"Rabbi?"

"Yes, Oscar."

"Rabbi Binder, do you believe in God?"

"Yes."

"Do you believe God can do Anything?" Ozzie leaned his head out into the darkness. "Anything?"

"Oscar, I think—"

"Tell me you believe God can do Anything."

There was a second's hesitation. Then: "God can do Anything."

"Tell me you believe God can make a child without intercourse."

"He can."

"Tell me!"

"God," Rabbi Binder admitted, "can make a child without intercourse."

"Mamma, you tell me."

"God can make a child without intercourse," his mother said.

"Make *him* tell me." There was no doubt who *him* was.

In a few moments Ozzie heard an old comical voice say something to the increasing darkness about God.

Next, Ozzie made everybody said it. And then he made them all say they believed in Jesus Christ—first one at a time, then all together.

When the catechizing was through it was the beginning of evening. From the street it sounded as if the boy on the roof might have sighed.

"Ozzie?" A woman's voice dared to speak. "You'll come down now?"

There was no answer, but the woman waited, and when a voice finally did speak it was thin and crying, and exhausted as that of an old man who has just finished pulling the bells.

"Mamma, don't you see—you shouldn't hit me. He shouldn't hit me. You shouldn't hit me about God, Mamma. You should never hit anybody about God—"

"Ozzie, please come down now."

"Promise me, promise me you'll never hit anybody about God."

He had asked only his mother, but for some reason everyone kneeling in the street promised he would never hit anybody about God.

Once again there was silence.

"I can come down now, Mamma," the boy on the roof finally said. He turned his head both ways as though checking the traffic lights. "Now I can come down . . ."

And he did, right into the center of the yellow net that glowed in the evening's edge like an overgrown halo.

[1959]